De-Whitening Intersectionality

De-Whitening Intersectionality

Race, Intercultural Communication, and Politics

Edited by Shinsuke Eguchi,
Bernadette Marie Calafell, and Shadee Abdi

LEXINGTON BOOKS
Lanham • Boulder • New York • London

Published by Lexington Books
An imprint of The Rowman & Littlefield Publishing Group, Inc.
4501 Forbes Boulevard, Suite 200, Lanham, Maryland 20706
www.rowman.com

6 Tinworth Street, London SE11 5AL, United Kingdom

British Library Cataloguing in Publication Information Available

Library of Congress Cataloging-in-Publication Data Available

ISBN 978-1-4985-8822-5 (cloth : alk. paper)
ISBN 978-1-4985-8824-9 (pbk : alk. paper)
ISBN 978-1-4985-8823-2 (electronic)

∞™ The paper used in this publication meets the minimum requirements of American National Standard for Information Sciences—Permanence of Paper for Printed Library Materials, ANSI/NISO Z39.48-1992.

Contents

Acknowledgments vii

Foreword ix
Ashley Mack

Introduction: De-Whitening Intersectionality in Intercultural Communication xvii
Bernadette Marie Calafell, Shinsuke Eguchi, and Shadee Abdi

SECTION I: THE POLITICS OF THEORIZING

1 Intersectionalities in the Fields of Chicana Feminism: Pursuing Decolonization through Xicanisma's "Resurrection of the Dreamers" 3
Michelle A. Holling

2 Lethal Intersections and "Chicana Badgirls" 25
Jaelyn deMaría

3 Black Feminist Thought, Intersectionality, and Intercultural Communication 45
Aisha Durham

4 Intersectional Assemblages of Whiteness: The Case of Rachel Dolezal 59
Dawn Marie D. McIntosh

5 Doing Intersectionality under a Different Name: The (Un)intentional Politics of Refusal 83
Santhosh Chandrashekar

SECTION II: PERSONAL NARRATIVES

6 Making it Real Plain: Ruminations on De-Whitening Intersectionality in Academia From the Monstrous Queer Chicana Who Makes White Straight People Uncomfortable 99
Bernadette Marie Calafell

7 A Local *Gay Man/Tongzhi* or A Transnational *Queer/Qu-er/Kuer*: (Re)organizing My Queerness and Asianness through Personal Reflection 101
Andy Kai-chun Chuang

8 *What Are you*? Embodying and Storying Categorical (Un)certainty 119
Benny LeMaster, Amber Johnson, and Miranda Olzman

9 Bodies that Collide: Feeling Intersectionality 139
Sachi Sekimoto, Christopher Brown, and Justin Rudnick

10 Microaggressions in Flux: Whiteness, Disability, and Masculinity in Academia 159
Haneen Ghabra and Shahd Al Shammari

SECTION III: TRANSNATIONAL CIRCUMFERENCES

11 Remembering Julia de Burgos: Faithful Witnessing as Decolonial Feminist Performance 183
Sara Baugh-Harris

12 De-Whitening Intersectionality through *Transfeminismo* 203
Raquel Moreira

13 Dark Looks: Sensory Contours of Racism in India 223
Pavithra Prasad and Anjana Raghavan

14 "We Had to Sink or Swim": Privileging and Intersectionalizing Racialized Ethnic Identifications among Asians and Asian Americans 243
Yea-Wen Chen

15 Crazy Sexy Asian Men! Masculinities in *Crazy Rich Asians* 263
Zhao Ding and Kamela Rasmussen

Index 283

About the Editors 287

About the Contributors 289

Acknowledgments

Collectively, we as the coeditors would like to thank all the chapter contributors to this edited collection. Without your rigorous and intellectual work, this book would not be possible. Also, we thank Nicolette Amstutz at Lexington Press for her continuous support throughout this book's publication process. Without your having originally approached us for collaboration, this book would not be possible. Moreover, we would like to extend our appreciation to Lexington Press's editing and production teams for ensuring the quality of this edited collection. Thank you so much!

Shinsuke Eguchi would like to thank both of my coeditors Drs. Bernadette Marie Calafell and Shadee Abdi for their unconditional, loving, and supportive friendships. I also credit Drs. Nicole Files-Thompson, Dawn Marie D. McIntosh, Rachel A. Griffin, Tina M. Harris, Leilani Nishime, Tom Nakayama, Bryant Keith Alexander, Sachi Sekimoto, Andy Kai-Chun Chuang, Fatima Zahrae Chrifi Alaoui, Benny LeMaster, Robert Gutierrez-Perez, Amber Johnson, Satoshi Toyosaki, Ahmet Atay, Ashely Mack, Raquel Moreira, Andrew Spieldenner, Gust A. Yep, Ralina L. Joseph, Nina M. Lozano, Dana L. Cloud Chuck Morris, Yea-Wen Chen, Trina Wright, David Oh, Gloria Pindi, Zhao Ding, Erin D. Watley, Hannah R. Long, Godfried Asante, Haneen Ghabra, Jimmie Manning, Christopher Brown, Sarah Amira De la Garza, Leland Spencer, Susana Martinez Guillem, Marco Briziarelli, Ilia Rodriguez, Jaylen deMaria, Yangsun Hong, Michael Lechuga, Myra Washington, David Weiss, Michelle A. Holling, Jeffery Q. McCune Jr., Lisa Flores, Karma R. Chávez, Stacey Sowards, Deborah J. Borisoff, Mary Jane Collier, Kent A. Ono, and Bryan J. McCain for your support during the course of this particular project. Furthermore, I dedicate my efforts on de-whitening intersectionality to all who struggle every day against racism, cisheterosexism, and classism. Thank you and love you all!

Bernadette Marie Calafell would like to thank my dear friends and coeditors Dr. Shinsuke Eguchi and Dr. Shadee Abdi for their consistent and unconditional friendship, love, patience, and support. Additionally, thanks to Joshua Michael Calafell, Raven, Dr. Ashley Mack, Dr. Dawn Marie McIntosh, Scarlett Harrington, Miranda Olzman, Paula Martin-Noble, Dr. Santhosh Chandrashekar, Dr. Tom Nakayama, Dr. Nina Lozano, Dr. Raquel Moreira, Dr. Fatima Chrifi Alaoui, Dr. Robert Gutierrez-Perez, Dr. Andy Chuang, Dr. Sara Baugh-Harris, Cassidy Ellis, Cristy Dougherty, Caleb Green, Taisha McMickens, Wanda Lakota, Charles LuLevitt, Dr. Lisa Flores, Dr. Karma Chávez, Dr. Lisa Calvente, Dr. Jessica Johnson, Dr. E. Cassandra Dame-Griff, Dr. Jonathan Rossing, and Dr. Juliane Mora, and Sarah Gonzalez Noueiry for their friendship, love, and kindness. Thank you to Faris Badwan and the Horrors for motivating my writing. Thank you to Roy Wood for always being my unwavering advocate. I'll see you on the other side. I dedicate this book to Josh who continues to show me to all the possible layers of love and friendship, reminding me that it's a good life. I'll be your Sheri Moon if you'll be my Rob Zombie. Always.

Shadee Abdi would like to thank her colleagues, friends, and coeditors, Dr. Bernadette Marie Calafell and Dr. Shinsuke Eguchi for their unwavering support, care, mentorship, and guidance throughout this project and far beyond. Further, Shadee would like to dedicate this project to all the strong, brilliant, impressive women of color who continue to de-whiten intersectionality every second of every day. For this reason, and for all uniquely challenging me to be a better academic/ally/advocate/scholar/teacher/friend, a very special thank you goes out to Dr. Fatima Zahrae Chrifi Alaoui, Dr. Raquel Moreira, Dr. Nivea Castaneda, Dr. Pavithra Prasad, and Dr. Michelle A. Holling. Finally, I would like to thank all those who work toward de-whitening intersectionality in their daily lives. It is a process that requires hard work, dedication, and courage. I will continue to fight with and alongside you, forever.

Foreword

Intersectionality and the Colonizing Forces of Whiteness in Feminist Communication Studies

Ashley Mack

In the midst of the 2016 U.S. presidential primary election, Democratic nominee hopeful Bernie Sanders was gaining ground with younger voters. Hillary Clinton, the eventual nominee, capitalized on growing critiques of Sanders, who describes himself as a democratic socialist and campaigned primarily on economic issues, as a myopic class reductionist by invoking the ethos of intersectionality in her campaign rhetoric (Foran, 2016). On March 6, 2016, Clinton posted a series of tweets that deployed terminology related to "intersectionality" to describe Flint's water crisis, in which lead contamination killed twelve people in the majority African American city. However, she did so in a manner that completely divorced intersectionality from its meaning and origins in black feminist thought and activism.

Clinton's first tweet stated, "Flint's water crisis is an example of the combined effects of intersecting issues that impact communities of color" (HillaryClinton, 2016a). The tweet was accompanied by a graphic that showed various concepts "intersecting" with systemic racism, including unemployment, poverty, pollution, health disparities, food deserts and malnutrition, under investment and neglect, crumbling infrastructure, lost resources and budget cuts, and decline in manufacturing jobs. The graph was followed up by a tweet stating, "When we talk about the Flint water crisis, we also have to talk about its root causes—economic, racial, and other. #DemDebate" (HillaryClinton, 2016b). Finally, a third tweet shared another depiction of "intersecting" ways we might solve these issues. At the center of the graph was the phrase "investing in communities of color." Surrounding this phrase was another web of "intersecting" concepts including but not limited to accountable leadership, infrastructure investments, universal health care, and environmental protection. The tweet stated, "We face a complex, intersectional set of challenges. We need solutions and real plans for all of them.

#DemDebate" (HillaryClinton, 2016c). Taken as a whole, the series of tweets functioned as an attempt by Clinton's campaign to portray the former U.S. secretary of state as the more nuanced candidate with regard to various forms of structural inequality.

While Clinton used the terms "intersecting" and "intersectional," her tweets and the accompanying graphs are an example of the ways that, as it gains ubiquity, intersectionality as a theoretical framework for understanding the intersections of power and identity becomes diluted and misappropriated in U.S. popular culture and mainstream U.S. politics. "Intersectionality," a term coined by Kimberlé Williams Crenshaw (1989, 1991)—but conceptually introduced by a multitude of black and women of color feminists in the twentieth century—theorizes that we need to consider the social location and embodied standpoint of those that experience multiple axes of domination simultaneously. While originally theorized in relation to the unique and often erased experiences of black women, intersectional considerations of power and identity at multiple axes of domination are not relegated to only experiences of women of color. As opposed to single axis approaches to analyzing oppression, intersectionality theorizes the multiplicity of embodied oppression amid various places "where power comes and collides, where it interlocks and intersects" ("Kimberlé Crenshaw on Intersectionality," n.d.).

Clinton was certainly identifying interrelated issues impacting communities of color (which are related to interlocking power systems). However, her use of intersectionality relied on framing it as simply a metaphor for "complexity" or for seeing issues as "intersecting." Her use of intersectionality, therefore, was an attempt at virtue signaling and not necessarily an active engagement with intersectionality as a black feminist theory of power and identity at multiple axes of domination. While Clinton recognizing that multiple issues intersect to cause problems for communities of color is not problematic on its own, as a white woman her deployment and co-optation of the terms of intersectionality to mean whatever she wanted it to mean colonizes and erases the work of women of color while failing to actively engage decades of their scholarship and academic contributions. Her non-interactive engagement with Crenshaw's theory of intersectionality, but desire to use it in a virtue signaling rhetoric that benefits her campaign through performative "wokeness," highlights how white feminist colonization of black and women of color feminist and queer theories occurs (Lugones, 2013).

The popularization, and resignification, of intersectionality in the U.S. public sphere has increased dramatically in the last decade (Nash, 2019). Throughout digital activism on platforms such as Twitter, and popular feminist digital trade publications such as *Jezebel* and *Teen Vogue*, "intersectional feminism" is often purported as the dominant feminist framework. Memes declaring "Feminism without intersectionality is just white supremacy" and

"My feminism will be intersectional or it will be bullshit" circulate on Instagram, and multiple news articles reference Crenshaw and the term in their analysis of the intersections of race and gender. In some ways, the popularity of intersectionality is exciting and necessary. National public conversations about the multiplicity of identity and the ways in which interlocking systems of domination work in tandem to create conditions of oppression for the multiply marginalized are much needed. But what understandings of intersectionality are being mainstreamed? And perhaps, more importantly, who gets to set the terms for the ways scholars and activists deploy the concept?

Some claimed Clinton's use of intersectionality in her campaign was a positive development in political discourse. As an article in *The Atlantic* on March 9, 2016, notes, Clinton's

> public advocacy of an intersectional approach to politics brings the concept further into the political mainstream. It could introduce the term to new audiences, and shape the way politicians, particularly on the political Left, think and talk about, as well as offer solutions to, inequality and discrimination. (Foran, 2016, para. 8)

While the article may be correct that Clinton's use of terminology invoking the ethos of intersectionality may have brought the concept further into mainstream U.S. political conversations, Clinton's co-optation and misuse of intersectionality reveals the ways that useful, critical, and radical concepts can be taken up on a neoliberal logical plane where they are incorporated into a lexicon of hyper individualism and capital, becoming everything and nothing at once. Co-optation and misappropriation are rhetorical strategies of whiteness. As Sirma Bilge (2014) notes, such engagement with "intersectionality" incorporates and dilutes the radical critiques of black feminist theories "into the neoliberal governance of diversity and minority difference, to which the questions of knowledge production and dissemination are integral" (p. 175). Simultaneously, such maneuvers symbolically functioning to re-center whiteness, white feminism, and white women's experiences and knowledges.

In an interview with Columbia Law School, Crenshaw describes some of the ways that intersectionality has been misunderstood and misused as it has entered further into popular consciousness:

> It's not simply that there's a race problem here, a gender problem here, and a class or LBGTQ problem there. Many times that framework erases what happens to people who are subject to all of these things. Some people look to intersectionality as a grand theory of everything, but that's not my intention. If someone is trying to think about how to explain to the courts why they should not dismiss a case made by black women, just because the employer did hire

> blacks who were men and women who were white, well, that's what the tool was designed to do. If it works, great. If it doesn't work, it's not like you have to use this concept. The other issue is that intersectionality can get used as a blanket term to mean, "Well, it's complicated." Sometimes, "It's complicated" is an excuse not to do anything. ("Kimberlé Crenshaw on Intersectionality," n.d.)

The mainstreaming of intersectionality in the broader U.S. public sphere has occurred alongside its popularization within the U.S. Women's Studies discipline and white Western feminist theories, frameworks, and ideas (Nash, 2019). Yet, as was the case with Hillary Clinton, the mainstreaming of intersectionality within predominately white Western feminist theories and U.S. Women's Studies programs has meant that intersectionality has been deployed in various ways that not only dilute its radical potential but work to re-center dominant power relations (Bilge, 2014). In fact, like other theories put forward by black feminist or women of color feminists, intersectionality has often faced co-optation and misappropriation. Specifically, as Eguchi, Calafell, and Abdi argue in the introduction to this edited volume, the colonizing forces of whiteness often results in total eclipse of the critical analysis of racist systems in "whitened" intersectional critiques.

In her book *Black Feminism Reimagined* (2019), Jennifer C. Nash charts the institutional and academic deployments and uses of intersectionality in U.S. academic contexts, and argues that while intersectionality has emerged as a dominant concept within U.S. Women's Studies programs, it is also positioned as a potential threat to the coherence of feminism. Nash argues that because of the ubiquity and co-optation of intersectionality, black feminists in U.S. academic spaces have been preoccupied with a kind of defensiveness over intersectionality. Such constative histories seek for a "true" theory or history of intersectionality. However, Nash argues this defensive theoretical posture also restricts black feminisms from developing potential liberating futures.

The defensiveness surrounding the misuse and appropriation of intersectionality is not without cause. Even within critical and cultural communication studies scholarship, intersectionality has often been deployed as a disembodied analytic rather than a description of embodied lived experience and knowledge about existing at multiple axes of domination, or theory in the flesh (Gutierrez-Perez, 2019). For example, white feminist critiques in communication studies have previously argued that scholars in feminist communication studies should always forefront sex/gender but "in the context of multiple axes of power" (Hayden & O'Brien Hallstein, 2012, p. 97). Such treatment of identity as disarticulated ignoresprimary arguments of black feminist theories of intersectionality as the embodiment of identities at multiple axes of domination and oppression, and contributes to the ongoing erasure of racial analysis in feminist communication scholarship.

Furthermore, passive citation of intersectional considerations and performative positionality statements by white scholars eschew active engagement with women of color feminist or queer of color theories. In such manifestations, misuse of intersectionality can become a performative alibi white feminist scholars deploy as they identify their unique identity position as "white, heterosexual, able-bodied, women," while continuing to re-center white feminist theories, causes, and histories. María Lugones (2013) contends that white scholars who provide brief moments of reflexivity about racial privilege often do so as a "diversity disclaimer" and proceed to non-interactively engage with the theories produced by scholars of color while non-reflexively erasing difference and centering whiteness (pp. 68–69).

The mainstreaming and popularization of intersectionality has also led to multiple academic and activist critiques of the concept and its popular and academic use. For example, Weheliye (2014) warns that academic uses of intersectionality can be too rigidly wielded to a type of neoliberal identity politics that renaturalizes racial and ethnic categorization in ways that constrain liberatory politics. Jasbir K. Puar (2017) similarly argues that

> No matter how intersectional our models of subjectivity, no matter how attuned to locational politics of space, place, and scale, these formulations—these fine tunings of intersectionality, as it were, that continue to be demanded—may still limit us if they presume the automatic primacy and singularity of the disciplinary subject and its identitarian interpellation. (p. 206)

There are also a series of critiques from critical race scholars that have attempted to assess whether or not intersectionality is a theory that can encompass the nuances of power in modern society. Tommy J. Curry, author of *The Man-Not* (2017), has consistently waged polemical critiques of black feminists, and the ubiquity of intersectionality more broadly, arguing that intersectionality is theoretically problematic because it presumes that black men have male privilege in society. According to Curry, black men are also oppressed by white patriarchy and in some cases black women possess privilege and status where black men do not.

But intersectionality need not succumb to singular identitarian politics so common in U.S. public discourse, nor does it need to sacrifice an analysis of how white patriarchy contributes to the domination and oppression of black men. Despite activists and critical race theorists criticizing the deployment and use of intersectionality, is still desperately needed as a means of examining the multiple ways power and identity intersect *at multiple axes of domination and oppression*. This need is further exasperated within the exigence of our current political climate in the U.S. within the ongoing terror of Donald Trump's presidency. Since 2016, the rising tide of fascism and white nationalism in the U.S., alongside ever-present (and, to be clear, bipartisan) racism, xenophobia, transphobia, misogyny, and homophobia necessitates intersectional considerations. In 2019, at least twenty-two trans women or gender non-confirming people have been murdered or killed through violent means in the United States, a majority of whom are black trans women (Human Rights Campaign, 2019). The forced imprisonment of migrants at the U.S./Mexico border and the increasing violence against LGBTQ and women migrants in ICE custody mandates considerations of power and identity as interlocking and mutually constitutive (Parshall, 2018).

De-Whitening Intersectionality: Race, Intercultural Communication, and Politics works to resist the colonizing function of whiteness in contemporary feminist theory and communication studies. By focusing on theorization by those at the margins—those whose embodied experience of oppression is fundamentally intersectional at multiple axes of domination—this volume begins the work of untangling and resisting the re-centering of whiteness in the deployment of intersectionality in critical and cultural communication studies. By centering women of color, queer people of color, and trans people of color theorizing intersectionality, while simultaneously critiquing the whitening of intersectional theories and methods, this edited book becomes an invaluable resource for feminist and queer scholars to resist the whitening and diluting impulses of white Western feminisms and critical communication theories.

WORKS CITED

Bilge, S. (2014). Whitening intersectionality: Evanescence of race in intersectionality scholarship. In W. D. Hund & A. Lentin (Eds.), *Racism and sociology: Racism analysis yearbook 5* (pp. 175–205). Berlin: Lit Verlag/Routledge.

Crenshaw, K. W. (1989). Demarginalizing the intersection of race and sex: A black feminist critique of antidiscrimination doctrine, feminist theory and antiracist politic. *University of Chicago Legal Forum, 1989*(1), 139–67.

Crenshaw, K. W. (1991). Mapping the margins: Intersectionality, identity politics, and violence against women of color. *Stanford Law Review, 43*(6), 1241–99. doi:10.2307/1229039.

Curry, T. J. (2017). *The man-not: Race, class, genre, and the dilemmas of black manhood.* Philadelphia, PA: Temple University Press.

Foran, C. (2016, March 9). Hillary Clinton's intersectional politics. *The Atlantic.* Retrieved from: https://www.theatlantic.com/politics/archive/2016/03/hillary-clinton-intersectionality/472872/.

Gutierrez-Perez, R. (2019). Theories in the flesh and flights of the imagination: Embracing the soul and spirit of critical performative writing in communication research. *Women's Studies in Communication*. doi:10.1080/07491409.2018.1551 695.

Hayden, S. & O'Brien Hallstein, D. L. (2012). Placing sex/gender at the forefront: Feminisms, intersectionality, and communication studies. In K. R. Chávez, & C. L. Griffin (Eds.), *Standing at the intersection: Feminist voices, feminist practices in communication studies* (pp. 97–124). New York, NY: SUNY Press.

HillaryClinton. (2016, March 6). Flint's water crisis is an example of the combined effects of intersecting issues that impact communities of color. [Tweet]. Retrieved from https://twitter.com/hillaryclinton/status/706649487696130048?lang=en.

HillaryClinton. (2016, March 6). We face a complex, intersectional set of challenges. We need solutions and real plans for all of them. #DemDebate [Tweet]. Retrieved from https://twitter.com/hillaryclinton/status/706649487696130048?lang=en.w

HillaryClinton. (2016, March 6). When we talk about the Flint water crisis, we also have to talk about its root causes—Economic, racial, and other. #DemDebate [Tweet]. Retrieved from https://twitter.com/hillaryclinton/status/7066494876961 30048?lang=en.

Human Rights Campaign. Violence Against the Transgender Community in 2019. (n.d.). Retrieved October 30, 2019, from https://www.hrc.org/resources/violence-a gainst-the-transgender-community-in-2019.

Kimberlé Crenshaw on Intersectionality, More than Two Decades Later. (n.d.). Retrieved October 30, 2019, from https://www.law.columbia.edu/pt-br/news/2017/ 06/kimberle-crenshaw-intersectionality.

Lugones, M. (2003). *Pilgrimages/peregrinajes: Theorizing coalition against multiple oppressions*. New York: Rowman & Littlefield Publishers.

Nash, J. C. (2019). *Black feminism reimagined: After intersectionality*. Durham, NC: Duke University Press.

Parshall, H. (2018, November 30). *The crisis at the border is an LGBTQ issue. Here's why*. Human Rights Campaign. Retrieved from https://www.hrc.org/blog/the-crisis -at-the-border-is-an-lgbtq-issue-heres-why.

Puar, J. K. (2017). *Terrorist assemblages: Homonationalism in queer times*. Durham, NC: Duke University Press.

Weheliye, A. G. (2014). *Habeas viscus: Racializing assemblages, biopolitics, and the black feminist theories of the human*. Durham, NC: Duke University Press.

Introduction

De-Whitening Intersectionality in Intercultural Communication

Bernadette Marie Calafell, Shinsuke Eguchi, and Shadee Abdi

With a lot of passion, intellectual frustration, and excitement, three of us come from different intellectual and political spaces to co-edit this book *De-whitening Intersectionality: Race, Intercultural Communication, and Politics*. As the collective, we are the *queer people of color* who value the conceptualization and performance of *intersectionality*. It speaks with the way in which simultaneous technologies of differences (e.g., race, ethnicity, gender, sexuality, class, nation, and the body) construct our everyday lived experiences. Who we are, what we do, and how we make sense of those actions, are intersectional. Kimberlé Crenshaw (1989, 1991) first coined the term "intersectionality." She accounted for the simultaneous operations of race, gender, and class that shape nuanced particularities of everyday institutional experiences for black women. The legal institution that essentially focuses on women as *white women* and blacks as *black men* ignores, erases, and marginalizes the issues and concerns of black women who are historically oppressed by both racism and sexism at the same time. Hill Collins (1990) extended Crenshaw's work of intersectionality to the matrix of domination. The institutional oppressions of race, gender, and class are always already interconnected to other classifications such as sexuality, religion, and the body. Thus, Crenshaw (1989, 1991) and Hill Collins's (1990) theorizings of intersectionality have impacted various disciplines (e.g., Sociology, Psychology, Education, Critical Racial and Ethnic Studies, and Women's, Gender, and Sexuality Studies).

In Communication Studies, a number of scholars of color who interrogate culture, power, and communication (e.g., Abdi & Calafell, 2017; Abdi & Van Gilder, 2016; Calafell, 2007, 2012, 2013, 2015; Chávez, 2012, 2013; Eguchi, 2015, 2020; Eguchi, Calafell, & Files-Thompson, 2014; Griffin, 2014; LeMaster, 2015; Johnson, 2014; Yep, 2013) have utilized the conception of intersectionality to identify with and critique the complex, contradictory, and fluid practices of race, gender, and class. However, intersectionality, aligned with women of color feminist tradition, has also been an intellectual site of *controversy* as well (e.g., Yep, 2010; Yep & Chivers, 2017). For example, King (2015) argues that intersectionality is often constructed as passé by graduate students who are often in search of the "hot" new theory that holds cultural currency. This has further interpersonal consequences as women of color scholars get treated as atheoretical or become the recipients of microaggressions. At least one of the editors Bernadette Marie Calafell can attest to this experience, which left her wondering when did critiquing women of color became radical, critical, and cutting edge?

At the same time, Puar (2007) has suggested scholars who appropriate the use of intersectionality as a checklist of identity markers simultaneously obfuscate the logics of whiteness that organize the normative system of social institution. Whiteness is a discursive practice that re-centers and resecures the invisible and universal power of white supremacy that subordinate people of color (e.g., Nakayama & Krizek, 1995; McIntosh, Moon, & Nakayama, 2019). Such Puar's observation points to the way in which we everyday observe the misuse of intersectionality as an alibi of whiteness. For example, when we challenge scholars and practitioners, particularly white feminists, who use a raceless paradigm of intersectionality as their major conceptual lens, they typically reply to us with the following remarks; "I am looking at the intersection of gender, sexuality, and class. So, race is not a major concern of my study"; "whiteness wasn't present in the field because all participants talk about their struggles with patriarchy"; "whiteness is irrelevant in our field work in [a name of country in Africa] because everyone else was black. Why are you bringing up whiteness?" These comments insinuate what Bilge (Aiello et al., 2013) has critiqued that the conception of intersectionality appropriated particularly by white feminists re-centers the logic of color-blindness as whiteness as an invisible and universal power. Despite claims of inclusion and social justice through the utilization of intersectionality, such discursive readjustment sustains the historical marginalization of women of color, queer, and nonbinary people of color, and people of color occupying intersectioning positionalities. Bilge (2014) names this unfortunate situation as *whitening intersectionality*.

The whitening of intersectionality highly troubles us. As Yep (2010) has argued before us, we are frustrated with how some scholars and practitioners conceptualize and operationalize intersectionality as if it is about negotiations of multiple identities. We are concerned with scholars who feel entitled to no guilt and shame, while using intersectionality without honoring the genealogy of women of color feminism. Given that "race" cannot be separated from women of color, queer, and nonbinary people of color, and people of color, occupying and acknowledging intersectional positionalities in scholarship should be the ethical responsibility. However, by using intersectionality, some scholars and practitioners want to be hip, cool, and edgy even though what they are doing are racist and settler-colonialist moves. They even feel entitled to chastise people who question and critique their usages of intersectionality as an alibi of whiteness. By reinserting *white privilege*, they are reinforcing the color-blind systematic and institutional inequalities that make and remake experiences of women of color, queer, and nonbinary people of color, and people of color occupying intersectional positionalities.

For these reasons, in this edited book, we invest our energies in decentering the logics of whiteness that characterize intersectional research in Communication Studies. More precisely, we call for a re-centering of difference by exploring the origin of intersectionality, in addition to distinguishing between uses of intersectionality that appear inclusive versus actually enacting inclusion. Drawing on Calafell and Moreman (2010) and Warren (2008), we approach the concept of differences as driving mechanisms of power relations that reproduce and reconstitute historical and systematic inequalities. Differences are social and performative sites of ideological struggles that alter, shape, and reinforce the hierarchical politics of identity. Hence, we are interested in showcasing culture-specific and text-specific nuances of knowledge for women of color, queer, and nonbinary people of color, and people of color occupying intersectional positionalities who have been marked as *Others*. We explicitly reorient disruptive possibilities of intersectionality as a conceptual lens that decenters white, Western, patriarchal, and/or heteronormative productions of communication theory and research. In what follows, we offer our conceptualization of "de-whitening" intersectionality that methodologically emphasizes race, intercultural communication, and politics. The organization and contents of this book also follows.

"DE-WHITENING" INTERSECTIONALITY

We approach the concept of *de-whitening* as a critical praxis of decentering the logics of whiteness that organizes the production of knowledge in and across personal, institutional, and academic contexts. Whiteness that maneuvers throughout temporal paradoxes between the past, the present, and the future is a very sneaky product because it is often invisible or easily unidentifiable (e.g., McIntosh, Moon, & Nakayama, 2019; LuLevitt & Calafell, 2019). Such strategic fluidity of whiteness is a discursive practice of white modernity that maintains the inferiority of people of color as *backward*. White supremacy is an active force of whiteness that may even look like "liberal" and "progressive" (Ono & Cheung, 2019). For example, the contemporary assimilation of cisgender gays and lesbians into the nation-state is a white modernity that marks U.S. exceptionalism (Eguchi & Calafell, 2020). The liberalism of whiteness that promotes gay and lesbian rights allows the United States to maintain its global, imperialist superiority over non-Western, nonwhite nations (Puar, 2007). Accordingly, *whiteness is dangerous*. Its power, influence, and consequences can be very subtle, ambiguous, and ambivalent. Hence, it is important for scholars to actively marginalize the changing landscape of whiteness that shape ways of knowing about culture, power, and communication.

Orienting such methodological praxis of de-whitening in this book, we strongly emphasize on three following concepts: race, intercultural communication, and politics. *Race* is a socially constructed category of meanings assigned to the body, skin color, and physical appearance (Delgado & Stefancic, 2012; Omi & Winant, 2014). Institutions essentialize differences in order to conceptualize and operate racial categories such as American Indian or Alaska Native, Asian, black, and white. To name a couple, the racialized term Latina/o/xs include various nationalities, ethnicities, body appearances, and skin colors is complex and contradictory (Calafell, 2007). In addition, the term "Asian" has been historically contested because its term points to such large and vague regions that cannot exactly pinpoint who "Asians" are (Eguchi, 2013). However, the socially constructed meanings of race are ongoing dynamic processes of culture, communication, and power that reflect an ever-changing landscape of society. Showcasing the multiracial complexities of professional golfer Tiger Woods, Nishime (2012) argues that naming practices of mixed-race subjects that challenge the material boundaries of racial categories explicate the way in which race is a fluid construct. At the same time, Joseph (2018) also approaches race as a strategic performance. She suggests the way in which some black women perform racial ambiguities to pass the racial lines for survival under the white patriarchal control. Thus, as we consider the de-whitening of intersectionality, we cannot ignore the complexities and contradictions of race that operate with/in differences as the matrices of domination.

We also emphasize the *intercultural communication* that reproduces and reconstitutes the complexities and contradictions of race in and across local, national, and global contexts. When we say intercultural communication, we strongly refuse a social scientific approach that controls, determines, and predicts the relationships between culture and communication. Instead, by intercultural communication, we mean the way in which relationships between culture and communication always already explicate, elucidate, and elaborate complex and messy processes of power (Eguchi, 2019; Halualani & Nakayama, 2010). For instance, all people of color do not have the same relationships with the white, Western, colonialist, and imperialist supremacy that organizes the U.S. institutional lives. As Tuck and Yang (2012) have advocated for decolonization, we must account the historical continuum of colonization that politicizes and contextualizes each racial and ethnic minority group's positionality differently. In fact, the settlers from multiple locations continue to occupy the lands that belong to indigenous people for so long (Na'puti & Bevacqua, 2015). Migrants from non-Western, nonwhite spheres also act as colonial settlers who participate in the white, Western colonialist system that recycles the replacement of indigenous populations. From this perspective, we recognize that the everyday operation of power that shapes institutional experiences is never neat and clear; it is always already messy and ambiguous. Thus, as we de-whiten intersectionality, we elaborate such dynamic of intercultural communication that complicate the technology of race working with/in differences.

In addition to our emphasis on race and intercultural communication, we intentionally highlight *politics* because there is nothing apolitical about intersectionality. More precisely, the U.S. preferred logics of individualism that color-blinds structural issues of power (e.g., racism, cisheterosexims, and classism) reproduce and reconstitute the major problem associated with the reappropriation of intersectionality. U.S Americans are always already taught to believe that success is based on an individual trait and attitude and has nothing to do with the titled scale of race, gender, sexuality, nation, class, and the body (Halberstam, 2011). The cultural myth of American dream reinforces such individualism that ignores the historical and contemporary realities of power, privilege, and oppression (Eguchi, Files-Thompson, & Calafell, 2018). Under such ideology at play, some scholars and practitioners, particularly white feminists, have the audacity to reappropriate the conception of intersectionality that intends to situate the racialized, gendered, and classed knowlegde(s) embedded in the material realities of women, nonbinary, and queer people of color. The misuse of intersectionality that ignores, erases, and marginalizes complexities and contradictions of race in and across intercultural communication contexts is the product of whiteness that strategically maintains white supremacy. The position of scholars and practitioners who choose not to politicize their uses of intersectionality through the matrix of domination is political. They are comfortable with the way power works or the way it is.

Therefore, by situating race, intercultural communication, and politics, we revitalize a space to de-whiten intersectionality. Our intellectual and political move follows Crenshaw's (2012, 2017) calls to better attend to intersectionality's origins that illuminates and contests systemic privilege. This book underscores that to play well with intersectionality, scholars must be attentive to its origins and implications. The chapters in *De-Whitening Intersectionality: Race, Intercultural Communication, and Politics* explicitly or implicitly point to our goal.

ORGANIZATION AND CONTENTS OF THE BOOK

This book consists of three sections: "The Politics of Theorizing," "Personal Narratives," and "Transnational Circumferences." Chapters that fall under "The Politics of Theorizing" pay particular attention to the complex and contradictory tensions of power that surround the politics of theorizing to de-whiten intersectionality in and across the lines of difference. In chapter 1, "Intersectionalities in the Fields of Chicana Feminism: Pursuing Decolonization through Xicanisma's "Resurrection of the Dreamers," Michelle A. Holling turns to Ana Castillo's monograph *Massacre of the Dreamers* (1994) to develop current understandings of Chicana feminism and its emphasis on intersectionality. This chapter emphasizes culturally grounded ideas that centralize difference. In chapter 2, "Lethal Intersections and "Chicana Badgirls," Jaelyn deMaría examines alternative meaning systems, which revealed complicated intersectionalities articulated in *Chicana Badgirl* counter-narratives that complicate and resist the reproduction of whiteness. deMaría hopes to deconstruct mainstream narratives of violence and to amplify alternative counter-narratives of survival. In chapter 3, "Black Feminist Thought, Intersectionality, and Intercultural Communication," Aisha Durham locates contemporary intersectionality scholarship and black feminist thought by identifying new stewards whose research exemplifies the advocacy-oriented analytic in intercultural communication. In chapter 4, "Intersectional Assemblages of Whiteness: The Case of Rachel Dolezal's Whiteness," Dawn Marie McIntosh critiques the case of a former NAACP (The National Association for the Advancement of Colored People) president Rachel Dolezal who becomes publicly known for identifying as a black woman. This chapter showcases how the case of Dolezal denotes where whiteness has neutralized intersectionality to remove whites' accountability to racism. In chapter 5, "Doing Intersectionality under a Different Name: The (Un)Intentional Politics of Refusal," Santhosh Chandrashekar challenges the assumption that power is a minor analytic in the deployment of intersectionality and any attempt by white feminists to use intersectionality constitutes its misappropriation. In so doing, Chandrashekar suggests a transparent extension of intersectionality by nonblack feminists.

Chapters 6 through 10 methodologically centralize performative techniques of personal narratives that de-whiten the use of intersectionality. This theme, "Personal Narratives," starts with Bernadette Marie Calafell whose short piece "Making it Real Plain: Ruminations on De-Whitening Intersectionality in Academia from the Monstrous Queer Chicana Who Makes White Straight People Uncomfortable" explores how white faculty strategically embrace and appropriate intersectionality while simultaneously working against Others. In chapter 7, "Local *Gay Man/Tongzhi* or a Transnational *Queer/Qu-er/*

Kuer: (Re)organizing My Queerness and Asianess through Personal Reflection," Andy Kai-chun Chuang argues the necessity of bringing (Other) bodies and better attending to intersectionalities to de-whiten queer (intercultural) communication scholarship by sharing his personal experiences. In chapter 8, "*What Are You*? Embodying and Storying Categorical Uncertainty," Benny LeMaster, Amber Johnson, and Miranda Olzman draw on their lived experiences as racially ambiguous subjects embodying queer and nonbinary sexual and gender identities to de-whiten intersectionality. This chapter situates whiteness that emerges as a cultural force seeking to apprehend racial ambiguity through dictates of contextual sameness or to destroy and belittle racial ambiguity through contextual renderings of difference. In chapter 9, "Bodies that Collide: Feeling Intersectionality," Sachi Sekimoto, Christopher Brown, and Justin Rudnick use the insights from the visceral metaphor of intersectionality as a point of "collision." So, they interrogate the sensuous materiality of inhabiting one's body as a social subject at the intersection of multilayered histories, positions of privilege, and intercultural interactions. In chapter 10, "Microaggressions in Flux: Whiteness, Disability and Masculinity in Academia," Haneen Ghabra and Shahd Al Shammari demonstrate the way in which Middle Eastern transnational feminisms are constantly in flux as they performatively share their experiences with the hope that they create safe spaces for our Otherized students. This chapter nicely transitions to next theme "Transnational Circumferences."

Chapters that fall under the last theme reconsider the ways that de-whiten intersectionality in and across transnational contexts. In chapter 11, "Remembering Julia de Burgos: Faithful Witnessing as Decolonial Feminist Performance," Sara Baugh-Harris argues the way in which Carmen Rivera's play *Julia de Burgos: Child of Water* models memory that can be used to disrupt white, colonial systems of power. This chapter reads Rivera against calls to de-whiten intersectionality. In chapter 12, "De-whitening Intersectionality through *Transfeminismo*," Raquel Moreira traces the development of *transfeminismo* in Brazil, an epistemological and political project that critically embodies the concept of intersectionality. In chapter 13, "Dark Looks: Sensory Contours of Racism in India," Pavithra Prasad and Anjana Raghavan draw a conceptual map of relations between caste-based patriarchy and anti-blackness, furthering an understanding of intersectional identities as shifting, fluid, and locational, specifically in relation to the global south. In chapter 14, "'We Had to Sink or Swim': Privileging and Intersectionalizing Racialized Ethnic Identifications among Asians and Asian Americans," Yea-Wen Chen examines voices of racialized Asian ethnics about their experiences with (re-) racialization and pan-Asian organizing. In so doing, this chapter discusses de-whitening racialized ethnic identifications across intersecting oppressions. Lastly, in chapter 15, "Crazy Sexy Asian Men! Masculinities in *Crazy Rich*

Asians," Zhao Ding and Kamela Rasmussen interrogates the desirable images of Asian men and masculinities portrayed in *Crazy Rich Asians* (2018) through the conceptual lens of intersectionality. This chapter challenges the hierarchy of masculinities presented in the film that draws attention away from white cis-hetero-patriarchal masculine norms.

With these lineups of chapters, *De-Whitening Intersectionality: Race, Intercultural Communication, and Politics* aims to create an intellectual space through which scholars argue, reimagine, and practice de-whitening of intersectionality furthermore. However, we acknowledge that this book is neither a complete nor a perfect vision. Our visions presented in this book advance just some of the many potential passages toward de-whitening intersectionality. Recognizing this shortcoming, it is our hope (as the queer of color collective) that our coediting of this book adds to ongoing questions and critiques that intersectionality operates as a checklist of multiple identities resecuring whiteness as an invisible and universal power. We reiterate that we should never forget how intersectionality emerged to begin with in addition to distinguishing between uses of intersectionality that seem inclusive versus actually enacting inclusion. The de-whitening of intersectionality is only doable when we as intersectional scholars and practitioners continue to question and critique the appropriation of intersectionality.

REFERENCES

Abdi, S. & Calafell, B. M. (2017). Queer utopias and a (feminist) Iranian vampire: A critical analysis of resistive monstrosity in A Girl Walks Home Alone at Night. *Critical Studies in Media Communication, 34*(4), 358–70. DOI:10.1080/15295036.2017.1302092.

Abdi, S. & Van Gilder, B. (2016). Cultural (in)visibility and identity dissonance: Queer Iranian-American women and their negotiation of existence. *Journal of International and Intercultural Communication*, *9*(1), 69–86. DOI: 10.1080/17513057.2016.1120850.

Aiello, G., Bakshi, S., Bilge, S., Kahaleole Hall, L., Johnston, L., Pérez, K., & Chávez, K. (2013). Here, and not yet here: A dialogue at the intersection of queer, trans, and culture. *Journal of International and Intercultural Communication, 6*(2), 96–117. DOI: 10.1080/17513057.2013.778155.

Bilge, S. (2014). Whitening intersectionality: Evanescence of race in intersectionality scholarship. In W. D. Hund, & A. Lentin (Eds.), *Racism and sociology: Racism analysis yearbook 5* (pp. 175–205). Berlin: Lit Verlag/Routledge.

Calafell, B. M. (2007). *Latina/o communication studies: Theorizing performance.* New York: Peter Lang.

Calafell, B. M. (2012). Monstrous femininity: Constructions of women of color in the academy. *Journal of Communication Inquiry, 36*(2), 111–30. DOI: 10.1177/0196859912443382.

Calafell, B. M. (2013). (I)dentities: Considering accountability, reflexivity, and intersectionality in the I and the we. *Liminalities: A Journal of Performance Studies, 9*(2), 6–13. http://liminalities.net/9-2/calafell.pdf.

Calafell, B. M. (2015). *Monstrosity, performance, and race in contemporary culture.* New York: Peter Lang.

Calafell, B. M. & Moreman, S. (2010). Iterative hesitancies and *Latinidad*: The reverberances of raciality. In R. Halualani, & T. K. Nakayama (Eds.), *Handbook of critical intercultural communication* (pp. 400–416). Hoboken, NJ: Wiley-Blackwell.

Chávez, K. R. (2012). Doing intersectionality: Power, privilege, and identities in political activist communities. In N. Bardhan, & M. P. Orbe (Eds.), *Identity research and communication: Intercultural reflections and future directions* (pp. 21–32). Lanham, MD: Lexington Books.

Crenshaw, K. (1989). Demarginalizing the intersection of race and sex: A black feminist critique of antidiscrimination doctrine, feminist theory, and antiracist policies. *The University of Chicago Legal Forum, 1*(8), 139–67.

Crenshaw, K. (1991). Mapping the margins. *Stanford Law Review, 43*(6), 1241–99.

Crenshaw, K. (2012). From private violence to mass incarceration: Thinking intersectionally about women, race, and social control. *UCLA Law Review, 59,* 1418–71.

Crenshaw, K. (2017). Race liberalism and the deradicalization of racial reform. *Harvard Law Review, 130,* 2298–319.

Delgado, R. & Stefancic, J. (2012). *Critical race theory: An introduction* (2nd ed.). New York: New York University Press.

Eguchi, S. (2015). Queer intercultural relationality: An autoethnography of Asian-Black (dis)connections in White gay America. *Journal of International and Intercultural Communication, 8*(1), 27–43. DOI: 10.1080/17513057.2015.991077.

Eguchi, S. (2019). Transnational LGBTQ pride: Whiteness, health, and wellbeing in VICELAND's *Gaycation. China Media Research, 15*(3), 83–92.

Eguchi, S. (2020). Sticky rice politics: Impossible possibilities of queerness in and across *Yellow Fever* and *Front Cover. Women's Studies in Communication, 43*(1), 67-84. DOI: 10.1080/07491409.2019.1696435.

Eguchi, S. & Calafell, B. M. (2020). Introduction: Reorienting queer intercultural communication. In S. Eguchi & B. M. Calafell (Eds.), *Queer intercultural communication: The intersectional politics of belonging in and across differences* (pp. 1–16). Lanham, MD: Rowman & Littlefield.

Eguchi, S., Calafell, B. M., & Files-Thompson, N. (2014). Intersectionality and quare theory: Fantasizing African American men's same-sex relationships in *Noah's Arc: Jumping the Broom. Communication, Culture, & Critique, 7*(3), 371–89. DOI: doi:10.1111/cccr.12054.

Eguchi, S., Files-Thompson, N., & Calafell, B. M. (2018). Queer (of color) aesthetics: Fleeting moments of transgression in VH1's *Love & Hip-Hop: Hollywood Season 2. Critical Studies in Media Communication, 35*(2), 180–93. DOI:10.1080/15295036.2017.1385822.

Griffin, R. A. (2014). *Pushing into precious*: Black women, media representation, and the glare of the White supremacist capitalist patriarchal gaze. *Critical Studies in Media Communication, 31*(3), 182–97. DOI: 10.1080/15295036.2013.849354.

Halberstam, J. (2011). *The queer art of failure*. Durham, NC: Duke University Press.

Halualani, R. T. & Nakayama, T. K. (2010). Critical intercultural communication studies: At a crossroads. In T. K. Nakayama & R. T. Halualani (Eds.), *The handbook of critical intercultural communication* (pp. 1–16). Malden, MA: Wiley-Blackwell.

Hill Collins, P. (1990). *Black feminist thought; Knowledge, consciousness, and the politics of empowerment*. New York: Routledge.

Johnson, A. (2014). Confessions of a video vixen: My autocritography of sexuality, desire, and memory. *Text and Performance Quarterly, 34*(2), 182–200. DOI: 10.1080/10462937.2013.879991.

Joseph, R. L. (2018). *Postracial resistance: Black women, media, and the uses of strategic ambiguity*. New York: New York University Press.

LeMaster, B. (2015). Discontents of being and becoming fabulous on RuPaul's Drag U: Queer criticism in neoliberal times. *Women's Studies in Communication, 38*(2), 167–86. DOI: 10.1080/07491409.2014.988776.

Lethabo King, T. (2015). Post intersectional and post identitarian anxiety in the neoliberal corporate university. *Feminist Formations, 27*(3), 114–38. DOI: 10.1353/ff.2016.0002.

LuLevitt, C. & Calafell, B. M. (2019). Reverberations of familial and cultural histories: Performances with and again whiteness. In D. M. D. McIntosh, D. G. Moon, & T. K. Nakayama (Eds.), *Interrogating the communicative power of whiteness* (pp. 46–65). New York: Routledge.

McIntosh, D. M. D., Moon, D. G., & Nakayama, T. K. (2019). Introduction: Introducing twenty-first century whiteness or "everything old is new again". In D. M. D. McIntosh, D. G. Moon, & T. K. Nakayama (Eds.), *Interrogating the communicative power of whiteness* (pp. 1–12). New York: Routledge.

Muñoz, J. E. (1999). *Disidentifications: Queers of color and the performance of politics*. Minneapolis: University of Minnesota Press.

Nakayama, T. K. & Krizek, R. L. (1995). Whiteness: A strategic rhetoric. *Quarterly Journal of Speech, 81*(3), 291–309. DOI: 10.1080/00335639509384117

Na'puti, T. R. & Bevacqua, M. L. (2015). Militarization and resistance from Guåhan: Protecting and defending Pågat. *American Quarterly, 67*(3), 837–58. DOI: 10.1353/aq.2015.0040.

Nishime, L. (2012). The case for Cablinasian: Multiracial naming from *Plessy* to Tiger Woods. *Communication Theory, 22*(1), 92–111. DOI:10.1111/j.1468-2885.2011.01399.x.

Omi, M. & Winant, H. (2014). *Racial formation in the United States* (3rd ed.). New York: Routledge.

Ono, K. A. & Cheung, A. Y. (2019). Asian American performance in White supremacist representation. In D. M. D. McIntosh, D. G. Moon, & T. K. Nakayama (Eds.), *Interrogating the communicative power of whiteness* (pp. 15–28). New York: Routledge.

Puar, J. K. (2007). *Terrorist assemblages: Homonationalism in queer times*. Durham, NC: Duke University Press.

Tuck, E. & Yang, K. W. (2012). Decolonization is not a metaphor. *Decolonization: Indigeneity, Education & Society, 1*(1), 1–40.

Warren, J. T. (2008). Performing difference: Repetition in context. *Journal of International and Intercultural Communication, 1*(4), 290–308. DOI: 10.1080/17513050802344654.

Yep, G. A. (2010). Toward the de-subjugation of racially marked knowledges in communication. *Southern Communication Journal, 75*(2), 171–75. DOI: 10.1080/10417941003613263.

Yep, G. A. (2013). Queering/quaring/kauering/crippin'/transing "other bodies" in intercultural communication. *Journal of International and Intercultural Communication, 6*(2), 118–26. DOI: 10.1080/17513057.2013.777087.

Yep, G. A. & Chivers, N. T. (2017). Intersectionality. In Y. Y. Kim, & K. McKay-Semmler (Eds.), *International encyclopedia of intercultural communication* (pp. 1532–37). West Sussex, UK: Wiley-Blackwell.

Section I

THE POLITICS OF THEORIZING

Chapter 1

Intersectionalities in the Fields of Chicana Feminism

Pursuing Decolonization through Xicanisma's "Resurrection of the Dreamers"

Michelle A. Holling

Over twenty years ago, I began studying Chicana feminism—"a nationalist and feminist struggle against racism and sexism, designed to improve the position of Chicanas in American society" (García, 1989, pp. 220–21). Chicana feminism was and remains a means to know them/us/me and, as important, to (w)rite them/us/me into a disciplinary field in which they/we/me had been invisible. That is, throughout most of my graduate education, there was no published literature in communication about Chicanas and, there were less than a handful of articles that examined the rhetoric of Chicanos. Such an absence made me question if they/we/me had a place in the field of communication and if Chicana feminist theory, when integrated, would be perceived as instructive to understandings about the field and its subfields. Scholarship over the years has since made significant inroads not only to fill the gaping hole in knowledge but also to demonstrate Chicana feminism as a heuristic for the study of communication.[1] Within Chicana feminism lies the affirmation of racial, ethnic, gendered, and classed identities and voces[2] [voices] that speak of cultural struggles and resistance.

In addition to the widely known and cited Chicana feminist voces of Gloria Anzaldúa and Cherríe Moraga are many other less-known Chicana feminists who began putting pen to paper to articulate a set of experiences that pointed to triple oppression[3] or, the triumvirate of race, class, and gender oppression. Although rarely heard nowadays, triple oppression was the terminology adopted by Chicana feminists preceding what many now recognize as "intersectionality" (Crenshaw, 1993) or the matrix of domination (Hill Collins, 1991). By turning to Chicana feminists, the point is not a matter of whose claims to intersectionality are *the* basis for intersectionality, but rather how particular racial-ethnic, gendered, classed, and sexed identities structure and offer unique understandings about intersectional matrices, power, resistance, and levels of oppression. Moreover, in thinking about how to enlarge current understandings of Chicana feminism and its emphasis on intersectionality, I turn to the voz [voice] of Ana Castillo in particular, her monograph *Massacre of the Dreamers* (1994).[4]

She is considered "one of the most outspoken voices for the 'colonized woman'" and her book is "a work that explains more clearly than any other the historical, philosophical, and political underpinnings of contemporary Chicana writing" (Milligan, 1999, pp. 19–20). In *Massacre*, Castillo theorizes Xicanisma and its possibilities for reinvigorating Chicana feminism which "has fallen prey to theoretical abstractions" (1994, p. 11). Although she at times explains Xicanisma as conceptually referring to Chicana feminism, Castillo harkens to indigenisma, feminine principle, and activista and feminista impulses to advance an alternate view. Her use of "X" is a gesture to the racial-indigenous roots that metaphorically and literally ground Xicanas subsequently predating nascent appearances of "x." Xicanisma contains within it an expanded perspective on intersectionality as both repressive and restorative that is racially ethnically situated, cognizant of forces of oppression, guided by conscientización, and a (re)turn to ethnic-cultural practices that seek to decolonize Xicanas. Xicanisma, therefore, contributes to this volume's goal of de-whitening intersectionality given the primacy placed on culturally grounded ideas and emphasis on difference that is firmly steeped in a "MexicAmerIndian"[5] identity. Castillo's ideas offer points of connection for (critical) (inter-)cultural scholars interested in decolonization, cultural practices, and, of course, intersectionality.

Before turning to her work, I first revisit pivotal Chicana feminist writings from the Chicano movement period to familiarize readers with how Chicanas were thinking and writing about triple oppression. I then move inward by synthesizing a sampling of scholarship in communication that made inroads to establish Chicana feminist frameworks, ones that implicated intersectionality. From Chicana feminism, I turn to Castillo's notion of Xicanisma and advance intersectionality, as both repressive and restorative, concluding with final thoughts.

CHICANA FEMINISM IN THE FIELD(S)

As a trope, "field(s)" acknowledges various material sites in which Xicanas have labored. For example, there are historical battlefields in which Malinche, soldaderas, and adelitas found themselves laboring to survive; agricultural fields in which Dolores Huerta and many unnamed Chicana (and Filipina) migrant workers challenged exploitative conditions and resisted treatment experienced from agribusiness; and fields of struggle, cultural and ideological, occurring within the Chicano and women's movements. Extended discussions of each type of field that burgeons Chicana feminism is beyond the scope of this chapter. I do, however, provide an overview of Chicana feminism from the fields, historically and contemporarily, that (re)inscribes a set of experiences, knowledge, and theories foretelling triple oppression.

Early Feministas

Culture-based infusions of Chicana feminism date to Chicana writings in which scholars, poets, and writers drew from a colonized history and archetypes arising in and from it to begin theorizing the specificities of Chicana feminism. La Virgen de Guadalupe, la Malinche, la adelita, and la soldadera are key archetypes[6] who were "products of their environment and producers of history"[7] (Williams, 1998, p. 218). The first two are products from a history of conquest(s) and subsequent colonization that sought to deny the indigenous origins of both Tonantzin[8] better known as la Virgen and Malinalli or Malintzin better known as la Malinche, supposed traitor to her race due to her alliance with Hernán Cortés. Not until Chicana feminists' writings are different interpretations of those two archetypes rendered, but in particular of Malinche as a producer of history and feminist prototype for Chicanas.[9] In terms of la adelita and soldaderas, as participants in the Mexican Revolution, they retain symmetry to la Virgen and Malinche. Adelitas, as with la Virgen, historically are adored and venerated, whereas soldaderas and Malinche are positioned in and at the service of others,[10] despite their acumen and strategic maneuverings in actual war times.

Turning to the archetypes not only affirms a cultural legacy left for contemporary Chicanas, but they also intimate a distinct understanding of intersectionality as pointing to conditions of conquest, colonization, and religiosity. Such a view directs attention to the interaction of conditions that produce cultural domination on the basis of race, class, and gender; indicate oppressor/oppressed relationship that brings about subordination; and orient scholars to discern intersectionality as temporally inflected by conditions that then bear upon identities and subjectivities. The mix of conquest, colonialism, and religion had lasting impacts on Chicanas' insurgency of the 1960s who turned to soldaderas and Malinche for inspiration and who contended with the strictures of la Virgen, all of which brought about particular tensions.

One such tension is that of the buena mujer [good woman] and mala mujer [bad woman], an additional way that Chicanas' identities are scripted dichotomously along sexual[ized], gendered, racialized, and classed ways (Castillo, 1994; Holling, 1994, 2000; NietoGomez, 1997). As a derivative from the intersection of conquest, colonization, and religiosity, the dichotomy of buena-mala mujer later played out along the lines of Chicana loyalists and Chicana feminists that parallels the cultural values attached to La Virgen and the ascribed traitorous behavior of La Malinche, respectively. In brief, "loyalists viewed Chicanas who called themselves feminists as allies of a middle-class women's movement who advocated individualistic upward mobility rather than struggle against race/class domination. Feminists . . . argued that the struggle against male domination was central to the overall Chicana/o movement for liberation" (Segura & Pesquera, 1988/1990, p. 74). The split was an ideological and hence a cultural one in that loyalists were traditionalists, emphasized Chicana/o familial values and gendered roles, and "believed that racism not sexism was the greater battle" (Castillo, 1994, p. 34). Chicana feminists, on the other hand, identified racism, sexism, and classism as triple oppressive factors that impeded their social and familial mobility. Perceived as mujeres malas, Chicana feminists' tenuous alliance with each of the Chicano and women's movements would both fall short in addressing the layered forms of oppression experienced by Chicanas (Holling, 1994); thus, their formation of distinct organizations[11] and their own feminist movement.

Chicana feminists' writings during movement periods indicate a growing awareness of what was then termed "triple oppression"; the three levels of oppression based on race, class, and gender that produce social inequalities. Reflecting on her own participation in the Chicano movement, Ana Castillo (1994) identified racism, sexism, and sexist-racism "as ways that oppressed socially and economically" (p. 33). Triple oppression may attribute to economic-structural dimensions and/or be "reproduced ideologically and socioculturally" (Segura, 1990, p. 58). Important to note is that triple oppression presumes interplay, rather than an additive approach to understanding social inequities. Segura (1990), for example, emphasizes the interactive consequences experienced by Chicanas who are subordinated socially and economically on the basis of race, class, and gender relative to men of color and white counterparts, within and outside of the home. A survey of Chicana feminist writings is apt to find both perspectives of triple oppression (i.e., economic-structural and ideological-cultural). Ideologically, Chicana feminists bore responsibility for challenging hierarchical views of triple oppression in which racism was perceived of utmost importance (a viewpoint among Chicanos) or, challenging the view that sexism compromised cultural notions of familia [family] or Chicanas' femininity in identifying as feminists (Longeaux y Vázquez, 1973). A prime example of a Chicana feminist's effort to unseat a hierarchy of triple oppression is Cherríe Moraga's (1981) autobiographical poem “La Güera.” In comparing her lesbianism to her mother’s brownness, she realizes both are poverties and “the danger lies in ranking the oppressions. The danger lies in failing to acknowledge the specificity of the oppression” (p. 29). Her cautionary words are significant in that she warned against viewing oppressions as a competition and, in doing so, encouraged feminists, Chicanas or otherwise, to identify points of commonalities amid distinctions that differently anchor oppression as a means toward solidarity. Moreover, Moraga, among others, expands triple oppression to account for sexuality as another axis of which Chicana lesbians contended.

Cataloguing Chicana feminists’ herstorical[12] legacies and more broadly Chicana feminists’ writings is Alma García’s (1997) *Chicana Feminist Thought: The Basic Historical Writings*, culled from prose, poetry, conferences, and newspapers. It remains a premier, if not primer, on the ways that Chicanas experienced racist-sexist and/or racist-sexist-classist oppression that was a basis for their activism, resistance, and theorizing. The purposes of Chicana feminists’ writings are complex given desires to challenge restrictive cultural ideologies, to create a sense of place given bicultural identifications, to craft identities and subjectivities uniquely their own as revealed in scholarly writings, and to alter imbalances of power (Castillo, 1994; Dicochea, 2004; Flores, 1996; Holling, 1994, 2000). Ana Castillo characterizes Chicana feminists’ writings as “un tapiz,” a “tapestry of conscientización” (1994, p. 171). She names writings by herself, Gloria Anzaldúa, and Cherrie Moraga who revision culture through inventional resources of metaphors, subversion, and word play.

The invention inherent in Chicana feminists’ writings becomes apparent when considering, for example, Pat Mora’s (1990) poem “Legal Alien” or Ana Castillo’s (1994) motif of “countryless woman” that speak to resulting feelings from triple oppression. Implied in each motif are layers of displacement. One layer is from justice-oriented movements in which Chicanas’ concerns with triple oppression were not wholly embraced thus necessitating them to break away and foment change on their own behalf. There is also displacement from nation-states, United States and Mexico, in which Ch/Xicanas although legally possessing U.S. citizenship, remain perceptually as “alien” or “countryless” consequently exist outside of representational boundaries, left to navigate bicultural identifications. Mora explains, “American but hyphenated,/viewed by Anglos as perhaps exotic,/perhaps inferior, definitely different,/viewed by Mexicans as alien,/their eyes say, ‘You may speak/Spanish but you’re not like me’ ” (p. 376). Ascribed a “foreign-like identity” (Castillo, 1994, p. 39) are resulting traumas of assimilation and internalized racism produced from colonial relations in a U.S. context and lack of acceptance in a Mexican context that produce a countryless woman. Ultimately, Chicanas are tokenized: “A handy token/sliding back and forth/

between the fringes of both worlds/by smiling/by masking the discomfort/of being pre-judged/bi-laterally" (Mora, 1990, p. 376).

Intersectional Chicana Feminist Perspectives

The marginality Chicanas experienced in U.S. society regrettably extends into the field of communication wherein the appearance of scholarship that centralizes them was slow to manifest even as scholarship about Chicanos was published (Holling, 2008). I turn to select seminal works and scholars for two reasons.[13] Early scholarship indicates a disciplinary micro-herstory of Chicana feminist ideas by communication scholars that reflects their work as "archeologists," a role Castillo (1994) encourages. In such a capacity, scholars excavate Chicana writings, along with their own experiences, to develop theoretical frameworks by which to study voces [voices] of difference. As I argued elsewhere, "the use of difference to herald identities historically stereotyped, scorned, and/or negated is significant in light of public discourses that exert control (or attempt to) over how" Chicanas are understood by publics at large (Holling, 2008, p. 304). Second, the selected essays are ones that to date have received varying degrees of attention. The collective "we" have failed to apprehend key moments in which scholars theorize what I term an intersectional Chicana feminist perspective on theoretical and methodological levels for the field of communication. Therefore, digging up seminal essays is to know (and, possibly adopt) scholars' early accountings of intersectionality that surfaced most in (inter)culture, rhetoric, performance studies, and Latin@ communication during a "decade of repoliticalization" (Holling, 2008).[14]

The contours of an intersectional Chicana feminist perspective begin with a critical orientation that concerns itself theoretically with voz [voice], through which power struggles and resistance surface, and with materiality. The principle of voz highlights embodiment and contributes to decolonizing efforts. She who speaks reclaims her (cultural) truths, speaks through different linguistic tongues (e.g., English, Spanish, Spanglish, Nahuatl, etc.), expresses experiences of triple oppression, instructs how a marginalized population has proceeded in their pursuit for justice, and disrupts colonialist efforts to silence and erase Chicanas. This is much like the reclamation of Malinalli who possessed "the gift of the voice" (De La Garza, 2004, p. 108); this is much like the efforts of Chicana scholars to have their writings and acts of speaking reflect their "effort to live and become that which has been silenced in [her] life" (Martinez, 2000, p. 130); and, this is much like some who have contributed to the development of Latina/o performance as a way of expanding disciplinary voices heard (Calafell, 2003). In each/all instances, countering silences obviously relies upon voz (and/or vocalities) and sources of knowledge.

Chicanas' bodies[15] and experiences are the sources from which they produce insights and acknowledge their material realities that belie intersectionality. Martinez (2000) asserts, Chicana experiences "become the site of interrogation whereby we may come to better understand how a racist-sex ist-classist-homophobic-assimilationist culture works so as to more effectively counteract it" (p. 106). Evident is that intersectionality anchors Chicana feminist theorizing, whether multilayered or the triumvirate of race, class, and gender. Depending on which scholarly work is consulted, other manifestations of intersectionality come to the fore.[16] Flores (2000), for example, extends identity categories to mean the "interconnectedness of gender, race, class, and heterosexuality" (p. 693). Differently is De La Garza (2004) who, in thinking through labels attributed to women of Mexican descent, notes "four primary dimensions . . . religion, sexual mores, social class, and race" (p. 13) that due to their ideological force intersectionally constrain Mexican-Chicana women (p. 32). Methodologically, Chicana scholars draw on personal narratives, auto-ethnography and biography, and personal experience as a basis for knowledge production as well as a means to analyze culture (Calafell, 2003, 2005; De La Garza, 2004; Flores, 2000; Martinez, 2000).[17] In so doing, the body is a means through which loss, memory, and "queer temporality,"[18] among other possibilities, come to the fore (Calafell, 2003). As "sources of political power" (De La Garza, 2004, p. 123), Chicana feminists act as "cultural scribes" (Flores, 2000, p. 692) writing to tell of their own experience and cultural history in order to "challenge the neo-colonial practices which shape the lives of Chicana/os" (Flores, 2000, p. 693). Endeavoring as they do, an array of Chicana feminist scholar[s] in diverse disciplinary fields bring forth and highlight Chicanas' voces [voices] yet, re/membering they are "one voice among many" (Flores, 2000, p. 695).

Chicanas' knowledge and experiences, existing in archives or catalogued in anthologies and literature, are a basis for theorizing Chicana-centered frameworks. Ones developed include Chicana critical rhetoric (Dicochea, 2004) or subject/ivity, identity, and agency (Holling, 2000) that provide a means by which to analyze Chicanas' writings, news-like publications, and fictional literature, respectively.[19] Dicochea and Holling each merge Chicana feminist studies with critical veins of rhetoric in order to herald Chicanas' "unique body of knowledge" (Dicochea, 2004, p. 78) as influenced by their material realities that range from economic or educational inequalities to culturally constraining ideologies. Their scholarship also indicates the ways in which Chicana feminist writings convey resistive and transformative possibilities for living.[20]

Complicating the principle of voz (and, intersectionality) is Garza (2011) who offers a way to include and move beyond the potentialities (and limitations) of a singular voz [voice] by turning to vocalities[21] related to the Mexica legend of Coyolxauhqui. Garza explains that vocality not only gives "voices its rhetorical emphasis" (p. 37), it also "attempts to account for the ways in which subjects of discourse become creators, innovators, or producers of discourse, in order to forge new articulations that aim to expand agency and empowerment through calls for consciousness" (p. 41). Although the term "intersectionality" does not appear in Garza's theorization of vocality, there is a sense that uni-, multi-, and hypervocality form a type of intersectionality that highlights power (i.e., struggles over which layering of vocality acquires prominence). Layerings of vocality may be compounded based on textual, narrative, or experiential voicings from Chicanas that overlap thereby revealing the urgency behind voice(s) and indicating possible conflicts or tensions inherent in or following from the interaction of vocalities.

From this concise survey of scholarship that advances an intersectional Chicana feminist perspective, some observations. Intersectionality appears in triumvirate form and extends to account for sexuality that harken to early feministas. Martinez (2000) and Calafell (2003), for example, weave sexuality and queerness, respectively into their monographs that deepens their reflections on processes of assimilation, for instance. What becomes evident among the works discussed under this section is the incremental movement to expand intersectionality as race, class, and gender. The modicum of attention on sexuality and queerness might also be contextualized and hence understood as a reflection of the literature selected and/or as the state and development of scholarship within the field in particular moments. In addition, vocalities (Garza, 2011) or ideological layerings (e.g., De La Garza, 2004; Holling, 2000) indicate robust intersections that are culturally situated and beckon attention to the ways that race, class, and gender play out in these formations of intersectionality. Next, intersectionality in Chicana feminists' lives reflects and urges deep-seated grappling with the ways that identity categories and ideologies overlap to position them against that which they resist. This point is crucial; *intersectionality exceeds mere (ac)counting of identities*. To engage intersectionality as simply a matter of overlapping identities is not only reductive, it abandons a focus on power that animates the lives of individuals. Instead, intersectionality is a modus operandi that has, and continues, to play a role in Chicana feminists' activism, organizing, and efforts to create social change. A contemporary example is the Esperanza Center that views optimism, holistic approach, intersectionality, relationality, and historicity as key components to its methodology to social justice (deTurk, 2015). Further complicating intersectionality is the work of Castillo, who identifies other facets that affect Chicanas' identities and provides entry points to reinvigorate Chicana feminism.

"WE ARE A GOD-DAMN WALKING MIRACLE"

The epigraph, voiced by Inez Talamantez (qtd. in Castillo, 1994, p. 221), opening this section pays homage to the resilience of Xicanas, who persist and survive (while aiming to thrive) amid oppressive forces that seek to squelch her/our spirit. Two aims compose this final section—one is to advance what I label repressive intersectionalities that enliven the meaningfulness of Talamantez's words thus providing a backdrop to apprehending the necessity of Ana Castillo's conception of Xicanisma. The second aim is to elaborate on the contours of Xicanisma and its ideas for what I term restorative intersectionalities that hold relevance for the everyday and, as important, suggest a pathway toward decolonization. Scholars in communication view decolonization as important move to pursue and reveal in Chican@-Latin@ communication (Flores, 2000; Holling & Calafell, 2011; Martinez, 2004). Thus, Castillo's work revalues cultural facets that seek to restore Xicanas' spirituality, reclaim sexuality, and redress the harms committed in, by, and through culture at large.

Repressive Intersectionalities

Massacre of the Dreamers provocatively compels reflection about the agent(s) and victims of violence. To massacre indicates full-on assaults against individuals, populations, or groups in order to usurp their power, agency, and way of being. Following from a massacre are the relations of colonizer/colonized in the case of Xicanas and its significant impacts on knowledge received and learned. As a consequence, perpetuated is "systematic and determined ignorance" among Xicanas, who have been denied access to their historical-cultural knowledges and "white dominant society," who have suppressed the histories and literature of marginalized peoples (Castillo, 1994, p. 5). The repressive forces affecting Xicanas, historically and contemporarily, are macro level and point to an understanding of intersectionality shaped by colonial legacies.

Forces that repress Xicanas are distinct yet, also intersect to include nationalism, machismo, capitalism, and Catholicism that inhibit conscientización. While page limits prevent me from going into immense detail on each factor, I offer some elaboration. A problematic of nationalism—whether from a movement period as in the Chicano movement or nation-state—is its premise of ethnic and racial identification to the subordination of other identity categories that resulted in the marginalization of Xicanas. More broadly, nationalism is exclusionary and "always find[s] justification for manipulation of power" (Castillo, 1994, p. 226). The nationalism of the Chicano-era movement, and by extension the nation-state, results in a "countryless woman"

(Castillo, p. 21). She is accorded no space within la causa as a feminista and representationally absent in the United States; her visibility becomes possible if she opts to subscribe to "Hispanic," a flattener of difference that names Spain as the "paternal cultural progenitor" (Castillo, p. 28). Displacement then produces alienation, demoralization, dominant/subordinate relations, racial rejection and/or invisibility, consequences that necessitate a pathway to conscientización.

A by-product of the aforementioned forces is perceptions of Xicanas' role as producers-reproducers that create a contemporary manifestation of being colonized. That is, economic (among other) systems co-opt and control Xicanas', extending to marginalized womens', labor and bodies.[22] The role of producer-reproducer certainly has a political economy bent considering the relationality of "the domineering husband, the sexist activist, and el patrón" (Castillo, 1994, p. 58) to Catholicism as it hails from Christianity, nationalism, and capitalism respectively, that perpetuate women as "productive/reproductive entit[ies] within U.S. Mexican society" (p. 36). Capitalism may be broadened to include global economic forces in light of neoliberal policies (e.g., NAFTA) wherein corporations have readily available and exploitable labor forces that perpetuate economic inequities based on race and gender. A concern of Castillo is the absence of conscientización—for some but not all women—that "makes the maquiladora an ideal worker for the semi-legal, exploitative operations of multi-national factory production" (p. 38). In the case of factory workers,[23] if conscientización is not developed, discerning discrimination remains possible; the challenge is coping or resisting it. In the absence of conscientización, it may be fostered through labor activism (p. 47), as an act that challenges "white supremacist patriarchy" (p. 58), and building solidarity with marginalized women globally (p. 61).

With the intensification of capitalism so too has women's oppression as they have been viewed as "property" (Castillo, 1994, p. 64), a notion that surfaces with the appearance of machismo attributable to "tribal societies" (p. 70) in particular. The intersection of machismo, a means through which patriarchy manifests, with Catholic doctrine enforces the "reproducer" role of Xicanas that leads to a repression of their spirituality and sexuality. Such repressions, particularly the (con)scripting of heterosexual desire serve men, are premised on domination and power, and objectify women (Castillo, p. 127). For Xicanas to reclaim both spirituality and sexuality would challenge systems that have long benefited.

"There is no utopia" for Xicanas, not to mention "brown women," when one resides in a world that colonizes Xicanas spiritually, mentally, physically, and sexually (Castillo, 1994, p. 145). The process of colonization brought with it transformative forces, such as those elaborated upon, that deleteriously affect Xicanas. Colonization vis-à-vis internalized racism has also enforced a presumption that Xicanas possess no right to their perspectives (Castillo, p. 175). As a consequence, they seek to overcome cultural "self-contempt" and writing inferiority (p. 168), lest they adopt "white writing"[24] (p. 167). Intimated here, but also throughout *Massacre of the Dreamers* are levels of oppression based on race, ethnicity, class, gender, language, and skin color that "all determine identity and predict one's fate in the United States" (Castillo, p. 29). Where various forces literally and metaphorically massacre Xicanas, or seek to, in light of a history of subjugation, racism, ethnocentrism, and imperialism, Castillo is hopeful about possibilities. The title of her final chapter—"Resurrection of the Dreamers"—completes her vision. It is not of a religious orientation; rather, a recovery of knowledge and practices, suppressed due to forces previously reviewed, that she discusses across different chapters as ways to promote Xicanas' conscientización that aims for human liberation.

Restorative Intersectionalities

Castillo's hopefulness for a future other than what it is garners strength from the fact that Xicanistas have a history of activating themselves and those around them. She identifies "the activista" of the 1960–1970s era and the generation that came of age during the Reagan–Bush era because their "flesh, mind and soul serve[d] as the lightning rod for the confluence of her consciousness" (1994, p. 93). Activism is a path toward conscientización and, so too is higher education (although it sometimes requires Xicanas viewing themselves as "educatable,"[25] a hurdle to overcome given socializing messages that convey otherwise, p. 50). Regardless of the path taken toward conscientización, it and related practices is of necessity for Xicanas to recover their creative powers that aid in attaining larger aims to sustain themselves and those around them. From the perspective of Xicanisma, an understanding of intersectionality as restorative is suggested; the intersectional axis being spirituality, sexuality, and identities (e.g., race, class, gender). The first two replenish Xicanas' identities that put her on a path of conscientización and embolden her.

To begin, self-defining as a Xicanista "is a rejection of colonization" (Castillo, 1994, p. 12) in that her point of origin so to speak anchors in its meaning. Contrary to what Xicanas experienced in previous social justice movements, Castillo advocates that Xicanisma resist hierarchical ideologies, not be elitist nor woman-identified nor quick to attack or retaliate against those who contend with their own spiritual distancing (p. 224). The presence of any undercut a resurrection of the dreamers. Instead, Xicanisma is a way to reclaim the erasure of mestizas and Chicanas as well as counter perceptions of them/us as recently immigrated absent a colonial history (p. 23). Fending off erasures harkens possibly to a primordial period when considering the following: "The basic premise of Xicanisma is to reconsider behavior long seen as inherent in the MexicAmerIndian woman's character, such as, patience, perseverance, industriousness . . . we do not reject these virtues. . . . [they] may be considered strengths" (p. 40). Castillo's assertion functions not as an "essentialist rhetoric of exclusion" (Carson, 2004, p. 123) instead, as a means to ground Xicanas in their racial-ethnic (and gendered) heritage. In so doing, they/we embark on a reclamation of culturally based practices and ways of being that enable Xicanas to carry on their work not only as "obreras culturales" [cultural workers] (Castillo, p. 94) but also as "cultural guerrillas" (Castillo, p. 220) who work adamantly to subvert that which undermines their/our sense of being. The collectivist orientation and multilevel responsibility to the self, others, allies, and the environment that informs Xicanisma derives from "an ever-present consciousness of our interdependency" rooted in Xican@ culture and history (Castillo, p. 226) that enables Xicanas, and extending to men and non-Mexicans, to understand themselves. Toward that end, Castillo holds out a vision where Xicanas, and brown women generally, would no longer experience exploitation, predatory behavior, self- and other hatred, or objectification. Ultimately, "*our* vision as Xicanistas expects peace. . . . not the opposite of war, [rather] the achievement of balance" (Castillo, p. 225).

Viewing intersectionality as restorative (or as repressive) is a perspectival shift that recognizes when identities are influenced by cultural strategies that enrich the individual, she derives strength that assists her in combating inequalities. The cultural strategies Castillo names are a form of "self-care." My reticence with such phrasing has most to do with its depoliticized middle-class overtones in which those with means, who feel beleaguered by a state of affairs in daily life that overwhelm, literally turn further inward to tend to the individual consequently away from structural matters that necessitate attention.[26] Nonetheless, Xicanas' self-care entails culturally based strategies such as dreams, visions, brujeria, and curanderisma, or language alchemy to reclaim an embodied connection to that which has been suppressed. Self-care for Xicanas begins with reclaiming their indigenisma and "reinsert[ing] the forsaken feminine into consciousness" (Castillo, 1994, p. 12). These interrelated practices help to counteract the spiritual imbalance created from centuries old dualisms that hail from religious doctrine and nationalism. Indigenismo, for example, has long been repressed due to Christianity and Chicanas' conditioning to forget about their indigenous roots (Castillo, p. 87). However, by learning and embracing indigenismo, Xicanas learn about themselves and accept "oneself as an individual and of her/his people" (Castillo, p. 6). Indigenismo invokes the feminine based on who it implicates, namely, Coatlicue, "the serpent skirt and mother of many deities"[27] (Garza, 2011, p. 39). Mexican society transforms Coatlicue into Tonantzin, who due to Spanish colonization is transformed into La Virgen de Guadalupe, later appropriated during the Chicano movement to advance nationalistic aims. Through such transformations, the feminine is imbued with the negative and dichotomizes Xicanas' roles as either the "buena mujer" or the "mala mujer" contra to the power that inhered in Mexica female deities. As Garza (2011) writes, "Mexica female cultural mythic, religious, and historical figures have become symbolic of the struggle for Indigenous [sic] female empowerment, and the right to self-determination" (p. 39). Thus, Castillo asserts the feminine "is best recognized in our devotion to Tonantzin/La Virgen de Guadalupe"[28] (p. 88).

The feminine principle "is concerned with preservation, protection—especially of the young and less fortunate—and affiliations of communities for the common good" (Castillo, 1994, p. 87). It also exists within males and females, and "may be generally termed as the absence of machismo—all the qualities that have been negated, denied, denigrated, and made to be essentially valueless by our society" (Castillo, p. 82). By embracing indigenismo and the feminine, Xicanas begin to heal their traumatized, spiritual, and sexual selves; in so doing, she communicates her rejection of institutionalized religion, which has encouraged women's submissive and secondary status and repressed women's sexuality yet, men's expression of it (p. 107) subsequently, beginning her decolonization. Proclaiming spirituality rather than religiosity becomes "an act of insurrection to the system" (Castillo, p. 147) as Xicanas' agency manifests through their ability to define what is "needed to give [them] courage" (Castillo, p. 145). Xicanas may draw on homeopathic or non-Western methodologies such as curanderas or brujas, sweat lodges, along with rituals such as creating altars, lighting candles, burning copal, or baños (bath infused with herbs and spirits to "remedy physical or emotional ills," p. 160), or resurrecting Mexica goddesses to aid spiritual healing and cleansing. For example, curanderas are "a specialized healer" of the body who diagnosis ailments, whereas brujas are "a spiritual healer or psychic" (Castillo, p. 156), each of whom are differently skilled based on specialties related to healing.[29] Evident is that spirituality is an individualistic endeavor given the array of methodologies or cultural practices and rituals available to Xicanas. The spirituality that Castillo advocates is woman-centered and values Xicana's creatix ability (e.g., not being shameful of menses instead accepting it as a symbol of fertility and divine power, p. 123). By reconnecting to spirituality, which anchors Xicanas in the body, they simultaneously begin to challenge their expected role as reproducers. Their sexuality historically and contemporarily through religion, and Catholicism in particular, "has enforced female sexual repression" (Castillo, p. 128) outside of the confines of reproduction. Xicanisma encourages recognition of the functions of heterosexual desire that are at the expense of Xicanas embracing their sexuality and desires. Phrased otherwise, heterosexual desire is designed to serve men, offers no role models of sexual relationships other than that of domination and power, and objectifies women (p. 127). Instead, Castillo encourages Xicanas "to explore our erotic selves while attempting to remain true to the Mexican/Chicana/Latina/India/mestiza aspects of our sociopolitical identity" (p. 141). Ultimately, whatever forms Xicanas adopt to practice spirituality and pathways taken to reconnect to her sexuality should maintain the goal of restoring the feminine and address their contemporary needs.

CONCLUDING REMARKS

The aim of this chapter has been to present manifestations of intersectionality from Chicana and Xicana feminist perspectives that remind readers of the triple oppressive force of racism, sexism, and classism that initially shaped Ch/Xicanas' view of intersectionality. In so doing, this chapter contributes to a goal of this collection—"de-whitening intersectionality" (Eguchi, Calafell, & Abdi). Its timeliness contributes to and advances "race(ing) intercultural communication" (Moon & Holling, 2016, p. 3). Either/both moves, as with this chapter, convey concern, if not take umbrage with, uses of intersectionality that strip it of its politicized orientation, reduce it to identity politics, and/or adopt it for decorative branding purposes in organizational settings (Blige, 2013; Crenshaw, 2015). Whether in the classroom, at conferences, or in organizational settings, when scholars apply intersectionality as though it is merely a mechanism for articulating identities that intersect does the theory and its origins a disservice. Recall Crenshaw's (2015) originating idea, "intersectionality is an analytic sensibility, a way of thinking about identity *and* its relationship to power" (para. 6, emphasis added). Apprehending power becomes apparent through manifestations of intersectionality politically, structurally, or representationally that produce subordination among women of color given their identities (Crenshaw, 1993). A question that comes to mind is in what ways might those very identities that intersect be not only a basis for subordination or repression, as discussed, but also restorative? Carrying out Crenshaw's view of intersectionality "requires paying proper attention to historical contingencies, to specific contexts, and the purposes of specific arguments" (Blige, 2013, p. 420).

With "historical contingencies" and "specific contexts" in mind, I turned my attention to Chicana and Xicana feminism across different periods. Chicana feminism during movement period names triple oppression that they experienced in structural-economic ways and in sociocultural, ideological terms. A result were tensions (e.g., buena/mala mujer) Chicanas navigated and exposed in their writings that subsequently revealed Chicanas' writing as multifunctional and inventional. This first field of knowledge indicates intersectionality as affected by conditions of conquest, colonization, and religiosity that produce cultural domination based on race, class, and gender. Next, analyzing Chicanas' writings and/or cultural archetypes are Chicana feminist scholars in communication whose work indicates intersectional Chicana feminist perspectives. Apparent from the literature are formations of intersectionality as interconnected identities (i.e., gender, race, class, and [hetero]sexuality), ideological layerings (e.g., religion, sexual mores, social class, and race), and vocalities (i.e., uni, multi, and hyper), each of which foreground matters of voz [voice] and power. The varieties of intersectionality implicate identity matters and power thus engaging in a "politic of disruption" (Moon & Holling, 2016). The final perspective on intersectionality is from Xicanisma.

A Xicana feminist view of intersectionality, as conceived from Ana Castillo's monograph *Massacre of the Dreamers* (1994), assumes an accounting of macro forces as sites in and from which triple oppression surfaces and identifying micro approaches for counteracting the effects from structures. Carrying out that view of intersectionality also works in the service of "a politic of disruption" (Moon & Holling, 2016, p. 3) precisely due to its disrupting the (mis)taken-for-granted use of intersectionality as micro oriented. Instead, attention to the macro-micro tension (Holling & Moon, 2016, p. 185) implicated in intersectionality provokes questions about the conditions that enable racist-sexism to persist or about the power dynamics that enable or constrain individual actions in the face of structural inequities; both of which, for example, help advance the call for race(ing) intercultural communication (Moon & Holling, 2016, p. 3). Alternatively, a decolonial frame, in the sense of disrupting various dominant and Chicano histories (consult Pérez, 1999), informs a Xicana feminist view of intersectionality. One way is Xicanisma's recovery of cultural knowledge and practices that herald from their racial-ethnic-gendered history. Another way is Xicanisma's acknowledgement of Xicanas' stance as "countryless woman" (Castillo, 1994) that indicates disaffinity with the notion of nation (and culture as nation, see Halualani, Mendoza, & Drzewiecka, 2009) that is not only static but exclusive of intersectional identities that inhibit "cultural guerrillas" (Castillo).

Finally, I further discerned intersectionality as repressive and as restorative which contribute to intercultural communication and race. Despite being presented as dualities, likely an unintended consequence of Western thinking, intersectionality as both repressive and restorative is a perspectival shift to accepting them as dialectical, a stance in better alignment with critical intercultural communication (Martin & Nakayama, 1999) and with Castillo's conception of Xicanisma, which is "based on wholeness not dualism" (p. 226). For instance, where nationalism, machismo, capitalism, and Catholicism were identified as distinct forces that repress Xicanas and inhibit conscientización, Castillo's vision of Xicanisma, along with its embrace of indigenismo, the feminine, and cultural practices and rituals, are restorative thereby providing a pathway to conscientización, an awakening central to decolonizing oneself. More specifically, repressive intersectionalities operate on a macro level wherein structural forces and ideologies repress on the basis of, for example, race, ethnicity, class, gender, language, and skin color, attributable to colonial legacies. Xicanas consequently experience displacement from themselves, communities, and society given dichotomized roles as producer/reproducer. Restorative intersectionalities are enacted on a micro level; they are individual in the sense of the diverse racial-ethnic cultural practices and rituals that may be selected to promote self-care. It is needed given the lingering impact of a colonial history on Xicanas' spiritual and sexual selves that affect their racial, gendered, classed, and sexed identities. The idea is that through Xicanas' ability to restore themselves bears implications for communities based on the interdependent and collectivist orientation of Xicanisma and those who avow the identity of Xicana. Intersectionalities in the way proposed (i.e., repressive and restorative) encourages scholars to discern possibilities of decolonization as arising from that which individuals are encouraged to disassociate (e.g., indigenismo). In so doing, new insights and knowledge may arise about the "cultural-individual dialectic" (Martin & Nakayama, 1999) that bear upon the production of knowledge and cultural transformation.

NOTES

1. Consult my retrospective essay (2008) in which I chronicle the development of Chicana/o-Latina/o communication.

2. Elsewhere, I and coauthor Bernadette Calafell asserted that voces [voices] is a trope operating within Latin@ communication that highlights marginalized speaking subjects who self-assert using cultural forms of expression, who operate from a personal-performative stance that is contextually bound and responsive to "ideological barriers," and who write "within and against marginalized and dominant discourses" (Calafell & Holling, 2011, p. xix).

3. Predating "triple oppression" is Frances Beal, who coined "double jeopardy." It is a means to elucidate the intersection of being "black and female" (1970, p. 382).

4. University of New Mexico Press, which published the 1994 edition from which I work, rereleased a twentieth edition of *Massacre of the Dreamers*.

5. Castillo (1994) uses the label to represent the racial and ethnic composition of women of Mexican descent and "to assert both our indigenous blood and the source, at least in part, of our spirituality" (p. 10).

6. In addition to those named, Chicana feminist scholars in communication theorize by returning to Mexica deities such as Coatlicue or Coyolxauhqui (Garza, 2011).

7. Writing on the subject of Chicano [sic] cinema, Williams theorizes "type," a resistive possibility to the promulgation of stereotypes in media during the 1960–1970s. She writes that type "represent[s] both the historical and material situation of that minority and its very real differences from the dominant society" (pp. 216–217) subsequently, characters as type would be represented as "products of their environment," positioned between cultures, and "produced by and producers of history" (p. 218).

8. For a more complicated rendering of Tonantzin consult De La Garza (2004).

9. Consult, for example, Calafell (2005), Candelaria (1980), or Del Castillo (1997) who argue Malinche as a transgressor of limited gendered roles ascribed in narratives about her.

10. During Spanish conquest, soldaderas were servants who took soldiers' pay in exchange for food and supplies (Salas, 1990) whereas during the Mexican Revolution, both soldaderas and adelitas were military soldiers and strategists (Cantú, 1990). Adelitas were later immortalized in corridos [akin to ballads], a site of their cultural reformation narratively.

11. One example is the establishment of Comisión Femenil Mexicana in 1970, a national Chicana organization that developed in part as a response to the marginalization of Chicanas' contributions in social movements of the time (Comisión Femenil Mexicana, 1973).

12. The term "herstorical" (and herstory) privileges and records women's experiences from a feminist perspective. Such an act resists the notion of hetero-patriarchal, masculinist rendering of history in which men are perceived as active agents in the production of "History." Following Lerner, "History" with a capital "H" references the "recorded and interpreted past" (1986, p. 4) that has excluded women's contributions consequently, not viewing them/us as central to "History-making" (p. 5).

13. Those in mind include Dolores Tanno, Sarah Amira De La Garza, Lisa A. Flores, Jacqueline Martinez, Bernadette Calafell, Perlita Dicochea, and myself. Coincidentally, with the exception of Dolores Tanno, all named authors, shared time and space(s) while at Arizona State University perhaps indicative of sensibilities and sensory affinities to do work as Chicana feminists in the southwest.

14. I acknowledge, yet treat secondarily, publications by Flores (1996), Palczewski (1996), Sowards (2010, 2012), or Enoch (2004, 2005), for example. These are important works to be clear for each advances understandings about Chicana feminist writings from distinct historical junctures and diverse fields. Yet, some of the essays also evince an Anzalduaean shift in the study of Chicana feminism and read most as Chicana feminist oriented criticisms.

15. I have in mind Moraga and Anzaldúa's (1983) "theory in the flesh" in which flesh and blood concretize what Chicanas specifically, but all women of color generally, experience that serves as a basis for theorizing.

16. For example, Darrel Enck-Wanzer's (2006) work on the Puerto Rican Young Lords informed his postulating intersectional rhetoric as <bodies+words+images> or, the various formulations of intersectionality contained in Chávez and Griffin's (2012) edited collection.

17. With the exception of Flores, the other scholars noted interrogate Mexican (American) and Chican@ culture using distinct approaches to interrogate their

experiences as Chicanas. For example, De La Garza's monograph reflects a spiritual journey as a means of finding and examining herself and her culture that she supplements with her four seasons approach and art as mediation that provide a methodology for embarking on auto-ethnographic work.

18. My read of Calafell's advancement of "queer temporality" is that it is produced from reminiscing or nostalgia which privileges memory and it is a way to disidentify. Queer temporality is employed by individuals who have been ignored or misrepresented within dominant discourse subsequently challenging those discourses, creating community, and offering counter-narratives.

19. More recently, scholars have analyzed letters authored by Chicanas such as Gloria Anzaldúa and Dolores Huerta revealing their unique rhetorical functions inflected by intersections of race, class, gender, and/or nationality as well as by cultural ideologies and archetypes, consult Palczewski (1996) and Sowards (2010; 2012).

20. Evidence of Chicana feminist writings as transformative also appear in *Chicana/Latina Education in Everyday Life* edited by Delgado Bernal, Elenes, Godinez, and Villenas (2006).

21. Garza (2011) names three vocalities—univocal, "it emphasizes one particular line of argument or perspective" or when a singular medium is used; multivocality, an individual or group assertion of voice through multi-mediums; and hypervocality, "an excessive, ubiquitous, over-saturation of voice" (p. 42).

22. As examples, Castillo names corporations' encouragement of Filipina workers to sterilize (p. 61), depleted wage earnings among women of color in the United States (p. 36), and an underpaid labor force in Mexico due to maquilas, products of which Mexicanas produce and whose labor is exported across the border due to policies such as NAFTA.

23. Castillo's central focus throughout *Massacre of the Dreamers* is Xicanas yet, broadens when she speaks of maquilas [factories]. Due to its exploitative nature, along with her commitment to exploring racial-ethnic identities particularly where colonization has played a role in identity formation, she recognizes the implicature of all brown women working in factories in Juárez, Southeast Asia, or metropolitan cities such as Los Angeles or New York (Milligan, 1999, p. 23).

24. Generally, "white writing" is standard English; however, Castillo, drawing from Ivan Argűelles, explains it as periodically politically correct, safe, sanitized, and absent passion (1994, p. 168).

25. Seeing oneself as "educatable" is an issue that has confronted not only Mexican (Americans) but all "impoverished" women of color (pp. 50, 52). Dominant groups' perceptions of Mexican Americans as "educatable" is complicated by historical instances of educational injustices such as with the *Mendez v. Westminister* and *Lemon Grove* cases.

26. For more on the politicization shift of self-care readers may consult Harris (2017).

27. Coatlicue "the earth goddess, goddess of fertility. She also represents death" (Castillo, 1994, p. 106). As the "serpent skirt" (Garza, 2011), her powers included controlling knowledge, immortality, and fertility (Castillo, p. 106).

28. Castillo acknowledges that Xicanas may continue their practice of Catholicism and religious rituals due to the influence on identity yet, may reorder the value of La Virgen to be above God.

29. Curanderas may specialize in any or all of the following as sobaderas (i.e., gives massages), yerberas (i.e., expert in use of herbs), or parteras (i.e., midwives). A contemporary manifestation is the ChicanoBrujo who "reflects a therapeutic subjectivity that engages in a decolonial practice of healing an identity that struggles against the legacy of colonialism and its impact(s)" (Holling & Calafell, 2007, p. 65).

REFERENCES

Beal, F. M. (1970). Double jeopardy: To be black and female. In R. Morgan (Ed.), *Sisterhood is powerful: An anthology of writings from the women's liberation movement* (pp. 382–96). New York: Random House.

Blige, S. (2013). Intersectionality undone: Saving intersectionality from feminist intersectionality studies. *Du Bois Review*, *10*(2), 405–24.

Calafell, B. M. (2003). *Latina/o communication studies: Theorizing performance*. New York: Peter Lang.

Calafell, B. M. (2005). Pro(re-)claiming loss: A performance pilgrimage in search of Malintzin Tenépal. *Text and Performance Quarterly*, *25*(1), 43–56. DOI: 10.1080/10462930500052327.

Calafell, B. M. & Holling, M. A. (2011). Introduction. In M. A. Holling & B. M. Calafell (Eds.), *Latina/o discourse in vernacular spaces: Somos de una voz?* (pp. xv–xxv). Lanham, MD: Lexington Books.

Candelaria, C. (1980). La Malinche, feminist prototype. *Frontiers, A Journal of Women Studies*, *5*(2), 1–6.

Cantú, N. (1990). Women, then and now: An analysis of the adelitas image versus the Chicana as political writer and philosopher. In T. Córdova, N. Cantú, G. Cardenas, J. García, & C. M. Sierra (Eds.), *Chicana voices: Intersections of class, race, and gender* (pp. 7–10). Colorado Springs, CO: National Association for Chicano Studies.

Carson, B. D. (2004). The Chicana subject in Ana Castillo's fiction and the discursive zone of Chicana/o theory. *Bilingual Review/La Revista Bilingüe, 28*(2), 109–26.

Castillo, A. (1994). *Massacre of the dreamers: Essays on Xicanisma*. Albuquerque, NM: University of New Mexico Press.

Chávez, K. R. & Griffin, C. L. (Eds.). (2012). *Standing at the intersection: Feminist voices, feminist practices in communication studies*. Albany, NY: SUNY Press.

Comisión Femenil Mexicana. (1973). In D. Moreno (Ed.), *La mujer: En pie de la lucha* (pp. 271–72). Mexico: Espina del Norte Press.

Crenshaw, K. W. (1993). Beyond racism and misogyny: Black feminism and 2 Live Crew. In M. J. Matsuda, C. R. Lawrence III, R. Delgado, & K. W. Crenshaw (Eds.), *Words that wound: Critical race theory, assaultive speech, and the first amendment* (pp. 111–32). Boulder: Westview Press.

Crenshaw, K. (2015, September 24). Why intersectionality can't wait. *The Washington Post.* Retrieved from https://www.washingtonpost.com/news/in-theory/wp/2015/09/24/why-intersectionality-cant-wait/?utm_term=.0fb7ab794079.

De La Garza, S. A. (2004). *María speaks: Journeys into the mysteries of the mother in my life as a Chicana.* New York, NY: Peter Lang.

del Castillo, A. R. (1997). Malintzín Tenepal: A preliminary look into a new perspective. In A. Garcia (Ed.), *Chicana feminist thought: The basic historical writings* (pp. 122–26). New York: Routledge.

Delgado Bernal, D., Elenes, C. A., Godinez, F. E., & Villenas, S. (Eds.). (2006). *Chicana/Latina education in everyday life: Feminista perspectives on pedagogy and epistemology.* Albany, NY: State University of New York Press.

de Turk, S. (2015). *Activism, alliance building, and the Esperanza Peace and Justice Center.* Lanham, MD: Lexington Books.

Dicochea, P. R. (2004). Chicana critical rhetoric: Recrafting la causa in Chicana movement discourse, 19701-1979. *Frontiers: A Journal of Womens Studies, 25*(1), 77–92.

Enck-Wanzer, D. (2006). Trashing the system: Social movement, intersectional rhetoric, and collective agency in the Young Lords organization's garbage offensive. *Quarterly Journal of Speech, 82*(2), 174–201.

Enoch, J. (2004). *Para la mujer*: Defining a Chicana feminist rhetoric at the turn of the century. *College English, 67*(1), 20–37.

Enoch, J. (2005). Survival stories: Feminist historiographic approaches to Chicana rhetorics of sterilization abuse. *Rhetoric Society Quarterly, 35*(3), 5–30.

Flores, L. A. (1996). Creating a discursive space through a rhetoric of difference: Chicana feminists craft a homeland. *Quarterly Journal of Speech, 82*, 142–56.

Flores, L. A. (2000). Reclaiming the 'other': Toward a Chicana feminist perspective. *International Journal of Intercultural Relations, 24*, 687–705.

García, A. M. (1989). The development of Chicana feminist discourse, 1970-1980. *Gender & Society, 3*, 217–38.

García, A. M. (Ed.). (1997). *Chicana feminist thought: The basic historical writings.* New York: Routledge.

Garza, T. (2011). The rhetorical legacy of Coyolxauhqui: (Re)collecting and (re) membering voice. In M. A. Holling, & B. M. Calafell (Eds.), *Latina/o discourse in vernacular spaces: Somos de una voz?* (pp. 31–56). Lanham, MD: Lexington Books.

Halualani, R. T., Mendoza, S. L., & Drzewiecka, J. A. (2009). "Critical" junctures in intercultural communication studies: A review. *The Review of Communication, 9*(1), 17–35.

Harris, A. (2017, April 5). A history of self-care: From its radical roots to its yuppie-driven middle age to its election-inspired resurgence. *Slate.* Retrieved from http://www.slate.com/articles/arts/culturebox/2017/04/the_history_of_self_care.html

Hill Collins, P. (1991). *Black feminist thought: Knowledge, consciousness and the politics of empowerment.* New York, NY: Routledge.

Holling, M. A. (1994). *La virgen o la malinche: Rhetorical tension in the Chicana feminist movement.* Unpublished thesis, San Francisco State University.

Holling, M. A. (2000). *Extending critical rhetoric and feminist theory: Rhetorical constructions of Chicana subject/ivity, identity and agency.* Unpublished dissertation, Arizona State University.

Holling, M. A. (2008). Retrospective on Latin@ rhetorical-performance scholarship: From "Chicano communication" to "Latina/o communication?" *The Communication Review, 11*, 293–322. DOI: 10.1080/10714420802511218.

Holling, M. A. & Calafell, B. M. (2007). Identities on stage and staging identities: ChicanoBrujo performances as emancipatory practices. *Text and Performance Quarterly, 27*(1), 58–83.

Holling, M. A. & Calafell, B. M. (2011). Tracing the emergence of Latin@ vernaculars in studies of Latin@ communication. In M. A. Holling & B. M. Calafell (Eds.), *Latina/o discourse in vernacular spaces: Somos de una voz?* (pp. 17–29). Lanham, MD: Lexington Books.

Holling, M. A. & Moon, D. G. (2016). Conclusion—Continuing a politic of disruption: Race(ing) intercultural communication. In D. G. Moon and M. A. Holling (Eds.), *Race(ing) intercultural communication: Racial logics in a colorblind era* (pp. 184–86). New York: Routledge.

Lerner, G. (1986). *The creation of patriarchy.* New York: Oxford University Press.

Longeaux y Vázquez, E. (1973). Soy Chicana primero. In A. García (Ed.), *Chicana feminist thought: The basic historical writings* (pp. 197–99). New York: Routledge.

Martin, J. N. & Nakayama, T. K. (1999).Thinking dialectically about culture and communication. *Communication Theory, 91*, 1–25.

Martinez, J. (2004). Forward. In S. A. De La Garza (Ed.), *María speaks: Journeys into the mysteries of the mother in my life as a Chicana* (pp. xi–xii). New York, NY: Peter Lang.

Martinez, J. M. (2000). *Phenomenology of Chicana experience and identity: Communication and transformation in praxis.* Lanham, MD: Rowman and Littlefield.

Milligan, B. (1999). An interview with Ana Castillo. *South Central Review, 16*(1), 19–29.

Moon, D. G., & Holling, M. A. (2016). Introduction – A politic of disruption: Race(ing) intercultural communication. In D. G. Moon & M. A. Holling (Eds.), *Race(ing) intercultural communication: Racial logics in a colorblind era* (pp. 1–8). New York: Routledge.

Moraga, C. (1981). La güera. In C. Moraga, & G. Anzaldúa (Eds.), *This bridge called my back: Writings by radical women of color* (pp. 27–34). New York: Kitchen Table Women of Color Press.

Moraga, C. & Anzaldúa, G. (1981). Theory in the flesh. In C. Moraga & G. Anzaldúa (Eds.), *This bridge called my back: Writings by radical women of color* (p. 23). New York: Kitchen Table Women of Color Press.

NietoGomez, A. (1997). La Chicana—Legacy of suffering and self-denial. In A. García (Ed.), *Chicana feminist thought: The basic historical writings* (pp. 48–50). New York: Routledge.

Palczewski, C. H. (1996). Bodies, borders, and letters: Gloria Anzaldúa's "Speaking in tongues: A letter to 3rd world women writers". *Southern Communication Journal, 62*, 1–16.

Pérez, E. (1999). *The decolonial imaginary: Writing Chicanas into history*. Bloomington, IN: Indiana University Press.

Salas, E. (1990). *Soldaderas in the Mexican military*. Austin, TX: University Texas Press.

Segura, D. A. (1990). Chicanas and triple oppression in the labor force. In T. Córdova, N. Cantú, G. Cardenas, J. García, & C. M. Sierra (Eds.), *Chicana voices: Intersections of class, race, and gender* (pp. 47–65). Colorado Springs, CO: National Association for Chicano Studies.

Sowards, S. K. (2010). Rhetorical agency as *haciendo caras* and differential consciousness through lens of gender, race, ethnicity, and class: An examination of Dolores Huerta's rhetoric. *Communication Theory*, *20*, 223–47. DOI: 10.1111/j.1468-2885.2010.01361.x.

Sowards, S. K. (2012). Rhetorical functions of letter writing: Dialogic collaboration, affirmation, and catharsis in Dolores Huerta's letters. *Communication Quarterly*, *60*(2), 295–315. DOI: 10.1080/01463373.2012.669341.

Williams, L. (1998). Type and stereotype: Chicano images in film. In C. E. Rodríguez (Ed.), *Latin looks: Images of Latinas and Latinos in the U.S. media* (pp. 214–20). Boulder, CO: Westview Press.

Chapter 2

Lethal Intersections and "Chicana Badgirls"

Jaelyn deMaría

INTRODUCTION

The roots of this chapter grew from an intersection of mass tragedy and art. The *Chicana Badgirls: Las Hociconas* art exhibit opened at 516 ARTS Gallery in Albuquerque, New Mexico, on January 17, 2009. At the same time that Chicana artists were speaking loudly about parallel issues related to violence against women in connection to the exhibit, women's bodies were being uncovered on Albuquerque's West Mesa and they were being identified, one by one. They were urban, most were Chicana,[1] women, aged fifteen to thirty-two. The women were missing for years and were missed by their families and friends. They were dynamic human beings who lived and loved. However, they were labeled with loaded terms that disregarded their humanness, their positions in their families, and the complexities of their existence. Mainstream narratives focused on particular aspects of their identities as if a twisted justification for their murders. Labels like "poor," "prostitute," and "woman" intersected tragically on brown bodies. The women of the West Mesa were scrutinized by the media and criminalized in the public narrative. However, it is not even clear what their crimes were, except possibly, and not in all cases, submitting to men to provide sexual acts for money. Two of the victims were fifteen years old—how could they be criminals in an act they couldn't even consent to under the law? What does the more complicated past of these women tell about why they made the particular choices they did despite the risks they knew were present on the streets? Wasn't the real risk inherent in being Chicana, female, and poor?

When Crenshaw (1991) wrote "Mapping the Margins: Intersectionality, Identity Politics, and Violence Against Women of Color," she observed that racism and sexism clearly intersect in the lived realities of real people. She brought attention to intersecting patterns of racism, classism, and patriarchy in relationship to violence against women of color. She argued that "Because of their intersectional identity as both women and of color within discourses that are shaped to respond to one or the other, women of color are marginalized within both" (Crenshaw, 1991, p. 1244). Crenshaw points to expectations put on women to resist rape and protect their chastity, which became foundations for legal understandings in the United States and are still present in lingering practices in the U.S. legal system. "Legal rules thus functioned to legitimize a good woman/bad woman dichotomy in which women who lead sexually autonomous lives were usually least likely to be vindicated if they were raped" (Crenshaw, 1991, p. 1266). Some of these same narratives are reflected in New Mexico, where people have endured and survived more than 500 years of colonial intersections that continue to be financially supported by the sale, trade, and imprisonment of brown bodies for sexual and other purposes. Some of those traumas are identified through art and addressed with cultural remedies, while some linger at the crossroads of physical violence, race, class, and law. I write these words nearly thirty years after Crenshaw wrote "Mapping the Margins" and more than ten years after eleven young women were killed and buried on Albuquerque's West Mesa. The killer has not been brought to justice for the crimes (Perez & Browman, 2018) and it is clear that these women were not the first nor last to experience violence in this place in similar ways.

INTERSECTING ROOTS

I identify with the women whose bodies were buried on the West Mesa. I grew up in Albuquerque, I am Chicana, I was a wild young woman running the streets of Albuquerque and taking risks at the same time the killer was collecting victims. I cannot help but think that it could have been me, it could have been my family grieving for their daughter. I managed to walk away from Albuquerque's street culture, go to college, and avoid addiction, but I also, literally, walked many of the same paths that these women did. I personally know some of their family members and friends, we ran in some of the same circles. Regardless of all of the intersecting identities I embody, if I had gone missing, I would have the same labels as all of these women. They were more than these labels, and they didn't have time nor opportunity to overcome their temporary situations. Perhaps it makes it easier for the public to sleep at night to think that the women made bad choices that led to their deaths, that their identities explained the violence inflicted upon them, the violence that took their last breath. For me, it was difficult to understand the depths of this tragedy through mainstream narratives about a serial killer who murdered prostitutes. However, a visual, alternative narrative that was collectively built by *Chicana Badgirls*, better reflected some of the complexities we live as Chicana women, in life and in death. This narrative helped me understand how patriarchy, colonialism, and violence lust for brown bodies.

In this chapter, I share insights gained by exploring the parallel narratives, connections, and intersections between the *Chicana Badgirls* art exhibit and the real tragedy of violence in Albuquerque. The purpose of this chapter is to uncover meaning systems related to Chicana artistic expression and identity. I interviewed artists who participated in the exhibit about their attitudes, beliefs, and perceptions of Chicana art and identity, and specifically about identity labels associated with the overall exhibit to understand more about how those labels are imposed, co-opted, and recreated by communicating through artistic expression. The exhibition itself gave voice to Chicana identity through the public presence of Chicana art in a public gallery setting. Understanding more about the attitudes, perceptions, and opinions of these particular artists may inform a larger conversation about how art is used to communicate interculturally and respond to violence.

CHICANA INTERSECTIONALITY AND ART

Interdisciplinary Chicana scholars have written about Chicana art and intersectionality from multiple perspectives (Anzaldúa, 1999, 2012; Pérez, 2007; Gaspar de Alba, 1998, 2014; Latorre, 2010) and countless Chicana artists have communicated about intersectionality through their art. However, there is a further need to understand Chicana visual narratives and to develop knowledge about how art challenges patriarchy, power structures, and racist systems through co-optation of myths, codes, and symbols. This understanding has the potential to inform discussions and practical application of art as an anti-colonial avenue to communicate and redefine reality.

The *Chicana Badgirls* exhibition grew from an act of solidarity with artist Alma López and her controversial work depicting *La Guadalupana* in a bikini of roses, which was on display at the Museum of International Folk Art and was met with intense controversy in Santa Fe. That controversy led to an exhibition of five artist's work titled, *Las Malcriadas . . . Coloring Out of the Lines* (2001) at Pola López' Emanations Gallery in Santa Fe, New Mexico. "What was at stake then and what is being addressed now is the right to create work that represents our experience as Latina artists whose work is based on the lived reality of the struggles we encounter" (*Chicana Badgirls: Las Hociconas Exhibition Catalog*, 2009). Through the exhibit, artists were able to engage in dialogue with the Catholic Church, other artists, the greater community in New Mexico, and beyond. López suggests that the show was about much more than *La Virgen* in a bikini; it addressed issues dealing with feminism, religion, and sexuality. She argued that people were "able to see that there was another side to the story and able to grow from that" (P. López, personal communication, March 20, 2009). She further ties the experience into the *hocicona*[2] concept,

> Not being able to hold your tongue—that's the voice I'm talking about. I have to address this, I just can't accept this. Our grandmothers would have just held their tongue, and that's the way we were raised, but we're from a different time and different generation and we thought we need to speak our minds, but still with respect. (P. López personal communication, March 20, 2009)

Chicana Badgirls cocurator Pérez' book, *Chicana Art: The Politics of Spiritual and Aesthetic Altarities* (2007), explores recurring symbols used by Chicanas to artistically articulate spiritual and political themes in Chicana art. She explores the Chicana artistic landscape in a way that offers interpretation about how art offers a stage for reimagining and recreating historical reality through artistic communication. Specifically, she explores spirituality, and, through her research, approaches the spiritual apparitions she sees in Chicana art as "culturally hybrid, often do-it-yourself, noninstitutional spiritualities . . . as a gesture of yearning and *ofrenda*, or offering, toward greater personal integrity, empowerment, and social justice" (Pérez, 2007, p. 2). This offering is exemplified through the multiple voices that come together in collaborative expressions in exhibitions like the *Chicana Badgirls* show. These collective showings provide a microphone to Chicana artists who, as described by Peréz, "won't stay quiet, who won't make nice, who won't pretend that everything's okay when it's not" (*Chicana Badgirls: Las Hociconas Exhibition Catalog*, 2009). Peréz (2007) points to connections between spiritual and social struggles in Chicana art and suggests that it often speaks to an unaffiliated spirituality that addresses a colonized history by reenvisioning it. She further suggests that work in the *Chicana Badgirls* show redefines imposed definitions, with or without permission, offering a resistive, collective act of self-empowerment (Peréz, 2007).

Gaspar de Alba (1998) questioned the categorization of Chicana art and the stratifying definition of "subculture" in her book, *Chicano Art Inside/Outside the Master's House: Cultural Politics and the CARA Exhibition*. Gaspar de Alba (1998) introduced a model of alter-Nativity as she "question(s) the hierarchical assumptions that organize cultures into 'sub' categories" (Gaspar de Alba, 1998, p. 15). She argues that the art and style displayed by oppressed groups often exist to challenge power and are rejected and subjugated by the mainstream, partly due to their resistive nature. The specific exemplification of the *Chicano Art: Resistance and*

Affirmation, 1965-1985 (CARA) Exhibition, which opened in the early 1990s, is employed to examine how this presentation of Chicana/o "alter-culture" managed to cross borders.

> For many who saw the show, mainstream reviewer and *Raza* viewer alike, CARA signified the first time they had ever seen Chicano/Chicana art in a mainstream museum. Some interpreted it as trespassing, others as breaking through the walls of the master's house. (Gaspar de Alba, 1998, p. 22)

As the door was pried open, there became an opportunity to critique the restrictive reality of "freedom of expression" and twenty years later shows like "Qué Chola" (2019) find space at the National Hispanic Cultural Center. Gaspar de Alba (1998) argues that loss of cultural memory results in the loss of dignity, yet, by maintaining complicated identities in the face of overwhelming pressure to assimilate, the structure of resistance is reinforced and Chicanas prove that they can subversively stand up for, reinvent, and honor the complications in our intersections. In a discussion about taking the national stage at "the master's house," referring to the mainstream art world, Gaspar de Alba (1998) engages the concept of "alter-culture" in a way that challenges the theories of "subculture." In the overall discussion of negotiating avenues of expression, art is presented as a means of reasserting power and breaking down the walls of oppression in order to transform the "sub" status to one of "alter." The house was divided again as Gaspar de Alba (1998) brought gender politics to issue. She found irony in the angry screams for equality coming from the mouths of those who did not see the glaring unequal representation of women in the CARA show. "To ignore gender, however, in the struggle for civil and human rights is to perpetuate the objectification and abuse of women" (Gaspar de Alba, 1998, p. 122). It is argued that, while class, race, and culture cannot be divorced from gender politics, sexism has tendencies of infecting and intersecting with all levels of multiple, overlapping power structures.

ARTISTIC INTERPRETATION OF INTERSECTIONALITY

Disempowering labels are often imposed upon people; however, artists are able to communicate in ways that more accurately reflect lived intersectionalities and complexities of existence. Dominant visual narratives often normalize and center Whiteness. However, as a decolonial practice, narratives from the margins can be methodologically useful to theorize intersectionality and to resist the reproduction of Whiteness. *Chicana Badgirls* defiantly crossed physical, social, cultural, and emotional borders with their creative explorations of Chicana experiences in a multivocal exhibition of artistic offerings in *Chicana Badgirls: Las Hociconas*. Eighteen artists conspired to bring a show together that celebrated loudmouth women who refuse to be silenced. Three generations of women spoke up to honor *Chicana Badgirl* experiences and spoke out against injustice and violence in a celebration of creativity, resistance, and healing. This chapter illustrates how artistic ways of knowing communicate complex, intersecting understandings about identity and provide space for responses to damaging, disempowering narratives imposed on brown bodies. Violence is a symptom of the systemic colonial view of women as disposable sexual labor. Lived experiences in intersectionality are a matter of life and death for young, poor, women of color.

I attended the opening of the *Chicana Badgirls* show as a freelance reporter in January 2009. I was personally impressed by the reflections of diverse Chicana experiences I saw there and the visual messages resonated with me. I wanted to know more, so I employed a Chicana anti-colonial praxis model. Looking through this lens, I spent time with the art and conducted a thematic visual analysis, looking specifically at themes of violence and sexuality within the context of resistance. I also asked the artists to grant me an in-depth interview about their work and specifically about what it means to them to be a "Chicana Badgirl." I began to set up interviews and scheduled them for future dates. A few weeks later, a woman who was walking her dog on Albuquerque's West Mesa found a human bone. The discovery led to months of investigation, during which time more and more bones were unearthed (Perez & Browman, 2018). The ongoing events were on the minds of many of the artists and myself as we sat down to talk.

Chicana art offers an alternative reading of culture and I explore it here to find meanings. This research is done with the goal of understanding more about artistic counter-narratives and how they are strategically enacted to respond to violence and to create change. *Chicana Badgirls* cocurator Delilah Montoya spoke about connections that were evident in the ways intersectionality is experienced by young Chicana women in life and in death.

> They're all Chicanas, and when the first one was found, immediately we hear people saying, 'Oh, they're just prostitutes,' 'they're just drug addicts,'—*badgirls*, and that's what happens to a bad girl—they get killed and buried up in the West Mesa . . . You know, they're poor, they're prostitutes and therefore the police departments, the people in power don't feel as though they really need to move on this because they've turned them into monsters already . . . And so what it does, is it talks about how we're disempowered, even in our deaths we become disempowered. (D. Montoya, personal communication, March 18, 2009)

Montoya also discussed the "official response" to the systemic disappearances of young Chicana women. She asked,

> How is it possible by any stretch of the imagination that thirteen[3] women disappear and nothing is investigated until one of their bones comes leaping out of the ground? How is that possible that the police department didn't see that something was going on? If those thirteen women had disappeared from the heights or an affluent neighborhood—two women, one woman—there would have been a formal investigation as to what was occurring there, but, no, it didn't happen for those Chicana bad girls. (D. Montoya, personal communication, March 18, 2009)

She goes further to talk about how the women advocated for themselves after their deaths. "The bone did come up. They unburied *themselves* out of the ground and they could not be ignored, so in many ways they are the *hocicona*," she said. "The earth has a memory, the mother spoke, she didn't forget what was buried inside of her . . . the Mother has a memory and it cannot be erased, lies cannot be covered up. You look at the ground and you will see the memory that is still etched in that ground" (D. Montoya, personal communication, March 18, 2009).

Montoya took a revisionist standpoint in her own contributions to the *Chicana Badgirls* show. She rewrites myths, "because it is the myths that hold on to concepts and ideas throughout generations, and what myths do more than anything else is teach, they are teaching tools that are handed down from one generation to the next" (D. Montoya, personal communication, March 18, 2009). Montoya presented a visual narrative connected to the well-known Mexican/Chican@ myth of *La Llorona*, the Weeping Woman, and to the mythological figure, Lilith, in her piece titled, "La Llorona in Lilith's Garden." *La Llorona* wanders near waterways in search of her missing children, who she is sometimes accused of killing, and Lilith refused to submit to Adam and is described as a demon in ancient myths. The significance of this work ties in closely to the theme of the show. According to Rabbi Hammer,

> Lilith means "the night," and she embodies the emotional and spiritual aspects of darkness: terror, sensuality, and unbridled freedom. More recently, she has come to represent the freedom of feminist women who no longer want to be "good girls." (Hammer, 2008)

Montoya looks at these mythic women as dynamic personalities, who deserve a second look. *La Llorona* and Lilith are "badgirls" of mythology. This revision allows them to be seen in a more complex way.

Figure 2.1 "La Llorona in Lilith's Garden" by Delilah Montoya. Full-wall installation photographed as seen at the Chicana Badgirls: Las Hociconas exhibit in 2009. *Source*: Reprinted with permission of Delilah Montoya. (Photo by Jaelyn deMaría).

In New Mexico, we grew up knowing about *La Llorona*, but the version differed greatly. The story I grew up with told about how the children drown in the *acequia* because they didn't listen to their parents about the dangers and their mother's soul continues to wander the banks of the *acequias* searching for them. Because we lived right next to an *acequia* in Albuquerque's North Valley, it was told multiple times as a way to keep us safe and away from the ditches, especially at night. I was raised by a group of loving, overprotective women and their version made sense to me. However, as I grew, I learned many other versions of the myth. Some of the versions connect more clearly to the Sixth Omen of the Aztec, which tells of a woman's voice whose screams pierced the nights of Tenochtitlán (modern day Mexico City), warning the people of the violence of the forthcoming Spanish colonization. I first heard this version from a cab driver in Mexico City who pointed out the window at a waterway that flowed through Xochimilco and said, "*Esas son las lágrimas de La Llorona* (these are *La Llorona's* tears)." He said that the Omens became reality for the people and that she still cries today. Some believe that the screams came from Coatlique, the goddess of childbirth, who still weeps and cries around bodies of water, screaming for her lost children. Some say the screams come from *La Malinche* herself, who embodies the intersections of coloniality and sexuality. And some say that we will continue to confront her in our dreams, in our art and in our scholarship until we reconcile her narrative (Moreman & Calafell, 2008; Pérez, 2002). Some of the versions of the story demonize her and label her as a jealous murderess who killed her children out of spite because her lover cheated on her and left. In these versions,

> She was shameful, she was s*in verguenza* (without shame)—and those were the words that would get thrown at us if we didn't behave in the way that it was felt

> it was appropriate for a young woman. She was really trapped in this situation. If things were different she would have probably walked away, taken her things and said, 'I don't need this.' That wasn't presented as an option in the story . . . she was an unwed mother, trapped a man with sexuality and she did all these things that made her 'evil' and ends up as this monster that is wondering the streets. It's all of our story. Because we've all experienced that—the pain of somebody not wanting you or the pain of raising your child alone because the relationship didn't work out. The pain of not having the resources you need to do whatever it is that you need to get done. The pain of watching the person you love go with somebody else. These are things that we all experience, so her story is all of our story. (D. Montoya, personal communication, March 18, 2009)

Montoya also realized that there is something transformative about the myths and she empowers herself to retell the stories from a different angle. In conversation about her piece, "La Llorona in Lillith's Garden," she said,

> I did it pointedly to where the image is very beautiful, because we are beautiful and the stories that are there can have another meaning to it, so it was my way of subverting something that was supposed to be horrific and reinventing it or revisiting it and giving it a revisionist history where she becomes something that is powerful and something that is beautiful and something that we need to rethink because what *La Llorona* goes through is something that is very familiar to who we are as women. (D. Montoya, personal communication, March 18, 2009)

She also tells stories about the beginnings of *Mestizaje* in which the Old World God, and the New World God angrily pull and push against each other and suggests, "that's where we come from, from that anger" (D. Montoya, personal communication, March 18, 2009).

The degree to which women are sexualized and demoralized as whores and temptresses builds on a structure that sets up women to be stripped of dignity and power. Gaspar de Alba (1998, 2014) points to the image of *Malinche* and how she is evoked to illustrate how depictions of her as an Eve-like temptress who betrayed her people is used to imply that the same constructed traits can be applied to all women. Power is negotiated and regained as Chicana artists take back the authority to tell her story. By recreating history and defining the present, women empower themselves to be equal partners in conversations that often exclude, objectify, and over-sexualize women's voices in the context of a virgin/mother/whore trilogy. Calafell (2005) writes about how Malintzin's story is historically twisted by narratives about Hernan Cortés that both ignore her contributions and slay her character. "She has no narrative, instead others write over her story with their narratives, seeking to fix Malintzin in the virgin/whore dichotomy in national memory" (p. 49). Calafell and other contemporary artists and scholars rebirth her story symbolically, physically, and in various expressions of culture and scholarship. In the spirit of resistance, "Rather than the chaste virgin, the weeping mother, and the treacherous whore, *La Lupita*, *La Llorona*, and *La Malinche* are now configured as powerful icons of Chicana resistance to cultural hegemony and patriarchal domination" (Gaspar de Alba, 1998, p. 143). Like *Malinche*, who symbolically refused to take on any more oppressive violation of her image and is reconstructed to be the venerated mother of *Mestizaje*, other similar patterns emerge as women continue to produce culture in borderlands and other hybrid places and spaces (Anzaldúa, 2007). The myth of *Malinche* has been twisted, embraced, and constructed to tell the story of the origin of a *Mestizo* union. Some see her as a betrayer, others see her as a loving mother, and others still see her as a murderess. Chicana artists are engaging in revisionist writing of myth and reconstructing the images of *la Malinche*, *la Llorona*, *la Guadalupana*, Lilith, and others to resist oppression and violence and to gain the narrative power to tell the story from an "alter" *feminista* perspective. New Mexico artist Maye Torres also spoke about a particular violence that is imposed on brown bodies and connects the murders to patterns of disrespect and silence. She said,

> In a situation like this, I think it's time for women to speak up. We're tired of being beaten, we're tired of being verbally abused, were even tired of being told what we can and can't do anymore . . . people will say, 'she's just a bad girl,' she deserved it. So those kinds of thought processes that are old and ancient have to go. (M. Torres, personal communication, March 20, 2009)

The good girl/bad girl binary continues to situate women at the intersections of violence and imposes alien identities on Chicana bodies.

Diane Gamboa offered work from her *Alien Invasion* series, which raises the question, "Why is it that Mexicans are considered aliens, when people from other places are considered immigrants?" Speaking of the women she depicts in her art, she said,

> These women are coming from another planet and people are so fearful of us as *aliens* so, the only thing that could be worse is if they are women aliens . . . So they're badass women from outer space that are coming here to hopefully help out our planet, help out Mother Earth and change some attitudes in everyone's mind. (D. Gamboa, personal communication, April 10, 2009)

Her characters are intended to be seductive—they are here to "probe men, trying to figure out why men are so violent and why it is that they have such disrespect and disregard for women" (D. Gamboa, personal communication, April 10, 2009). In a similar way, Gloria Anzaldúa interrogates alien intersectionalities and "uses the alien as a means to describe the bodily and psychic horrors of a legacy of colonialism" (Calafell, 2005, p. 60). Multiple colonizations and shifting, layered alien identities are imposed upon Malinche's descendants who now live in places like Albuquerque, New Mexico; however, we continue to resist and shape our own identities in the face of overwhelming pressure to assimilate or be destroyed. Calafell (2015) considers how monstrosity offers an alternative lens to think about decolonialism. "Monsters act as archetypes or myths that serve to guide a community" (Calafell, 2005, p. 56). Therefore, decoloniality embraces monstrosity as an intersectional identity while also recognizing survival as a privilege given the real psychic trauma and physical violence that we continue to experience in our homelands.

Muñoz's contributions bring murders and disappearances involving women in Ciudad Juarez, Mexico, to issue. In a large visual installation piece, Muñoz included hundreds of words, which she located in various media reports about the issue. When the viewer steps back from the work, a collaged police badge is revealed. "It's calling out to the investigators and it's calling out to the community, saying why are you letting this continue?" Montoya said (D. Montoya, personal communication, March 18, 2009). Muñoz crossed international borders through her artistic offering to the murdered and disappeared women of Ciudad Juarez. However, she did not know how relevant that voice would be to Albuquerque at that time the show opened. Her protests against violence are now in the name of the women of the West Mesa too. "This is for the women of Juarez who never got a chance to be badgirls," she said at the opening of the show, "It's the story of injustice within an unjust system . . . I hope this is fuel. That it gives permission to express who we are, because we have the chance to," she said (C. Muñoz, personal communication, January 17, 2009).[4]

TRANSNATIONAL INTERSECTIONS

Gaspar de Alba (2010) focuses on the violent murder and disappearance of women in Ciudad Juarez. In "Poor Brown Female: The Miller's compensation for 'free' trade" (2010), she points to a mostly U.S.-supported economic system in which, "the real criminals are not just the perpetrators of the crimes, but the powers and interests being served by the brutal slayings of poor, brown females" (Gaspar de Alba, 2010, p. 63). Employing logic of victim blaming, some of the theories about who did the killings and why are that, "The victims were leading double lives as prostitutes" or "The victims dressed provocatively in short dresses and high heels" (Gaspar de Alba, 2010, p. 67). In this way, the murdered women in Ciudad Juarez are blamed for their own death just as the women of the West Mesa were.

> Accused of leading *una doble vida*, the double life of a good girl (student or employee) and a bad girl (sex worker) who goes out drinking and dancing after her shift at the *maquiladora*, the victims are seen as "asking for it," both because of the company they keep and the way they dress." (Gaspar de Alba, 2010, p. 67)

She writes that silence is an accomplice to the murders because as long as the public remains ignorant or silent about what is going on in Ciudad Juarez, no real work could be done to stop the killings or to identify motives behind the systemic killing of poor, brown women. However,

> When the news is too sensational to keep quiet—such as when a woman's dead and mutilated body is discovered wrapped in a blanket and dumped at the intersection of two major streets in Juarez—then it is time to blame the victim because, . . . 'she asked for it,' trashy, slutty, ignorant *indita* that the media and the social discourse make her out to be. (Gaspar de Alba, 2010, p. 84)

Gaspar de Alba also makes contradictions on the border visible with the inclusion of several sets of photographs that show contrast between multinational corporations and institutions and the *colonias* where most of the women lived. The visual images "exemplify the extremes between what is important and what is unimportant that all who cross and converge there must negotiate on a daily basis" (Gaspar de Alba, 2010, p. 85). Lozano (2019) examines the relationships between *feminicidio*, globalization, and free trade and identifies the murders in Juarez as inherently systemic, which is in contrast to assigning fault to a single serial killer or to the multiple theories that were developed to explain the killings. Recognizing the systemic origins of violence may also lead to more holistic experiences of justice, because punishing or jailing a particular murderous perpetrator will not eliminate the normality of a system that supports that violence.

VISUAL INTERSECTIONS

Holling (2014) specifically addresses violence against women of color in "'So My Name Is Alma, and I Am the Sister of …': A Feminicidio Testimonio of Violence and Violent Identifications." This particular *testimonio* is recorded in Ciudad Juarez. Holling argues that "ultimately, a feminicidio *testimonio* is a means not only to respond to violence but also to produce new witnesses" (Holling, 2014, p. 313). In the same ways that oral, transcribed *testimonios* can produce witnesses, I argue that art can be a form of visual *testimonio* in that it can produce new witnesses, and sometimes in emotional ways that other forms of communication cannot. Holling (2014) recognizes visual communication, and especially photography, as having power to transform listeners into witnesses. She describes how photographs of missing and murdered women from Juarez were hung on the walls of the room where they sat to listen to Alma's narrative about her sister who disappeared and about the specific acts of violence that she experienced and witnessed. Holling argues that the photographs "transform listeners to witnesses" because by being present with the photographs, listeners are no longer detached from the victims through abstraction "as the photographs solicit listeners' recognition of those pictured as once-living beings. More emphatically, the girls and young women are humanized and present in spite of their absence at the hands of (un)known assailants" (Holling, 2014, pp. 321–22). Holling also discusses Alma's thoughtful actions as she brought forth her sister's photograph after she gave her *testimonio*. She argues that the photograph allowed for a process of humanization, in contrast to dehumanizing legal and media landscapes. Photographs have also been a meaningful component of the overall narrative about the women found on Albuquerque's West Mesa.

At first, the women's mug shots from some of the women's previous arrests were used by the media as a way of illustrating the story and identifying the women by name and attaching them to their criminalized images. Some news outlets replaced the original mug shots with photographs from yearbooks or those provided by families in later stories, but the arrested images of young women resonated and continued to criminalize them even in their deaths. In December 2010, Albuquerque police released six photographs of young women, most of them unconscious, lying with their mouths open and their eyes closed. The public was asked to help identify their images. Then, in 2016, police released two more still frames from a video of women who may have appeared on a sex tape recorded by one of the suspects in the murders (Perez & Browman, 2016). While some of the women in the photographs released by police were found alive, the collection of images the public has seen reinforce a particular visual narrative about sexuality, criminality, and death. Ruth Trinidad Galván (2016), who worked with her students at the University of New Mexico to bringing awareness to the West Mesa murders through art and public memorial, writes, "Dominant narratives both in Juárez and Albuquerque that suggest women live 'risky' lifestyles that don't merit our attention or 'justify' their deaths must be challenged as sexist, heteronormative, and racist" (Galván, 2016, p. 348).

In contrast to the mainstream narratives, over the ten years since the first bone unearthed itself from the mesa dirt, many forms of memorial art have been created. The story is rewritten as we see the beauty of the woman's existence represented in the form of butterflies, angels, and other symbols of freedom and flight.[5] The images of these woman's mug shots that were

Figure 2.2 During the memorial marking ten years since the woman's bones were unearthed, notes were written to the women by loved ones and family members and tied to the fence that surrounds the burial site. *Source*: Photograph taken by Jaylen deMaria.

originally run with the articles reporting their deaths were replaced with smiling images from happier times; making viewers witness to their humanness. The memorials recognized the violence, but responded to it through beauty, respect for life, and spirit. The living children and grieving families were also remembered in the art. The poetic and beautiful ways they were remembered there provided opportunity for balance in the public memory and in visual rhetorics of disappearance. Their lives mattered and no amount of intersections in their identities justified the violence imposed upon them. The young women were remembered in love because of their complications and not despite them. The city of Albuquerque promised a park to be built on the site in their memory, but at the time of this chapter's submission date, no park has been built. The city did remove the memorial that was collectively built by family and friends of the women in preparation for the future park.

PATTERNS OF VIOLENCE

The memorials also reminded the public that there are still more missing women. Some women who disappeared from Albuquerque during the same time period are still not found and many more Chicana and Native/Indigenous women go missing every day in different parts of the world in a violent pattern that cannot be denied. The Urban Indian Health Institute reported that, in 2016, New Mexico was the state with the highest number of cases (78) of missing and murdered Indigenous women in the United States; Albuquerque is listed as the city with the second highest number (37); and Gallup as the location with the most cases that were not in law enforcement records (20) (Lucchesi & Echo-Hawk, 2018). The report reveals a "data crisis" in demonstrating that out of 5,712 cases of murdered and missing Indigenous women reported in 2016 (which is a number that is still under reported), only 116 cases were entered into the U.S. Department of Justice database (Lucchesi & Echo-Hawk, 2018). "The study's intention is to provide a comprehensive snapshot of the MMIWG crisis in urban American Indian and Alaska Native communities and the institutional practices that allow them to disappear not once, but three times—in life, in the media, and in the data" (Lucchesi & Echo-Hawk, 2018, p. 2).

New Mexico's rankings indicate the urgent need for attention to violence against brown bodies. It is not clear if this report even includes Chicana women in the collected data, but lived experience suggests that we encounter some of the same violence at our intersections. As an example, the report (Lucchesi & Echo-Hawk, 2018) quotes a representative from the Santa Fe Police who wrote, in a response to a request for data, "[Many] Native Americans adopted Hispanic names back during colonial times . . . Our crime

Figure 2.3 Photographed in 2018, the memorial site on Albuquerque's West Mesa reminds viewers that many women who disappeared during the same time period are still missing. *Source*: Photograph taken by Jaylen deMaria.

Figure 2.4 Photographed in 2009 at Robinson Park, in Albuquerque, New Mexico. *Source*: Photograph taken by the author.

systems are not flexible enough to pick out Native Americans from others in the system . . . it would be impossible to compile any statistically relevant information for you" (p. 16). Federal recognition of tribal affiliations has historically, and possibly intentionally, ignored intersectionality as a way of creating divisions in traditional communities in the Southwest and borderland regions of the United States. The divisions also prevent seeing a larger pattern of systemic, transnational violence against poor brown bodies. "In this way, it is possible that American Indian and Alaska Native women and girls indigenous to the land the city is located on may not even be included in the city's data on American Indian and Alaska Native people, and their deaths and disappearances go uncounted on their own homeland" (p. 17). It is also important to note that if Chicanas and other detribalized or unrecognized Indigenous women were included in the data, the overall numbers would be much higher.

CONCLUSION

This chapter considers art as a vehicle to move conceptual understandings of intersectionality toward more complicated realities. It responds to calls for a collective reenvisioning of culture informed by critical/feminist theory (Moon, 1996) and to calls for a "disruption" in communicative flows of color-blind normality (Holling & Moon, 2015). Moon (1996) defines culture as a contested space where a plurality of perspectives creates place for constructions of multivocal meanings. She writes, "This contested nature of 'culture' often gets lost in homogenizing views of 'culture as nationality' where dominant cultural voices are the only ones heard, where the 'preferred' reading of 'culture' is the only reading" (Moon, 1996, p. 75). Moon and Holling (2015) observe that "intercultural communication scholars have been notoriously silent on issues of race. Even during historical moments such as the Civil Rights era, few intercultural scholars took up what was certainly the most important issue of the day" (Holling & Moon, 2015, p. 3). A "politic of disruption" goes further to provide space to envision ways forward. "In the so-called 'post-racial' era not only are disrupting notions of colorblindness crucially important, but also are imagining new ways of thinking through racial matters" (Holling & Moon, 2015, p. 4). As exemplified in the *Chicana Badgirl* visual narrative, art offers space for deconstructing imposed identities as well as space for constructing decolonial discussions that acknowledge, confront, and challenge colonial normalities of violence enacted upon women's bodies.

The women whose bodies were buried on the West Mesa experienced real violence in their deaths and even after the women died fighting, they were still dishonored because of narratives that were imposed upon them. Crenshaw (1989, 1991) wrote about how dominant narratives often provide legal justification for rape and violence against women. Specifically pointing to aspects of a woman's "moral character" as justification given for violence against her.

> A woman's sexual history, for example, is frequently explored by defense attorneys as a way of suggesting that a woman who consented to sex on other occasions was likely to have consented in the case at issue. Past sexual conduct as well as the specific circumstances leading up to the rape are often used to distinguish the moral character of the legitimate rape victim from women who are regarded as morally debased or in some other way responsible for their own victimization. (Crenshaw, 1991, p. 1270)

Specifically, as in the case with the women of the West Mesa, the woman's past acts, real or fabricated, are used to justify murder. And while nothing can bring back the lives that are lost, there is a possibility to build a new normal that does not justify or encourage violence. Crenshaw recognizes counter-hegemonic potential in rising up from these intersections. She writes, "Yet implicit in certain strands of feminist and racial liberation movements, for example is the view that the social power in delineating difference need not be the power of domination; it can instead be the source of social empowerment and reconstruction" (Crenshaw, 1991, p. 1242). Specifically, she notes, "Clearly, there is unequal power, but there is nonetheless some degree of agency . . . And it is important to note that identity continues to be a site of resistance for members of different subordinated groups" (Crenshaw, 1991, p. 1297).

Complicated intersectional identities were articulated in *Chicana Badgirl* counter-narratives that decolonized spirituality, sexuality, and survival at a time when the colonial violence of patriarchy was being uncovered on the West Mesa. The art visually articulated an alternative interpretation of reality that is not built within the context of Whiteness and patriarchy, but rather resists its reproduction and complicates dominant narratives. I believe that reenvisioning culture is strategically enacted through art. Powerful counter systems of symbols are created when historically grounded contexts are rewritten. The artists whose work appeared in the *Chicana Badgirls* exhibition exemplify a multivocal revision of meaning. Art becomes a space for performance, interpretation, resistance, and reinvention and it is constructed through verbal and nonverbal language. Multiple voices make up the Chicana Badgirl experience, we speak loudly in our collective refusal to be silent. This work contributes to the conversation about how to strategically communicate resistance and power. Silent, yet screaming, the visual creations of eighteen artists made a statement. It just so happened that these screams came at a time that served to gain understanding into what happened to the twelve lost lives[6] whose bodies were unearthed on the West Mesa. Their memories still live as Chicanas continue to work toward justice and then toward collective healing and empowerment. As a matter of survival, we are crafting our identities to resist physical violence and cultural death. The colonial patriarchal system that we live in supports myths about women and sexuality, which penetrate legal and social systems. This chapter asserts that Chicana women are more than disposable sexual labor, we are humans that deserve to live.

NOTES

1. Here I use the word "Chicana" to reflect "Chicana Badgirl" solidarity, although, in other places, I use Xicana. The "X" is a strategic decolonial move. While the definition is multidimensional, complicated, and contested, I draw from urban place-based understandings and lived experiences of Indo-Hispano/C(X)hicana culture centered in Albuquerque, New Mexico.

2. The word *hocicona* crossed physical, political, and cultural borders to arrive in New Mexico in its twisted form. Directly translated, *hocico* is a snout or muzzle (Hocico, 2019), but its intended meaning has been hijacked and redefined.

3. At the time of this interview, police speculated that there were thirteen bodies, but further investigation put the final count at eleven and one fetus.

4. This quote was also published in deMaría, J. (January 21, 2009). Las Chicas Chicanas Malas en Denuncia/Chicana Bad Girls Speak Out. *MAS New Mexico.*

5. These are some of the symbols I observed at the memorial and burial site on the West Mesa.

6. This chapter is written with respect to and in loving memory of Jamie Barela, Monica Candelaria, Victoria Chavez, Virginia Cloven, Syllania Edwards, Cinnamon Elks, Doreen Marquez, Julie Nieto, Veronica Romero, Evelyn Salazar, Michelle Valdez, her unborn child, and all of the missing and murdered women and men from North to South. Jaelyn deMaría is also in gratitude to the *Chicana Badgirl* artists who shared their thoughts and their art. Of course, many thanks go to the editors of this collection for providing space and intentions for understandings.

REFERENCES

Anzaldúa, G. (2007). *Borderlands / La Frontera.* San Francisco, CA: Aunt Lute Books.

Calafell, B. M. (2005). Pro(re-)claiming loss: A performance pilgrimage in search of Malintzin Tenépal. *Text and Performance Quarterly, 25*(1), 43–56. doi:10.1080/10462930500052327.

Calafell, B. M. (2015). *Monstrosity, performance, and race in contemporary culture.* New York: Peter Lang.

Chicana Badgirls: Las Hociconas Exhibition Catalog. (2009). Albuquerque, NM: 516 ARTS. http://www.516arts.org/images/stories/PDFs/chicana_badgirls_catalog.pdf.

Crenshaw, K. W. (1989). Demarginalizing the intersection of race and sex: A black feminist critique of antidiscrimination doctrine, feminist theory, and antiracist politics. *University of Chicago Legal Forum,1989*(1), 8th ser., 139–67. Retrieved January 23, 2019.

Crenshaw, K. W. (1991). Mapping the margins: Intersectionality, identity politics, and violence against women of color. *Stanford Law Review,43*(6), 1241–99. doi:10.2307/1229039.

deMaría, J. (2009, January 21). Las Chicas Chicanas Malas en Denuncia/Chicana bad girls speak out. *MAS New Mexico.*

Galván, R. T. (2016). Collective memory of violence of the female brown body: A decolonial feminist public pedagogy engagement with the feminicides. *Pedagogy, Culture & Society,24*(3), 343–57. doi:10.1080/14681366.2016.1166149.

Gamboa, D. (2009). Interview by phone from Los Angeles. April 10, 2009.

Gaspar de Alba, A. (1998). *Chicano art: Inside/outside the master's house: Cultural politics and the CARA exhibition.* Austin: University of Texas Press.

Gaspar de Alba, A. (2010). Poor brown female: The miller's compensation for "free" trade. In *Making a Killing: Femicide, Free Trade, and La Frontera* (pp. 62–93). Austin, TX: University of Texas Press.

Gaspar de Alba, A, (2014). *(Un)framing the "Bad Woman": Sor Juana, Malinche, Coyolxauhqui, and Other Rebels with a Cause.* Austin, TX: University of Texas Press.

Hammer, J. (2008, October 17). Lilith, lady flying in darkness. Retrieved January 23, 2019, from https://www.myjewishlearning.com/article/lilith-lady-flying-in-darkness/.

Hocico. (2019). *Oxford dictionaries: Spanish Oxford living dictionaries.* Retrieved January 23, 2019, from https://es.oxforddictionaries.com/translate/spanish-english/hocico

Holling, M. A. (2014). "So my name is Alma, and i am the sister of … ": A feminicidio testimonio of violence and violent identifications. *Women's Studies in Communication,37*(3), 313–38. doi:doi.org/10.1080/07491409.2014.944733.

Holling, M. A., & Moon, D. G. (2015). Continuing a politic of disruption: Race(ing) intercultural communication. *Journal of International and Intercultural Communication, 8*(2), 81–85. doi:10.1080/17513057.2015.102532.

Latorre, G. (2019). New approaches to Chicana/o art: The visual and the political as cognitive process. *Image and Narrative: Online Magazine of the Visual Narrative*, (2), 111.

Lopez, P. (2009). Interview by phone from Los Angeles. March 20, 2009.

Lozano, N. M. (2019). *Not one more!: Feminicidio on the border.* Columbus, OH: Ohio State University Press.

Lucchesi, A. & Echo-Hawk, A. (2018). Missing and murdered indigenous women and girls (Rep.). Retrieved January 23, 2019, from Urban Indian Health Institute website: http://www.uihi.org/wp-content/uploads/2018/11/Missing-and-Murdered-Indigenous-Women-and-Girls-Report.pdf.

Moon, D. G. (1996). Concepts of "culture": Implications for intercultural communication research. *Communication Quarterly, 44*(1), 70–84. doi:10.1080/01463379609370001.

Montoya, D. (2009). Interview in Albuquerque, New Mexico. March 18, 2009, January 17, 2009.

Moreman, S. T. & Calafell, B. M. (2008). Buscando para Nuestra Latinidad: Utilizing La Llorona for cultural critique. *Journal of International and Intercultural Communication, 1*(4), 309–26. doi:10.1080/17513050802344647.

Muñoz, C. (2009). Interview in Albuquerque, New Mexico, January 17, 2009.

Pérez, L. E. (2007). *Chicana art: The politics of spiritual and aesthetic altarities.* Durham, NC: Duke University Press.

Perez, N. & Browman, R. (2016, October 5). Police worried, looking for women in old sex tapes made by man investigated in West Mesa Case. *Albuquerque Journal.* Retrieved January 23, 2019, from https://www.abqjournal.com/860097/police-looking-for-women-in-old-sex-tapes.html.

Perez, N. & Browman, R. (2018). Albuquerque Journal special report: West Mesa murders. *Albuquerque Journal.* Retrieved January 23, 2019, from https://www.abqjournal.com/community-data/west-mesa-murders.

Torres, M. (2009). Interview in Albuquerque, New Mexico, March 24, 2009.

Chapter 3

Black Feminist Thought, Intersectionality, and Intercultural Communication

Aisha Durham

Returning from faculty leave, I faced a cutout in the front office entryway. The conference banner boxed me and two-few black graduate students as promotional material for my department. I stared at the frozen smiles, remembering the all-white feminist division conference table where a photographer was egged to snap us young women of color awkwardly curling, camouflaging into the wood paneling to avoid "capturing" like I had been years earlier as one of the two-few black graduate students advertised on the homepage for my department.

The department, division, and the discipline capture then reconfigure black knowledge-bodies to advance race-awareness with representations of difference that do not significantly change the structure nor the ideological frames supporting white-centered communication. *Recall my reflection of the still black-and-white photos.* The recent cyber-rally around #communicationsowhite (Chakravartty, Kuo, Grubbs, & McIlwain, 2018) along with the collective call to "de-whiten" intercultural communication in this book reminds me of the "difficult dialogues" about race raised by Houston, Davis, and James (2012) and others more than three decades ago. In this chapter, I return to Houston and other scholars working in the black feminist tradition to remap—if not reclaim—intersectionality. I describe disciplinary whitening outlined by Bilge (2013, 2014). I suggest dislocation and depoliticization are whitening techniques employed to render intersectionality legible outside of the discipline and as an interchangeable identity category only. By remapping intersectionality, I also work to reconnect and re-center contemporary black feminist scholarship that exemplifies the advocacy-oriented approach in critical intercultural communication today.

INTERSECTIONALITY

Intersectionality is a racially rooted feminist analytic approach used to describe the *differential impact of power* and an inclusive, activist-informed liberating praxis of meaningful political engagement by minoritized groups situated within interlocking systems of power. Germinal queer black feminist theorizations about power using metaphors of matrices, multiple jeopardy, and moving cars at race-gender traffic crossings have consistently illustrated the futility of single-axis analyses as well as the incommensurability of black womanhood historically (e.g., Guy-Sheftall, 1995). And, as a key component of black feminist thought, intersectionality recognizes the shared experiences of the *socially situated* self to generate embodied theory and critical interpretive methodology in what Houston (2000) calls community-cognizant scholarship.

Hill Collins and Bilge (2016) identify six core ideas of intersectionality: (1) social inequality as multifaceted and multiplicable, (2) power as interpersonal, disciplinary, cultural, and structural, (3) relationality as a both/and rather than either/or dynamic, (4) context as sociopolitical and historical, (5) complexity as nuanced understanding, and (6) social justice as engaged activism to challenge uneven power relations. These core ideas echo key concepts and the distinguishing features of black feminist thought. As a critical social theory, black feminist thought is dialectical, experiential, group oriented (i.e., standpoint), dialogical and collaborative, dynamic (in its analysis of social conditions, power, and within-group experience), and committed to social justice (Collins, 2000). This commitment underscores black feminism. Both Hill Collins and Bilge acknowledge activism as an optional component of an intersectional project. They do so to embrace the critical approach as well as its praxis for academics, activists, and artists alike performing political work within and outside of the academy. Social justice marks a significant distinction between intersectionality in general and its deployment within the intellectual tradition of black feminist thought.

Distinguishing intersectionality from black feminist thought does not sever its ties to that intellectual tradition. It is always already unapologetically associated with it because black women have served as the principle "stewards" (Hancock, 2016) of the racially rooted feminist analytic (Bliss, 2016; Nash, 2019). Still, the two are not interchangeable. This distinction opens different configurations or mappings of intersectionality that might not hinge on black feminist thought even as its recent articulation comes from Crenshaw (1989, 1991), the black feminist critical race theorist who is credited for coining the term. I say recent because Crenshaw and others identify similar conceptualizations by black women that predates *Mapping the Margins* by a century (Bell Scott, Hull, & Smith, 2015; Guy-Sheftall, 1995). The work by activist-journalists Ida B. Wells and Maria Stewart at the close of the nineteenth century are two notable examples referenced in intercultural communication (Davis & Houston, 2002). Moreover, sociologists Thornton Dill and Baca Zinn (1996) collaborate to develop a similar framework from their theorization of multicultural feminism around the same time when intersectionality is codified. I point to Thornton Dill and Baca Zinn to identify alternate articulations of intersectionality across different disciplines and between women of color, and to highlight different women of color archives in which the analytic approach has been developed and continues to be applied (Dill & Zambrana, 2009).

There is risk in refusing to reclaim intersectionality as black feminist. Claim conveys possession. Hancock (2016) considers whether intersectionality is a form of intellectual property that can be claimed by black women or a meme that can be copied, altered, and adapted without any attention to inequality and gendered racism, or its roots in black feminism specifically (pp. 1–37). The question the political scientist poses is an important one. To take up intersectionality as intellectual property might mean conceding to the capitalist-racial logic of ownership and slaveability that undergirds academic knowledge production, including those claiming to "advance" the approach with white-centered feminist theory. At best, this option operates on hopeful inclusion—a marginal one that might include an irreverent reference to Crenshaw without citing or contextualizing her conceptualization within black feminist thought. In my own research, I can recall the tension with claiming the third wave as a part of hip-hop feminism (Durham, 2007, 2014). The third wave inherited a whitewashed model and its birth was legitimated by incorporating intersectionality at the expense of their young women of color counterparts whose theorization of power had been grafted from the same language of movement feminism (Durham, Cooper, & Morris, 2013). Here, claiming was not tied so much to gaining recognition, inclusion, or token visibility *within* an existing exploitative, parasitic paradigm more than it was *reclaiming* intersectionality as an integral part of a black feminist project that produced hip-hop feminist scholarship.

The in-between space or interstice where intersectionality cannot be claimed as intellectual property nor embraced as a "free" signifier about multiple apolitical identities is the place where Hancock locates the steward. In two related passages, Hancock (2016) suggests:

> If we think of a steward as someone entrusted with caring for valuables that she does not herself own, then my role is to not only disavow ownership of intersectionality, but to remember that while I am permitted to use it, I must do so ethically, which entails producing projects that hopefully leave intersectionality scholars better equipped to engage in knowledge production projects in intersectionality studies. (p. 23)

> Stewardship means drawing some boundaries while simultaneously relaxing into the ambiguities of newer formulations—a delicate feat. But accepting all definitions, all critiques, or all rehabilitations simply because they mention more than one category of difference in their text will indeed limit intersectionality studies from transforming the world in ways it was intended to. (p. 200)

Hancock harkens to my hesitation with marrying hip-hop feminism to the third wave because of its celebration of difference. In the same vein as Hill Collins, Hancock holds a healthy tension in order to make space for practical applications and new iterations of intersectionality at the same time reminding us of its political impetus as a racially rooted analytic of power developed by feminists of color to advance liberation. *Liberation is the work.* To "hold on" intersectionality as property stymies that work (Nash, 2019). The core ideas, ethical considerations, and the activist orientation honed within black feminism guide my critique concerning the twin whitening technique of dislocation and depoliticization of intersectionality in intercultural communication. More than a mere defensive reaction to decentering, de-whitening is a charge of stewards of intersectionality working in the black feminist intellectual tradition.

(DE)WHITENING INTERSECTIONALITY IN INTERCULTURAL COMMUNICATION

The difficult dialogues that black feminists bravely broach decades earlier about gendered racism and interlocking power lay the groundwork for future intersectional analyses in intercultural (and feminist) communication and anchor the advocacy-oriented approach for what Houston later describes as "liberatory scholarship" whose aim is to celebrate, empower, and transform (Davis & Houston, 2002, p. 12; Houston, 2000). In the Foreword to *Standing in the Intersections*, Houston (2012) cautions white contributors about employing intersectionality to enhance their citational reputation without collective transformation. Use your white privilege to center those marginalized and excluded, she adds. Houston also signals what Bilge names in an online forum published in the *Journal of International and Intercultural Communication*: whitening intersectionality. Bilge argues recontextualizing intersectionality through feminist studies without including its postcolonial and antiracist critiques of disciplinary whiteness, citing intersectionality without critical engagement with antiracist feminist theorization, and canonizing (queer) white scholars as both antecedents to and theoretical refiners of the racially rooted analytic together form a "genealogical recalibration" of intersectionality (Bilge, 2013, p. 417). This technique has three strategies: the denial of race, the equation of race with nonwhiteness, and the acknowledgment of race as an interchangeable, replaceable identity only. Dislocation and depoliticization is a twin technique of whitening in intercultural communication that resemble strategies that Bilge identifies in disciplinary feminism.

Whitening: Dislocation

Compared to other interdisciplinary fields where culture, power, and identity are organizing concepts, intersectionality appears to be a late adoption in intercultural communication.[1] No articles are present in the *Journal of Intercultural Communication*. There are less than a dozen studies published in the *Journal of Intercultural Communication Research* and the *International Journal of Intercultural Relations* collectively (within the last three years only).[2] Moving beyond a requisite Collins or Crenshaw citation or the mentioning of multiple identities, Han and Groves Price (2015) provide a notable exception in describing the lived experience of Chinese, Japanese, and Indonesian immigrant women in Korea by addressing both interpersonal and structural power relations among Asian men and women across class, ethnicity, and cultural citizenship from an intersectional feminist-informed critical race framework. Han and Price take up intersectionality similar to earlier book-length applications, such as the aforementioned *Standing in the Intersections* (Chávez & Griffin, 2012) and *The Handbook of Critical Intercultural Communication* (Halualani & Nakayama, 2010). Han and Price notwithstanding, the relative absence of intersectionality as a racially rooted analytic of power in these three leading journals suggests simple erasure (or the denial of race) is a strategy of whitening in the field.

Dislocation can serve as a whitening technique. By dislocation, I am recalling when and where (and with whom) intersectionality can enter the field. Circle back to Collins and Crenshaw. The two stand outside of the reference field of intercultural communication. To incorporate them can imply that intersectionality lives elsewhere rather than being housed and honed by communication theorists of color. Here, researchers can claim they are performing new intellectual bridge-work by bringing intersectionality to intercultural communication.[3] The so-called new discoveries, however, could reenact the very genealogical recalibration that Bilge describes. *We been here.* To be clear, reading across disciplines is not necessarily dislocation. Both transdisciplinarity and interdisciplinarity are integral to the intellectual richness of black feminist thought. That said, dislocation functions as a whitening technique when (intercultural) communication is assumed to be a theoretical white domain to analyze difference through the adoption of elsewhere-intersectionality without a meaningful engagement of queer-black feminist scholarship at home. Disciplinary dislocation appears in most of the intercultural communication journal references where intersectionality is cited, and it serves as a primary whitening technique that erases the far-reaching theoretical and methodological contributions by queer women of color whose development of intersectionality across inquiry areas has informed the study of power, culture, and identity in intercultural communication.

Foregrounding interlocking power marks the "critical turn" in intercultural communication (Moon, 2010). It also underscores much of the recent scholarship about intersectionality featured in the *Journal of International and Intercultural Communication* published in JIIC within the past five years. Take J. Johnson's (2013) research about CeCe McDonald, a black woman who faced institutional violence because of race-gender criminalization after confronting antiblack transphobic violence on a Minneapolis city street. Johnson places Collins and Crenshaw in conversation with Houston and Allen to address cisprivilege and cissexism using black feminist-informed intersectionality. "For intercultural communication (IC) scholars committed to the study of power, oppression, and privilege, the case of CeCe McDonald holds particular relevance: it illustrates the pervasiveness of cisgender privilege, the use of identity to justify violence, and the importance of intersectional analyses for challenging privilege and oppression," Johnson adds (p. 136). Bilge, Chávez, and others also discuss racialized gender and sexual difference in the same JIIC special issue tackling queer theory and intersectionality. I point to Johnson, Bilge, Chávez, and others because they mine queer feminist of color archives to examine culture and identity.

The increase in representation of politically grounded intersectional approaches in JIIC does not happen simply because more folks are employing them. *We been here.* In their study assessing disciplinary and "citational whiteness" in communication, Chakravartty, Kuo, Grubbs and McIlwain (2018) argue for more nonwhite and non-U.S. researchers to be cited as knowledge bearers and included as editorial board members to de-whiten the discipline. (Again, they echo what Houston and Allen address earlier.) The JIIC editorship of Halualani exemplifies that call for women of color to transform the field, considering it has been under her previous JIIC editorship where many of the articles about intersectionality have been published. Under her editorship, there is a noticeable shift from apolitical interchangeable identity found in previous journals to an intersectional analysis of identity situated within interlocking systems of power. By staging critical conversations with communication theorists of color across distinct areas, she has broadened how we could imagine the field and how we could conceive of power, culture, and identity from a politically grounded intersectional approach (e.g., Alexander et al., 2014).

De-whitening: Relocation

Critical intercultural communication closely aligns with the advocacy-oriented intersectionality developed in black feminist thought. To my mind, there are three stewards whose experiential, embodied, democratizing research reflect this intellectual tradition: Manoucheka Celeste, Amber Johnson, and Robin Boylorn. The three represent what we might call the third generation of black feminist intercultural communication. They de-whiten intercultural communication when they draw from the theorizations, interpretive approaches, and representational forms established and cultivated by black feminist scholars from Marsha Houston, Olga Davis, Navita James, and Brenda Allen to Tina Harris, D. Soyini Madison, Ralina Joseph, Robin Means Coleman, E. Patrick Johnson, and Bryant Keith Alexander. *Granted, genealogies are always rife with omissions.* Including Celeste, Johnson, and Boylorn as stewards is meant to relocate intersectionality within a black feminist tradition and to remap intersectionality within (critical) intercultural communication, which culls inquiry areas, such as media, performance, and rhetoric to explore culture, identity, and power.

Manoucheka Celeste. From her body of work, de-whitening has entailed an explicit naming of women of color archives as a part of her political project of remembering (and re-centering) through citations, the insistence of transnational cultural politics or glocalized contexts in which culture is consumed and produced, and the unapologetic postcolonial framing of intersectionality as an immutable feature of black feminist thought (Celeste, 2015, 2018a). These commitments are concretized in her recent book, *Race, Gender, and Citizenship in the African Diaspora: Travelling Blackness* where Celeste explores racialization as a meaning-making communicative process of identity that gains currency across different boundaries in political and pop cultural spheres (Celeste, 2017).

There is a major contribution that Celeste makes to intersectionality in intercultural communication. She sutures "black" with "immigrant" thereby offering new insights about how immigrant blackness functions as a form of double outsiderness within discussions of citizenship and national belonging in intercultural communication. Celeste disrupts the homogeneity of blackness where African American and black cannot be read as interchangeable nor as a mere ethnic, racial marker without addressing U.S. geopolitical power in relationship to Haiti (and other Caribbean countries) and its black citizens within the nation-state. Addressing the precarity of black life, for example, Celeste applies the feminist trope of the wailing woman to demonstrate the ways black women's public grief is a form of political redress not only for onlookers to bear witness to black pain but also to incite collective resistance regarding the state-okayed killing of black folks (Celeste, 2018b). Her cultural analyses of unnamed or lesser-known black women juxtaposed to popular ones, such as Beyoncé, Mia Love, and Celia Cruz all address the ideological and affective "work" of black women's representations and performances in a transnational context.

Amber Johnson. Performance is privileged in the work of Johnson whose embodied approach to pedagogy and cultural analyses also troubles blackness by using it as a generative site to explore gender and sexuality when they use personal experience and performative enactments in media to underscore vulnerability, uncertainty, and the kind of affectivity Celeste describes. Where Celeste identifies the wailing woman in entertainment and news media, Johnson conceptualizes the homo coon as a black genderqueer performance in social media that highlights the both—and dynamic of intersectional analyses. For Johnson, to read the social media sensation Antoine Dodson as a coon or buffoon caricature only is to ignore the ways Dodson delinks femininity from women and masculinity from straight men. To recognize how Dodson mines his meme to market himself in entertainment media means there may be agency in his performance even as he is vulnerable to violence *because of* his performance. Johnson points to possibility. Here, they address intersectionality in terms of situated identity that has the potential to disrupt binaries and discussions of power that can be hierarchical and be productive (from the bottom-up) in critical intercultural communication (Johnson, 2013).

Forgoing binaries (and certainty) for fluidity, flexibility and vulnerability is a central feature of Johnson's intercultural research. From transfuturism to trans-pedagogy, Johnson (LeMaster & Johnson, 2018) uses contact zones of the classroom and the street to cultivate creative, collaborative, and affirming spaces where we can recognize our humanity and forge community. Traveling to Ghana, for example, Johnson grapples with their perceived whiteness because of citizenship and complexion even as they embrace diasporic blackness in an autoethnographic account (Johnson, 2016b). Using lived experience to engage in politics, Johnson's performance-based artivism of the Justice Fleet best demonstrates black feminist intersectionality as praxis (Johnson, 2016a). Coming from the classroom where students have been frozen by guilt, trauma, or shame, Johnson uses art to move through their feelings. By transforming a moving truck to a "mobile network of experiences," Johnson literally meets people where they are—physically and emotionally ("Justice on Board," 2019). Reporter Germain writes:

> In the last year alone, Johnson's work with The Justice Fleet has yielded a number of noteworthy ethnographic insights around intercultural communication and identity negotiation. For such heavy, unquestionably complicated topics, creating a playful atmosphere might seem counterintuitive. But, Johnson says, playfulness, laughter and creativity make room for vulnerability, and vulnerability plays a critical role in transformation. (Germain, 2019)

The investment in employing "mobile" art as an intimate vehicle for critical reflection and personal-political transformation defines a black feminist-informed intersectional approach to analyzing power and advocating social change. Like Johnson's cocreated "forgiveness quilt," their main contribution to de-whitening intercultural communication is by theorizing the performative and by showing advocacy-oriented intersectional scholars that our cultural lives are singularly unique but interwoven and interconnected (e.g., Johnson, 2016a).

Robin Boylorn. Relocating the situated body as *the site* to explore culture, identity, and power as an outsider-within anchors intersectionality research by Boylorn who bridges critical autoethnography (i.e., interpersonal) with critical intercultural communication to emphasize the complexity and contradictions of the human condition.[4] Like Celeste and Johnson, Boylorn (2006, 2011) stages everyday interactions through poetry and life narratives to connect, to reflect, and to intervene in taken-for-granted conversations about blackness. Her development of crunk feminism from hip-hop feminism (Cooper, Morris, & Boylorn, 2017), quare autoethnography (Boylorn, 2014) and intersectionality (Johnson & Boylorn, 2015) as theory and method from communication and performance studies theorist E. Patrick Johnson, and her embodied approach to interpret media representations using autoethnography or what I refer to as textual experience (Durham, 2014) all connect the personal (to critical theory) to culture.

The autoethnographies Boylorn writes are relational, dynamic, dialogic, and dialectical. Again, they are endemic of intersectionality rooted in black feminist thought. In a collaborative analysis framed by quare intersectionality, for example, Boylorn and Johnson (2015) discuss black lesbian visibility in a popular webseries, *Between Women*. It is her article, "From Here to There," however, that can be read as a companion piece where Boylorn (2014) advances a quare autoethnographic method when she rereads remarkable moments to recall how she imagined and later scripted lesbians. In her book *Sweetwater*, Boylorn (2017) reconnects with southern rural black women from "The Bottom." Any scent of nostalgia is soured by a remembering of good-bad men and mean-loving women who shape Boylorn's "blackgirl" becoming. Through remembering Boylorn mines the performative possibilities that bring together black women across difference and bring together the past with the present. *It is her narrative quilting.* Boylorn notes, "Auto/ethnography is an accountability check for me. By looking at myself through an introspective and retrospective lens, I have to take responsibility for my actions and attempt, through personal narrative, to correct them" (2014, p. 324). The bridge that Boylorn narratively builds is significant to de-whitening intercultural communication because she locates her work within the black feminist tradition by privileging the situated body to sense gaps in culture and identity and by theorizing power from lived experience across different representation forms and communication fields.

CONCLUSION

The charge to de-whiten intersectionality in the field of intercultural communication and the discipline writ large is one that has been championed by researchers of color who have identified the white institutional logic and structural barriers that delegitimize and erase our scholarly contributions. In the prominent journal venues where intercultural research is housed, intersectionality either lives elsewhere or it is welcomed without any meaningful attention to power. Drawing from Bilge, I suggested dislocation coupled with depoliticization served as a formidable whitening technique in intercultural communication. To remap the development of whitening, then, I attempted to relocate contemporary scholarship within intercultural communication and connect them to the advocacy-oriented black feminist-conceived analytic articulated by Houston and Davis decades earlier. I pointed to who we might call the third generation of black feminist intersectional scholars. Celeste, Johnson, and Boylorn are the new stewards of intersectionality because they not only embrace the complexity of situated identity, but they also adopt representational forms of autoethnographic cultural criticism, poetic narrative, and performance-based artivism already celebrated in black feminism. Most important, these stewards treat intersectionality as a racially anchored analytic approach that examines the differential impact of power to develop an inclusive, liberating praxis that recognizes the black body can stage political redress, can be a vehicle for transformation, and serve as a site for critical inquiry about identity in intercultural communication.

NOTES

1. Keyword searches of the terms "intersectionality" and "intersectional" from 2011 to 2018 were performed in four leading journals in intercultural communication: *Journal of Intercultural Communication*, *Journal of Communication Research*,

Journal of International and Intercultural Communication, and *International Journal of Intercultural Relations*.

2. For example, In Srividya Ramasubramanian's study about television imagery and racialization, she suggests the model minority image works to privilege whiteness and erase systemic racism that Asians experience because of controlling images. Here, intersectionality is not referenced but differential power anchors her argument in, "Television Exposure, Model Minority Portrayals, and Asian-American Stereotypes: An Exploratory Study," published in the *Journal of Intercultural Communication*.

3. In some cases, moving intersectional analyses outside of the United States is a way to avoid to perceived provincialism of race and the citational politics surrounding black feminist claims to intersectionality.

4. Writing with Mark Orbe, Robin Boylorn describes critical autoethnography and its engagement with theory. "We talk about autoethnography as a critical method by using three central features of critical theory, which include: to understand the lived experience of real people in context, to examine social conditions and uncover oppressive power arrangements, and to fuse theory and action to challenge processes of domination. We also elaborate on the ways in which individual autoethnographies are in conversation with one another and offer a commentary on the intersection of identity, culture, and relationships." See R. M. Boylorn & M. P. Orbe (Eds.), *Critical Autoethnography: Intersecting Cultural Identities in Everyday Life* (p. 20). New York: Routledge.

REFERENCES

Alexander, B. K., Arasaratnam, L. A., Durham, A., Flores, L., Leeds-Hurwitz, W., Mendoza, S. L., . . . Halualani, R. (2014). Identifying key intercultural urgencies, issues, and challenges in today's world: Connecting our scholarship to dynamic contexts and historical moments. *Journal of International & Intercultural Communication, 7*(1), 38.

Bell Scott, P., Hull, A., & Smith, B. (2015). *But some of us are brave: Black women's studies* (2nd ed.). New York: The Feminist Press at CUNY.

Bilge, S. (2013). Intersectionality undone: Saving intersectionality from feminist intersectionality studies. *DuBois Review: Social Science Research on Race, 10*(2), 405–24.

Bilge, S. (2014). Whitening intersectionality: Evanescence of race in intersectionality scholarship. In W. D. Hund, & A. Lentin (Eds.), *Racism and sociology*. Munster: LIT Verlag.

Bliss, J. (2016). Black feminism out of place: *Signs: Journal of Women in Culture & Society, 41*(4), 727–49.

Boylorn, R. M. (2006). E pluribus unum (out of many, one). *Qualitative Inquiry, 12*(4), 651–80.

Boylorn, R. M. (2011). Gray or for colored girls who are tired of chasing rainbows: Race and reflexivity. *Cultural Studies, Critical Methodologies, 11*(2), 178–86.

Boylorn, R. M. (2014). From here to there: How to use auto/ethnography to bridge difference. *International Review of Qualitative Research, 7*(3), 312–26.

Boylorn, R. M. (2017). *Sweetwater: Black women and narratives of resilience, revised edition*. New York: Peter Lang Incorporated, International Academic Publishers.

Celeste, M. (2015). Black women and U.S. pop culture in the postidentity era: The case of Beyoncé Knowles. In C. R. Rodriguez, D. Tsikata, & A. Adomako Ampofo (Eds.), *Transatlantic feminisms: Women and gender studies in Africa and the diaspora* (pp. 137–58). Lanham, MD: Lexington Books.

Celeste, M. (2017). *Race, gender and citizenship in the African Diaspora: Travelling blackness*. New York: Routledge.

Celeste, M. (2018a). Black media studies. *Feminist Media Histories, 4*(2), 38–43.

Celeste, M. (2018b). 'What now?': The wailing black woman, grief, and difference. *Black Camera, 9*(2), 110–31.

Chakravartty, P., Kuo, R., Grubbs, V., & McIlwain, C. (2018). #CommunicationSoWhite. *Journal of Communication, 68*(2), 254–66. doi:10.1093/joc/jqy003.

Chávez, K., & Griffin, C. (Eds.). (2012). *Standing in the intersection: Feminist voices, feminist practices in communication studies*. Albany, NY: SUNY Press.

Collins, P. H. (2000). Distinguishing features of black feminist thought. *Black feminist thought knowledge, consciousness, and the politics of empowerment* (2nd ed., rev. 10th anniversary ed., 21–43). New York: Routledge.

Cooper, B. C., Morris, S. M., & Boylorn, R. M. (2017). *The crunk feminist collection*. New York, NY: The Feminist Press.

Crenshaw, K. (1989). Demarginalizing the intersection of race and sex: A Black feminist critique of antidiscrimination doctrine, feminist theory, and antiracist politics. *University of Chicago Legal Forum, 1989*, 139–67.

Crenshaw, K. (1991). Mapping the margins: Identity politics, intersectionality, and violence against women. *Stanford Law Review, 43*(6), 1241–99.

Davis, O. I. & Houston, M. (2002). *Centering ourselves: African American feminist and womanist studies of discourse*. Cresskill, NJ: Hampton Press.

Dill, B. T. & Zambrana, R. E. (2009). *Emerging intersections: Race, class, and gender in theory, policy, and practice*. New Brunswick, NJ: Rutgers University Press.

Durham, A. (2007). Using [living hip hop] feminism: Redefining an answer (to) rap. In G. D. Pough, E. B. Richardson, A. Durham, & R. Raimist (Eds.), *Home girls make some noise!: Hip hop feminism anthology*, 304–12. Mira Loma, CA: Parker Publishing.

Durham, A. (2014). *Home with hip hop feminism: Performances in communication and culture*. New York: Peter Lang.

Durham, A., Cooper, B. C., & Morris, S. M. (2013). The stage hip-hop feminism built: A new directions essay. *Signs: Journal of women in culture and society, 38*(3), 721–37.

Germain, J. (2019). Art in motion: Through the justice fleet, Amber Johnson empowers people to heal. *STLMade*. Retrieved from https://thestl.com/culture/art-in-motion/.

Guy-Sheftall, B. (1995). *Words of fire: An Anthology of African-American feminist thought*. New York: New Press.

Hualani, R. T. & Nakayama, T. K. (2010). *The handbook of critical intercultural communication*. Malden, MA: Wiley-Blackwell.

Han, E.-J. & Price, P. G. (2015). Uncovering the hidden power of language: Critical race theory, critical language socialization and multicultural families in Korea. *Journal of Intercultural Communication Research, 44*(2), 108–131. doi:10.1080/17475759.2015.1028427.

Hancock, A. (2016). *Intersectionality: An intellectual history*. New York, NY: Oxford University Press.

Hill Collins, P. & Bilge, S. (2016). *Intersectionality*. Malden, MA: Polity Press.

Houston, M. (2000). Writing for my life: Community-cognizant scholarship on African-American women and communication. *International Journal of Intercultural Relations, 24*(5), 673–86.

Houston, M. (2012). Difficult dialogues: Intersectionality as lived experience. In K. R. Chavez, & C. L. Griffin (Eds.), *Standing in the intersection: Feminist voices, feminist practices in communication studies,* ix–xii. Albany, NY: Suny Press.

Johnson, A. (2013). Antoine Dodson and the (mis) appropriation of the Homo Coon: An intersectional approach to the performative possibilities of social media. *Critical Studies in Media Communication, 30*(2), 152–70.

Johnson, A. (2016a). The justice fleet: Fostering healing through art, dialogue and play. Retrieved from https://www.thejusticefleet.com.

Johnson, A. (2016b). Negotiating more, (mis)labeling the body: A tale of intersectionality. In R. M. Boylorn, & M. P. Orbe (Eds.), *Critical autoethnography: Intersecting cultural identities in everyday life* (pp. 81–95). New York: Routledge.

Johnson, A. & Boylorn, R. (2015). Digital media and the politics of intersectional queer hyper/in/visibility in between women. *Liminalities: A Journal of Performance Studies, 11*(1), 1–26.

Johnson, J. R. (2013). Cisgender privilege, intersectionality, and the criminalization of CeCe McDonald: Why intercultural communication needs transgender studies. *Journal of International and Intercultural Communication, 6*(2), 135–44.

Justice on Board. (2019). News. Retrieved from https://www.slu.edu/news/social/justice-fleet.php.

LeMaster, B., & Johnson, A. L. (2018). Unlearning gender—Toward a critical communication trans pedagogy. *Communication Teacher*, *33*(3), 189–98.

Moon, D. G. (2010). Critical reflections on culture and critical intercultural communication. In R. T. Halualani, & T. K. Nakayama (Eds.), *The handbook of critical intercultural communication,* 34–52. Malden, MA: Wiley-Blackwell.

Nash, J. (2019). *Black feminism reimagined: After intersectionality*. Durham, NC: Duke University Press.

Ramasubramanian, S. (2011). Television exposure, model minority portrayals, and Asian-American stereotypes: An exploratory study. *Journal of Intercultural Communication*, *26*(1), 1–17.

Zinn, M. B. & Dill, B. T. (1996). Theorizing difference from multiracial feminism. *Feminist Studies, 22*(2), 321–31.

Chapter 4

Intersectional Assemblages of Whiteness

The Case of Rachel Dolezal

Dawn Marie D. McIntosh

INTERSECTIONAL ASSEMBLAGES OF WHITENESS: THE CASE OF RACHEL DOLEZAL'S WHITENESS

I remember where I was when I first heard of Rachel Dolezal. I flipped on the morning news, sipped my coffee, and listened to broadcasters explain how the NAACP president of the Spokane Washington chapter was a white woman masquerading as a black woman. I watched the coverage in amazement and then disregarded Dolezal as mentally unstable. My initial reaction mirrored white women's ability to remove accountability with my affiliation to Dolezal as a fellow white woman and our hetero-feminine whiteness. Often whites do this by deflecting racist actions of whites as isolated incidents by mentally disturbed white people (e.g., Calafell, 2015; McIntosh, 2018). Ableism is employed by whiteness to disassociate Whites' accountability with racism. I enacted these practices to absolve myself.

In my following class, I used the Dolezal case for a discussion on race as a performance, but I still maintained an unreflexive relationship to her. A few months later, I had my third child and did not give Dolezal another thought until almost a year later. In a conversation with a respected biracial black feminist friend, she challenged me, "Dawn, why haven't white people confronted Rachel Dolezal?" There was a small pause, and she answered for me. She went on, "I'll tell you why, most white people are like, 'Heck no! I ain't going anywhere near that woman.'" I meditated on our conversation for weeks. Respectively, I acknowledged the privilege I had to simply disregard Dolezal. Dolezal's racial deceit did not affect me personally, but it should have. As my friend reminded me, "She is your people, Dawn; you need to deal with her." Dolezal challenged my whiteness, which is exactly why I felt no compelling affect toward her. To not take ownership of Dolezal absolves white feminists from the discomfort of white fragility she ignites. DiAngelo (2018) explains white fragility is the emotive reactions that white people have when challenged in terms of race or held accountable to racism. In thinking longer on why more white scholars did not take up the case of Dolezal, I realized that it was not the fear of white discomfort that sealed our lips. No. It is here, in the complexity of Dolezal's intersecting identities and her improvised performance of blackness that the depoliticizing of intersectionality proved to succeed. Dolezal's whiteness was not illusive; it was justifiably erased.

Bilge (2013, 2014) cautions that the theory of intersectionality intensely grew in popularity becoming appropriated by mainstream, typically white, scholars across many different disciplines. The popularity of intersectionality is proven through the absorption of the theory by white scholars, where the notion of intersectionality is not read through race, but instead through intersections of other fore-fronted identities (e.g., Nightingale, 2011; Anthias, 2013). With intersectionality becoming so mainstream, the foundation of the theory, the intersection of race and gender, is lost. In turn, the whitening of intersectionality prohibits the magnitude of intersectionality by appropriating it to function *for* whiteness (Bilge, 2013, 2014). Bilge (2014) explains it best to which I reference her at length here,

> The removal of whiteness from the scope of race component of intersectionality enables race-free analysis to claim intersectionality, in which gender and class function as structures and experiences unfettered by race (whiteness). Not accounting for how whiteness inflects gender, sexuality, class and so on also reinforces the impression that race is optional in intersectional analytics. (p. 24)

The whitening of intersectionality reveals a trend to allow for white scholars to overlook their racial privilege and focus solely on their marginalization. This is troublesome and harkens toward racist and homophobic feminist practices. The appropriation of intersectionality by white scholars has spearheaded social justice conversations where white people at large are often allowed to focus on their marginalization and reward themselves as social justice activists, all the while, never acknowledging their role in oppression. In walks Rachel Dolezal and white scholars are tongue-tied.

The Dolezal case is material proof of whiteness' appropriation of intersectionality. I use the phrase "the Dolezal case" to refer to Rachel Dolezal, her book and movie, and the media circulating her. In terms of the scholarly conversations that derived around Dolezal, they are hardly critical. Most research regarding Dolezal examines race as identity markers and racial identifiers (Morning, 2018; Orbe, 2016), rhetorics around racial categories or co-cultural racial organization (Roth, 2016; Orbe, 2016), and the primarily focus was of transraciality and racial fluidity (Brubaker, 2016a, 2016b; Roth 2016; Tuvel, 2017). The only critical conversation I found was Bey and Sakellarides's (2016) work in which they examine how Dolezal's problematic blackness demonstrates the current harmful cultural assumptions of what constitutes blackness.

Collectively, the research on Dolezal is missing intersectional readings challenging interpoles of her identities and her improvised blackness through a critical lens on her whiteness. Dolezal's intersection of denied privilege and falsely claimed marginalization is certainly not a new narrative of whiteness. Rather the case of Dolezal denotes where whiteness has neutralized intersectionality to remove whites' accountability to racism. Nash (2008) claims there remains unexplored avenues for intersectionality like "the ways in which privilege and oppression intersect, informing each subject's experiences" (p. 12). Yep (2016) also calls for more examination of "both marked and unmarked intersections so more nuanced operations of power in society can be revealed" (p. 88). Responding to their calls, this chapter walks readers through the depoliticizing critiques of intersectionality and how these critiques serve as workings of whiteness. Next, I build on Yep's (2010, 2016) notion of thick intersectionality and Puar's (2012) notion of intersectional assemblages to understand intersectional workings of whiteness through what I coin, intersectional assemblages of whiteness. Finally, I use intersectional assemblages of whiteness to read the case of Rachel Dolezal.

THE GENEALOGY OF INTERSECTIONALITY

I begin by reiterating the genealogy of intersectionality came from feminists of color (for more on genealogy of intersectionality, see: Collins & Blige, 2016; Combahee River Collective, 1983; Crenshaw, 1990; Lorde, 2012; hooks, 1982; Moraga & Anzaldúa, 2012; Moraga, 1983). So, its nucleus is a theorization of raciality/race. However, before its given name, feminists of color employed intersectionality within their claims of how their many positionalities work within/through their lives and furthermore each of these positionalities intersect and are indivisible to form their lived realities. The theoretical groundwork for intersectionality was established by (queer) women of color (Anzaldúa, 2012; Moraga & Anzaldúa, 2012; Moraga, 1983). My point here is to emphasize the origins for this scholarship grew from the materiality of the subjective Other. In doing so, I hope to remind readers, intersectionality was manifested to place marginalized identities at the center and enunciate these experiences in relationship to workings of power. First coined by Crenshaw (1990), intersectionality was developed to provide a methodological tool to recognize the workings of identity politics in judicial/legal settings and critical law studies. Crenshaw claims that the problems with identity politics is not the recognition of difference but the ignoring of difference *within* groups. Through her articulation of intersectionality, she traced the places where race and gender intersect in the lives of black women to shape structural, political, and representational aspects of violence against them (p. 1244).

For Crenshaw (1990), intersectionality provides a theoretical lens to both articulate and read how identities intersect in sociopolitical manners that marginalize women of color both through racism and sexism. Intersectionality manifests a consciousness of the multiplex of identities working simultaneously against/with a politics of power. Patricia Hill Collins (2002) theorization of the matrix of domination builds on the articulations of power by noting how systems of power work intersectionally to marginalize bodies that differ from the normative (p. 18). The matrix of domination denotes the intersectional nature of oppression and how systems of power interconnect through macro and micro levels of social institutions to impact beings in various ways. Taken together, these theoretical lenses propelled intersectionality, as McCall (2008) claims, to be "the most important theoretical contribution that women's studies, in conjunction with other fields, has made so far" (p. 1771). Indeed. Intersectionality is employed across multiple disciplinary fields, multiple countries, and multiple contents. The fame of intersectionality is where critiques and developments of the theory have flourished and floundered. I now momentarily address the critiques of intersectionality.

Intersectionality, as developed by Crenshaw (1990), orchestrates from a binary understanding of power. In other words, identities are situated from either a marginalized or privileged orientation. Discursively intersectionality, then, is dependent on binary understandings of power. In other words, the intersections of identities must be read from an either/or relation to hegemony. This theoretical premise births an essentialist critique of intersectionality. The postmodernist critique is twofold. First, there is a crisis of identity limitlessness where the list of social locations is boundless. Crenshaw, herself, alluded to this very issue when she first developed intersectionality by claiming it must not be seen "as some new, totalizing theory of identity" but rather called for scholars to expand this work into other intersections "such as class, sexual orientation, age and color" (pp. 1244–45). Zack (2007) adds, "Theoretical endorsements of intersectionality as an intellectual project impose no limits on the numbers of kinds of possible intersected identities" (p. 199). Furthermore, as Yuval-Davis (2013) augments, with the boundless nature of identities which intersections of identities should take primary focus?

Second, intersectionality is critiqued for the essentializing nature of categorization necessitated by intersectionality, the boundaries these categories create, and margins these categories then maintain (Nash, 2008). When researching such subjects as white womanhood how do I accurately define the identities of white womanhood while not reducing my claims to an essentialists critique? Arguably for those employing intersectionality from a privilege perspective to articulate embodied politics of power, this critique is the most prevalent because it serves to remove privileged accountability. These challenges fed an anti-essentialism trend that the intricacies of one's identities must be always read subjectively and fluidly. From this perspective, no one person will have the same intersectional realities with another; even the same person's identities alter contextually (e.g., nationality and nation place) and through time (e.g., age and ageism) (Yuval-Davis, 2006). This fluidity critique left those employing intersectionality to possibly be reductionist in nature and conclusively bleak. Looking to Muñoz's (1999) framing of "the race, class, and gender mantra" (p. 166), Yep (2010) alludes to this essentialist critique of intersectionality through an intersectional-methodological framing by claiming that intersectionality, conceived from this manner, suggests "a simplistic, formulaic, 'roster-like approach,' that simply lists the individual's race, class, gender, sexuality, and nationality" (p. 173). Yep (2016) later details, "In this process, it tends to homogenize people inhabiting similar intersections" (p. 87).

These critiques of intersectionality and the theoretical development that grew from them are not born from misguided thought, nor are they entirely absent of positive growth for the theory, but culture and communication scholars must be vigilant to remain reflexively accountable to these critiques. The current cultural state paints a telling picture of what overindulgence in anti-essentialism manifests. These consequences have created a "post" ideology that establishes paramount harms for marginalized Others and erases the material realities of their experiences. Alexander and Mohanty (2013) clarify my point here best claiming:

> Postmodernist discourse attempts to move beyond essentialism by pluralizing and dissolving the stability and analytic utility of these categories of race, class, gender, and sexuality. This stability often forecloses any valid recuperation of these categories or the social relations through which they are constituted. If we dissolve the category of race, for instance, it becomes difficult to claim the experience of racism. (xvii)

In many respects, the erasure of difference through anti-essentialism was the racist realms of white feminism's history repeating itself here, or what Bilge (2013) referred to as *disciplinary feminism* (pp. 408–9). The insurgence to incorporate intersectionality into Euro-American academics served to depoliticized intersectionality or whiten it (Bilge, 2014). These academic critiques and the saturation of intersectionality in academic disciplines grew from a neoliberal goal to "legitimize" its academic accountability with the end goal to create an intersectionality grand theory or standardized methodology for academic capital. One is left to question, why a theory developed by feminists of color must go through such labors for legitimization?

Cho, Crenshaw, and McCall (2013) astutely respond, "It is far from mere coincidence that current debates about intersectionality's capacity to represent anyone other than black women bear a striking resemblance to courts' discomfort with centering black women in class-action lawsuits" (pp. 791–92). With "the key feature of feminist analysis of intersectionality to decenter the normative subject of feminism" (Brah & Phoenix, 2004, p. 78), the critiques of intersectionality functioned to remove the accountability of whiteness and race. More so, these grandiose critiques function to discipline marginalized methodologies as mere navel gazing or narcissistic (Calafell & Moreman, 2009; Calafell, 2010). We must listen to the wisdom of feminists of color that never proposed to essentialize one's experiences because intersectionality is inseparable from the body and affects. Rather, Moraga and Anzaldúa (2015) call scholars to rein anti-essentialism in from unraveling reality because "the physical realities of our lives all fuse to create a politic born out of necessity" (p. 21). Grillo (1995) challenges, "Essentialism is not always a bad thing . . . the question is whether the essentialism, which is sometimes unavoidable, is explicit, is considered temporary, and is contingent" (p. 21).

Anzaldúa (2007) suggested identity should be conceptualized through the history behind it (p. 307). Building here Madison (1993) reminds us, "Theories of the flesh means that the cultural, geopolitical, and economic circumstances of our lives engender particular experiences and epistemologies that provide philosophies about reality different from those available to other groups" (pp. 213–14). Identity scholarship must research lived experiences through history, context, and time. Rendering contingent-essentialism is not limiting but an acknowledgment of the cultural narrative that is negotiated historically, contextually laden, and timely. Intersectionality, then, must remain vigilant to observe the multiplex of intersecting identities but be allowed to be contingently essentialist with respect to context, time, and those involved in the relation. My claim here strikes similar to Yep's (2010, 2016; also see Yep & Chivers, 2017; Yep & Lescure, 2018) theorization of "thick intersectionality." Yep (2010) demonstrates the need for intersectional incorporation of space, time, and the body in relation which brings us toward an affective awareness in intersectional analysis.

Certainly, these critiques have propelled valuable conversations around intersectionality and challenged scholars to do the immense labor to demonstrate on the page the intersectional particularities of power laden on/through the body. However, these critiques also demonstrate how scholars, particularly unreflexive white scholars, lay claim to marginalized theories and whitewash them. Cho, Crenshaw, and McCall (2013) claim, "Assessing intersectionality's value against the expectations of a grand theory seems off the mark since we do not understand intersectionality's use or objectives to be realized only through a full-fledged grand theory or a standardized methodology" (p. 789). In the end, the critiques noted here of intersectionality arise from a desire to move a theory of identity into standardized methodology and grand theory. These moves in intersectionality confiscate its foundation as a racial theory that sought to locate the workings of racism and sexism for women of color. I note these specific critiques of intersectionality at length here because these critiques offer ideological insights into the workings of whiteness.

The very notion of devaluing intersectionality is a function of whiteness to loosen the authority intersectionality holds in dismantling it. Furthermore, whiteness reminds us of the detrimental harms that ripple from overlooking race in intersectional analysis. The erasure of race in intersectionality research prompts "silencing, exclusion, or misrepresentation of subordinated groups" (Bilge, 2014, p. 407). Notably, intersectionality is not only attacked by white scholars but also by black male scholars, demonstrating whiteness works not only through whites but as a function of patriarchy within people of color as well (e.g., Curry, 2014, 2017). As these critiques of intersectionality demonstrate, race and racism are removed intentionally from a race-based theory in order to offer white's unaccountable access to intersectionality. These critiques denote how the appropriation of intersectionality derives the functionality of whiteness. In the following section, I look to these critiques and utilize the scholarship that arose from the critiques of intersectionality as a new theoretical articulation of whiteness.

INTERSECTIONAL ASSEMBLAGE OF WHITENESS

At its core, whiteness is cultural workings to empower white raciality, performatives of whites, and racism. Whiteness as Nakayama and Krizek (1995) noted is discursively strategic and dynamic with the primary aims to maintain white supremacy at the center. Warren (2003) moves whiteness from solely discursive tactics toward a thinking of whiteness as a performative accomplishment. Alexander (2004) flushes this further when he claims whiteness is an act, an embodied performance that is scripted not based on one's skin, but on the enactments of whiteness. Moving whiteness toward discourses of the body forces an acknowledgment to see "whiteness as politically organized not only racially but also through our gender, ability, sexuality, age, class, and nationality" (McIntosh, 2018, p. 95). McIntosh (2018) contests "to trace the embodiments of whiteness, one must examine the intersections of our identities in relation to whiteness" (p. 95). Intersectionality uproots whiteness research from a singular model of racial study to denoting how the workings of whiteness, and race for that matter, are intermingled with all our identities removing the possibility of understanding whiteness on singular grounds. McIntosh, Moon, and Nakayama (2019) claim, "The communicative power of whiteness must be mapped from an intersectional reading of it" (p. 5). In sum, intersectionality serves as an essential component to understanding the workings of whiteness on and through the body.

Whiteness is also a cultural entity of power that works through a collection of other norms of hegemony to maintain power. For example, Yep (2003) claims whiteness is a coconspirator with heterosexuality. Lugones (2007) correlates whiteness with colonialism and heteronormativity. McIntosh (2017) claims that heteronormativity and whiteness "share the same cultural workings of power" (p. 162). Hill Collins's (2002) notion of the matrix of domination moves understandings of whiteness from linear perspectives toward understanding how multiple oppressions function complexly together in order to maintain dominance. Whiteness, like intersectionality, works simultaneously through multiplex-interlocking social locations and matrix of cultural mechanisms of power. The complexity of these theoretical layers is flattened and simplified by the limitations of language. In turn, like intersectionality, whiteness becomes confined to binary modes and one-dimensional notions of power. A theoretical resolve is an orchestration of whiteness as intersectional assemblage. Whiteness as intersectional assemblage requires a more complex reading of whiteness and a multifaceted demonstration of its workings.

I approach assemblage following closely to Puar's (2012) defining principles of assemblages. Puar calls for us to be less concerned with defining what assemblages are but focusing more on what assemblages do (p. 57). From this ideological approach, I define assemblages as the workings of bodies in relation, bodies as both material enfleshment and the matter of bodies, and the doings of bodies in relation to space(s). Whiteness as intersectional assemblage provides a theoretical lens to reading whiteness from both privileged and marginalized positionalities, while simultaneously calling for the contextual and relational manifestations of power to be unearthed. Whiteness scholarship needs these types of moves to propel us toward dissuading whiteness' elusive affective void. I am not suggesting for a removal of the material norms of whiteness directly linked to frames of identities. Rather, I am advocating for the complexity of whiteness to be read through relations of positionalities of bodies and the affective, relational, spatial, and contextual realms whiteness infiltrates.

Yep's (2010, 2016) conceptualization of "thick intersectionality" challenges scholars to move beyond the identity mantra and toward a contextual and affective understanding of power in relation to bodies. Building here on Yep's point, Puar (2012) takes a slightly different critique of intersectionality by claiming that "many of the cherished categories of the intersectional mantra—originally starting with race, class, gender, now including sexuality, nation, religion, age, and disability—are the products of modernist colonial agendas and regimes of epistemic violence, operative through a Western/Euro-American epistemological formation through which the notion of discrete identity has emerged" (p. 54). In turn, Puar suggests intersectionality as assemblage which allows for identity(ies) to rather be "identification"—to be a process. She clarifies, "Where categories—race, gender, sexuality—are considered events, actions, and encounters between bodies rather than simply entities and attributes of subjects" (p. 58). For Puar, "identities are multidirectional, liminal" (p. 59). While I support Puar in striving to see identity outside of Western fixity and instead as more processual norm of identification, I am weary of assemblage theory's ability to "not only misrepresent the importance of race in original architecture of intersectional thought and activism, by minimizing it, but also contribute to making race analysis optional in current scholarship" (Bilge, 2014, p. 17).

Puar (2012) challenges that it is difference in doing, in being with, and difference with, that structure the significance and signifying of simultaneous privileged and marginalized identification. Calafell (2014) cautions to always remember how practices of theorization can and do colonize the work of feminists of color. While there is probability in theorizing the fluidity of difference, we cannot overlook the reality that intersections of identities are always constructed against or with difference as defined by the normative. Taking Puar's (2012, 2017) logic that identity is manufactured only through relation and maintains no constraints but is in a constant state of becoming, variations of variations, then how do we explain the limitations placed on the materialized bodies of color? Or furthermore, how do we then account for the discursive limitlessness provided to white bodies from the absence of configurations of whiteness? While history and relationality are components, the linguistic framings of nonwhite are undeniably a confining global discursive that evolves from the neoliberal politics of our ever-growing globalized market. Whiteness, then, thrives in the limitless notion of identity as a constant state of becoming. Perhaps what assemblage is awaking here is yet another proof of whiteness. Whiteness as the "doing of assemblage" is, in essence, a manner of reading how non-formative identity maintains discursive absence through a constant relation to organizations of power. Thus, the assemblage of whiteness is the becoming of intersectional whiteness.

Intersectional assemblage of whiteness, then, is a call to acknowledge the mechanisms of power that function fluidly and affectively to maintain elusiveness and superiority. McIntosh (2014) references the absence of affectivity in whiteness as a means to maintain power. Building on Carrillo Rowe's (2008) work, McIntosh (2014) claims the only way to locate affective raciality in/by/through whiteness is to foster affective attentiveness from normative positions. The affective workings of whiteness' ability to remain in a constant state of becoming is exactly how whiteness maintains its power. In turn, I am not debunking intersectionality as assemblage here in its entirety but again cautioning the use of this proposed theoretical expansion of intersectionality by Western white scholarship to remove whiteness. Intersectional assemblages' function as/are whiteness. So, intersectional assemblages of whiteness are always and already present in the relations, in the becoming, in the affective undertones, and embodied vibrations.

As suggested by Yuval-Davis (2006), "There is a need to differentiate carefully between different kinds of difference" (p. 99). Specifically, intersectionality used by culture and communication scholars must move the larger focus of intersectionality from an examination of "differences from" to "differences within." Whiteness scholarship is hindered by binary notions of whiteness where it locates whiteness in relation to people of color, a naïve interrogation. Rather, we need to locate the intersectional assemblages of whiteness within the differences of white bodies and furthermore within the differences of bodies of color. Puar (2012) claims, "One of the big payoffs for thinking through the intertwined relations of intersectionality and assemblages is that it can help us produce more roadmaps of precisely these not quite fully understood relations between discipline and control" (p. 63). Yep (2016) provides four defining features for doing thick intersectionality, which I used as theoretical jumping points to locate the intersectional assemblages of whiteness by white bodies (for more see pp. 89–90). The remainder of this chapter will walk readers through what I have keyed the four primary workings intersectional assemblages of whiteness, utilizing the Dolezal case to prove these workings of power.

RACHEL DOLEZAL'S INTERSECTIONAL ASSEMBLAGES OF WHITENESS

Intersectional assemblages of whiteness expose the processual nature of whiteness—the becoming of whiteness through intersections and contextual relations of bodies—to empower normativity.

The performance of Dolezal's biracial-ness, albeit being false, denotes the reality of how identities are always in a perpetual state of becoming. My point here is not to demonstrate that intersectional assemblages prove Dolezal as a biracial black woman or embodied blackness, nor to defend her claims to transraciality. Rather, the case of Dolezal and the mediated hype surrounding her "outing" is cultural proof of the overall reality that all our identities are in a constant state of negotiation and how this propels the current state of racial fragility. Race is a negotiation that is factored contextually, spatially, affectively, and relationally. Certainly, many people of color were suspicious of Dolezal's "blackness." *The Rachel Project* provides multiple examples of women of color being suspicious of Dolezal's claims to blackness. But the assemblages of whiteness empowered Dolezal's blackness in order to erase the realities of whiteness. Accounting for the fluidity of identity negotiations, we are challenged to see her identities flushed through not only her presentation of self, but affective and contextual aspects of the performance of blackness she presented. In doing so, assemblages of whiteness function to empower whiteness by deconstructing the material realities of race and racism.

If we accept that identities are "processual, fluid, and [in an] ever-changing nature of becoming" (Yep, 2016, p. 90), then Dolezal's racial embodiments must be read against micro and macro contextual backdrops. In these ways, Dolezal exemplifies how race is intersectionally contingent and always becoming. For these matters, she did embody black straight feminine performatives on a micro level through her everyday enactments (her hair, clothing choices, the art she studied, the communities she affiliated). On these micro levels, Dolezal demonstrates the unapologetic and unreflexive reality of white bodies' fluidity of raciality. Dolezal's whiteness is permitted to fluctuate and change without acknowledging her white body. The disregard she continues to maintain of whiteness serves as a symbol of how whiteness has responded to the fluidity of race.

Intersectional assemblages of whiteness seized the notion of identity's fluidity to empower white supremacy. First, saturation of whiteness function to empower Dolezal's racial fluidity and her appropriating black performance. The proximity to which Dolezal's body is placed is significant to these racial readings. As one scholar in response to Dolezal stated, "[Dolezal] couldn't have gotten away with this in places like D.C., Atlanta, or New Orleans. But in Spokane, where just over 2 percent of the population is black, the calculus is different" (Patton, June 17, 2017, para 23). Contextual proximity of whiteness here demonstrates how Dolezal's performance of blackness worked through the intersectional assemblages of whiteness. Dolezal's blackness is *not* authentic but does not have to be because her blackness is juxtaposed to a saturation of whiteness. Jones concludes, "It's so lonely in these places where you're the only one, or one of the few. You might not ask questions. You just say, 'Hey Black person, lets [sic] sit down and have coffee.' " (Patton, June 17, 2017, para. 14). Intersectional assemblages of whiteness clarify how affective powers of whiteness function through isolation toward bodies of color/bodies of difference from the normative.

Furthermore, since Dolezal is performing black hetero-feminine embodiments there is less surveillance of her. Patriarchy protects definitive properties of masculinity but femininity, especially women of color femininity, is available for mis-appropriation. Likewise, heteronormativity makes queer performatives suspect. Since Dolezal enacts performatives of a straight black mother, heteronormativity cloaks her in normalcy. Thus, it is not that Dolezal's blackness needs to be proven rather that intersectional assemblages of whiteness function to authenticate Dolezal through the proximal inundation of whiteness, patriarchy, and heteronormativity that affectively authenticates Dolezal's hetero-feminine blackness. Perhaps, more significantly, these intersectional assemblages of whiteness empower Dolezal, as a white woman in a saturated space of whiteness, to appropriate blackness and people of color through her deceptive embodied performance of black straight femininity.

Another intersectional dimension of the assemblages of whiteness is in the fluidity of racism. Dolezal's accounts of racism provide a crystalized moment of how whiteness work to destabilize racism in order to remove the tangible realities of racism. According to Dolezal, she experienced acts of racism while president of the NAACP that many questioned the validity of even prior to being exposed as white. She claims nooses, hate mail, and suspicious men from local white supremacist groups infiltrated her home and workspace after being nominated as president of the NAACP. The racism Dolezal articulates in both her book and documentary are not mundane moments of her lived experiences. Micro-racism is acknowledged struggles experienced daily by people of color and carry grave significance since they are never validated as racist behaviors. Dolezal's accounts of racism, rather, are always overt acts directly linked to her positions she held in the black community. Whiteness functions here to remove racism from embodied experience and rather to macro spaces of positions of power.

Micro-racism is the lived experiences of bodies of color. Dolezal demonstrates how whiteness functions to remove racism as a function from a micro perspective. The acts of racism constructed by Dolezal remove the correlation of racism to race or in her case her "blackness." Instead racism becomes constructed as affiliated solely with the social role's people hold. In Dolezal's case, as president of the NAACP she experienced acts of racism. The case of Dolezal reveals how whiteness positions racism as solely functioning from a macro level. In turn, racism on a micro-everyday consciousness can be nullified. Intersectional assemblages of whiteness challenge us to understand the contextual framings of racism, are confined to macro narratives, and serves as a cautionary reminder how racism becomes removed from lived experiences of one's race.

In addition, Dolezal's discursive claims to experiencing racism denote how intersectional assemblages of whiteness disassociate racism from white bodies.

Dolezal's accounts of racism are constantly hearkened by her as a means to prove herself as black. In true colonizing manners, she appropriates experiences of marginalized people for her advantage. Intersectional assemblages of whiteness function through heteronormativity, whiteness, and racism to allow Dolezal, as a white woman, to claim victimization of racism. Whiteness thrives by white bodies never acknowledging our historical and personal role in racism. Instead, neoliberal whiteness re-centers itself by whites situating themselves as part of the fight against marginalization and experiencing marginalizing harms due to their social justice plight. Dolezal's disassociation with her whiteness perpetuates the larger macro narratives of white privilege to victimization rather than acknowledging white folks' role in racism. Perhaps best captured by Dolezal herself in speaking about white privilege, " 'I think there's definitely a stereotype of White privilege, and that stereotype gets expanded to mean rich, not oppressed, not suffering, et cetera. And yes, it's a misperception.' The undeniable existence of White privilege, she argues, does not preclude the possibility of White pain" (Aitkenhead, February 25, 2017, para. 34). Whiteness flourishes in spaces where it can re-center privilege through victimization.

As Dolezal demonstrates rather than acknowledging herself as white and partaking in whiteness, she instead removes her accountability in whiteness and claims she understands racism because she too has experienced it. Dolezal represents how whiteness relationally capitalizes on post-race and anti-essentialism logics. In turn, whites can disassociate with the material realities of privilege. Dolezal's case demonstrates how race and whiteness must always be acknowledge and accounted for because whiteness like identity is "incomplete and full of possibilities" (Yep, 2016, p. 90). People of color called on Dolezal to admit of her fraudulent racial performative for reasons of reflexive apologetics. Whites not surprisingly never call for Dolezal to acknowledge herself as white. The narratives that surfaced around Dolezal by white people need to be conversations discussing how race remains in state of frantic verification and what that means for whites. When whiteness is placed in fragile states of becoming it weakens its fixed normativity. To be clear, I am not saying that Dolezal's performance of black femininity is one to celebrate the fluidity of race. What I am emphasizing here is intersectional assemblages of whiteness necessitate identity as discursively fixed in order to perpetuate dominant norms of power. Intersectional assemblages of whiteness capitalize on the fluidity of race in order to remove whites personal accountability to being white, white supremacy, and racism. Intersectional assemblages of whiteness function through the fluidity of identity and the interlocking marginalization of patriarchy, heteronormativity, and whiteness to overlook micro realities of marginalization and rather lean on these macro narratives to insert themselves into these experiences of marginalization, removing the material realities of racism and whites accountability to it.

Intersectional assemblages of whiteness demonstrate how whiteness capitalizes on messy fragmented fluidity to empower white supremacy and marginalize Others.

There is nothing "messier" than Rachel Dolezal's everyday experiences. The mere fact that Dolezal finds it ethically and personally appropriate to perform as a black woman moves understandings of blackface to new disturbing levels. However, her racial aesthetic of black femininity was accepted, by most, until she is revealed to be a white woman performing as a black woman. Dolezal inhabited many different roles throughout her life: daughter to poor white strictly religious white parents, white sister to adopted black brothers and black sisters, graduate student at Howard university, white wife and pregnant mother to a black man and then single divorced white mother to black boys, black hairdresser, artist, college instructor, activist, and president of the NAAPC. Throughout her life and the telling of her experiences, Dolezal has always differentiated herself from whiteness (for more, see Dolezal, 2017). However, it was not until much later in her life after graduate school, after her marriage, after the birth of her first son and divorce did Dolezal identify herself as black (Morning, 2017, p. 9). Notably, Dolezal's embodiment of black femininity was a learned improvised performance over many years. Her deceptive embodiment moved beyond presentation of self. Dolezal claimed to have a black father. Introducing many people to a black man that she claimed as her father, and those that did not meet him personally, met him via the framed picture of her with him in her office. Dolezal leans on the messiness of lived experiences to project herself as biracial and justify her blackness. Yep and Lescure (2018) note thick intersectionality challenges scholars to regard how "individuals inhabit and perform multiple and simultaneous identities in fluid, open, messy, fragmented, emerging affectively charged, lived and embodied ways" (p. 4). Attending to this notion of thick intersectionality challenges an acknowledgment that contextually and in many moments of her life, Dolezal improvised black femininity as a white woman. Intersectional assemblages of whiteness ask culture and communication scholars to read how whiteness functions relationally and affectively in this messy fragmented fluidity to empower white supremacy and marginalize people of color.

Dolezal's consumption of difference grew from a disdain for her own white impoverished, religious extremist household (Dolezal, 2017). It must be emphasized here, her access to whiteness was never relinquished despite distinguishing from it. In fact, her improvisation of blackness was very much understood through her relationship with white heteronormative patriarchy. Dolezal's childhood, as she tells it, mirrors the lessons of white heteronormative patriarchy most U.S. white children endure (see Dolezal, 2017). Violent white fathers, passive white mothers, white parents "saving" colored children are all the relational experiences of learning white culture and furthermore how to embody whiteness (for more here, see McIntosh, 2017). Interestingly, even when describing herself before her outing, Dolezal claims she was "not just perceived as Black, but Black and 'uppity' " (Aitkenhead, February 25, 2017, para. 12). Dolezal's explanation of her blackness maintains a correlation to what she lacked in her whiteness, class. On the other hand, her whiteness morphed her blackness through articulations of class. Blackness is often whitened by affiliations with classism.

As she grows, her racial disassociation with whiteness denotes how whiteness remains imbued on all bodies despite their acknowledgment of it. The Dolezal case signifies the desire of white bodies for difference in order to find solace in our own emotional displacement. My point here is not to understand Dolezal's "transraciality" but rather to expose how whiteness functions through her improvised blackness. Each of her experiences as a white woman in relation to black siblings, black lovers, black colleagues, black mentors, and black friends certainly positioned Dolezal's whiteness in abject manners. Conley (2001) explains his whiteness was learned from growing up in a constant state of abjection from normative white experiences. Unlike Conley, Dolezal did not read these experiences as a means to understand whiteness but rather how to perform blackness. Thus, she understands how to perform black femininity, but she learns these embodiments through the social script of white femininity.

With that said, Dolezal never loses her access to whiteness nor her embodiment of whiteness. For example, she is never scripted as an angry woman of color because she always affectively engages white femininity through her improvisation of black femininity. Rather Dolezal demonstrates the ideology of whiteness is imbued within white people no matter how they racially perform. Dolezal's embodiment of blackness articulates how intersectional assemblages of whiteness allows whiteness to function through relations of others by means of appropriating Othered experiences in order to remove the accountability to whiteness.

Furthermore, Dolezal's embodiment of black femininity is a lived contradiction to her acknowledgment of whiteness. The claim of race as a social construct is Dolezal's premise to her justification of her racial transformation and defense for why she can claim to be black. After first reading about race as a social construct, she states, "I felt free, like I was no longer coerced into claiming 'whiteness' because that was the 'honest' or right thing to do (out of obligation to my parents and previous social conditioning)" (Morning, 2017, p. 9). She adds, "I knew White wasn't my state of mind, and this gave me permission to stop repressing and be exactly who I am" (p. 9). Interestingly, her transformation and identification as black contradicts her underlining claim of transraciality. She rejects the fixity of whiteness but embraces the fluidity of her racial performative choices. White is fixed as a state of mind, but her whiteness is permitted to be transformed from her. The intersectional assemblages of whiteness expose the intersectional pulls of everyday messiness of whiteness here and where affective privilege lies in Dolezal's racial embodiments. Dolezal's rejection of herself as white discounts the permanence of her access to whiteness.

The Dolezal case is certainly a messy example of our lived experiences with identity performances. But her "untidy blackness" is a clarifying template to how whiteness functions to remove whites' accountability to our raciality in our everyday lives. Whites can simply grant ourselves "permission to stop repressing and be exactly who I am" (Morning, 2017, p. 9). We can stop feeling the accountability to our white racist realities and instead be anyone we want to be. Intersectional assemblages of whiteness expose how affective attentiveness to whiteness is not only absent but justifiably removed. Additionally, Dolezal's account reminds us how intersectional assemblages of whiteness excuse whites of all acts of cultural appropriation under the guise of finding our "true-selves." Performative freedom without performative reflexivity, this is intersectional assemblages of whiteness embodied.

The intersectional assemblages of whiteness reveal how the role of affectivity, affective investment, and relationality operate to allocate white entitlement and justify cultural appropriation.

Affect motivates embodied performances of identities. The motivation of our identity become saturated by our evocative emotive response to our lived experiences and exposes the role politics of power play in our affective affiliation toward our performances of our identities. In the Dolezal case, one can question her affiliation with blackness but cannot deny the endured affective investment she places on/in blackness. Her affective investment in blackness and emotive denial of her whiteness is an interesting moment of whiteness as assemblage.

Dolezal (2017) writes, "Imagining I was a different person living in a different place was one of the few ways—drawing was another—that I could escape the oppressive environment I was raised in" (p. 11). Dolezal did not necessarily desire to be black as much as she writes of a deep desire for difference, difference from her white parents in this case (p. 11). Within and through this desire is an intersectional assemblage of whiteness where difference is desired by the center. As means to mark her own displacement and find acceptance by constructing her identity as abject, Dolezal colored herself with brown crayons. Desire of difference is a foundation for assemblages of whiteness. hooks (2012) alludes to this desire of Otherness in the objectification and exotification of Othered bodies. hooks note, "One dares—acts—on the assumption that the exploration into the world of difference, into the body of the Other, will provide a greater, more intense pleasure than any that exists in the ordinary world of one's familiar racial group" (p. 310). Dolezal's desire for blackness mirrors these same racial consumptions that hooks speaks of. But there is an interesting shift in the affective relation to blackness located through Dolezal's desires that complicates whiteness' desire to objectify and consume people of color, and rather, a desire to displace the center by becoming the Other.

Along these same lines, Dolezal (2017) addresses notions of blackface and cultural appropriation. For her, cultural appropriation is directly connected to affective investment. She claims, "While living in West Jackson, I dedicated no small amount of thought and reflection to understanding cultural appropriation and examining my life to ensure that I was making authentic choices, not offensive or insincere ones" (p. 93). Whiteness works here strategically to pull on anti-essentialist ideologies that deconstruct the material realities of cultural appropriation into realms of legitimacy based on emotive relations. For Dolezal, she found affective relations of approval when the local black hairstylist offered to braid her hair as an invitation to embody black femininity (pp. 93–95). The intersectional assemblages of whiteness pulsate through affective entitlements that justify a cultural appropriation through genuine relations with difference. Whiteness fluidly absorbs cultural Otherness through discursive justifications of "authenticity" and more so through an affective investment in becoming the Other.

Similarly, Dolezal's affective ties with black femininity are strengthened by her disassociation from whiteness. She claims,

> Whiteness feels foreign to me. It was awkward, how people saw me when I was a child and how some people see me now, so I have to interact with that disconnect at times. The very idea of whiteness, upon which the worldview of race was built, established the propaganda of White as righteous, pure, and superior. I reject this worldview and am not a member of, as James Baldwin called them, "people who think they're White." (Morning, 2017, p. 9)

Dolezal's emotive relationship to her whiteness is not a new idea. Whiteness feels foreign to all whites, that is the point of normative framings of whiteness as affective absence. White culture exists through an affective lack (see McIntosh, 2014). Since whites do not see themselves as having a culture, the desire for community is orchestrated through Dolezal's longing to become a part of the black community. For whiteness, affective lack is replaced with affective belonging through the annexation of difference. Dolezal's affective rejection of whiteness emphasizes that whites do not have to acknowledge their racial investment in privilege. Furthermore, her justification for the appropriation of black femininity demonstrates how easy and acceptable whiteness makes appropriating Others. Instead Dolezal's acquisition of difference demonstrates how intersectional assemblages of whiteness are universally affectively absent and permits cultural appropriation in affective racial absence through justifications of "feeling authentic."

Intersectional assemblages of whiteness operate by removing the geopolitical responsibility and historical consequences from whites.

While Dolezal acknowledges the terrible history of racism inflected on black bodies in regard to the United States, she believes that her employed separation from whiteness erases her implication with white bodies in this history. This is perhaps the worst perpetuation of post-race, color-blindedness afforded to a white body. To completely disregard white racial history because one is affectively drawn to blackness is a powerful pulse of intersectional assemblage of whiteness, where one's whiteness is disassociated by means of white appropriation of Otherness. Consequently, her appropriated performance of black femininity flattens the robust history tied to black feminist politics. Similar to the problematic flaw in most white feminist politics, Dolezal pulls on her relationship to patriarchy, heteronormativity, and classism and her disassociation to whiteness as a means to understand the embodied politics of difference experienced by black straight women. However, intersectional assemblages of whiteness demonstrate that these cultural politics cannot be separated from the affective affiliation with race. Black straight women experience patriarchy, heteronormativity, and classism differently than white straight women. Thus, the historical and contextual relationship to black feminist performatives cannot ever be accurately embodied from a white woman politic.

Material realities of bodies despite the affective affiliation toward difference do not lose their embodied histories in relation to the specific geopolitical and historical contexts. It does not matter the affective draws of relations, whiteness propels itself toward the center when whites disregard our embodied histories of colonization, racism, and xenophobia. Dolezal's geopolitical and historical contexts specific to her story is couch in the current Black Lives Matter movement. Her voice, constructed as a "black" mother, surfaces as a leader against violence to black men's bodies. Her negotiations here would have made much more cultural sense had she reflexively acknowledged that it was *her people* inflicting these harms. The complexity to purposefully overlook her whiteness in order to pursue social justice demonstrates how the intersectional assemblages of whiteness function.

As a "black mother," her voice is muted by meeting cultural expectations contextually and historically to speak against racist acts of police brutality. Furthermore, Dolezal's intersecting identities as "black" feminine single mother with the undertones of her still very present whiteness serves black masculinity along with white heteronormativity. Again, black feminism is erased by a white woman's voice vigilantly speaking for black masculinity, a space where white women find solace in racial affective relations. Important black feminist narratives are silenced by the Dolezal case. Even through her exposure, intersectional assemblages of whiteness function to stifle conversations about black women's realities "by a louder, more scandalous story that was ultimately about whiteness" (Bey & Sakellarides, 2016, p. 34). In the current pulse of covert racism, Dolezal as a white woman masked in a black woman's body contextually and historically degrade the value of her social justice plight.

In the end, Dolezal denotes intersectional assemblages of whiteness must always be a point of acknowledgment when understanding how race functions. Her rejection of her whiteness removes the material realities of racism she speaks against. Like the critiques of intersectionality, at some point, whites must acknowledge the material experiences of our lives are always part of our becoming. However, this becoming is never removed from our past. No matter the affective relation, whiteness pulsates through whites and is further strengthened when we unreflexively disregard this history as emotively shaping our current affective longings and relational pulls.

CLOSING CHALLENGES

Scholars of culture and communication must acknowledge the critiques of intersectionality as functions of patriarchy, heteronormativity, and whiteness to prohibit reflexive social justice. In this day of post-race and color-blind racism, intersectional assemblages of whiteness expand ideological understandings of whiteness toward an everyday, affective, relational action that reminds scholars of its constant state of becoming that is empowered by identities' fluidity and messy voids of abstraction. I agree with Puar (2012) that if we are "to dismiss assemblages in favor of retaining intersectional demitarian frameworks is to dismiss how societies of control tweak and modulate bodies as matter, not predominantly through signification or identity interpellation but rather through affective capacities and tendencies" (p. 63). Intersectional assemblages commit us to the fluidity and affectivity of identities. Like thick intersectionality, intersectional assemblages of whiteness encourage us to also acknowledge the intersectional material realities present through these identification processes of multiplex identities in relation to whiteness. I am a proponent for affective, contextual, and embodied incorporations into intersectional analysis. But the intensities of intersectional identities must always be read in relation to normative politics of race, without doing so, we whiten intersectionality's genealogy and "not only misrepresent the importance of race in the original architecture of intersectional thought and activism, by minimizing it, but also contribute to making race analysis optional in current scholarship" (Bilge, 2014, p. 17). When examining articulations of identities that occupy simultaneously privileged and marginalized bodies, or even the more daunting challenge of researching primarily privileged orientations, intersectionality is a viable theory only if race remains a centerfold of the research analysis. Reflexivity is crucial for intersectionality to remain ethical and relevant. Intersectionality from privilege vantage points require reflexive engagement (for more on reflexive intersectionality see: Jones, 2010; Jones & Calafell, 2010; McIntosh & Hobson, 2013). Eguchi (2015) and Eguchi and Baig (2018) demonstrate how reflexive intersectionality as a methodological practice organically extrapolates the affectivity present within and through identification in contextual moments.

I spent a considerable amount of time engaging with the history, critiques, and current pulse of intersectionality, I did so with the intended goal to provide a clear picture of *how* these critiques of intersectionality are functioning as norms of whiteness. Interestingly, Dolezal pulls on these same essentializing and postmodern critiques to justify her racial transformation. The Dolezal affair stands as the current white feminism example of erasing difference. In the Dolezal case, intersectional assemblages of whiteness justify rejecting privilege by embodying/appropriating difference. Dolezal's whiteness, or whiteness in general, is always already present despite her disassociation as white. My point here is despite her affinity toward blackness and negative sentiment toward her whiteness these affective affiliations never remove her accessibility to whiteness. More so, her successful disavowal to whiteness further perpetuates white supremacy to justify unreflexive affective affinity by the normative toward Otherness. Even if Dolezal's racial performances of blackness were culturally accepted, she always was/is white and performs through an affective affinity of whiteness as well.

Certainly, on micro levels she endured overt racists attacks against her and in these ways her whiteness became suspect as all white women that disrupt white hetero-patriarchy. But the macro norm of whiteness allocates the larger narrative of whiteness ability to excuse whites' accountability in our historical role in racism and pardon our affective investment in whiteness. Dolezal pulls on the fluidity of identities and in doing so also engages the fluidity of whiteness. The intersectional assemblages of whiteness expose how whiteness is strengthened by racial discursive fluidity in relation to the contextual presence of other bodies as fixed. Intersectional assemblages of whiteness pierce holes in the Dolezal affair forcing an accounting for how whiteness functions through her identity fluidity, contextual and relational embodiments, affective racial affinities, and historical accounts of white woman performing blackness in social activist's roles.

The erasure of race within intersectional analysis and essentialist critiques of intersectionality denotes the entrenched power of whiteness. Given that whiteness functions through discursive allusivity, embodied performances, relationally, historically, affectively, and contextually, intersectional assemblages of whiteness is an exciting new terrain to unearth complex strategies of whiteness and also practical resolutions. However, culture and communication scholarship utilizing intersectional assemblages of whiteness must remain vigilant to never allow these theoretical incorporations to depoliticize intersectionality. We accomplish this by always examining the purport of identity labels in relation to race (e.g., white sexuality not whiteness propelled through sexuality) that affectively shape each contextual moment of relations between matter and beings as they become in contexts and time.

Intersectional assemblages of whiteness, like thick intersectionality, opens doors to locate whiteness. Thus, it is in the everyday messiness, the everyday performances, the complexities of our simultaneous marginalization and privileges that we cannot and should never reject or overlook the workings of hegemony functioning by our embodied acts. The Dolezal case is an accountable example to whites of how intersectional assemblages of whiteness can affectively entrance whites so far away from our unflushed realities that we no longer are responsible for our relationships with privilege and our reflexivity with our performances of hegemony. In reality, my initial reaction to Dolezal was no different than her appropriation of blackness. By disregarding her through white ableist logics, I affectively dissociated myself from whiteness to absolve my affective white discomfort. Intersectional assemblages of whiteness draw attention to these affective terrains of disavowal. No longer can I disregard the actions of white people like Dolezal. Instead, I hold them as part of my problem, my progression in acts of whiteness. If not, I am participating in the intersectional assemblages of whiteness to remove racism from white affective relationality and accountability by associating myself through an affinity for difference. My hope is this chapter unties the tongues of more white scholars in culture and communication, myself included, because there are many more Rachel Dolezal's that excuse their whiteness through affective affinities for difference.

REFERENCES

Aikenhead, D. (2017, February 25). Rachel Dolezal: I'm not going to stoop and apologise (sic) and grovel. *The Guardian*. https://www.theguardian.com/us-news/2017/feb/25/rachel-dolezal-not-going-stoop-apologise-grovel

Alexander, B. K. (2004). Black skin/White masks: The performative sustainability of Whiteness (with apologies to Frantz Fanon). *Qualitative Inquiry*, *10*(5), 647–72.

Alexander, M. J. & Mohanty, C. T. (2013). *Feminist genealogies, colonial legacies, democratic futures*. London and New York: Routledge.

Anthias, F. (2013). Hierarchies of social location, class and intersectionality: Towards a translocational frame. *International Sociology, 28*(1), 121–38.

Anzaldúa, G. E. (2007). Making alliances. *Sexualities & Communication in Everyday Life: A Reader, 1*.

Bey, M. & Sakellarides, T. (2016). When we enter: The blackness of Rachel Dolezal. *The Black Scholar, 46*(4), 33–48.

Bilge, S. (2013). Intersectionality undone: Saving intersectionality from feminist intersectionality studies. *Du Bois Review: Social Science Research on Race, 10*(2), 405–24.

Bilge, S. (2014). Whitening intersectionality. *Racism and Sociology, 5*, 175.

Brah, A. & Phoenix, A. (2004). Ain't IA woman? Revisiting intersectionality. *Journal of international women's studies, 5*(3), 75–86.

Brubaker, R. (2016a). *Trans: Gender and race in an age of unsettled identities*. Princeton: Princeton University Press.

Brubaker, R. (2016b). The Dolezal affair: Race, gender, and the micropolitics of identity. *Ethnic and Racial Studies, 39*(3), 414–48.

Calafell, B. M. (2010). When will we all matter? Exploring race, pedagogy, and sustained hope for the academy. In D. L. Fassett, & J. T. Warren (Eds.), *The Sage handbook of communication and instruction*, 343–59. Sage.

Calafell, B. M. & Moreman, S. T. (2009). Envisioning an academic readership: Latina/o performativities per the form of publication. *Text and Performance Quarterly, 29*(2), 123–30.

Cho, S., Crenshaw, K. W., & McCall, L. (2013). Toward a field of intersectionality studies: Theory, applications, and praxis. *Signs: Journal of Women in Culture and Society, 38*(4), 785–810.

Crenshaw, K. (1990). Mapping the margins: Intersectionality, identity politics, and violence against women of color. *Stanford Law Review, 43*, 1241.

Collins, P. H. (2002). *Black feminist thought: Knowledge, consciousness, and the politics of empowerment*. London and New York: Routledge.

Collins, P. H. & Bilge, S. (2016). *Intersectionality*. John Wiley & Sons.

Conley, D. (2001). Universal freckle, or how I learned to be White. *The making and unmaking of whiteness* (pp. 25–42). Durham: Duke University Press.

Curry, T. J. (2014). Black studies, not morality: Anti-black racism, neo-liberal cooptation, and the challenges to black studies under intersectional axioms. *Emerging Voices of Africana: Disciplinary Resonances*.

Curry, T. J. (2017). *The man-not: Race, class, genre, and the dilemmas of Black manhood*. Philadelphia, PA: Temple University Press.

DiAngelo, R. J. (2018). White fragility: Why it's so hard for white people to talk about racism. Boston, MA: United States: Beacon Press.

Dolezal, R. & Reback, S. (2017). *In full color: Finding my place in a Black and White world*. Dallas, TX: BenBella Books, Inc.

Eguchi, S. (2015). Queer intercultural relationality: An autoethnography of Asian–Black (dis)connections in white gay America. *Journal of International and Intercultural Communication, 8*(1), 27–43.

Eguchi, S. & Baig, N. (2018). Examining embodied struggles in cultural reentry through intersectional reflexivity. *Howard Journal of Communications, 29*(1), 33–48.

Grillo, T. (1995). Anti-essentialism and intersectionality: Tools to dismantle the master's house. *Berkeley Women's LJ*, *10*, 16.

Hooks, B. (1982). Aint IA woman. *ARGUMENT*, *24*(JUL), 534–41.

Jones, R. G. (2010). Putting privilege into practice through "intersectional reflexivity:" Ruminations, interventions, and possibilities. *Reflections: Narratives of Professional Helping*, 122.

Jones, R. G., Jr. & Calafell, B. M. (2012). Contesting neoliberalism through critical pedagogy, intersectional reflexivity, and personal narrative: Queer tales of academia. *Journal of Homosexuality*, *59*(7), 957–81.

Lorde, A. (2012). *Sister outsider: Essays and speeches*. Berkley, CA: Crossing Press.

Lugones, M. (2007). Heterosexualism and the colonial/modern gender system. *Hypatia*, *22*(1), 186–219.

Madison, D. S. (1993). "That was my occupation": Oral narrative, performance, and Black feminist thought. *Text and Performance Quarterly*, *13*(3), 213–32.

McCall, L. (2008). The complexity of intersectionality. In *Intersectionality and beyond* (pp. 65–92). Routledge-Cavendish.

McIntosh, D. M. D. (2014). White feelings, feeling straight: Cultivating affective attentiveness for queer futurities. *QED: A Journal of Queer Worldmaking*, *1*(3) 154–58.

McIntosh, D. M. D. (2017). Victims, protectors, and possibilities for change: White womanhood and the violence of heteronormativity. *QED: A Journal in GLBTQ Worldmaking*, *4*(2), 162–69.

McIntosh, D. M. D. (2018). From white ladies to white trash mamas: (Re)Locating the performances of white femininity. In *Interrogating the Communicative Power of Whiteness* (pp. 108–30). London and New York: Routledge.

McIntosh, D. M. D. & Hobson, K. (2013). Reflexive engagement: A white (queer) women's performance of failures and alliance possibilities. *Liminalities: A Journal of Performance Studies*, *9*(4), 1–23.

McIntosh, D. M. D., Moon, D. G., & Nakayama, T. K. (Eds.). (2018). *Interrogating the communicative power of whiteness*. London and New York: Routledge.

Moraga, C. (1983). *Loving in the war years: Lo que nunca pasó por sus labios*. South End Pr.

Moraga, C. & Anzaldúa, G. (Eds.). (2015). *This bridge called my back: Writings by radical women of color*. Suny Press.

Morning, A. (2017). Race and Rachel Doležal. *Contexts*, *16*(2), 8–11.

Morning, A. (2018). Kaleidoscope: Contested identities and new forms of race membership. *Ethnic and Racial Studies*, *41*(6), 1055–73.

Muñoz, J. E. (1999). *Disidentifications: Queers of color and the performance of politics* (Vol. 2). University of Minnesota Press.

Nakayama, T. K. & Krizek, R. L. (1995). Whiteness: A strategic rhetoric. *Quarterly Journal of Speech*, *81*(3), 291–309.

Nash, J. C. (2008). Re-thinking intersectionality. *Feminist Review*, *89*(1), 1–15.

Nightingale, A. J. (2011). Bounding difference: Intersectionality and the material production of gender, caste, class and environment in Nepal. *Geoforum*, *42*(2), 153–62.

Patton, S. (June 17, 2015). Rachel Dolezal case leaves a campus bewildered and some scholars disgusted. *The Chronical of Higher Education*. https://www.chronicle.com/article/Rachel-Dolezal-Case-Leaves-a/230947.

Puar, J. K. (2012). "I would rather be a cyborg than a goddess": Becoming-intersectional in assemblage theory. *PhiloSOPHIA*, *2*(1), 49–66.

Puar, J. K. (2017). *Terrorist assemblages: Homonationalism in queer times*. Duke University Press.

Roth, W. D. (2016). The multiple dimensions of race. *Ethnic and Racial Studies*, *39*(8), 1310–38.

Rowe, A. C. (2008). *Power lines: On the subject of feminist alliances*. Durham: Duke University Press.

Tuvel, R. (2017). In defense of transracialism. *Hypatia*, *32*(2), 263–78.

Warren, J. T. (2003). *Performing purity: Whiteness, pedagogy, and the reconstitution of power*. New York: P. Lang.

Yep, G. A. (2003). The violence of heteronormativity in communication studies: Notes on injury, healing, and queer world-making. *Journal of Homosexuality*, *45*(2–4), 11–59.

Yep, G. A. (2010). Toward the de-subjugation of racially marked knowledges in communication. *Southern Communication Journal*, *75*(2), 171–75.

Yep, G. A. (2016). Toward thick (er) intersectionalities: Theorizing, researching, and activating the complexities of communication and identities. *Globalizing Intercultural Communication: A Reader*, 86–94.

Yep, G. A. & Chivers, N. T. (2017). Intersectionality. *The International Encyclopedia of Intercultural Communication*, 1–6.

Yep, G. A. & Lescure, R. (2018). A thick intersectional approach to microaggressions. *Southern Communication Journal*, 1–14.

Yuval-Davis, N. (2006). Intersectionality and feminist politics. *European Journal of Women's Studies*, *13*(3), 193–209.

Yuval-Davis, N. (2013). A situated intersectional everyday approach to the study of bordering. *Euborder-scapes Working Paper, 2*.

Zack, N. (2007). Can third wave feminism be inclusive? Intersectionality, its problems, and new directions.

Chapter 5

Doing Intersectionality under a Different Name

The (Un)intentional Politics of Refusal

Santhosh Chandrashekar

Perhaps no single concept captures the tensions that have haunted Western feminism as much as intersectionality. From calls to move past it—what some scholars have critiqued as post-intersectionality (Cho, 2013)—to pleas to at least apply it in conjunction with something else (Carbado, 2013), the broad range of anxieties that intersectionality evokes make clear the historical fault lines of feminism that have only come to be intensified in a neoliberal academy (King, 2015). Given that these anxieties continue to reverberate everywhere from the classroom to conferences and in academic publications, it is important to unpack them in all their diverse manifestations.

In this chapter, I attempt such a task by looking at one of the less-discussed ways in which intersectionality is refused, especially by white feminists but also by some nonblack feminists of color. For some time now, I have noticed both within the classroom as well as in academic work a refusal by some feminists to deploy intersectionality because of its foundation in black women's experiences. This rejection is not the same as theoretical arguments that posit intersectionality as too specific—that is, too black—and, therefore, ungeneralizable. Rather, the refusal I am interested in exploring presents itself as an ethical-political move that intentionally chooses not to participate in the appropriation of black feminist thought. Put differently, the argument presents itself somewhat in this way: Intersectionality is based in the experiences of oppression faced by black women. Too often, white (or nonblack) feminists have appropriated black women's labors and experiences and made them their own, which has marginalized black women. Given this history and our positionality as white/nonblack feminists, we refuse to participate in this trend.

Following this argument, which I term the "well-intentioned refusal of intersectionality," intersectionality is either bypassed as a theoretical and methodological framework or evoked *only* if the theorist is examining an issue that predominantly affects black women. What such a move hides, nevertheless, is how intersectionality is already structurally manifest in a given situation and gets renamed under the guise of avoiding it. Although this move is well intentioned[1] and attempts to challenge the problematic legacies of academic feminism in particular, my concern is that it also unwittingly participates in the marginalization of one of the most signal contributions of black feminist thought based on a misreading of the concerns that black feminists have raised. If the appropriation of intersectionality by white Western feminists and others—what Sirma Bilge (2014) labels the whitening of intersectionality—is a problem, I am concerned that the move to avoid intersectionality is also an issue that needs urgent attention as it fosters a distancing from black feminism at best and a disengagement at worst, even as it rebrands intersectionality. I believe that this move weakens/whitens the feminist project.

Surely, the black feminist intervention emblematized in intersectionality was never about the reification of racial borders. Rather, it sought to demonstrate how race and gender constituted interlocking systems of oppression in the lives of black women that rendered them invisible or hypervisible as subjects of law (Cooper, 2015). As such, their experiences of oppression could not be understood through a race- or gender-only approach or an additive combination of the two. If this is indeed the case, then I believe that it is important not to abandon but to instead engage intersectionality as a theoretical, methodological, and political project that is foundationally linked to black feminism and that can, with attentive usage, illuminate the lives of others whose experience of oppression is also located at the intersection of multiple axes of social stratification.

I begin the next section by briefly reviewing intersectionality. I avoid providing an extensive review of the debates surrounding it. Rather, I focus my attention on the critique that black women are the primary subjects of intersectional theorizing. After this, I turn to Chris Linder's book, *Sexual Violence on Campus: Power-Conscious Approaches to Awareness, Prevention, and Response* (2018), as it emblematizes the well-intentioned refusal of intersectionality that I am concerned with. Linder posits "power-conscious approach" to study the problem of sexual violence on campuses. According to the author, a power-conscious framework calls attention to "*dominant* group members' investment in power, rather than attempting to center and speak for women of color" (p. 15; italics in original). In making this argument, Linder presents power-conscious approach as a move that helps avoid the appropriation of black feminist work, which is precisely the maneuver that this chapter attempts to unpack.

I use comparative reading as a method to draw attention to the premises that ground power-conscious framework by reading it against Kimberlé Crenshaw's (1989, 1991) articulation of intersectionality and an essay by Devon Carbado (2013) that chart a divergent path. Comparative reading juxtaposes two or more texts to tease out the premises that underlie them. Inspired by the comparative turn within literature and cultural studies that sought to center a transnational and interdisciplinary framework in the study of cultural texts (de Zepetnek, 2007), comparative reading applies the same principles as it tries to compare and contrast texts against each other.

I undertake this work with humility. As a South Asian who travels under the sign of "man"[2] and who now lives in the United States, I have often grappled with the founding of intersectionality in black women's experiences and figuring out ways to translate it ethically to understand the oppressions facing brown bodies in North America, who are the focus of my work. While I continue to be vigilant to charges of appropriation, especially in the citational practices and the coalitional politics that we produce, I have also found intersectionality to be a robust theoretical and political framework that can illuminate how race, gender, and sexuality, among others, intersect in the lives of people of color in general and women and queer subjects of color in particular to produce different experiences of power and oppression. Furthermore, and given my own indebtedness to black feminist thought, I believe that intersectionality is not a spent force, as is often articulated, but will continue to be an indispensable analytic insofar as racism and sexism, among others, continue to intersect in people's lives.

WHEN RACE AND GENDER INTERSECT

The phenomenon that we now recognize as intersectionality has a long history in black feminist thinking and activism (Cooper, 2015). Black feminists drew attention to the ways in which race and gender intersected in the lives of black women to create compound experiences of oppression that remained untheorized through a gender- or race-centric framework that were hegemonic in women's rights and anti-racist organizing, respectively. As early as 1851, Sojourner Truth highlighted this phenomenon when she asked members of a Women's Convention in Ohio, "Ain't I a woman?" (Painter, 1996) that illuminated how the privileges of normative gender had been denied to black women. Truth's utterance was aimed at not just the male hecklers who argued that women were unequipped to the rigors of voting, but also at white women suffragist who sought to silence her as they believed that her presence might foreground abolition as an issue over the struggle to secure women's rights to vote.

Over a century later, it was again to this phenomenon that the Combahee River Collective Statement drew attention to (Smith, 2000). A gathering of primarily black feminist lesbians, the collective rejected what it saw as separatist tendencies arising in white feminism by arguing that gender oppression could not be seen as separate from racial oppression when viewed through the subject position of black women. The collective played a key role in not only developing an anti-oppression politics that took identity seriously, but was also one of the earliest systematic articulation of a black feminist position that refused to treat gender and racial oppression as separate.

But it is legal theorist Kimberlé Crenshaw (1989, 1991, 2011) who is widely credited with systematizing intersectionality as a concept. In her path-breaking 1989 article, Crenshaw explored the ways in which race and gender intersected in the lives of black women to leave them hypervisible or invisible as subjects of law. Through her reading of three cases involving black women plaintiffs, Crenshaw demonstrated how courts relied on black men as race representatives and white women as gender representatives in arbitrating claims of race and sex discrimination, thereby denying black women legal redress. Crenshaw also tracked this same tendency in feminist theory and anti-racist organizing, which relied on white women and black men, respectively, as representatives of sex- and race-based discrimination. As she argued (1989):

> Because the intersectional experience is greater than the sum of racism and sexism, any analysis that does not take intersectionality into account cannot sufficiently address the particular manner in which Black women are subordinated. Thus, for feminist theory and antiracist policy discourse to embrace the experiences and concerns of Black women, the entire framework that has been used as a basis for translating "women's experience" or "the Black experience" into concrete policy demands must be rethought and recast. (p. 140)

In her subsequent work, Crenshaw has expanded her focus to include nonblack women of color and other populations whose experience of oppression cannot be understood without deploying an intersectional framework. In "Mapping the Margins," Crenshaw's (1991) analysis included an explicit engagement with the case of a Latina fleeing her abusive partner and refused admission into a homeless shelter because of her lack of fluency in English. In the same article, she also drew attention to how restrictive immigration regimes trap migrant women of color in abusive situations. More recently, and taking incarcerated women as a case in point, Crenshaw (2011) has suggested that there is no reason to believe that women of color are intersectionality's only subjects. It is against this backdrop of an expansive deployment of intersectionality as charted out by Crenshaw herself that I explore the refusal of intersectionality under the premise that it represents the appropriation of black women's intellectual work and labor.

Before I turn to Linder's work, it is important to recognize a point that is central to my analysis. I agree with Cooper (2015) that intersectionality is not a theory of identity but an analytic to understand the operation of power and the differentiated experience of oppression it creates. In her excellent entry on intersectionality, Cooper argues that some of the critiques of the concept participate in a problematic reading of intersectionality as a heuristic to apprehend the production of identity and subjectivity in all their complexity rather than as an analytic that can help us understand how aspects of one's identity makes them invisible or hypervisible as subjects of law. If intersectionality is understood the way Cooper (2015) presents it, then I believe that it can open up ways to understand how power and oppression are generated at the intersections of race and gender, among others, rather than as a theory of identity and subjectivity.

REBRANDING INTERSECTIONALITY

I first heard about Linder's book from a graduate student during a discussion of the political and ethical fallouts of nonblack feminists using intersectionality. The book was presented as an example of a work that tried to chart a different path against the history of white feminists appropriating the concept for their own purposes. While the student made it clear that they were providing neither a positive nor a negative assessment of the work (they had just heard about the book and thought it was worth mentioning as an example of the phenomenon under discussion), what intrigued me immediately was a theoretical framework titled "power-conscious approaches." However well-intentioned such a move is, two questions came to my mind immediately: (1) What is intersectionality if not power conscious? and (2) If intersectionality is indeed invested in understanding power, then why the need for a separate framework? Later, as I read the work, another question eventually surfaced: given that Crenshaw spends a substantial part of her 1991 article drawing attention to how feminist and anti-racist critique of rape laws as well as remedial frameworks exclude black women but also other women of color, and given that Linder is also interested in the issue of sexual violence, why not extend intersectionality to address the issues she[3] is interested in exploring instead of deploying a new framework?

Before I tease out some of the ways in which Linder's work participates in what I am terming the well-intentioned refusal of intersectionality, some clarifications are in order. First, the work contributes to the growing corpus of literature on the pervasiveness of sexual violence on college campuses and the ways in which institutions fail to attend to this pressing issue. In this, her work is laudable, much needed, and full of insights which can help colleges and universities address sexual violence in a manner that is ethical and receptive to the needs of survivors while also holding perpetrators responsible for their actions.[4] Furthermore, the work is full of insights that take seriously the intersection of race and gender and other dynamics that black feminists call our attention to. As such, my engagement of Linder's work is not a critique of her project. Rather, I am primarily interested in the use of "power-conscious approaches" as a theoretical framework in lieu of intersectionality and what is lost through this maneuver. Second, Linder has used intersectionality as the primary theoretical framework in other places to analyze the issues facing "minoritized" (2018, p. 14) student groups in general (e.g., see Linder, 2019). Hence, I limit my attention to the monograph as it encapsulates the phenomenon I am interested in.

Power-conscious approaches is a theoretical framework that amalgamates critical consciousness and intersectionality with an eye toward understanding the operation of power at the individual, institutional, and cultural levels (Linder, 2018). Drawing on bell hooks' work on engaged pedagogy, which draws extensively from Paulo Freire's theorization of conscientization, Linder argues that critical consciousness comprises two dimensions of awareness: self-awareness and an awareness of systems of domination. Intersectionality is posited as a call to examine the intersections of oppressions such as racism, sexism, and classism. According to Linder, a power-conscious framework, which builds on critical consciousness and intersectionality, calls for an analysis of power to bring an end to oppression.

Linder notes that three assumptions and six tenets are the constituent parts of a power-conscious framework. The three assumptions are (1) power is omnipresent; (2) power and identity and inextricably linked; and identity is socially constructed. The six tenets are (1) to engage in critical consciousness and self-awareness; (2) consider history and context; (3) change behaviors based on reflection and awareness; (4) name and call dominant members' investment in and benefit from systems of domination; (5) interrogate the role of power in individual interactions, policy development and practice; and work in solidarity to eradicate oppression.

Linder (2018) suggests that while a power-conscious framework borrows from intersectionality, it is distinct from the latter for two reasons. As this lengthy quote elaborates:

> Although some tenets of a power-conscious framework are rooted in similar assumptions as intersectionality, a power-conscious framework focuses explicitly on the relationship of people with power to systems of oppression. Scholars created intersectionality to center the experiences of women of color . . ., so

> using it in other contexts risk misappropriating the scholarship. I do not intend to use a power-conscious framework *in place of* intersectionality or to indicate that intersectionality *only* focuses on race and gender . . . However, far too many white people—and white women specifically—have misappropriated and misused intersectionality by using it to examine oppression broadly rather than focusing explicitly on racism and sexism and their varied intersections . . . I use a power-conscious framework to call attention to dominant group members' investment in power, rather than attempting to center and speak for women of color. (pp. 14–15; emphasis in original)

It appears to me that two substantive presumptions undergird Linder's elaboration of a power-conscious framework. First, that power-conscious approaches explicitly center an analysis of power with an eye toward how those with power benefit from domination. Conversely, the idea here is that intersectionality is more focused on the experiences of oppression as faced by women of color. Put differently, power-conscious framework seems to be offered as the constitutive opposite—a complimentary framework, if you will—of intersectionality that focuses on the role of power. This renders intersectionality as an analytic that is not sufficiently invested in an examination of power but rather only its effects (namely oppression). The second presumption is the claim that any use of intersectionality that attends to perpetrators rather than those who are oppressed risks misappropriating the framework. This presumption delimits intersectionality as an analytical framework that somehow cannot be, with attentive usage, elaborated to illuminate how power not only oppresses women of color but, through this very process, also invariably benefits others who are also intersectionally constituted, albeit differently. Both presumptions fall apart under closer scrutiny.

Let us begin with the first presumption that power and oppression are substantially different that they necessitate different analytical frameworks. Even a cursory look at Crenshaw's work demonstrates that intersectionality is as much invested in unmasking the operation of power at multiple levels as it is in highlighting the effects that such articulations have in compounding oppression for black women and other women of color. This is because in so much as power is integral to the production of oppression, any analysis of the latter cannot afford to ignore the role of power. Linder is certainly right in that intersectionality approaches this question from the perspective of women of color, especially black women. But I am not sure if this necessarily means that it cannot be extended to account for how the interlocking of racism and patriarchy oppresses other bodies as well as benefits racial- and gender-privileged subjects.

By way of an example and given that Linder's work also focuses on sexual violence, let me revisit Crenshaw's analysis of statist and feminist and anti-racist critique of rape (1991). I am specifically interested in how questions of power and oppression appear therein as the proverbial two sides of the same coin. In her 1991 article, Crenshaw posits structural, political, and representational intersectionality that help capture different dimensions of intersectionality. If structural intersectionality refers to the ways in which the location of women of color at the intersection of race and gender make their experiences of domestic violence, rape, and redress different than that of white women, political intersectionality refers to how women of color are situated within two categories that follow conflicting agendas (Crenshaw, 1991). Representational intersectionality refers to the cultural constructions of women of color, which through their skewed representations produce "intersectional disempowerment" for women of color (Crenshaw, 1991, p. 1245).

In each of these iterations, Crenshaw is interested in how the intersections of racism and patriarchy create unique conditions for women or color. Yet, at the same time, her analysis demonstrates an acute awareness of power dynamics. In her discussion of structural intersectionality and rape, Crenshaw not only posits that rape crisis centers are structurally unequipped to attend to the needs of women of color but also names the source of this problem: standards around which the work of such centers is organized are largely white and middle class, thereby benefitting subjectivities that are also constituted at these intersections. Furthermore, in the political intersectionality section where the bulk of here analysis of rape occurs, Crenshaw is interested in how both feminist and anti-racist critiques of rape and remedial frameworks ignore black women. Nevertheless, her analysis does not shy away from naming who benefits from such arrangements.

Given Linder's argument that a power-conscious framework focuses on those with access to power rather than just the victims, Crenshaw's reading of the Mike Tyson rape trial is especially pertinent here. Crenshaw notes that within the black community, racial solidarity was deployed on behalf of Tyson while Desiree Washington, his black accuser, was vilified. This extreme polarization is the result of how black male victimization as sexual aggressors has come to dominate discussions on sexual assault within the black community with very little attention spared to the condition of black women. This phenomenon, as Crenshaw notes, persists even when the accuser is a black woman.[5] Put differently, the compound marginalization suffered by Washington both from whitestream society (Grande, 2003) and from her own black community cannot be understood without denaturalizing the support that Tyson received (also see Griffin, 2013). This is because conceptions of racism and discrimination are organized around the black male subject and consequently is seen as a more pressing issue over the violence facing black women. An analysis of power is integral to this task as it unmasks who benefits when black women are allowed to slip through the cracks. In addition, Crenshaw notes that the vitriol directed toward Washington also came from black women, who found her claims ingenuous. Reading her work in the era of #MeToo, one cannot help but marvel at how astutely she anticipates some of the tensions around sexual violence such as victim-blaming that the #MeToo movement has forced into the open (e.g., see Zarkov & Davis, 2018).

The point I am belaboring here is that an intersectional analysis is always already about power, not just oppression. While Crenshaw's focus is on women of color, especially black women, her analysis does not preclude an attention to power but rather necessitates it. Rape crisis centers are needed because rape is a central technology of maintaining racial and gender power, which is constructed and enforced often in the interest of whites and males by a host of ideologies and institutions. Such centers do not cater to the needs of women of color (oppression) because they are organized around the needs of white, middle-class survivors (power). Feminist and anti-racist critiques of rape devalue the experiences of women of color (oppression) because they articulate narrow conceptions of gender and racial oppression which are themselves organized around the needs of the most privileged within these oppressed categories, namely white women and black men (power). Though appearing decentered, an analysis of power animates intersectionality in the same way that an analysis of race and whiteness structures critical race theory even as it is oriented toward centering the experiences of people of color.[6]

This brings me to the second claim that Linder (2018) advances, which is that "Scholars created intersectionality to center the experiences of women of color . . ., so using it in other contexts risk misappropriating the scholarship" (p. 14). Put differently, this claim seems to suggest that women of color are the subjects of intersectionality, while a power-conscious framework might better serve to illuminate the role of white male perpetrators and the systems that empower them. While this may appear true at the surface level, I am not sure that this binaristic approach stands closer scrutiny.

To make my point, I want to draw attention to an essay that challenges the understanding that intersectionality is specific to black women or should focus *primarily* on the intersection of race and gender. In his essay titled *Colorblind Intersectionality*, Carbado engages masculinity, whiteness, and sexual orientation, which are precisely the subjectivities and issues traditionally seen as outside the purview of intersectionality. Through an analysis of a case in which a casino fired its white queer female bartender for not adhering to its grooming policy, an examination of gay rights advocacy against the Don't Ask, Don't Tell policy, and finally an assessment of racial justice interventions, Carbado elaborates color-blind and gender-blind intersectionality that demonstrate how whiteness helps to produce a social category but is invisible and unarticulated as also an *intersectional* subject position (emphasis mine). In doing so, Carbado's work challenges the claim that intersectionality is only about women of color by highlighting how whiteness is also "intersectionality unmarked" (p. 823). As he articulates toward the end:

> It is erroneous to conceptualize intersectionality as a theory whose exclusive focus is the intersection of race (read: nonwhite) and gender (read: nonmale). Moreover, there are significant costs to doing so. Framing intersectionality as only about women of color gives masculinity, whiteness, and maleness an intersectional pass. That, in turn, leaves colorblind intersectionality and gender-blind intersectionality unnamed and uninterrogated, further naturalizing white male heterosexuality as the normative baseline against which the rest of us are intersectionally differentiated. (2013, p. 841)

Following Carbado (2013), what I am suggesting here is that if women of color's experiences of oppression is constituted at the intersection of racism and patriarchy (Crenshaw, 1991), then the power accrued by white straight men and other privileged subjects is also generated at the "intersection" of whiteness, masculinity, and heterosexuality, among others. If intersectionality can help us in arriving at a more nuanced understanding of oppression, then there is no reason to believe that it cannot be extended to apprehend power. As a result, I am not convinced that a power-conscious framework is more suitable for this task than intersectionality.

In the end, it appears to me that the real concern is whether white women (and nonblack feminists of color) can use intersectionality. The answer, as always, is contextual. The real issue then is not who is using intersectionality but what they have done with it. It feels reasonable to suggest that (1) as long as the citational chain of intersectionality as emerging from black feminist work is not lost, (2) as long as the researcher is transparent about their own positionality, (3) there is an explicit focus on unraveling different intersections that produce privilege and oppression, (4) and the researcher is animated with a commitment to ending oppression beginning from the most marginalized subjects, then I do not see any embargo within black feminist theorizing that prohibits nonblack people, including white theorists, from using intersectionality. Quite the contrary, as I believe that we must continue to extend intersectionality into new terrains even as we commit mistakes and learn from them. As Carbado (2013) suggests through his reading of Edward Said, applying theories to new domains and issues, even when risky, reinvigorates them. The real challenge is to do so in a way that the foundational impulse is not lost.

Furthermore, while a disengagement from intersectionality may help some scholars avoid the charge of misappropriating the concept, it also sidelines an important framework and may vicariously contribute to the growing trend of "posting" intersectionality by using or developing new frameworks, as Tiffany King (2015) so astutely demonstrated. Moreover, as people in the academic world know, an important way in which academics accrue visibility is through the number of times the theories and concepts developed by them are cited. This is a phenomenon that some term "reputational capital" (Moore, Newman, & Turnbull, 2001), which secures one's position in the academic world. While this may appear to be a minor issue to some, the repercussions of losing visibility in the academic world can hardly be ignored. In an "unintentional" way, the well-intentioned refusal of intersectionality may contribute to this phenomenon by intensifying the precarious situation facing black women academics, as several studies have pointed out.

DE-WHITENING INTERSECTIONALITY

It feels counterintuitive to argue that white feminists should not shy away from but rather embrace intersectionality in all its messiness. But this is precisely the argument that I have tried to advance. Recall that for Crenshaw (1989), the problem was not just that courts refused to acknowledge the specificity of black women's repression, but that they were also prohibiting black women from becoming class representatives for gender and racial discrimination. In the same vein, I am worried that by rendering intersectionality as only pertinent to black women, we may be participating in a similar trend whereby intersectionality is rendered as ungeneralizable.

Such a caution assumes heightened importance against the growing interest in intersectionality as a theoretical framework within the field of communication studies, particularly intercultural communication (Abdi & Calafell, 2017; Eguchi, Calafell, & Files-Thompson, 2014), even as whiteness and white masculinity continues to structure the discipline (Chakravartty, Kuo, Grubbs, & McIlwain, 2018). Given this state of affairs, I worry that the damage to intersectionality comes not just through the field embracing new competing frameworks at a time when intersectionality is gaining popularity,[7] or that white feminists might whiten intersectionality through a color-blind rendering of the concept (Bilge, 2014), but also through the framework being bypassed under the pretext of not misappropriating black feminist work. My fear is that the latter move paradoxically reinforces whiteness through the marginalization of a framework emerging in black feminism.

As a nonblack person of color whose relationship to intersectionality is also contested, I believe that a fully transparent and ethical extension of intersectionality that follows the right citational practice is preferable and can enhance the robustness of intercultural communication theorizing. While there is always a chance that the sort of "experiment" that I am advocating might fail or, worse, attract criticism for its blind spots, it may also teach us much in the process and contribute to a robust conversation that can only make the theories and our own understandings of them stronger.

NOTES

1. While intentions are important, they are also articulated within a forcefield of discourses that are often unrecognized. As Spivak's (1989) reminds us, intentions are akin to the formal set of rules that guide a game of tennis. But the outcome is determined not just by formal laws but also the rules of thermodynamics which are in operation but rarely recognized. In the same way, intentions might at best only help us capture part of the problem.

2. I borrow this framing from Sara Ahmed (2017), whose work attends to those who "travel under the sign of women." Such a framing helps denaturalize the essentialism that attends to such identities while also pointing to how bodies accrue privilege or become the targets of regimes of violence once they come to be read through a gendered-racialized framework. Likewise, my use of "man" gestures to how I am identified on an everyday basis but an identity with which I increasingly grow uncomfortable.

3. I use the pronouns she/her as preferred by Chris Linder. See https://faculty.utah.edu/u6018474-Chris_Linder/hm/index.hml

4. Linder's (2018) thrust seems to be to reorient our attention toward perpetrators of sexual violence, who are often not the focus of university interventions. While most policies and efforts are centered around the needs of survivors (and rightfully so), Linder brings up the important point that this focus might be giving perpetrators a pass. As such, she posits that a central focus of awareness, prevention, and response strategies should be to examine the role of perpetrators in sexual violence on college campuses.

5. I also draw attention to this excerpt because Linder (2013) notes that with the exception of Native American women, sexual assault faced by women across racial groups is likely to be intra-racial. If a focus on power means naming perpetrators and showing how they benefit from systems of domination (as Linder seems to suggest), then Crenshaw is already doing this by calling attention to how the black community mobilized around Tyson rather than Washington.

6. For example, see (Delgado & Stefancic, 2017).

7. Jasbir Puar's embrace of assemblages over intersectionality (2017) best emblematizes this trend, which has also been mirrored within the field of communication studies through emerging theories such as new materialisms and post-humanisms. These approaches render race as secondary vis-à-vis the materiality of matter. While new materialisms has much to offer, its use by white theorists can easily help avoid uncomfortable questions around race and center other analytics at a time when minoritized scholars have pushed the issue to the fore.

REFERENCES

Abdi, S. & Calafell, B. M. (2017). Queer utopias and a (Feminist) Iranian vampire: A critical analysis of resistive monstrosity in A Girl Walks Home Alone at Night. *Critical Studies in Media Communication*, *34*(4), 358–70.

Ahmed, S. (2017). *Living a feminist life*. Durham, NC: Duke University Press.

Bilge, S. (2014). Whitening intersectionality. In W. D. Hund, & A. Lentin (Eds.), *Racism and sociology* (pp. 175–205). Zurich, Switzerland: LIT Verlag.

Carbado, D. W. (2013). Colorblind intersectionality. *Signs: Journal of Women in Culture and Society, 38*(4), 811–45.

Chakravartty, P., Kuo, R., Grubbs, V., & McIlwain, C. (2018). #CommunicationSoWhite. *Journal of Communication, 68*(2), 254–66. https://doi.org/10.1093/joc/jqy003.

Cho, S. (2013). Post-intersectionality: The curious reception of intersectionality in legal scholarship. *Du Bois Review: Social Science Research on Race, 10*(2), 385–404.

Cooper, B. (2015). Intersectionality. In L. Disch & M. Hawkesworth (Eds.), *The Oxford handbook of feminist theory* (pp. 385–406). Oxford University Press.

Crenshaw, K. (1989). Demarginalizing the intersection of race and sex: A black feminist critique of antidiscrimination doctrine, feminist theory and antiracist politics. *University of Chicago Legal Forum, 1*, 139–67.

Crenshaw, K. (1990). Mapping the margins: Intersectionality, identity politics, and violence against women of color. *Stanford Law Review, 43*, 1241.

Crenshaw, K. (2011). From private violence to mass incarceration: Thinking intersectionally about women, race, and social control. *UCLA Law Review 59*, 1418.

Delgado, R. & Stefancic, J. (2017). *Critical race theory: An introduction*. New York University Press.

Eguchi, S., Calafell, B. M., & Files-Thompson, N. (2014). Intersectionality and quare theory: Fantasizing African American male same-sex relationships in Noah's Arc: Jumping the Broom. *Communication, Culture & Critique, 7*(3), 371–89.

Grande, S. (2003). Whitestream feminism and the colonialist project: A review of contemporary feminist pedagogy and praxis. *Educational Theory, 53*(3), 329–46.

Griffin, R. A. (2013). Gender violence and the Black female body: The enduring significance of "crazy" Mike Tyson. *Howard Journal of Communications, 24*(1), 71–94.

King, T. L. (2015). Post-indentitarian and post-intersectional anxiety in the neoliberal corporate university. *Feminist Formations, 27*(3), 114–38.

Linder, C. (2018). *Sexual violence on campus: Power-conscious approaches to awareness, prevention, and response*. Bingley, UK: Emerald Publishing Limited.

Linder, C. (2019). Power-conscious and intersectional approaches to supporting student activists: Considerations for learning and development. *Journal of Diversity in Higher Education, 12*(1), 17–26. https://doi.org/10.1037/dhe0000082.

Moore, W. J., Newman, R. J., & Turnbull, G. K. (2001). Reputational capital and academic pay. *Economic Inquiry, 39*(4), 663–71.

Painter, N. I. (1996). *Sojourner truth: A life, a symbol*. New York, NY: W.W. Norton & Company.

Puar, J. K. (2017). *Terrorist assemblages: Homonationalism in queer times*. Durham: Duke University Press.

Smith, B. (2000). *Home girls: A black feminist anthology*. New Burnswick, NJ: Rutgers University Press.

Spivak, G. C. (1989). A response to 'The difference within: Feminism and critical theory.' In Elizabeth A. Meese, & Alice A. Parker (Eds.), *The difference within: Feminism and critical theory* (pp. 207–20). Philadelphia: John Benjamins Publishing Company.

Zarkov, D. & Davis, K. (2018). *Ambiguities and dilemmas around# Metoo:# forhow long and# whereto?* London, UK: Sage.

Section II

PERSONAL NARRATIVES

Chapter 6

Making it Real Plain

Ruminations on De-Whitening Intersectionality in Academia From the Monstrous Queer Chicana Who Makes White Straight People Uncomfortable

Bernadette Marie Calafell

De-whitening intersectionality means taking it back from your appropriating self-serving ass. You throw around the word in your courses, but never actually have the students read any women of color, let alone Kimberlé Crenshaw. The same goes for border theory. Do you even know who Gloria Anzaldúa is? Or do you assume some dead European philosopher theorized it all? New materialist my ass.

You didn't want to be intersectional until you saw it as a means of possible coverage for your half-assed contributions and straight out racist behavior. Scapegoating ability on the backs of those who actually need accommodations. Don't use your paranoia to justify your racism and create scenarios in which you are the victim of people of color. So the theories of women of color don't matter in your class or research, just conveniently as a way to appropriate themselves for your identities that suddenly matter.

For you being intersectional gives you an excuse to not have to do any work, which means it becomes gendered labor for the women in the department to take up.

A particular day, though there are many, stands out, suddenly your so-called pain and feeling of being misunderstood and not heard (though your white tears and stories of victimhood literally dominate every conversation) took center stage as the white women stood around you to console you, while the tears literally rolled down my cheeks and Others of us held tightly to each other in disbelief. *The shitshow really is this bad.* She hugged you and showed you compassion, the kind that she never showed any of us Others. She, a poacher in her own right, had compassion for you, but the pain of Others was unintelligible and "unrelatable." Or maybe just uninteresting. No one for her research team here I guess. Our kind of difference didn't make the cut.

In shock, a friend who is present and offers an outside perspective tells me afterward, "This has never happened. This is not normal." Their words give me the power to believe in myself again.

That's right. I laugh. You have reached the most fucked up place on Earth. Where white fragility reigns and interracial marriage and international adoptions give privileged people a sense of security so they can tell themselves at night they can't possibly be racist all the while actively working against those with the least amount of power who just happen to be people of color.

Your fake platitudes about centering people of color where just that, fake. Because you were always the first ones to usher them out.

Your embrace of intersectionality not only whitens it, but misuses it as something to be weaponized in the name of whiteness.

Smile to my face some more while behind the scenes you all say you believe in anti-racism, but that doesn't mean centering the experiences of people of color. I'M THE UBER BITCH WHO MADE YOU TERRIFIED OF BEING CALLED A RACIST. I've got some news for you; if you think a person of color is gonna call you a racist, nine out of ten times you are one.

I go through cards as I pack, looking for what to save and to throw away. There it is a card from you, who specializes in and has commodified compassion, apologizing for not speaking up at the latest meeting featuring the latest microaggression.

It's meaningless as your words and performance of compassion ring hollow. You will be my friend, but only if my difference doesn't make you uncomfortable.

Then there was you who trafficked in dialogue and difference. Became yet another "nice" white diversity lady that makes the university go round and round. Difference and dialogue are great theoretically until they hit too close to home for you. The irony of someone who studies power refusing to advocate for the people of color leads me to tell you, "Your all lives approach to leadership has enabled all of this." White tears are shed that try to wash away my intersectional embodied critique. After eighteen years I deserved better. But from what I hear you reaped what you sowed.

When did family friendly mean taking your small child to happy hour? Why do I always get dirty looks when I use the word heteronormativity though you all claim to be so family friendly and critical? It sure doesn't seem particularly family friendly to abuse graduate students either.

How do mediocre white faculty succeed in the space? That's easy. They kiss ass and become administrators and faculty senate presidents.

I'm sorry my excellence intimidates you, because you sure ain't inclusive of it.

Something to remember me by.

Chapter 7

A Local *Gay Man/Tongzhi* or A Transnational *Queer/Qu-er/Kuer*

(Re)organizing My Queerness and Asianness through Personal Reflection

Andy Kai-chun Chuang

I have to admit that I never really planned my research trajectory in queer studies in the field of communication when I came to the United States for graduate school in 2006. My research has primarily focused on critical organizational communication, and I am always reluctant to write anything that may in/directly out myself in academia and in real life. Although I am far from my home country, Taiwan, most of the time, I am just not so sure that this is the attention I want in my life simply because I am not completely out. While I have identified myself as a gay man, I rarely call myself "queer" for many reasons. It is not that I am not informed by the history of the term "queer." It is not that I dissent from queer identity politics. It is more like my idea of queer politics is influenced predominantly by a "Western" context and further converges with the queer politics in Taiwan. I would not say that this is a crisis for me to identify and discuss queer politics. Instead, it gives me a chance to reconsider the concept of queer is not just simply "fixed and existing 'out there' " (Mumby, 2011, p. vii), but is a "more complex negotiations of everyday life" (Mitra, 2014, p. 65) under different cultural contexts.

As a foreign-born, but U.S. postgraduate educated scholar, my understanding of queer theory has predominantly shaped by interdisciplinary, particularly communication studies, scholars in the United States. Alexander (2008) points out that queer theory rearticulates gender, sexuality, identity, and cultural studies, and negotiates queer identity within heterosexual spheres. Eguchi and Asante (2016) argue that queer theory challenges the binary definition of homo/heterosexuality and provides sites of resistance to uncover the circulation of hegemonic power and domination from a hetero/

normative perspective (also see Sedgwick, 1990; Yep, Lovaas, & Elia, 2003; Yep, 2013). In other words, queer theory is a form of "academic activism" (Alexander, 2008, p. 108) and pays further attention to discovering and resisting normativity (Calafell & Nakayama, 2016). This makes queer theory not simply another term for lesbian, gay, bisexual, and transgender studies (LGBT), but can be a useful way to understand LGBT lives (Calafell & Nakayama, 2016). However, communication scholars also point out that queer communication scholarship that is intersectional is still overlooked and underrecognized even though the intellectual and political movement of queer theory has hugely impacted the field (Chávez, 2013; Eguchi & Asante, 2016). While most of my research agenda does not focus on queer politics directly, queer theory certainly influences how I address taken-for-granted everyday experiences in different communicative contexts.

Homosexuality had always been invisible, with no mention in the law and social welfare in Taiwan for a very long time (Chen & Wang, 2010). It was not until the onset *tongzhi*[1] movement started around early 1990s, and the term "queer" was formally introduced to the public around the same time in Taiwan (Ho, 2015; Huang, 2010). In 2010, a group of scholars and activists published research on Taiwanese queer studies in English from different foci, such as queer existence under global governance (Ho, 2010), human rights for LGBT or queer folks (Chen & Wang, 2010), and *tongzhi* identity formation and the politics of sexual shame (Huang, 2010). These different research foci further led to the debate on why and how queer theory needs to address cultural identity from a geopolitical difference perspective because the term "queer" from the West may not be transportable under different social contexts (Liu, 2010; Ho, 2015). Taiwan seems to afford more spaces and make huge progress for the ideas of human rights for LGBT or queer people in comparison with other major East Asian countries (Ho, 2010). After almost three decades of efforts of the onset *tongzhi* movement, Taiwan's Constitutional Court ruled that same-sex couple had the right to be legally married in May 2017, and the court further established a two-year deadline for legislation (Choy, 2019). Still, some Christian and conservative groups in Taiwan campaigned against the mandated changes, and the majority of voters rejected same-sex marriage in referendums in November 2018 (Choy, 2019; Ramzy, 2019) as the institutionalized heterosexuality continues to create the standard for legitimate, authentic, prescriptive, and ruling social, cultural, and sexual arrangement (Yep, 2003). After the long fight, lawmakers in Taiwan voted to legalize same-sex marriage in May 2019 as a first country in Asia (Ramzy, 2019).

Extending conversations from scholars in communication studies (Chávez, 2013; Eguchi, 2015; Eghchi & Asante, 2016; Moon & Holling, 2015; Yep, 2013; Yep & Chivers, 2017), this chapter provides an overview of the major challenges to queer (intercultural) communication studies in the United States. This overview pays particular attention on the necessity of bringing (Other) bodies and better attending to intersectionalities to de-whiten queer (intercultural) communication scholarship. Furthermore, I discuss the reconfiguring of the term "queer"/"qu-er"/"kuer" in Taiwan. Through autoethnographic storytelling, I attempt to demonstrate how constructions and practices of queerness are an ongoing complex process through discursive efforts in societal, cultural, and political spaces day by day. By doing so, this chapter further calls for an intersectional reflexivity on everyday experiences of (re) organizing queerness, Asianness, and communication.

CHALLENGES ON QUEER (INTERCULTURAL) COMMUNICATION SCHOLARSHIP IN THE UNITED STATES

As Calafell and Nakayama (2016) point out, queer theory is not described as a traditional sense of theory. Rather, it is an intellectual and political perspective scholars apply to challenge how knowledge is acquired and how we understand the nature of reality (Slagle, 2006). Not only does queer theory challenge the notion of normativity, assimilation, and essential identity, it further unpacks the circulation of hegemonic power and creates a possible space for resistance in favor of a more complex project (Calafell & Nakayama, 2016; Eguchi & Asante, 2016; Slagle, 2006; Yep, 2013). While queer theory has significantly impacted scholarship on sexuality studies, difference, and ways of knowing/reading body in the field of communication studies (Eguchi & Asante, 2016; also see Johnson, 2001; Yep, Lovaas, & Elia, 2003), the majority of queer (intercultural) communication scholarship is focused on making life more livable for queer people who are predominantly white, U.S. American, and middle-class (Chávez, 2013; Eguchi & Asante, 2016). This also reflects what intercultural communication scholars argue, that the intellectual knowledge of the field has been dominated and centered by white and Western experiences (Nakayama & Martin, 2007; Moon & Holling, 2015). Therefore, a politic of disruption, challenging the neglect of race in the queer (intercultural) communication and the myth of post-racial societies domestically and internationally is necessary to push the intellectual and political boundaries of theorizing race (Moon & Holling, 2015).

Queer scholars of color have long critiqued the whiteness of queer studies and the ways the raced body is erased (Arrizon, 2006; Johnson, 2003; Moreman, 2009), while others have attempted to make critical connections among postcolonialism and globalization (Altman, 1997; Binnie, 2004; Cruz-Malavé & Manalansan IV, 2002; Hawley, 2001). One ongoing criticism leveled against queer theory is that some Western knowledge fails to address the personal, institutional, and cultural lived experiences of LGBTQ people of color, who may retain communal ties of their racial and ethnic origin, or even beyond the U.S. borderlands (Calafell & Nakayama, 2016; Chávez, 2013; Eghchi & Asante, 2016, Yep, 2013). In this case, white gay male identities are hegemonically structured as the normative representative of queerness, and this normative practice is often at the cost of marginalized women, people of color, and transgender people, who remain relatively invisible in different localities (Calafell & Nakayama, 2016; Eguchi, 2015; Lee, 2003). In order to disrupt the hetero/homonormativity divide, Cohen (1997) argues that the heterosexual-homosexual divide needs to be challenged, and queer identities and communities need to be complicated through different social localities in order to address power circulations and intersectionality. As Crenshaw (1991) suggests, "[t]hrough an awareness of intersectionality, we can better acknowledge and ground the differences among us and negotiate the means by which these differences will find expression in constructing group politics" (p. 1299).

LGBTQ people of color also challenge the Western notion of coming out of the closet as a measurement of a progressive act of liberation (Calafell & Nakayama, 2016; Eguchi, 2015). Under this coming out of the closet paradigm, McCune (2008) argues the term turns to be "[a] niche phrase to articulate the universal threshold experience of sexual self-discovery and self fulfillment" (p. 298). This notion reinforces a rigid binary between heterosexuality and homosexuality and further assumes that homo/heterosexual identifications are singular and stable (Eguchi, 2015). Additionally, the risk for many LGBTQ people of color coming out of the closet is not only potentially losing their familial ties, but also the support from their racial and ethnic communities or their native countries (Calafell & Nakayama, 2016). As Cohen (1999) argues, "[q]ueer theorizing that calls for the elimination of fixed categories seems to ignore the ways in which some traditional identities and communal ties can, in fact, be important to one's survival" (p. 450). Therefore, the closet paradigm is not only a white middle- or upper-class construction, but further reproduces the white/Western modernity embedded within the U.S. American cultural imperialism (Calafell & Nakayaman, 2016; Eguchi, 2015). Chávez (2013) points out that Western queer identities and politics formations are described as gay imperialism or homonationalism and "can . . . operate imperialistically as the standard by which all others are evaluated, and they can become a rationale for imperialist expansion" (p. 87). Therefore, LGBTQ people of color have proposed alternative perspectives of queer theory to attend their intersectional identities, such as quare[2] studies (Johnson, 2001), kuaer[3] studies (Lee, 2003), or qu-er[4] studies (Ho, 2015). This political turn of queer theory demonstrates the necessity to challenge the idea of "all 'queers' of all races, ethnicities, and classes are shored under" as an umbrella term (Anzaldúa, 1987, p. 250).

While there have been an increasing number of queer of color communication scholarship, scholars have also called for bridging queer studies with critical intercultural communication to further examine the production and constitution of discursive differences from personal, societal, and cultural practices and representation (Chávez, 2013; Eguchi & Asante, 2016; Yep, 2013). Alexander (2005) argues that "[LGBTQ people of color's] bodies are always already racially historicized, sexualized, physicalized, and demonized" (p. 250), and these marginalized bodies as embodied texts require close reading and translating (Chávez, 2009). In this case, Yep (2013) stresses the meaning of studying "other bodies" is "a translation that resembles, honors, and respects" different viewpoints (p. 119), and this embodied translation may create necessary intellectual and political spaces of intersectonality in queer (intercultural) communication research. Although Eng, Halbaerstam, and Muñoz (2005) point out that queer scholarships should be built upon the intersectional perspective of race, gender, nationality, as well as sexuality, from multiple social, historical, political, and economic positions, Yep (2013) warns us that intersectionality should not be simply listed as categories of identity because it tends to create a superficial knowledge of Others. Instead, intercultural communication scholars have suggested "thick intersectionalities" to explore the complex perspectives of individuals' personal and intersectional lives because these experiences are fluid, subjective, imperfect, and emotional and should be understood within the context of history, geography, and politics (Yep, 2010; Yep, 2013; Yep & Chivers, 2017). Therefore, the concept of thick intersectionalities not only can help to explore queer (people of color) identity "as a messy interplay between social categories [and lived experiences]" but further disrupt white and Western productions of queer (intercultural) communication scholarships (Yep & Chivers, 2017, p. 4).

RECONFIGURING QUEER/QU-ER/KUER IN TAIWAN

Before the lifting of martial law in 1987, the obstacles LGBTQ people in Taiwan, similar to everywhere else around the world, often faced prejudice, hostility, and violence in society (Chen & Wang, 2010). The social and cultural changes were vibrant in the post-martial law era in Taiwan, and the resistance from sexual/gender minority was one of the tactics being utilized by social and political movements in Taiwan. Under this circumstance, Taiwanese gay movement started questioning the concept of coming out under traditional family-based Chinese value, and further triggered the debate on issue over "coming out *as what*—respectable citizens who are *just like* everyone else, or sexual subjects who affirm their erotic practices *despite* social stigma" (Ho, 2015, p. 122, also see Chu, 1998; Ho, 1994). As Taiwan's renowned sexuality studies scholar, Josephine Chuen-juei Ho, points out (2015), the term "queer" was formally brought to Taiwan in the early 1990s by a group of gay/lesbian writers for a Taiwanese leftist progressive magazine, *Isle Margins*.[5] One important notion of how the term "queer" being used in Taiwan is that it was not originated in the existing derogatory Chinese terms referring homosexuality; rather, it echoes to the pronunciation of queer in the creation of Chinese term, "*qu-er/kuer*" (酷兒) (Ho, 2015). The term "queer" often has less relevance for social activism in Taiwan, but denoted the fashionable meaning of a cool kid in Chinese, and for a while gay communities in Taiwan took this term to signify the youthful trendy cultural style without any knowledge of the shame, insult, or defiance the term referred to under the Western context (Ho, 2015) although most of times the term *tongzhi* (同志) is being used to denote homosexuals.

It is also worth noting, "the term qu-er/kuer was . . . reconfigured less in opposition to heteronormativity . . . than in resistance to growing homonormativity and feminist gender doctrine in Taiwan" (Ho, 2015, p. 123, also see Ning, 1998). Rather than simply residing with only gay and lesbian movements, queer/qu-er/kuer studies in Taiwan also focus on the decriminalization of sex work, the sex rights of teenagers, and the diversified families (Ning, 1998). Queer/Qu-er/Kuer studies in Taiwan relates itself to both marginalized sex emancipation movement and feminism movement and further challenges the need to disrupt essentialized binary roles and identities in the hegemonically constructed sex/gender hierarchy (Ho, 2015; Ning 1998). As Ho (2015) points out, queer/qu-er/kuer studies in Taiwan has provided a possible space to build alliances with sexual minorities and other marginal groups to challenge issues, such as same-sex marriage, gender mainstreaming, sex education, and HIV awareness. Qu-er/Kuer may have started with a relatively shallow meanings referring individualized cultural style, but it has built the site of collective resistance to challenge normalizing movements toward marginalized groups in Taiwan, such as the assault of growing global hegemony of morality increased toward queer representation and interaction through legal legislation (Ho, 2008, 2015). In this sense, qu-er/kuer works should be seriously reread and translated through our own culture and history in order to rediscover intersectional practices and knowledge and to provide new insights for both local and transnational contexts (Ho, 2015)

NARRATING MY QUEERNESS AND ASIANNESS

In this chapter, I identify myself as a Taiwan born, but U.S. postgraduate educated, transnational gay man of color, who is currently living and working in the United States. One significant aspect in my life right now is that I am the only member in my family living in the United States. In that vein, I still maintain the strong communal ties, particularly with my family members and friends, in my native country, although sometimes they jokingly say that I am an American now. In the meantime, I have also shared that I still don't feel confident speaking English and often feel that the colors of my hair, eyes, and skin define who I am in the United States (Cruz, McDonald, Broadfoot, Chuang, & Ganesh, 2018). The "who am I" question is real and even more complicated when I float around within gay community transnationally. When sexuality, sex, gender, and body are important facets of my overall identity, this creates an intersectional point to (re)organize the sense of belonging toward the self with larger social, cultural, political, and historical contexts (Eguchi & Asante, 2016).

Methodologically, I use autoethnographic approach to connect my personal narratives as spaces to link the self to the social, cultural, political, and historical (Holman Jones, 2005; Calafell, 2007). While the sharing of personal narratives as an inquiry is no stranger in the field of communication studies, Eguchi and Asante (2016) indicate that "the sharing of personal narratives as knowledge building has been marginalized [within] the discipline" (p. 173). As Yep (2013) argues, communication scholarship needs to create a new space for "other bodies" to articulate their embodied experiences (p. 124). Gutierrez-Perez (2018) further points out that these embodied experiences may be wicked and dangerous, which require researcher to "dive into their own flesh" to connect theory with material dimension in everyday life (p. 3). Hence, theories in the flesh "are embodied, experiential and intersectional theories of resistance and agency . . . from everyday life" (Gutierrez-Perez, 2018, p. 3, also see Calafell, 2009; Moraga & Anzaldúa, 1983) that offers "reality different from those available to other groups" (Madison, 1993, p. 214). With this in mind, I offer the following three short stories through my narratives to consider how my racialized body and local/global notions of queerness and identity intertwine together in the hope to contribute and complicate (dis)identifications of queerness and Asianness through intersectional analysis.

My Coming Out (to What) Story, Sort Of

"People asked me about my coming out story. I don't have any because technically I'm not out [to my parents]. Some people say I lead a double life or I'm not honest or brave enough to face who I really am. It is more than that. I have passed beyond the struggling of who I really am already. Although society moves forward, it doesn't mean that everyone has the luxury to make it happen. I am happy to celebrate and embrace the National Coming Out Day, but do remember it is a privilege to be able to come out."

This was the post by me on my Facebook wall a day after the National Coming Out Day in 2017. Reading many of my Facebook friends' posts on "coming out" triggered me, especially when a friend messaged me and asked my "coming out story." I don't remember how many times I have similar conversations with different people, and each time they just drag me to this black hole. It is not like I am completely hiding or lying about my sexual orientation. Most of my friends (within and outside of LGBTQ circle) know that I am gay. In the classroom, I often avoid talking about my sexual orientation to students unless related topics popping up during lectures or discussions. My philosophy has always been like this—it is a personal matter. I am the only person who makes the ultimate decision whether or not I am comfortable enough to reveal my sexual orientation. Besides, how would I know if I would get into trouble by coming out?

Oh yes, I got myself into a big trouble once!

While I was still not so sure whether or not I am gay when I was in the high school in Taiwan, I told one of my friends who encouraged me to tell him everything. After coming out to him, I was verbally abused by him almost everyday. I was called "abnormal," "a gross guy," and so on. He avoided me and made weird gestures when he saw me. He also told our friends that I was gay and demanded them to stop being my friends. It was the memory I didn't want to revisit. After that, I have always been very cautious about "coming out."

Another reason I maintain a low profile about my sexual orientation is certainly family related. As the only (male) child in my family, there are many expectations on my shoulders from extended family members and my parents' friends. "Are you having a girlfriend now?" "When are you going to get married?" "Your parents are waiting to be grandparents." You don't need to see me in person to picture my facial expressions when I am being asked all these questions. I am just not so sure how everyone would react if I came out from the closet. Family ties are important to me. My parents sponsored me financially and supported me spiritually all these years while I was in the graduate school in the United States. I have to be honest, if I ever came out to them around that time, the worst scenario would be they cut ties with me, and I might not be who I am today. Now, I work and support myself financially, but my parents are also my responsibility. I NEED to maintain this family relationship even though I constantly picture how things might turn when they realize their only son/child is gay. How would this change my relationship with them? I am not so sure what I would like to do. In the end, I choose to stay silent on this.

Friends in Taiwan most likely understand the hardship about whether or not to come out to family members. However, I have been called out by some of my white gay friends in the United States and have been told by them, "I am not honest" or "I should be proud of whom I am." One time I got into this argument with Billy, a gay friend who I have met after I came to the United States. He has been the one constantly criticizing me about not coming out to my parents. He insisted that if my parents loved me, they would accept anything I revealed to them. I responded, "Well, that's not how my parents or our society operates."

"Then, they don't DESERVE to be your parents! Cut them loose!" Billy said.

I have always rejected to such discourse, and particularly troubled by the universal experience of sexual self-discovery and self-fulfillment regarding coming out (McCune, 2008). It is harsh to simply say I should sever the relationship with my parents if they did not accept me as a gay. While I might not fully agree with what so-called the family value under Taiwanese/Chinese culture, I would also not want to be exiled by my family, particularly my parents, who are all I have. I don't simply stand where I am in my professional life by myself. Their support was and is an integral part of this life, and I am forever in debt to them. It is problematic that Western hegemonic discourse produces and reinforces this either or sexual identification, and it certainly raises following questions. Who made the demand for universal outness, and who made the decision for outness to be an affordable option to everyone without considering different social identities and lived experiences (Butler, 1993)? To what degree should we be out to count as fully "coming out?" Is "coming out" also considered as a type of self-empowerment for LGBTQ people of color who might damage communal ties with their racial and ethnic communities? The white and Western discursive notion to be "out" ignores that life of queer (people of color) does not always take place in the public domain (McCune, 2008). It is not about the shame, pain, discomfort, and anxiety of being in the closet; rather, it is a tactic of survival to just be who we are (McCune, 2008) in different junctures of our lives.

To this day, I still haven't "come out" to my parents and other extended family members. I feel that my mom probably senses something, but we both probably just pretend that nothing happens. It might not be the best way to resolve this, but I no longer worry too much about "coming out" to my parents. I have lived the life I want, and I don't need to perform something to reaffirm who I really am as a gay Asian/Taiwanese man.

Can You Be My Asian Bitch?

This is the story that has been told by different people with different versions. While the story may be similar, it deserves to be retold again under different contexts as I try to (re)organize queerness and Asianness through the discursive effort. So, here we go!

After living in the United States for almost fourteen years, I started realizing that no matter how I perform myself, I, as an Asian, will always be framed as a forever foreign under the white-black binary cultural context in the United States (Nakayama, 2012). When I first moved to Denver, Colorado, I rarely received attention from the predominantly white gay community, even in my mid-twenties. Western hegemonic discourses pen white gay men as representing the whole community because they are masculine, dominant, and powerful, while gay men of color are often portrayed as less attractive and desirable (Eguchi & Asante, 2016). Occasionally, I had white guys hitting on me in the bar, most likely because they love Asian guys. Here, I am using "love" in a very loose way because under the Western context, "Asian boy is a subcultural category referencing the racialized fetishes of an older white male for the diminutive and effeminized Asian male" (Lim, 2014, p. 27). To be fair, not all white guys that hit on me are older, but age is really just a number considering how old I was/am relatively speaking. Most of these encounters at gay bars ended sharply because I often did not perform this prescribed gender role, which is a feminized and subordinated Asian guy, in the hope of being chosen by white gay guys (Eguchi & Asante, 2016; Han, 2008). As Eguchi describes himself, "[o]nce when I open my mouth, I am clearly no longer a (queer) model minority" (Eguchi & Asante, 2016, p. 178). I fall into this not-so-model minority as well. "You don't really act like most Asians I talked to before, and you are pretty aggressive" was a comment I received from a white gay guy after our brief chat at a gay bar in Denver few years ago. Nowadays, my bar-hopping habit is replaced by the online dating apps, and those apps serve as the major gateway for me to get to know people. You can judge whatever you want, but I just don't have energy to even step into gay bars after teaching and working for a whole week. Oh, and I got a message!

"Hello, I am ___ years old white gay man. I like Asian guys. Where are you from?"
"Hi there, I am originally from Taiwan."
"Nice, I can be generous, too. Can you be my Asian bitch?"
"Thank you, but No!"

He did not keep pursuing after I said no, although he responded with a disappointed emoji. I was speechless by how blunt this guy was, though not surprised. This online encounter reinforced the discursive and material Western cultural ideology of Asian women/men because if we (Asians) perform our role as the good wife, we would be further rewarded by dominants (Fung, 2005; Hang, 2008). Nevertheless, I have long resisted to this stereotypical racialized and gendered aspects of gay Asian male who is feminine and submissive in general (Eguchi, 2011).

Eguchi (2011) also points out that some gay Asian men may not consider dating or even acknowledge the existence of nonwhite gay men. This does not resonate well for me because I never really limit myself to who I want to date, and it is really weird for me to say I only want to date Asian, Black, Latino etc.? Why do I have to label a racial preference? However, I also don't deny that my desire is influenced by Western hegemonic cultural ideology, toward certain types of men. I do like tall and athletic guys because these two characteristics make them look good. When tall and athletic gay men show their interest to me, I compliment their good physiques as a homonormative strategy to perform a certain degrees of submissive. Though not just to white guys, but other racial groups as well. This happens a lot, particularly after I moved to New York City. More gay men chat me up, and it is not simply just from one specific racial group, although I still constantly received the message, "I am attracted to Asians." But, I seem to stop and challenge the notion behind that message, as Muñoz (1999) argues that queer people of color desire this white ideal with a difference through the negotiations between desire, identification, and ideology, which is a disidentification toward the dominant script.

Are You a Tongzhi, Qu-er/Kuer, or Queer?

While I live and work in the United States most times of the year, I do go back to Taiwan at least twice each year. Maybe it is because I have been away from my home country for a while. I hardly know any gay bars existing, or it may be just because there is no such thing called the gay districts in major cities in Taiwan. Thanks to the online dating apps, I am able to get to know new gay friends in my home country. An interesting fact is that I receive more messages on dating apps once I mention I live in the United States. The curiosity kills the cat I guess.

A college student, Yi-chun, in my hometown chatted with me online for quite a while. In summer 2018 while I was in Taiwan, he and I decided to grab a coffee together and finally meet in person. He is in his very early 20s and full of energy. I am, on the other hand, close to 40 and look tired according to him. In the beginning, our conversation was centered on my expat experience in the United States. Then, Yu-chun asked me a question, "Do you identify as Tongzhi or Qu-er/Kuer?" "Well, we both know that Tongzhi denotes to gay and lesbian in Taiwan while qu-er/kuer is the term borrowed from queer in English without some historical background at that time. For me, qu-er/kuer is not just about being cool or LGBT movement, but should have a larger focus on social movements, exclusion and governance in Taiwan." At this point, I don't think Yu-chun really understood what I tried to explain. He protested a little bit, "Don't you think the whole deal of same-sex marriage is a significant effort from the qu-er/kuer movement in Taiwan?"

"Yes, pushing marriage equality and diversified family is important, but what's next?"

Part of me was thinking that maybe it's too complicated for a young college student to immediately realize that we, as Taiwanese/Asian gay men, take for granted a list of LGBT vocabulary, readings, and films from the West translated to us, and we further assume that this list is not only a common culture for same-sex communities across the global, but also constitutes local LGBT identities (Ho, 2015). After living in the United States for more than thirteen years, I have been able to observe the LGBTQ rights movement here closely. It is obvious that the so-called global influence of U.S. American homosexuality assumes that all LGBTQ people are in some middle ground and alike is an overstatement (Tang, 2001). There is also no singular U.S. American homosexuality because it is intersected by multiple social identities, race included (Tang, 2001). Even before the U.S. Supreme Court held in a decision to require all states to grant same-sex marriage in 2015, I have witnessed that how U.S. society aggressively debates this human right topic. At that time, I often wondered if Taiwan would ever allow same-sex marriage happen from legal perspective. If it happened, how much would it take for Taiwanese society to (re)negotiate between local circumstances and concerns in such important human rights topic (Tang, 2001)? Without a doubt, Taiwan is perceived as a gay rights pioneer in Asia, Still, the movement to legalize same-sex marriage faces challenge and resistance. While the constitutional court in Taiwan ruled the same-sex couples have the right to get married, in 2017, attacks from some nongovernmental organizations, particularly those affiliated with Christian groups, continue. Although the democracy is rooted deeply in Taiwan now, it has also been interpreted constantly as a majority rule to claim respect for diversity while simultaneously reaffirming mainstream values (Ho, 2008). Therefore, both global and local hegemonic discourses of morality have never stopped the assault on LGBTQ rights movement and queer representation in Taiwan (Ho, 2008). I, for once, debated with an extended family member who claimed that same-sex marriage would destroy the traditional family and cultural values, as well as the next generation in Taiwan.

Some younger Taiwanese qu-ers/kuers also seem to have a belief that once the marriage equality goes through in Taiwan all other problems within LGBT community will pull through eventually (Ho, 2015). Although Taiwanese LGBTQ rights movement have started establishing localized code of ethics recently, some Taiwanese qu-ers/kuers still (un)consciously take orthodox approach to only encourage the conformity and to discipline the dissent (Tang, 2001). The white and Western concept of queerness should not be simply brought to engender the local application or to theorize the indigenous understanding (Tang, 2001). As Muñoz (1999) points out, "Disidentification is about recycling and rethinking encoded meaning" (p. 31). While we are able to borrow agendas of queer movements from the West to empower our own positionality such as marriage equality in Taiwan, we need to further reconsider these movements from local perspectives culturally and historically (Ho, 2015). Are we prepared to reread marriage/family from a queer/ qu-er/kuer position "that has been historically constructed as unthinkable or impossible" (Eguchi & Asante, 2016, p. 176) in Taiwan? While we celebrate the recent victory of the freedom of same-sex marriage in Taiwan, the equality of building a same-sex marriage family, such as but not limited to legalizing surrogacy, same-sex couple's adoption, and/or transnational same-sex marriage, still needs to be addressed through our own culture and history. This reread should be the backbone to rediscover the local practices, traditions, cultures, and knowledge that could shed the invaluable insight for a new understanding of being a qu-er/kuer in Taiwan (Ho, 2015).

CONCLUDING THOUGHTS

In this chapter, my intention is not to demonstrate a fixed construction of queer identity under my transnational status across the Pacific Ocean. Rather, what does it mean for me to be a gay man/*tongzhi* living in a transnational queer/qu-er/kuer politics? As a gay man of color living and working in the United States, my everyday life experiences of oppression, assimilation, and resistance shape and shift in an interlocking systems between race, sex/gender, and class (Mitra, 2014). As I share my personal narratives, my body becomes a "matrix of domination" where my embodied performance is simultaneously privileged and oppressed within the Western cultural ideology (Hill Collins, 2009; Gutierrez-Perez, 2018). While my embodied performance is still grounded in the material realities in everyday life, retelling these personal stories from different entry-points further reveals different facets of interlocking matrix and further addresses the intersections of race, sexuality, body, and identity negotiation (Mitra, 2014; also see Howard, 2013).

Furthermore, a theory of disidentifications provides a useful angle to examine my embodied performance as a transnational gay man of color. As Eguchi and Asante (2016) assert, "[c]ommunication is an essential site for queer people (of color) and queer transnational migrants to rearticulate their subjectivities and possibilities in complex and shifting dynamics of culture" (p. 184). From this perspective, it is worth noting that I neither assimilate nor resist completely under the matrix of Western ideological hetero/homonormative. In the case of my coming out story, I challenge the notion of this (coming out) paradigm operates from the Western cultural and ideological discourse without considering the societal, historical, political, and cultural constraints. I also interrogate my embodied performance on racializng gay male desire through U.S. American heteronormative, patriarchal, and institutional discourses. I further problematize the localization-globalization dichotomy by arguing the meaning of being a *queer/qu-er/kuer* from a transnational context. We should not simply adopt the taken-for-granted concepts from Western queer politics without challenging privileges behind those philosophical assumptions. While nothing stated here is new, all these narratives, not taken seriously in the past, reaffirm that communication is an open-ended and shifting knowledge production process for (transnational) queer people of color to not only defix the larger and moral master narratives and to critique hegemonic circulations of power and privilege, but also to reveal the vulnerable self for the possible space to survive (Corey, 1998; Eguchi, 2015; Eguchi & Asnate, 2016).

Moreover, this chapter echoes communication scholars' calls for examining and challenging the discourse of "race as usual" in the intercultural communication scholarships (Moon & Holling, 2015, p. 4). In my narratives, I reflect the challenge that white and Western dominance communicates (dis)belonging through racial stereotypical labeling and demonstrates how I negotiate the space of belonging within the notion of "coming out" and "gay Asian man" through resistance. In the so-called post-racial era, it is important to not only disrupt the notion of color-blind discourse, but also self-position my subjectivity in the racial matters (Moon & Holling, 2015; Holling & Moon, 2015). As a communication scholar and a transnational gay Asian man residing in the United States, my self-positioning of narratives in this chapter is a critical move showcasing the embodied practice of race(ing) intercultural communication (Holling & Moon, 2015), and this embodiment further demonstrates the intersectional performance of my premature and struggled queer/qu-er/kuer identity construction and embraces the messiness of my everyday queer (intercultural) experience (Yep & Chivers, 2017). My transnational position in this chapter continues to bring the international/foreign perspective alongside U.S. domestic voice in the field of intercultural communication, which is, as Moon and Holling (2015) point out, not consistently heard in social and scholarly arenas.

In conclusion, this chapter builds upon previously published (queer) communication scholarship by seeking to further extend an intersectional lens to (re)organize my queerness and Asianness. I have attempted to gesture toward centering my experiences as a gay man/queer of color to question the Westernization of queerness. More spaces need to be created to produce the living theory for transnational queer people of color (Yep, 2013). As Muñoz (2009) asserts, "Queerness is not yet here" but should be "onward . . . and toiling in the present" (p. 1). As we continue to examine, critique, and theorize racialized queerness in the communication discipline, I hope for more spaces for other bodies emerging from an intersectional perspective beyond the conventional academic research to not only be read, be translated, but for other bodies to be able to talk back.

NOTES

1. It means "comrade" literally in Mandarin Chinese. Further denoting lesbian and gay or queer.
2. The African American vernacular of queer.
3. Influenced by Johnson (2001), Lee (2003) introduced "kuaer studies" to elaborate the transnational turns of sexuality, sex/gender, race, class, and body by focusing on local texts of Mandarin Chinese in Taiwan.
4. Qu-er or Kuer is the Mandarin Chinese pronunciation of queer (酷兒). According to Ho (2015), it was first introduced in Taiwan in the early 1990s. While the term was derived from queer, it has less relevance to stigma or queer movement from the West. Instead, qu-er/kuer is also denoted the fashionable meaning of "a cool kid" in Chinese.
5. This bimonthly magazine was launched in 1991 but was suspended in 1995 due to financial reason.

REFERENCES

Alexander, B. K. (2005). Embracing the teachable moment: The Black gay body in the classroom as embodied text. In E. P. Johnson & M. G. Henderson (Eds.), *Black queer studies: A critical anthology* (pp. 249–65). Durham, NC: Duke University Press.

Alexander, B. K. (2008). Queer(y)ing the postcolonial through the West(ern). In N. K. Denzin, Y. S. Lincoln, & L. T. Smith (Eds.), *Handbook of critical and indigenous methodologies* (pp. 101–33). Thousands Oaks, CA: Sage.

Altman, D. (1997). Global gaze/global gays. *GLQ, 3(4),* 417–37.

Anzaldúa, G. (1987). *Borderlands/La frontera: The new mestiza.* San Francisco, CA: Spinsters/Aunt Lute.

Arrizon, A. (2006). *Queering Mestizaje: Transculturation and performance.* Ann Arbor, MI: University of Michigan Press.

Binnie, J. (2004). *The globalization of sexuality.* London: Sage.

Butler, J. (1993). *Bodies that matter: On the discursive limits of sex.* New York: Routledge.

Calafell, B. M. (2007). Mentoring and love: An open letter. *Cultural Studies ↔ Critical Methodologies, 7*(4), 425–41.

Calafell, B. M. (2009). Rhetorics of possibility: Challenging the textual bias of rhetoric through the theory of the flesh. In E. E. Schell, & K. J. Rowson (Eds.), *Rhetorica in motion: Feminist rhetorical methods & methodologies* (pp. 104–17). Pittsburgh: University of Pittsburgh Press.

Calafell, B. M. & Nakayama, T. K. (2016). Queer theory. In K. B. Jensen, & R. T. Craig (Eds.), *International encyclopedia of communication theory and philosophy* (pp. 1–6). Hoboken, NJ: John Wiley & Sons.

Chávez, K. R. (2009). Embodied translation: Dominant discourse and communication with migrant bodies-as-text. *The Howard Journal of Communication, 20*(1), 18–36.

Chávez, K. R. (2013). Pushing boundaries: Queer intercultural communication. *Journal of International and Intercultural Communication, 6*(2), 83–95.

Chen, Y.-R. & Wang, P. (2010). Obstacles to LGBT human rights development in Taiwan. *Positions, 18*(2), 399–407.

Choy, G. (2019, March 19). Explained: Gay rights, LGBTQ and same-sex marriage in Asia. *South China Morning Post.* Retrieved from http://www.scmp.com.

Chu, W.-C. R. (1998). Coming out or not: Postcolonial autonomy and "gay" activism in Taiwan. *Taiwan: A Radical Quarterly of Social Studies, 30,* 35–62.

Cohen, C. (1997). Punks, bulldaggers, and welfare queens: The real radical potential of queer politics? *GLQ, 3*(4), 437–65.

Cohen, C. (1999). *The boundaries of blackness: AIDS and the breakdown of Black politics.* Chicago, IL: University of Chicago Press.

Corey, F. C. (1998). The personal against the master narrative. In S. J. Dailey (Ed.), *The future of performance studies: Visions and revisions.* (pp. 249–53). Washington, DC: National Communication Association.

Crenshaw, K. W. (1991). Mapping the margins: Intersectionality, identity politics, and violence against women of color. *Stanford Law Review, 43,* 1241–99.

Cruz-Malavé, A. & Manalansan IV, M. F. (Eds.). (2002). *Queer globalizations: Citizenship and the afterlife of colonialism.* New York, NY: New York University Press.

Cruz, J. M., McDonald, J., Broadfoot, K., Chuang, A. K.-C., & Ganesh, S. (2018). "Aliens" in the United States: A collaborative autoethnography of foreign-born faculty. *Journal of Management Inquiry.* Advanced online publication. doi: 10.1177/105649261879656.

Eguchi, S. (2011). Cross-national identity transformation: Becoming a gay 'Asian-American' man. *Sexuality & Culture, 15,* 19–40.

Eguchi, S. (2015). Queer intercultural relationality: An autoethnography of Asian-Black (dis)connections in white gay America. *Journal of International and Intercultural Communication, 8*(1), 27–43.

Eguchi, S. & Asante, G. (2016). Disidentifications revisited: Queer(y)ing intercultural communication theory. *Communication Theory, 26*(2), 171–89.

Eng, D. L., Halberstam, J., & Muñoz, J. E. (2005). Introduction: What's queer about queer studies now? *Social Text, 23*(3/4), 1–17.

Fung, R. (2005). Looking for my penis: The eroticized Asian in gay video porn. In R. Guins & O. Z. Cruz (Eds.), *Popular culture: A reader* (pp. 338–48). London: Sage.

Gutierrez-Perez, R. (2019). Theories in the flesh and flights of the imagination: Embracing the soul and spirit of critical performative writing in communication research. *Women's Studies in Communication, 41*(4), 404–15.

Han, C.-S. (2008). No fats, femmes, or Asians: The utility of critical race theory in examining the role of gay stock stores in the marginalization of gay Asian men. *Contemporary Justice Review, 11*(1), 11–22.

Hawley, J. (Ed.). (2001). *Postcolonial queer: Theoretical intersections.* Albany: State University of New York Press.

Hill Collins, P. (2009). *Black feminist thought: Knowledge, consciousness, and the politics of empowerment.* London: Harper Collins Academic.

Ho, J. C.-J. (1994). *The gallant woman: Feminism and sexual emancipation.* Taipei: Crown.

Ho, J. C.-J. (2008). Is global governance bad for East Asian queers? *GLQ, 14*(4), 457–79.

Ho, J. C.-J. (2010). Queer existence under global governance: A Taiwan exemplar. *Positions, 18*(2), 537–54.

Ho, J. C.-J. (2015). Localized trajectories of queerness and activism under global governance. In A. Tellis & S. Bala (Eds.), *The global trajectories of queerness: Re-thinking same-sex politics in the global south* (pp. 121–36). Netherland: Brill.

Holling, M. A. & Moon, D. G. (2015). Continuing a politic of disruption: Race(ing) intercultural communication. *Journal of International and Intercultural Communication, 8*(2), 81–85.

Holman Jones, S. (2005). Autoethnography: Making the personal political. In N. K. Denzin & Y. S. Lincoln (Eds.), *The Sage handbook of qualitative research* (3rd ed.). (pp. 763–91). Thousand Oaks, CA: Sage.

Howard, S. C. (2013). *Black queer identity matrix: Towards and integrated queer of color framework.* New York: Peter Lang.

Huang, H. T.-M. (2010). From glass clique to *tongzhi* nation: *Crystal Boys,* identity formation, and the politics of sexual shame. *Positions, 18*(2), 373–98.

Johnson, E. P. (2001). "Quare" studies or (almost) everything I know about queer studies I learned from my grandmother. *Text and Performance Quarterly, 21*(1), 1–25.

Johnson, E. P. (2003). *Appropriating blackness: Performance and the politics of authenticity.* Durham, NC: Duke University Press.

Lee, W. (2003). *Kuaering* queer theory: My autocritography and a race-conscious, womanist, transnational turn. *Journal of Homosexuality, 45*(2/3/4), 147–70.

Lim, E.-G. (2014). *Brown boys and rice queens: Spellbinding performances in the Asia.* New York, NY: New York University Press.

Liu, P. (2010). Why does queer theory need China? *Positions, 18*(2), 291–320.

Madison, D. S. (1993). "That was my occupation": Oral narrative, performance, and Black feminist thought. *Text and Performance Quarterly, 13*(3), 213–32.

McCune, J. Q., Jr. (2008). Out in the club: The down low, hip-hop, and the architexture of Black masculinity. *Text and Performance Quarterly, 28*(3), 298–314.

Mitra, R. (2014). Organizing foreignness: Of aliens, permanence, and shape-shifters. In S. C. Howard (Ed.), *Critical articulations of race, gender, and sexual orientation* (pp. 65–84). Lanham, MD: Lexington Books.

Moon, D. G. & Holling, M. A. (2015). A politic of disruption: Race(ing) intercultural communication. *Journal of International and Intercultural Communication, 8*(1), 1–6.

Moraga, C. & Anzaldúa, G. (1983). *This bridge called my black: Writing by radical women of color.* New York, NY: Kitchen Table.

Moreman, S. T. (2009). Rethinking Conquergood: Toward an unstated cultural politics. *Liminalities: A Journal of Performance Studies, 5*(5). http://liminalities.net/5-4/moreman.pdf.

Mumby, D. K. (2011). Organizing difference: An introduction. In D. K. Mumby (Ed.), *Reframing difference in organizational communication studies: Research, pedagogy, and practice* (pp. vii–xiv). Thousands Oaks, CA: Sage.

Muñoz, J. E. (1999). *Disidentifications: Queers of color and the performance of politics.* Minneapolis, MN: University of Minnesota Press.

Muñoz, J. E. (2009). *Cruising utopia: The then and there of queer futurity.* New York, NY: New York University Press.

Nakayama, T. K. (2012). Dis/orienting identities: Asian Americans, history, and intercultural communication. In A. Gonzalez, M. Houston, & V. Chen (Eds.), *Our voices: Essays in culture, ethnicity, and communication* (pp. 20–25). New York, NY: Oxford University Press.

Nakayama, T. K. & Martin, J. N. (2007). The "white" problem in intercultural communication research and pedagogy. In L. M. Cooks & J. S. Simpson (Eds.), *Whiteness, pedagogy, performance: Dis/placing race* (pp. 111–37). Lanham, MD: Lexington Books.

Ning, Y.-B. (1998). What is queer politics? *Gender/Sexuality Studies, 3/4,* 32–46.

Ramzy, A. (2019, May 17). Taiwan legislature approves Asia's first same-sex marriage law. *The New York Times.* Retrieved from http://www. nytimes.com.

Sedgwick, E. K. (1990). *Epistemology of the closet.* Berkeley, CA: University of California Press.

Slagle, R. A. (2006). Ferment in LGBT studies and queer theory: Personal ruminations on contested terrain. *Journal of Homosexuality, 52*(1/2), 309–28.

Tang, C. K. (2001). Transcending sexual nationalism and colonialism: Cultural hybridization as process of sexual politics in '90s Taiwan. In J. C. Hawley (Ed.), *Post-colonial queer: Theoretical intersections* (pp. 123–37). Albany: State University of New York Press.

Yep, G. A. (2003). The violence of heteronormativity in communication studies: Notes on injury, healing, and queer world-making. *Journal of Homosexuality, 45*(2/3/4), 11–60.

Yep, G. A. (2010). Toward the de-subjugation of racially marked knowledges in communication. *Southern Communication Journal, 75*(2), 171–75.

Yep, G. A. (2013). Queering/quaring/kauering/crippin'/transing "other bodies" in intercultural communication. *Journal of International and Intercultural Communication, 6*(2), 118–26.

Yep, G. A. & Chivers, N. A. (2017). Intersectionality. In Y. Y. Kim & K. L. McKay-Semmler (Eds.), *The international encyclopedia of intercultural communication* (pp. 1–6). Hoboken, NJ: John Wiley & Sons.

Yep, G. A., Lovaas, K. E., & Elia, J. P. (2003). Introduction: Queering communication: Starting the conversation. *Journal of Homosexuality, 45*(2/3/4), 1–10.

Chapter 8

What Are you?

Embodying and Storying Categorical (Un)certainty

Benny LeMaster, Amber Johnson,
and Miranda Olzman

Using intersectionality as theoretical framework, and autoethnography as method, we reflect on our (racially ambiguous) bodies in space and time and through a series of stories that tease the (in)conveniences of (mis)labeling that massage our understandings of self and/as other. Because of the contested nature of epistemology, we choose to tell stories that *disrupt* (rather than acquiesce), *reveal* (rather than eclipse), and create *possibility* (rather than inhibit) (Boylorn, 2011). For instance, one might assume that to de-whiten intersectionality, one must focus on race, with intention, absent intersecting frames of bodily intelligibility. Why? Race matters. Race matters differently depending on where one is differentially located along intersecting lines of identity and embodiment. Race continues to matter differently across time and through space. And race matters because whiteness' violent legacy has constructed—and continues to construct—a dehumanizing gaze projecting notions of bodily worth that mediate access to power and privilege. As such, the stories we share serve *disruptive* ends that *reveal* the limits of identity with the hope of fostering a sense of *possibility*.

We are three writers/artists who are often racialized in ambiguous terms and who differentially navigate white supremacist notions of (mono)racial purity informing racist notions of bodily worth (Lugones, 2003). And in this chapter, we explore matters of (ambiguous) race at the intersections of difference. Specifically, we find whiteness' apprehension of—and resistance to—racial ambiguity informs the ways in which our differential queer and nonbinary trans (QNBT) identities and embodiments are interpreted and, in turn, allowed or denied the capacity to thrive on their own terms. In the end, we chafe against the all-too-common refrain that titles this chapter: *What Are You*—a question predicated on the assumption of non/human difference

the further from whiteness and
the closer to blackness.
The white gaze disambiguates
acquiesces
eclipses
inhibits
possibility.

We write our bodies onto these pages, as a series of black words on white paper, pushing toward an integrated understanding of the body as a set of experiences couched within multiple categories. Many of those categories are rife with (un)certainty. Carving space for us to name and embrace those uncertainties emerges as a de-whitening gesture. De-whitening intersectionality presses us to interrogate race as a category that produces (un)certainty and that leaves us questioning how we understand our bodies beyond race—not in a post-racial beyond or a color-blind beyond, but rather in a beyond that always and already assumes whiteness disambiguates racial ambiguity so as to make meaning of intersecting lines of identity and embodiment. Said differently, whiteness asserts categorical certainty across intersections of difference. Using intersectionality and autoethnography to interrogate our own understandings of ambiguously racialized experiences opens the doors to de-whiten intersectionality by shifting beyond race alone and focusing on the myriad ways our bodies craft particular uncertainties. Again, *what are you?*

In what follows, we share stories that question hegemonic rhetorical constructions of race connected to gender. Informed by Calafell (2014), we approach rhetoric through embodiment as subjects rendered racially ambiguous in contextual times and spaces. All three of us are (mis)named and (mis) identified in ways that create tension, pain, and discomfort. We each pass as that with which we do not identify and are, as a result, forced to confront the limits of compulsory whiteness as a hegemonic structure asserting categorical certainty. To be clear, Benny is perceived as a racial question mark? Miranda is consistently mislabeled as Chicana or huh? And Amber is often asked if they are a biracial black and white person. Thus, we flirt with (un)certainty as racially ambiguous subjects and consider the many ways in which such flirtations can disrupt whiteness' performative constitution across intersections of difference.

Rather than focusing explicitly on race, we choose to focus on compulsory identity categories, and how, when chaperoned by whiteness, they create dialectical tensions rooted in convenience versus inconvenience, authenticity versus deception, static versus fluid, imagination versus constraint. Taken together, these dialectical tensions highlight our relative and collective embodied navigation of categorical (un)certainty. We accomplish this in three sections. First, we consider theory and method as we locate this project within intercultural communication. Next, using autoethnography, we collaboratively embody and story categorical (un)certainty. And finally, we close our chapter meditating on categorical (un)certainty as a critical point of departure for a reconceptualization of identity and embodiment.

INTERSECTIONAL AUTOETHNOGRAPHY

This project contributes to queer intercultural communication (QIC) research or the interdisciplinary study of intercultural communicative phenomena informed by, while centering, queer and trans-cultural production and performance. Chávez (2013) writes on the interdisciplinary connection focusing QIC research:

> The logics of race, class, gender, sexuality, coloniality, and culture, among others including language, ability, education, and nation, congeal to produce certain identities, modes of relating, ways of living, and manners of social organization not only as normal, but as normative. The normative is violent. (pp. 85–86)

QIC scholars study the rippling effects of normativity across intersections of difference. QIC scholarship is vast and has included areas of focus such as identity (Abdi & Van Gilder, 2016; Bie & Tang, 2016; Cheah & Singaravelu, 2017; Goltz, Zingsheim, Mastin, & Murphy, 2016; Van Gilder & Abdi, 2014; Johnson, 2013), transnational and diasporic queerness (Asante, 2019; Eguchi, 2014), relationality (Eguchi, 2015; Eguchi & Long, 2018; McCune, 2014), queer of color criticism (Abdi & Calafell, 2017; Eguchi, Calafell, & Files-Thompson, 2014; Eguchi, Files-Thompson, & Calafell, 2018; Howard, 2014), and mentoring and pedagogy (Calafell & Gutierrez-Perez, 2018; LeMaster, 2018; Pattisapu & Calafell, 2012), for instance. Notably, transness—and racialized cisheterosexism specifically—is undertheorized in QIC research (Griffin, 2014). A key exception includes Yep, Russo, and Allen (2015) who map critical intercultural means of communicating and affirming transness and gender diversity more generally. Across all of these works, intersectionality emerges as a core onto-epistemic framework focusing QIC scholarship.

Intersectionality emerged out of the materiality of black women's lived experiences as multiply oppressed (Collins & Bilge, 2016; Crenshaw, 1993). In their 1977 statement, the Combahee River Collective captures this sentiment when they pen, "[T]he major systems of oppression are interlocking. The synthesis of these oppressions creates the conditions of our lives" as queer black women (Smith, 2000, p. 264). Here, the Collective highlights the ways in which intersectionality provides an onto-epistemic anchor for interrogating power. In intercultural communication research, intersectionality provides a reflexive means for engaging human difference. This work is hard as it "requires scholars interact with their own privileges (or lack of it) and theoretical blind [sic] spots" (Griffin & Chàvez, 2012, p. 19). Yep (2015) proffers "thick intersectionalities" so as to provide "more complex and embodied ways of thinking about intersectionality" (p. 89). Thick intersectionalities, Yep (2010) writes, refers to the

> exploration of the complex particularities of individuals' lives and identities associated with their race, class, gender, sexuality, and national locations by understanding their history and personhood in concrete time and space, and the interplay between individual subjectivity, personal agency, systemic arrangements, and structural forces. (p. 173)

Thick intersectionalities provide a nuanced means to engage the complexity of human difference while refusing to reduce difference to singular or solitary categories. Still, whiteness is an elusive cultural force that asserts itself even as it is implicated. Evidenced in this volume, whiteness can reemerge even in intersectional scholarship. As a result, we turn to praxis-oriented research as a critical, embodied means to engage whiteness.

In his bid for a praxis-oriented approach to whiteness research, Toyosaki (2016) proposes three onto-epistemic points of focus. This approach shapes our project and helps us to engage the prior questions with the nuance they require. Praxis-oriented whiteness research (1) understands the living present as a space of communicative transformation, (2) affirms whiteness as a relational and intersubjective phenomenon, and (3) "develops webs of cultural narratives that function as 'social' critique of whiteness" (p. 255).

First, the living present is a reflexive space that understands communication as performatively constituted through a traditional—innovative dialectic (Warren, 2008). Understood in this way, the living present holds within it the capacity to intervene in whiteness, for instance, as a communicatively constituted performative phenomenon that draws on historically sedimented and embodied ideological cultural scripts (LeMaster, 2018). Eguchi and Asante (2016) remind us "intercultural negotiations of identity and practices of belonging are never a simple process of life learning and growth; they are on-going, complex, and paradoxical dialectics of life struggle in historical and ideological spaces" (p. 183). In this regard, our autoethnographic narratives embrace the living present as moments of cultural reification rife with transformative potential.

Second, whiteness is understood as an intersubjective and relational cultural phenomenon. How whiteness attempts to mediate our subjective sense of self through mundane disciplinary utterances—including *what are you*—points to the intersubjective and relational constitution of whiteness as it seeks to apprehend racial ambiguities. To de-whiten intersectionality requires naming and working against the pervasive ways whiteness seeks to identify itself through sameness while distancing nonwhiteness through difference that chafes against the limits of categorical (un)certainty. In this way, the relational constitution of our respective QNBT subjectivities and the respectability politics that seek to contain our gender potentiality is always and already augmented by racialized fantasies set in opposition to the white supremacist barometer distinguishing proper white manhood from proper white womanhood (binaohan, 2014).

Third, praxis-oriented whiteness research positions contradictory, complementary, and ambivalent cultural narratives in tension with one another in an attempt to nuance and contextualize whiteness across patterns of lived experience. In turn, the resulting narrative tapestry seeks to shift alongside and in tension with whiteness as a cultural phenomenon that is ontologically elusive yet defined through histories of material meaning making. Simultaneously, we center Martínez Guillem's (2016) critique of praxis-oriented whiteness research when she reminds us, "It is only when objective social conditions intercept subjective communicative interventions that people's praxis becomes a powerful historical force" (p. 266). Our narratives, thus, are informed not only by a subjective sense of self working toward awareness of whiteness in mundane communicative contexts, but also by a marked recognition of the ways our respective and collaborative materialities, as racially ambiguous subjects embodying QNBT subjectivities with access to higher education, hinder and enable particular communicative interventions across intersections of difference. To accomplish this, we turn to autoethnography.

Autoethnography is research, writing, storytelling, and method that connects the personal to the cultural, structural, and political (Boylorn and Orbe, 2014). Autoethnography can be conceptualized as "flesh to flesh theorizing," (Spry, 2001, p. 726) that draws our attention to many ways of (un)knowing via autopoetic narrative (Alexander & Warren, 2002), autocritography (Awkward, 1999), performance (Conquergood, 1985), and rhetorical autoethnography (Johnson, 2014). The goal of an autoethnographic text is to produce a creative yet critical articulation of lived experiences in a textual performance where different perceptions and standpoints of the same experiences enter into conversation (Conquergood, 1985, p. 9), and create new memories and new experiences that foster a space for understanding and possibility (Johnson, 2014). In the end, our embodying and storying of categorical (un)certainty, through autoethnographic means, helps us to de-whiten intersectionality.

EMBODYING AND STORYING CATEGORICAL (UN)CERTAINTY

I like karaoke
Not to sing
But to listen
To queer joy.

A Chubby Black Queen belts Lauryn Hill. Her vibrant orange eye shadow compliments the two perfectly symmetrical yellow puffs sitting atop her head. Glitter glistens across her dark black skin and across her broad, exposed chest. She stands tall Doo Wop-ping the recently renovated space. The only thing rarer than a queer bar is a renovated queer bar. The renovation marks a terrifying reality: They are competing with hipster bars encroaching and gentrifying our Fucking Spaces with "everyone is welcome" signs, which is really just neoliberal code for: We will gladly take your queer dollars.

I breathe and release. I get in my head. I wonder: *Is this my queer version of "GET OFF MY LAWN"*? Probably. Queer space matters (to) me. I close my eyes and raise my perfect vodka martini to my lips. I sip. I smile.

Taking in the week, the Chubby Black Queen's vocals, vodka. Queer joy is hard to find. Harder even to feel. Though I smile. Seeking. Joy. A connection with another.

It's been years since I've known intimate touch. A cliché rides the rim of my martini glass: It's been so long I've forgotten.

Words cut the Chubby Black Queen's vocals as I open my eyes and glance to my left.

He is a smidge drunker than me. I raise my left brow indicating confusion. *Excuse me*, I inquire. He points to my bomber jacket—an official New Kids on the Block Hangin' Tough World Tour production team jacket that once belonged to a man named "Howard." It remains my best thrift store purchase; he is *right* to compliment my jacket, I repeat to myself in an attempt to convince myself I am worth the attention. Positive affirmations are shit; but they work. I inhale and turn my body, hopeful for a hookup, or at the least, touch.

He grabs his drink and slides in close. Gin and garlic ride his breath. He is unemployed and riding his savings and happy, he insists. Having spent the better part of his life as a flight attendant, he has traveled the world. He loves Singapore the most. He is Latin but really just American, he insists. *May I run my fingers through your beard*, he insists. *Sure*, I quiz. No one has asked this of me. I am tense as his fingers run through my coarse beard. His face is perhaps too close. I am not good with boundaries. And I am, to put it plainly, thirsty. For touch. And connection. For queer joy. And thus confused.

A group of predictably drunk straight white women cheer for the Chubby Black Queen whose rendition of Lauryn Hill has ended. The drunk straight white women's cheers are amplified by the bachelorette they are celebrating. Queers roll eyes as the Chubby Black Queen swats away drunk straight white women "fans" and takes a seat. Queers roll eyes. Our joy is stifled by their jeers and cheers and cisheterosexist rituals.

His fingers pull me back to presence. *Excuse me*, I insist. *What are you*, he insists. My eyebrows furl in confusion. I am oddly affirmed when he follows up: *There is no way you are white.* I am stunned into silence uncertain how to respond. Rarely am I "seen" in my mixedness. Except when nearness eclipses the limits of a presumed stable racial formation.

I am Taiwanese and white.

You know, his fingers massage the skin anchoring my beard, *you'd look like a big ol' Buddha Chinaman if you shaved your beard.* His fingers turn to fists as he grabs my beard and pulls my face in close to his. His words shift to *tings* and *chongs*. He punctuates his nonsensical racist vitriol with a crooked smile as his name is called by the karaoke emcee. *It's my turn, cutie*.

He releases my beard and takes the stage. The song starts as a familiar racialized piano riff blares through the speakers—Kung Fu Fighting. *I dedicate this to my Chinaman in white face*. I toss back the remainder of my drink. I smile. I am not good with boundaries. And the bulldozing effect whiteness has on my mind and body and spirit.

I like karaoke
Not to sing
But to listen
To queer joy.

And whiteness stifles queer joy.

And the joy my beard brings my trans-feminine sense of self, despite being read as a white bear.

August 2002. I board my first international flight to Accra, Ghana, West Africa. Feet firmly planted on dusty gold soil, most conversation in Accra begin with Ghanaians asking me:

Ghanaian: Are you white?
Me: No
Ghanaian: Is your mother white?
Me: No
Ghanain: Is your father white?
Me: No.
Ghanaian: So your mother is white.

Me: No
Ghanaian: So your father is white.
Me: No.
Ghanaian, persistent still: Then what are you mixed with?
My witty comeback: Black and blacker.

Most of them laugh and look at me a bit twisted in disbelief. I am learning that maybe race is about skin, not story because, despite my story, they call me abruni, white. It stings a bit, this not being recognized.

2015: The stylist's chair is uncomfortable. They always are. They are not made for larger tushes. I am also excited though. She is pulling through my hair and examining it. I am trying to decide if I want extensions or not. I have had short hair for years and am contemplating growing it out but want to get extensions to see if it is worth the wait.

Stylist: What are you?
Me: Huh?
Stylist: What are you?

As she repeats herself, she is pulling my hair up and I can see her in the mirror gesturing to my hair.

Me: Uh, white.
Stylist: You're not.
Me: I am.
Stylist: This is not white people hair.
Me: Also Jewish.
Stylist: You should not be ashamed of your identity. This is not a white person's hair.

The entire time she is speaking to me, she is tugging my head around trying to demonstrate what she means. She keeps pointing to it nonstop.

Stylist: I am black and Jewish. I'm not ashamed. Stop being ashamed. I know hair. This is not white people hair.

In all honesty, I am at a loss of what to do. I do not want to protest too much but I do not want to claim identity I have no claim to. It finally takes pulling out my Ancestry.com DNA test to show her that I am not ashamed of anything.

Except, perhaps, taking this DNA test.

Whiteness is a "morphing social paradox" animated by a "slippery ontological nature," which renders it prolific precisely because of its absence (Toyosaki, 2016, p. 245).

IT (WHITENESS) IS AT ONCE EVERYWHERE AND NOWHERE

Whiteness scholars in communication have in turn sought epistemological anchors to help focus their pursuit for the elusively pervasive. Toyosaki (2016) finds communication scholars who study whiteness explore whiteness as: *nuanced*, *particular*, *contextual*, *historical*, *relational/intersubjective*, *intersectional*, *micro-meso-macro layered*, *consensus-conflict dialectical*, *reflexive*. Collectively, these epistemological anchors help us to *provincialize* whiteness—a processual research practice that in Yep's (2007) words "localizes, particularizes, contains and marks whiteness in its intersections by exploring how it operates and functions in time and space within a particular discursive context" (p. 174). Our narratives point to whiteness as an intersubjective phenomenon emerging at the limits of categorical (un)certainty.

What are you? A refrain that is both common and different to our respective experiences is often met with a foreclosing prescriptive:

- Brownness chaperoned by whiteness interpolates Benny as "Chinaman in white face," an anti-Asian racist ascription that concurrently masculinizes Benny's transness while framing whiteness as aesthetic through the signifier of the beard.
- Feeling the brunt of blackness prohibited by white beauty aesthetics exacerbated by gender and rendered invisible by locations, Amber's narratives locate the complex magnetic force fields of avowed and ascribed identities.
- Drawing on the shame and disappointment breathing in the accused and assumed body, Miranda highlights the presumption of being nonwhite and, in turn, accusations of being ashamed of being nonwhite when one, in fact, is white.

The converse emerges through disbelief and minimization.

August 2014. Twelve years after Ghana. I am teaching on a ship circumventing the Earth. A ship designed for learning. A ship designed to breathe a different kind of life into the traveling body. We are traveling learners, not tourists. The two-month voyage took me through Scandinavia, Northern Europe, Spain, and Portugal. I am not confused for white in any of these places. I am not asked if I am white or what I am mixed with by Swedes, Norwegians, Spaniards, Brits, or anyone else. I am not even approached or seen. In Sweden, I am invisible for the first time in my life. I do not stand on the receiving end of hungry stares wanting to peel back the skin on my body and consume my insides. I do not even get glances from passersby.

I am invisible. A minority who does not matter. Is this what it feels like to be in a place where blackness has no value? Does being black, even if only one drop, render the body invisible? Why do people assume me to be biracial in places where blackness is more prevalent, visible, contested? I think I know . . . and it stings too.

The final week of the voyage, we all feel like family—close, somewhat functioning dysfunction, a bit more curt in our words and actions. I let my guard down. They are smart like me. Aware like me. Critical like me. I let my guard down. I should not have let my guard down. I am learning, slowly, that they are not like me. And the words I have grown accustomed to hearing are not absent from this space. And to hear them in front of people who are not accustomed to the microaggressions that define a large part of my living life makes those microaggressions that much more powerful.

Throughout the voyage I am very open about my queer sexuality. I am not normative and perceived as a safe adult for many of the voyagers to confide in and talk to about their experiences. I am also teaching Race and Sexuality in Media. Then, I did not have the language to identify as gender fluid or left of masculine, but I am more masculine with my short haircut, masculine clothing, and athletic build.

Today I feel like being feminine (unexpectedly). I adorn my body in jewels, a femme jumpsuit, and make-up. I feel beautiful. I am standing at the water fountain speaking with a student when she, an older white woman, tells me, "You are looking exotically beautiful today." "Thank you," I say. I smile outside. I am not smiling inside. Her words sting. Exotic. Primitive. Not normal. Othered. Alone. My student's eyes grow wide. Suspended in disbelief. "What did she just say?" "Yeah, she said that." And yeah, it stings no matter how many times I have heard it. But it stings differently this time. We are on a ship designed for critical cultural reflection. But the cultural only seems to matter when it is an "other" worldly culture not from "our" world. It must be a higher culture. A different culture. Intranational difference is not meaningful enough. And that is not a part of the critical cultural component. Thus, I remain exotically beautiful.

A day later, as we approach the Sea Olympics, I am standing at the bar speaking with him, a white, forty-one-year-old male from a privileged background. He calls himself a good Catholic boy. She, a married, older, mother of a nine-year-old traveling with only her son, walks up. She wants to talk about Sea Olympics. She comes in close to ask her questions and smells my hair. She likes the way it smells. She pulls my head in closer, inhaling, and pressing me into her bosom. I can't breathe, but I can hear her breaths dragging in and out. "You smell so almondy and coconutty." She lifts my head and begins kissing the side of my face and telling me how good I smell and how beautiful I am. She asks her first question. "You look like someone with soul. I need help. The oldest and youngest lifelong learners are going to do a dance for Sea Olympics. Can you help us with choreography and music? Since you have soul." "Sure," with a dash of side eye. She comes in closer and starts to inhale deeply again. Then she licks my cheek. From jowl line to cheek bone. My face is wet. She pulls back and asks her second question, "What are you?" "I am . . ." To be honest, I don't know how to answer her question. I am so many things—a swimmer, a painter, a sensitive soul masquerading as tough, a dancer . . . Wait . . . she's pretty basic. She's talking about race. I clarify, "Do you mean racially? Oh, I am black.'" Long dramatic pause before she screams out, "No you're not!" "Yes. Yes I am." "No. No you're not. You're too pretty to be just black."

Her words sting. Wounds festering underneath the skin. I am too pretty to be *just* black. I have to be something else. I don't want to be something else. I want to be me. She will not let me be me. She wants me to be something else. Not *just* black. But something more. Something better. I am better. I am *better* because I am pretty. Damn.

Finally she leaves. His eyes are wide in disbelief. "What did she just say?" "Yeah, she said that." Our voyage isn't a critically cultural place for all who step foot in the realm of world travel. Some of us are shielded from other's difference. Some of us don't have to think about others. She does not. I feel the compounded sting still lingering from yesterday, from 2014, and from 2002 added to today.

In Ghana, I am asked if I am white by most Ghanaians I encounter. My skin and facial features signal some sort of difference. Something more. In Europe, I am invisible. When no one sees you, it does not matter if you are mixed or not; you are a nonfactor. A value-less entity. Aboard the ship, with white Americans, I am something more again. Exotic and too pretty to be *just* black. Why is being black *never* enough?

We're sitting at the large dinner table. A family holiday affair of sorts. Though, this is not my family. This is a family by marriage. Also, this is not my holiday. This is a holiday by marriage. And I look cute.

Points of fact: Where's the sticky rice? The chicken feet? The hierarchy that determines who sits where in relation to who?

Wine glasses clink as the *man of the house* approaches me and invites me to join him in the next room. His tight pants make me uncomfortable; his mane of hair is as aggressive as his wide gait. He is a wealthy playboy. A prick. *Hey man. Take a shot with me.* I oblige because it's free. I follow him to the next room where he reaches into his liquor cabinet and pulls out a bottle of tequila. *This is a $2000 bottle of tequila.*

I feign care: Gasp.
It tastes like . . . tequila.

I feign intrigue: Wow.
Will it get me drunker faster? I ask.
He blinks.
I am not good with straight white men. Especially wealthy playboys.
I feign intrigue: Huh.

A wave of trepidatious whispers announcing the day's politics escalates. The(ir) politics roll around my mouth like rusty screws.

What's the big *deal with a wall?*
I wouldn't want to serve [in the military] *with one of* those.

But *All Lives Matter.*

Intervention feels futile.

I toss back another shot of the playboy's tequila—he was distracted by the others in the next room talking politics. He sought a means to insert himself. A prick.

Well, I used to live there. And they're just so dirty. I just couldn't. Immigrants are just so disgusting, the playboy's daughter adds to the non-conversation.

The playboy salivates at the chance to affirm his daughter's xenophobic sentiment. She's a white girl who likes to feel "safe." By which I mean the Police State is her Daddy. The playboy a mere stand-in daddy.

I toss back another shot of the playboy's tequila—he's still distracted by "daddy's little girl."

I grew up in that neighborhood. I state. This is not a question.

It's just the worst, right? She asserts. The playboy prick raises a brow; will I cross his "little angel"?

Naw, it was perfect. To be surrounded by other immigrant families. That is the only place I ever felt at home. It is clear the(ir) family has once again forgotten that I am not like the rest. I punctuate the larger point casting our difference: *As a child of immigrants and growing up in an immigrant home.* The playboy prick's gaze is conflicted. Now that I have his attention, I pour another shot. His gaze turns fiery. I toss the shot back returning the gaze. *This gated community is rather terrifying in my experience. Remember that hilarious time your neighbors accused us* [my partner and I] *of being sex workers and called the police. Because of our gender presentation.*

Her backtracking would be funny if this weren't already a tragicomedy: *I mean, you're different. Not like them. You're just like us.*

I slam the shot glass on the table and stand. *I am literally nothing like you. And for my safety, I am going to excuse myself.*

I thank the playboy for his tequila. I clarify, however: *But for nothing else.*

My partner runs to join me as we walk. And walk. And we look cute. And out of place. But we're too drunk to drive. And so we walk in the hopes the neighbors won't do what they do best and call on Daddy to keep the outsiders out.

2013: I am in a performance workshop at the National Communication Association annual conference. In it, we are exploring identity—I am speaking about fatness and how I came to the meaning of my own fatness temporally.

We are on a break and taking a much-needed moment in-between movement and activity. We are chatting and discussing scholars we appreciate and need. They say (about a scholar I do not know), "She's another badass Chicana scholar like you." I ask, "Like who?" and they say, "Like you!"

I pause with discomfort and say, "I'm not, uh, I'm uh, just Jewish . . . well white, but Jewish."

"Get the fuck outta here!"

I am never sure where to go from here. My discomfort exists not in my own ambiguity. I have long since reached a space where I understand myself as existing in the "ish space." To me, this means I am Jew/ish, femme/ish, fat/ish, queer/ish, essentially I am never quite enough of whatever identity I occupy. Yet, I have never thought of this in terms of race—I was raised discussing my whiteness so it was always my assumption that was how others would see me. I never paused to think of what it would mean to be white/ish, or rather, white, but not white-passing.

Back in this moment though, my thoughts race. I do not want anyone to think I am attempting to pass for what I am not. I do not want to take up space that does not belong to me. Yet, I do not want to deny with vehemence lest it look as though I care about these moments of mistaken identity. Instead, I just say again, "I'm not Chicana, I'm just . . . Jewish." I am hesitant to say white. I worry about what perceptions will change about me.

When I get home from the conference, I share with my partner what happened. She turns kind of red and laughs. I ask her, "What's up?" She explains that when we were first dating in 2006 that she described me to her friends as Latina, resembling Callie Torres from *Grey's Anatomy.* When I move beyond the excitement of being compared to Sara Ramirez (she is ridiculously beautiful), I ask why she assumed this. She cannot quite pin it down though, just saying, "you just . . . don't look *that* white."

That. Just. Those words move in and out of conversations fluidly, slickly, slyly, over the high-pitched screech of a dog whistle. We rarely notice the qualifier when reading, listening, hearing, conversing about identity, until it qualifies our own. *Just* black. *That* white.

Laced in the narrative is the disappointment of being and becoming in a system designed to impede growth. We are not a disappointment, despite how our bodies are read at karaoke, on a ship, or in another country. We are not disappointments, despite not always having the capacity to correct comments riddled with mistaken identity. But our bodies highlight the way the system disappoints us everyday, in myriad ways.

2016: I struggle with what it means to be white, but not white passing. I struggle with what ambiguity means for my body in spaces designed to erase that which is not white. I struggle with my body and what it means to be declarative when I am constantly read as something else. I have a student come up to me after the first class. He asks if I am Latina. I tell him I am not. His eyes water as he begins to leave. I ask him if he is okay. He shakes his head but does not want to share. I promise him that his words will not hurt me, but I am not sure he will respond. There are multiple power dynamics present, but not all are clear and some require nuance. Shifting between and within teacher/student, racially ambiguous/visibly Latina turned white teacher/student of color delineates three moments of being and becoming where power isn't static, but rather expanding and shrinking within a system of emotions. He hesitates and shares, "I'm really disappointed. I was so excited to finally have a strong Latina professor."

I begin apologizing. I know this is not the first student I disappointed because of mistaken identity. However, I am not apologizing for my identity; I am not wrong in my body. But my body does create visceral responses when perceived racial ambiguity turns into whiteness and thus erases the dream many students of color have, to see themselves in their professors. I am apologizing for a system that fails students consistently.

Whiteness wants itself to be clear and present—centered—while simultaneously covert. Whiteness requires an entitlement to certainty. Because of this, ambiguity creates particular kinds of erasure and disappointment while de-centering whiteness. But the disappointment does not rest in my body, it rests in the systems that center performances of whiteness as idealistic and certain. There are not enough Latina professors. There are not enough professors that seek to decenter the performance of whiteness through their bodies. There are not enough interrogations into whiteness, certainty, and toxicity. However, my students ask questions that force me to interrogate the way whiteness impedes liberation in an act of emancipating (un)certainty. Consider, for example, the following exchange.

Him: I think you must be a black woman.
Me: Can you say a little more about why?
Him: Well, I know you don't look like me, but you do not talk like any white woman I know. They, they don't care about the same things you care about. They don't care about us.

We are talking about Black Lives Matter that day. The gravity of his words press. Race does not determine racial consciousness, but the white instructors in his life have not cared enough about black lives. He is certain that white people do not care about black lives. I want to be able to dispute this, but the evidence around us does not. The way that whiteness centers itself is so insidious that to even care about my black and brown students is to be rendered a person of color. Wash, rinse, repeat.

The way each of us experiences ambiguity often results in various types of erasure and violence. As these narratives articulate, ambiguity opens our bodies up to be interrogated in very violent ways. Ambiguity does not allow us to move more easily through the world, regardless of the potential fall back on whiteness, cisness, straightness, or other ways we are (mis)labeled. Ambiguity is not a safety net. The hairdresser narrative reinforces this notion. When Miranda said they were white, the hairdresser accused Miranda of trying to hide their "true" identity. In the end, people treat our bodies based on what they see, not what we say. If someone thinks we are something, and we tell them we are not, that doesn't mean they will change their behavior toward us. So instead, we answer questions that cultivate discomfort because we sit in our truths, however temporary or fleeting, and hold the blunt force of microaggressions designed to questions our authenticity. Wash, rinse, repeat.

Pedagogy of repetition.
Or, whiteness regardless.

Early on, I learned three things in conversion therapy.

One. There are two genders: Man and Woman.
Two. There is one sexuality: Procreative heterosexuality.
Three. Only white people can do gender right. Not well. Right.

Later, I learned three things in queer support groups.

One. There are two genders: Man and Woman; play with them.
Two There is more than one sexuality. You don't have to define your life by procreative standards.
Three. Only white queer people can play with gender right. Not well. Right.

Even later, I learned three things in transgender support groups.

One. *There are many genders:* They are yours to figure out.
Two. *There are many sexualities:* You do you; also, do who you want and how you want so long as it is consensual.
Three. *Only white people can embody gender right. Not well. Right.*

And with rare exception, I learned three things in communication classrooms.

One. There are two genders; deviation therein is an outlier and is thus inconsequential to communication understanding.
Two. There are two sexualities, which you will learn about in a voluntary safe zone training seminar. For deeper knowing, you can obtain a certificate that certifies your queer knowledge.
Three. Only white people know about gender and sexuality. And gender and sexuality can only be talked about in white peoples' languages, tones, and affects.

I now teach three things.

One. Gender is an imposed colonial structure. Its sole function is to control and thus to delimit potentiality (Lugones, 2011).
Two. Sexuality is dynamic, fluid, and felt. It is also apprehended, exploited, and abused. It is at once liberatory and oppressive across intersections of difference.
Three. The gender binary says more about race than it does about gender. Its sole function is to perpetuate a mythic standard distinguishing white manhood from white womanhood (binaohan, 2014).

To thrive, then, is to name and resist dictates of gender and sexuality defined and constrained through whiteness. Though the stakes are lethal. This, we must not forget. "Whiteness is a communication problem, and laboring for social justice necessarily involves interventions among communicators" (Toyosaki, 2016, p. 251). For whiteness is the only subject position afforded the capacity to live on its own terms for the terms of engagement for gender and sexuality were defined by whiteness.

CLOSING THOUGHTS: (UN) CERTAINTY AS POSSIBILITY

In this chapter, we three nonbinary and queer subjects draw on performance autoethnography in order to critically explore our lived experiences as racially ambiguous subjects. Informed by theories of intersectionality, these narratives lean into the synergistic force our unique, common, similar, different, and divergent identities and embodiments construct in context. As racially ambiguous subjects, the question of de-whitening intersectionality is complicated. It is complicated primarily because whiteness emerges as a prevalent force mediating the apprehension of categorical (un)certainty. In short, de-whitening that which determines our respective and collective points of material access and denial as racially ambiguous folks risks ironically enabling whiteness to emerge through an alleged absence—a key strategy of whiteness (Nakayama & Krizek, 1995; Yep, 2007).

Whiteness is an elusive colonial mechanism designed to denote and secure sameness while violently apprehending, violating, distancing, and destroying difference. Our respective racial ambiguities, however, afford us the capacity to shift between spaces and times in ways that are concurrently (de)humanizing, visible and erased, (dis)comforting. But be reminded, as articulated above, we present these stories in the living present, recognizing that the living present is a space for transformation, we affirm and critique whiteness as a relational and intersubjective phenomenon, and center Martínez Guillem's (2016) critique of praxis-oriented whiteness research (p. 266). Our narratives push us and the reader to find coherent value in the messy intersections of the racially ambiguous body embodying nonbinary gender subjectivities. If whiteness is a communication problem, as Toyosaki (2016) comes to understand it, then consider this our communicative intervention across intersections of difference, and situated within dialectical tensions including convenience versus inconvenience, authenticity versus deception, static versus fluid, and imagination versus constraint.

REFERENCES

Abdi, S. & Calafell, B. M. (2017). Queer utopias and a (feminist) Iranian vampire. *Critical Studies in Media Communication, 34*(4), 358–70. doi:10.1080/15295036.2017.1302092.

Abdi, S. & Van Gilder, B. (2014). Cultural (in)visibility and identity dissonance. *Journal of International and Intercultural Communication, 9*(1), 69–86. doi: 10.1080/17513057.2016.1120850.

Alexander, B. K. & Warren, J. T. (2002). The materiality of bodies: Critical reflections on pedagogy, politics, and positionality. *Communication Quarterly, 50*(3–4), 328–43. doi: 10.1080/01463370209385667.

Asante, G. A. (2019). Anti-LGBT violence and the ambivalent (colonial) discourses of Ghanaian Pentecostalist-Charismatic church leaders. *Howard Journal of Communications*. doi: 10.1080/10646175.2019.1590255.

Awkward, M. (1999). *Scenes of instruction: A memoir*. Durham, NC: Duke University Press.

Bie, B. & Tang, L. (2016). Chinese gay men's coming out narratives. *Journal of International and Intercultural Communication, 9*(4), 351–67. doi:10.1080/17513057.2016.1142602.

binaohan, b. (2014). *Decolonizing trans/gender 101*. Toronto, ON: biyuti publishing.

Boylorn, R. M. (2011). Gray or for colored girls who are tired of chasing rainbows. *Cultural Studies ↔ Critical Methodologies, 11*(2), 178–86. doi: 10.1177/1532708611401336.

Boylorn, R. M. & Orbe, M. P. (Eds.). (2014). *Critical autoethnography*. New York, NY: Routledge.

Calafell, B. M. (2014). Rhetorics of possibility. In E. E. Schell, & K. J. Rawson (Eds.), *Rhetorica in motion* (pp. 104–17). Pittsburgh, PA: University of Pittsburgh Press.

Calafell, B. M. & Gutierrez-Perez, R. (2018). (Critical) love is a battlefield. In A. Atay, & S. Toyosaki (Eds.), *Critical intercultural communication pedagogy* (pp. 49–63). Lanham, MD: Lexington.

Cheah, W. H. & Singaravelu, H. (2017). The coming-out process of gay and lesbian individuals from Islamic Malaysia. *Journal of Intercultural Communication Research, 46*(5), 401–23. doi:10.1080/17475759.2017.1362460.

Collins, P. H. & Bilge, S. (2016). *Intersectionality*. Malden, MA: Polity.

Combahee River Collective (2000). Combahee River Collective statement. In B. Smith (Ed.), *Home girls* (pp. 264–74). New Brunswick, NJ: Rutgers University Press.

Conquergood, D. (1985). Performing as a moral act. *Literature in Performance, 2*(5) 1–13. doi: 10.1080/10462938509391578.

Crenshaw, K. (1993). Mapping the margins. *Stanford Law Review, 43*, 1241–99.

Eguchi, S. (2015). Queer intercultural relationality. *Journal of International and Intercultural Communication, 8*(1), 27–43. doi:10.1080/17513057.2015.991077.

Eguchi, S. & Asante, G. (2015). Disidentification revisited. *Communication Theory, 26*(2), 171–89. doi: 10.1111/comt.12086.

Eguchi, S., Calafell, B. M., & Files-Thompson, N. (2014). Intersectionality and quare theory. *Communication, Culture & Critique, 7*(3), 371–89. doi: 10.1111/cccr.12054.

Eguchi, S., Files-Thompson, N., Calafell, B. M. (2018). Queer (of color) aesthetics. *Critical Studies in Media Communication, 35*(2), 180–93. doi:10.1080/15295036.2017.1385822.

Eguchi, S. & Long, H. (2018). Queer relationality as family. *Journal of Homosexuality*. doi:10.1080/00918369.2018.1505756.

Goltz, B. G., Zingsheim, J., Mastin, T., & Murphy, A. G. (2016). Discursive negotiations of Kenyan LGBTI identities. *Journal of International and Intercultural Communication, 9*(2), 104–21. doi:10.1080/17513057.2016.1154182.

Griffin, C. L. & Chávez, K. R. (2012). Standing in the intersections of feminisms, intersectionality, and communication studies. In K. R. Chávez, & C. L. Griffin (Eds.), *Standing in the intersection* (pp. 1–34). Albany, NY: State University of New York Press.

Griffin, R. (2014). Feminist consciousness and "unassimilated" feminisms. *Women's Studies in Communication, 37*(3), 254–58. doi:10.1080/07491409.2014.955429.

Howard, S. C. (2014). *Black queer identity matrix*. New York, NY: Peter Lang.

Johnson, A. (2013). Antoine Dodson and the (mis)appropriation of the homo coon: An intersectional approach to the performative possibilities of social media. *Critical Studies in Media and Communication, 30*(2), 152–70.

Johnson, A. (2014). Doing it. *Departures in Critical Qualitative Research, 3*(4), 366–88.

LeMaster, B. (2018). Pedagogies of failure. In A. Atay & S. Toyosaki (Eds.), *Critical intercultural communication pedagogy* (pp. 81–96). Lanham, MD: Lexington.

Lugones, M. (2003). *Pilgrimages/peregrinajes.* Lanham, MD: Rowman & Littlefield Publishers.

Lugones, M. (2011). Methodological notes toward a decolonial feminism. In A. M. Isasi-Daz & E. Mendieta (Eds.), *Decolonizing epistemologies* (pp. 68–86). New York, NY: Fordham University Press.

Martínez Guillem, S. (2016). The edges of praxis. *Journal of Multicultural Discourses, 11*(3), 262–68. doi: 10.1080/17447143.2016.1221410.

McCune, J. (2014). *Sexual discretion.* Chicago, IL: University of Chicago Press.

Nakayama, T. K. & Krizek, R. L. (1995). Whiteness. *Quarterly Journal of Speech, 81*(3), 291–309. doi: 10.1080/00335639509384117.

Pattisapu, K. & Calafell, B. M. (2012). (Academic) families of choice. In N. Bardhan & M. P. Orbe (Eds.), *Identity research and communication* (pp. 51–68). Lanham, MD: Lexington Books.

Spry, T. (2001). Performing autoethnography. *Qualitative Inquiry, 7*(6), 706–32. doi: 10.1177/107780040100700605.

Toyosaki, S. (2016). Praxis-oriented whiteness research. *Journal of Multicultural Discourses, 11*(3), 243–61. doi: 10.1080/17447143.2015.1073735.

Van Gilder, B. & Abdi, S. (2014). Identity management and the fostering of network ignorance. *Journal of Intercultural Communication Research, 43*(2), 151–70. doi: 10.1080/17475759.2014.892895.

Warren, J. T. (2008). Performing difference. *Journal of International and Intercultural Communication, 1*(4), 290–308. doi: 10.1080/17513050802344654.

Yep, G. A. (2007). Pedagogy of the opaque. In L. M. Cooks & J. S. Simpson (Eds.), *Dis/placing race* (87–110). Lanham, MD: Lexington Books.

Yep, G. A. (2010). Toward the de-subjugation of racially marked knowledges in communication. *Southern Communication Journal, 75*(2), 171–75. doi: 10.1080/10417941003613263.

Yep, G. A. (2015). Toward thick(er) intersectionalities. In K. Sorrells, & S. Sekimoto (Eds.), *Globalizing intercultural communication* (pp. 86–94). Los Angeles, CA: Sage.

Yep, G. A., Russo, S. E., & Allen, J. (2015). Pushing boundaries. In L. G. Spencer, & J. C. Capuzza (Eds.), *Transgender communication studies* (pp. 69–92). Lanham, MD: Lexington.

Chapter 9

Bodies that Collide

Feeling Intersectionality

Sachi Sekimoto, Christopher Brown, and Justin Rudnick

INTRODUCTION

Over three decades ago, Crenshaw conceptualized intersectionality as an analytical framework to account for the experiences of women of color whose lives are shaped by intersecting layers of racist and sexist domination (1989, 1991). The notion of intersectionality establishes a vantage point through which entangled and nuanced struggles of women of color—black women in particular—can be articulated and leveraged toward justice and equality in the context of law. Since its inception, intersectionality has been used widely by scholars in various disciplines, generating debates over its application, appropriation, and elaboration (e.g., Alexander-Floyd, 2012; Puar, 2012). While the influence of intersectionality as a conceptual tool is far reaching, the significance of utilizing intersectionality in the scholarship of culture and communication lies in the fact that an intersectional analysis may foster and encourage the act of knowing, relating, and feeling with and for others despite and beyond the social, cultural, and ideological differences that exist. That is, the notion of intersectionality should not simply account for the operation of structural and intersecting forms of oppression, but it should help students, scholars, and practitioners gain greater insight into how intersecting forms of oppression are felt, sensed, experienced, and lived. Intersectionality, in this case, is not simply an analytical framework for the critique of interlocking systems of oppression, but a tool with which we may gain insight into the lived experiences of marginalized subjects (e.g., Jones, 2010; Jones & Calafell, 2012; Eguchi & Baig, 2018; Yep, 2016).

Crenshaw (2003) uses the metaphor of "collision" to describe how multiple forms of oppression and discrimination strike women of color, as if they are standing at the intersection of oncoming traffic from multiple directions. The metaphor of collision invokes the sensory and felt dimensions of intersectionality: a collision involves a form of contact, which is likely to be forceful and violent, yet experienced differently by people based on the speed, direction, magnitude, and location of contact.[1] A collision can be fatal, unforeseen, anticipated, or routinized. Regardless of the likelihood and prognosis of survival, one comes out of a collision with a visceral memory of the contact, with a body that is forever changed by the velocity, gravity, and force of the collision. The metaphor of collision challenges the abstract approach to lived experiences of oppression, urging us to come to terms with the bodies through which we experience the operation of power, politics, and differences in everyday contexts:

> intersectionality is not simply a matter of how multiple identity categories intersect to shape one's social status . . . One's identity as a woman *and* person of color, for instance, does not occur in the abstract when multiple forms of oppression intersect to shape one's experience. Rather, the raced and gendered body *is* the intersection of multiple discourses and structures of oppression: *She* is the point at which racism and sexism collide. (Sekimoto, 2012, p. 234, emphasis in original)

When visceral and felt dimensions of social experience are considered, intersectionality can be conceptualized as an assemblage of literal and metaphorical impressions made on our bodies through multiple collisions (Ahmed, 2004; Massumi, 2002; Puar, 2007, 2012). This means to approach intersectionality not as a theoretical lens to interrogate the historical and systemic operation of power, but as the lived, ongoing condition of one's social and cultural existence filled with collisional encounters with others within the system of power. Types of collisions range from micro to macro level, as well as benign and tender to violent and deadly. Oppressive social interactions, including experiences of discrimination and violence, leave on our skin the felt sensations of harm, exclusion, and pain. On the other hand, empowering and nurturing social interactions also leave the literal and metaphorical marks on our skin in the forms of comfort, pleasure, mobility, sense of emotional security, and affective connection. One's social life is engraved with emergent and recurring felt sensations that become habituated or normalized over time—an "identity" emerges as an outcome of a series of recurring collisions, or the ways our bodies move to make contact with others, within the existing social and material environment.

The purpose of this chapter is to theorize intersectionality by attending to the felt dimensions of the collision (or contact) we make as social subjects. Rather than the categories of identity differences, we foreground the felt sensations and somatosensory experiences of living in and through racialized, gendered, and sexualized bodies (see Sekimoto & Brown, 2016, 2020; Sekimoto, 2018). Felt sensations are necessarily elusive, transient, and often escape linguistic fixity. At the same time, felt sensations that accompany social experiences are historically rooted and habituated. Our goal is to theorize intersectionality as a sensuous condition or event with rhythms, textures, movements, temperatures, and flows (Massumi, 2002; Puar, 2007; Saldanha, 2007) that substantiate and regulate the broader and systemic operation of power, hegemony, and oppression. That is, what we feel on and through our bodies—however personal or mundane it may seem—is both political and historical. Through our performative writing of sensory narratives, we set intersectional theorizing in motion, literally and metaphorically, by attending to the bodies that feel, move, and collide within the intersecting matrices of power (Pollock, 1998).

In the following, we first provide a brief characterization of thick intersectionality by Yep (2016) and develop our contribution to "thicken" its approach by attending to the felt sensations and somatosensory experiences of intersectionality. We then explain sensory narrative as our methodological approach, followed by three short narratives of visceral sensations of inhabiting racialized, gendered, and sexualized bodies by each author. Justin examines how bodily heat guides and induces a sense of resonance and dissonance surrounding racialized queer identity. Chris addresses the kinesthesia of black masculine performances of racial trauma and pain. Finally, Sachi unpacks her experience of childbirth and examines how her cultural memory, racial resistance, socioeconomic privilege, and gender ideologies collide into the sensation of labor pain and embodied act of birthing. We conclude by addressing the implications of adding a sensory layer to the theorizing of intersectionality in intercultural communication research.

THICK(ENING) INTERSECTIONALITY

Yep (2016) rightly critiques the approaches to intersectional theorizing that treat intersectionality as a grid of disembodied categories and resort to "the race/class/gender/sexuality mantra" that produces "a flat, formulaic, superficial, and 'roster-like approach' to intersectionality" (p. 87). By proposing the notion of *thick intersectionalities* (TI), he argues that scholars must attend to how people inhabit those categories in the fullness, voluptuousness, and nuances of their lived experiences. TI is characterized by four theoretical commitments, including (1) the refusal of "coherence and premature closure of identity," (2) the embracing of the "messiness of everyday experiences and interactions," (3) the focus on "the affective investments that people make in their identity performances," and (4) the understanding of identities as "embodied and lived by people within specific geopolitical and historical contexts" (pp. 90–92). For Yep, it is not enough to account for the categories of difference that pertain to individuals and groups; he urges us to closely examine the particularities and contradictions of how relations of power come to shape one's lived experiences and subjectivities. That is, the thick intersectional approach assumes one's agency to enact, perform, and transform one's identity, while simultaneously considering the influence and indeterminacy of how structural oppression manifests in one's lived experience.

Thick intersectionality adds depths, dimensions, and most importantly fluidity and movement to the understanding of people's lived experiences and identity positions. Lived experiences are not a sum of identity categories, but "a complex constellation of sensations, affective intensities, thoughts, perceptions, [and] memories" (Yep & Lescure, 2018, p. 5). The thick intersectional approach is necessarily holistic, biographical, and contextual. This chapter joins Yep's (2016) efforts to explicate cultural identity in its multidimensional, sentient forms. While Yep provided four prevailing characteristics of thick intersectionality, we propose to add another dimension or layer of lived experience—felt sensations and bodily feelings—to thicken intersectionality. We extend the notion of TI to explore the ways in which lived experiences of intersectionality may be fully captured in "the messiness, multidimensionality, and voluptuousness of identities as they are lived, expressed, and embodied" (p. 4). While Yep emphasizes affective intensities of lived experiences, we expand the scope of thick intersectionality by focusing on sensory experiences and felt sensations that substantiate and materialize the lived and situated sense of self. Intersectional identity is inhabited as an assemblage of felt sensations, bodily feelings, and dynamic corporeal materiality. In this chapter, we explore the assemblages of bodily feelings and intersubjective affectivities that give rise to lived experiences of intersectionality.

SENSORY NARRATIVE

Hunter and Emerald (2016) define sensory narrative as a sense-focused methodology that captures embodiment in ways that "move beyond telling stories of us *having* bodies to address us *as* bodies . . . emplaced, and whose movement and sensations are crucial to learning, knowing and understanding" (p. 28, emphasis in original). Sensory narrative, epistemologically and methodologically, aims to focus on the process of embodied, emplaced, and multisensorial knowing in stories that we engage and construct. All subjective experiences are necessarily multisensorial, engaging our multiple embodied senses simultaneously. The sensory narrative foregrounds the layers of multisensorial bodily sensations and feelings as a source of knowledge about self and the world. The sensory narrative aims to capture an embodied knowing, or an emplaced knowing that situates the embodied subject within all components of social and material environment (Howes, 2012). In this chapter, we develop intersectional narratives of our lived experiences by tuning into particular felt sensations and bodily feelings, letting our bodies search for words to describe what they feel.

Critical analysis that is purely discursive, ideological, or textual inadvertently feeds into the rationalist paradigm and upholds the imperialist construction of a racialized and sexualized Other (Conquergood, 1991). From a critical sensory perspective, any social analysis that privileges visible manifestations of power—in written texts, discourses, representations, and ideologies—overlook other crucially important dimensions of how hegemonic power is upheld through social interactions. The prevailing critique of identity politics is deeply influenced by the Western ocularcentric paradigm in which knowledge is established through the analytical process of looking at something (i.e., the body, discourses, images, texts, transcripts, and representations). However, various social logics function not because of its cognitive appeal and rationalistic order, but the "gut feeling" of implicit resonance and dissonance within one's lived experiences (Shotwell, 2011; Sullivan, 2014).

Through our sensory narratives, we echo Jones and Calafell's (2012) call for "intersectional reflexivity," or the act of acknowledging and reflecting on one's positions of privilege and marginality that shape intersectional identities (see also Jones, 2010; Eguchi & Baig, 2018). We expand the reach of intersectional reflexivity, however, by reflecting on what remains largely invisible yet felt (i.e., affect, sensation, gut feeling, and visceral memory) within and beyond the visible structures of power (i.e., discourses, representations, and ideologies). Instead of focusing on what we *think about* our bodies and embodiment, we focus on the direct bodily experiences of felt sensations of inhabiting a particular social body. We contend the structures of power are habituated and experienced normatively through our bodies in ways that are somatically felt, but not consciously recognized. In communication scholarship, the notion of self-reflexivity is still largely discussed in terms of cognitive reflexivity—to become conscious and cognizant of one's positionality and relations of power in society. In reflecting on the felt dimensions of intersectionality, we intend to engage the whole body, not just the cognitive mind. The significance of using sensory narrative as a method of self-reflexive inquiry is not about attaining the coherent "I" that thinks, speaks, acts, and reaches a conclusion about oppression, identity, or politics. Rather, sensory narrative allows us to examine the visceral and material conditions in which such coherency of the subject becomes possible in the first place. Thus, our goal is not to essentialize sensory experiences as they relate to one's identities, but to examine somatosensory experiences as a medium of social experience that give rise to the sensuous and embodied materiality of intersectionality as it is lived, felt, and experienced by the social and cultural subject.

SENSORY NARRATIVES OF INTERSECTIONALITY

Queer[2] Identities and the Resonance of Heat (Justin)

It's a warm summer night in late July when I park on a side street and turn off the car. 9:55 p.m.; the cover charge starts in five minutes, I'll have to buy my way in tonight. Walking briskly down the sidewalk, flip-flops flopping against the concrete, the familiar cacophony of the city reverberates through the air: smells of food and trash, the hum and buzz of traffic, laughter and shouts from people milling about the streets. This short walk from car to bar has become a ritual over the summer. Every Tuesday I make the trek, just before ten, to the Canteen: a queer bar in the downtown district with weekly karaoke. Tuesdays offer a chance to connect with friends, blow off steam, and drink away insecurities. Tuesday nights at the Canteen provide a needed spice to the banality of academic life in the summer.

As I approach the corner, a familiar scene unfolds: under the dazzling lights of the theatre marquee, I straighten my posture, raise my chin, pull back my shoulders, and push my chest out. This performance of strength and assuredness feigns enough confidence to carry me through the tumultuous sea of discomfort. All around me mull human manifestations of difference: mostly white heterosexual couples, men in expensive trousers and women in chic dresses, arms locked together en route to another destination, mingled with homeless persons, most of them black, asking for a few bucks or a cigarette. Through this bustle of people, I walk, in short khaki shorts and neon tank top, brown hair coiffed and white face painted with dark eyeliner and mascara. With every step, my body registers changes in temperature. Gentle waves of warmth are replaced by deep flushes of heat. I'm seen by no one, yet every almost-gaze sends a small shiver of shame up my spine. The heat of that shame "attaches to and sharpens the sense of what one is," a visceral, felt reminder of my whiteness and my queerness (Sedgwick, 2003, p. 37). All of this just three lanes of traffic away from the queer bar on the corner, dance beats tumbling out onto the patio and falling into the sidewalk around it. Sanctuary is so close.

After a short few minutes that feel like an eternity, I escape the perils of the outside and enter the Canteen. I relish the pause of this in-betweenness, the liminality of the ID check and cover charge payment. Separated from the uncertainty of the street, but not yet safely within the walls of our stronghold, I wait. My attention snaps into place as an amplified voice from the room on the other side of the swinging door announces something in Spanish. The microphone projects the sound into this waiting area, and as I hand my five bucks to the bouncer I slowly remember: Tuesday is Latinx night. Steeling myself, I push through the swinging door to the first bar. A drag queen is dancing on the stage to the right, but the bar is sparsely populated. Heads turn to greet me, only for eyes to look away as the whiteness of my skin glows neon beneath the pulsing lights. I'm not who they were waiting for, and this room is not mine, not tonight. I suddenly feel like a trespasser, a party crasher. The wrongness of being here presses upon me like a thick fog, and this chilled pressure makes me "feel 'out of place' where [I] have been given 'a place' " (Ahmed, 2006, p. 12). I feel cold and clammy as the display of confidence that carried me through the street falters. Calafell (2009) notes how whiteness, gender, and class status intersect in queer spaces like this to both magnify privileges and re-Other identifications, and I wonder how the intrusion of my white body disrupts the sense of safety and security for the Latinx queers here tonight.

Deflated, I quickly shuffle across the room and push through the doors that lead to the karaoke bar. What was a chill in the air gives way to a relieving and balmy atmosphere as the sound of synthesized pop music pumping from the room behind me succumbs to the smooth cadence of Frank Sinatra. Like most of the people crowded around this second bar, the room is brighter and whiter. I spot my friends in their usual haunt, a corner table with easy access to the patio door and bartender, and saunter over to the group to exchange quick hugs and occasional cheek kisses. Small, intimate touches to the face and back register an altogether different warmth as "the body returns to its ordinary buzz" (Stewart, 2007, p. 113). A glance at the older white man faltering through Frank's lyrics inspires me to roll my eyes and mumble "I'm not drunk enough for this," and I excuse myself to get a drink. I casually lean over the bar and order a vodka Sprite from the short, muscled bartender, who winks at me and replies with a "coming up, sweetie." The sense of *wrongness* of infiltrating the Latinx room fades away, and that coveted *comfort* sinks in. The bartender returns with my drink, and I exchange it for a card and smile as I request to "leave it open." I take a sip of the drink—strong, like they usually are here—and feel the tension in my shoulders start to melt. A gaze around the bar returns quick, furtive, flirtatious glances from a few other patrons, and my heart quickens in my chest. Here, abject bodies are "animated by possibilities at work in the . . . serendipitous" (Stewart, 2007, p. 117). Although I'm still too inhibited to flirt back, the possibilities before me send hot shocks of anticipation up my arms, and to my groin.

The night progresses much like any night at Canteen karaoke does. Drinks, music, "spilling the tea," laughter, and even more drinks fill my chest with a warmth and lightness as I momentarily forget about the stresses of life. What were brief exchanges of glances earlier in the night become prolonged gazes with beautiful men who pulse with heat, arousal, and desire as they walk past, stimulating a tightness in my pants. This is what I seek at the bar: the freedom to delight in forbidden passions or dark desires that pulse and thrive in the shadows of queer nightlife. I search for queer orientations, those ways of relating to others that "put within reach bodies that have been made unreachable by the lines of conventional genealogy" (Ahmed, 2006, p. 107). Every drink emboldens me, every passing look brims with yearning. Every tentative contact burns with the hotness of forbidden possibility.

Then, like a bubble burst, or an ear pop in a flight descent, the door separating (white) karaoke bar from Latinx night bar opens, and the Queen enters with a small group of followers. In the wake of the punctured threshold, deep beats of club music issue from the dance floor, suppressing the slow melody of poorly recreated Sheryl Crow. The pulsating music draws my attention, and I turn to watch the entourage cross the short distance to the patio door and disappear outside. As the doors to the dance floor swing shut and the pop music fades, I'm struck by a moment of sobering clarity. Ahmed (2006) notes that "the 'where' of queer is shaped by other worldly horizons—by histories of capital, empire, and nation—which give queer bodies different points of access to such worlds" (p. 176). The walls of this building provide sanctuary to us all, but I'm occupying an uneasy territory fraught with divisions.

Language is rife with relational colloquialisms centering temperature, from the ominous *cold shoulder* to the act of *warming up* to someone. As bodies move through the material and social world, they register temperatures in a kind of navigational way; hot and cold work to push and pull us toward or away from objects, spaces, and others. In deeply visceral and intuitive ways, the body comes to respond to temperature—and to respond *with* temperature. Shivers of cold, flashes of heat, clamminess or sweat, a "tingle in my cheeks" or the feeling when our "face is flushed" all illustrate a body's consciousness of the environment it occupies (Rudnick, 2018, p. 290). Our thermal registers are largely driven by bodily responses to shame, "the affect that mantles the threshold between introversion and extroversion" (Sedgwick, 2003, p. 38). In this sense, bodies who are rendered abject by the dominant social order, who are made to feel shame in the interest of policing identity performances, rely on temperature to gauge safety or access. Queer persons, for example, traverse a complex social and political terrain in which they collide with heterosexism. Queers of color collide with racism. Lower-class queers collide with classism. So many points of collision intersect and direct our movement through the world. Subjects are, therefore, rendered intelligible at the intersections of their various identities, and those intersecting subject positions produce a kind of heat signature that guides the centripetal and centrifugal forces directing human interaction.

Kinesthetic Feelings of Black Masculinity in Trauma (Chris)

The room is dark; only a makeshift stage is discernible. The audience, mostly white with a few people of color, sits quietly and waits in anticipation. The dim lightning suddenly illuminates areas of stages that brings the audience's attention toward an all-black, all-male cast. One man sits down to play the piano, using one hand to slowly move his fingers across the keys. He gently touches each key with his fingers, producing a solemn and sober tone that alters not only my perception of time and space, but also impels me to think about my skin, body, and innermost self. These black men, spoken-word artists and musicians alike, appear through the spectrum of light simultaneously with the somber tones of the piano and rhythms of their voices, (re)producing the spectacle of black masculinity—the entanglement of belittled and battered yet resilient raced, gendered, and sexualized subjectivities looms before my eyes. The intensity of the actors' performance is audible in the familiar rhythms and movements of their mouths, the vehicle of vernacular legacies of race-coded speech of blackness. Their presence also makes very real the sensations of the kinesthetic embodiment of black masculinity, possessing something that is felt and sensed as mobile, and still inert in pointing to the limitations of white hegemonic masculinity as a lens to view and understand black men. In essence, these performers enliven and elucidate the complexity of black men's negotiations, managing and feeling the tensions not only among their own intersecting subjectivities, but also with the whitening machines that historically neutralizes or facilitates the erasure of race.

Elsewhere, I have written about my everyday experiences of racial microaggressions (Brown, 2016; Sekimoto & Brown, 2016). However, I (re)experience my own sensory input and output as a black man not only through watching, but also feeling the psychic malaise of racism performed by others who look like me and *feel* as I do. This production, using Carl Jung's (1933) trope "Wounded Healers," is an original script and music score written and developed by Dr. Timothy Berry,[3] and performed by a cast of three talented, black male spoken-word artists. In Wounded Healers, these men are compelled to heal and nurse the black soul through the psychosis of white supremacy because their own bodies and souls have been already wounded and traumatized by it. The kinesthesia of black masculine performance, the movement of muscles in their eyes, mouths, shoulders, and other extremities with the onstage props, unleashes a dose of reality to the constraints of exercising freedom and liberation in a racist society. This is to say that while the spoken word represents the dominant form of expression of the performers, they straddle a range of sensory impulses and emotions through the rhythms, sounds, and movement of their bodies with the music, making racism *feel* real and sensorial.

As these men navigate the history of slavery, great migration and Civil Rights era, their performance emphasizes the taming of black masculinity in the face of its violent, hypersexualized, and aggressive constructions. These performers traverse the intersections of black masculinity, sexuality, social class, (im)mobility, and ability to voice how it feels to live under constant surveillance in white spaces that restrict their movement. The kinesthesia of their bodies—the movement of their eyes, the slow gait across the stage, the clenching of their fists causing their biceps to contract, and the loud tones and rhythms of spoken words evoking pain and trauma—manifests in understandings that their intersecting subjectivities have not only fallen prey to systemic racism but are deeply mired in white neoliberal cultural politics of difference to which *differences* don't matter.

In reenacting the African slave trade, one performer speaks of the cruelties of the conditions of transporting slaves by slowly unveiling the large shackles used by white slave traders to restrain the African slave. As he fastens the shackles around his wrists yielding a dull clicking sound that is heard with the dulcet but somber tones played on the piano, I feel and sense the pain of a dormant body unable to endure the weight of metal U-shaped cuffs, secured by a chain. As the performer stands in silence with shackles around his wrists and his eyes staring downward, I feel the trauma of having a motionless black body that involuntarily contorts to the will of white slave traders. Another performer then pulls out a large bullwhip consisting of a long handle and a braided lash. He speaks of how white slave masters asserted their dominance by whipping and flogging black slaves to strip away their humanity. With the crack of the whip, he produces a loud, piercing sound that causes me to slightly leap. The sound produces an adrenaline rush, a release of hormones moving through my body causing great stress and anger. These kinesthetic sensations within my body call upon me to imagine how the leather strap tore into the flesh of the black slave producing welts permanently etched in their body. After sensing through and within my body, I feel how whites' obsession with policing black male bodies produced a fragility of black masculinity—a permanent scar felt within the innermost self that persists in the trauma and pain of systemic white racism. Through the performance of pain of frequent assaults manifested in heterosexual prowess, these black males ultimately desire to feel and experience what it means to be fully human. While this performance is an avowed exploration of black masculinity paying little heed to the plight of black (trans) women, the artists are deeply indebted to the fact her story makes his story *feel* real—these stories altogether display the scars that are part of the natural healing process and remind us that struggles against white supremacy are still in progress.

The Birthing Body as a Site of Intersectional Collision (Sachi)

I still remember the sensation of an ice cube melting in my palm, as I closed my eyes and breathed slowly and deeply, counting my breaths in silence: one . . . two . . . three . . . four . . . five. The sensation of cold ice quickly turns into penetrating pain in my hand. I open my eyes and quickly release the melting ice cube into a bowl and wipe my hand with a dry towel. It takes five sets of inhaling and exhaling to hold the ice cube for just one minute. I repeat the set several times and try to engrave in my body the rhythm of slow breathing and awareness of sensations in my palm. It's not a pleasant experience, but it is absolutely doable, if only for one minute. This peculiar exercise is a practice of mindfulness for birthing—to be with pain, or as I find out later, to *be* pain (Bardacke, 2012).

Driven by the hormonal euphoria of the third trimester in my first pregnancy, I so naively decided to approach my childbirth as a phenomenological experiment with my body. Several months prior to giving birth to my son, I began reading about using mindful meditation in labor and delivery. I studied and practiced the principles of mindful meditation. I also learned that one minute is the longest duration of contraction even at its peak. If you are able to mindfully be with your pain for just one minute, you can rest until the next contraction occurs in less than 10 minutes. Sounds doable, right? I was not particularly concerned about being "natural" in my childbirth. My motivation for not using pain medication was not a political or ideological statement, but a naïve curiosity to experience what my body goes through in labor and delivery. It was about experiencing the sensation of birthing—including the pain—for exactly how it unfolded within my body.

My contraction started around midnight one week before my due date, and my water broke on the way to the hospital at 4:30 in the morning. My mindful meditation went out of the window—initially—as I endured my contractions in the hospital room. Fear, discomfort, and exhaustion took over my body and mind. Thank goodness for my doula who gave me a back massage every time the wave of pain and fear took over my body. She helped me try different positions, walk around the hallway, and gave me a peanut-shaped ball to encourage the baby to move, while my partner lovingly held my hand. For the first eight to nine hours after my partner and I arrived at the hospital, I was afraid of contractions, wanting to escape the pain. I was exhausted, uncomfortable, not knowing how things were going to turn out. Despite my efforts, my labor was slowing down at 8 cm after almost twelve hours. It was around 1:00 in the afternoon my doctor suggested that I go on a small dose of Pitocin to encourage more regular contractions. Thinking that Pitocin would worsen my pain, I was struck with a deep, paralyzing sense of fear. It's interesting how pain induces fear in the most instinctual way. It felt like my bones were frozen cold. I couldn't breathe.

When Pitocin started running through my veins, I decided I need to pull myself together, or I was going to lose myself in pain. I got into a "zen" position on the bed, sitting with my back straight up. I started breathing deeply and slowly, much slower and more concentrated than when I practiced with ice cubes. I focused on my breathing, but also tuned into my contraction. With all my senses and awareness, I tried to feel every detail of the sensation in my uterus, as if I was carefully tasting a delicious meal. Once I was completely tuned into my breathing and sensation—when I became the pain—the contraction felt like a wave, slowly rising in my uterus and taking over the entire belly down to my cervix, and slowly subsiding. I intently followed and tried to ride the wave, rather than resist or fight it. The wave was dynamic and warm, but it was no longer painful. When I reached this deep meditative state, the "I" became synonymous with the rhythmic movement of the laboring uterus, the widening cervix, and the dynamic sensation of birthing itself, being in synch with the body carrying out the revolutionary act of birthing a child. I savored the sensation of the birthing body with a deep sense of, for the lack of a better word, love. Through the sensation of my birthing body, I fully embraced my child in the womb and felt a deep connection with my mother (who was 5,000 miles away) who felt the same pain giving birth to me over three decades ago. For about one hour, I sat quietly without uttering a word or moan, going through contractions every few minutes in the transition phase of my labor when the pain was supposed to be most intense. I did not fight the pain; I became the pain itself. It was an extraordinary experience of becoming a body, a birthing body.

The meditative hour was truly euphoric and extraordinary, but the final stage of birthing is usually a bit more physically involved than sitting in silence. After quietly observing me breathe through contractions without a sweat, my doula suggested I try another technique called "abdominal lift and tuck" to move the baby down, which gave me an intense urge to push. I went through four contractions using this technique before my doula went to get the nurse. I was finally ready to push—or more precisely, I wasn't ready for anything, but my cervix was fully dilated, and the baby was correctly positioned to come out. My uterus was an amazing organ that worked like clockwork, naturally starting contraction at thirty-nine weeks of pregnancy. I also experienced the extraordinary sensation of becoming one with my labor pain, which was simultaneously experienced as becoming the body itself. In giving birth, I had to surrender to my body, allowing it to do what it does. However, in the very final stage of birthing, the willful, agentic "I" was called back (by my doctor, nurses, and doula), to follow the instructions and intentionally *use* my body, all the while enduring the excruciating pain. The pain was absolutely beyond anything "I" could tolerate, but my body still felt it. "I" pushed for about one hour. In the birth story my doula wrote, she said "after a few final strong pushes, Sachi birthed a beautiful baby boy at 3:49 p.m.!" I want to thank her for saying that "I" birthed him. The unified—and deeply cognitivist and rationalistic—sense of the "I" was deeply unsettled by the magnitude of my birthing experience. Childbirth is a whole-body experience; one cannot will her way out of the process, nor can she simply leave it to the body to take care of itself. In the embodied act of birthing a child, the duality of mind and body appears both pronounced and transcended. On the one hand, the duality is pronounced as the birthing mother imagines, makes sense, and attempts to control her body in labor within the existing medical practices and cultural discourses. On the other hand, the duality is transcended as the process of labor and delivery requires the birthing subject to work with, and ultimately surrender to, the way the biological body attempts give birth. Is it the body that gives birth? Or is it the birthing subject that gives birth? Such dualistic questions seem pointless, given how childbirth engages one's mind/body to the fullest extent.

Experience of childbirth encompasses complex interactions of biological, medical, social, socioeconomic, emotional, and cultural factors. My seemingly naïve but life-altering experiment with childbirth was largely enabled by my socioeconomic standing and privilege. I received proper prenatal care throughout my pregnancy, and my employment-based medical insurance paid for almost all of the medical expenses for pregnancy and birth. As a tenured faculty member, I was scheduled to have my paid maternity and parental leave for twelve weeks immediately following birth. I could afford the incredible support and service from the doula. Without medical or financial worries, I was able to focus on learning about childbirth and crafting my own birth plan. At the same time, living in the United States as a transnational migrant from Japan and being thousands of miles away from my country of origin, I was disconnected and removed from my cultural roots and communal support that I would have received otherwise. In retrospect, perhaps my desire to have a mindful childbirth was my way of experiencing birthing on my own terms and with my own body in ways that are resistive to how my Asian body is objectified and stereotyped on a daily basis. The return to the body in the process of birthing was simultaneously the recovery of my body as my own. It was a reclamation of my body as an active, willful, capable subject, rather than a passive object of racialization or gender stereotypes. While popular culture provides an ample supply of discussions about motherhood, it is rare to hear about the nuanced and mindful reflections on the bodily sensations of childbirth or the somatic feelings of living in a pregnant/postpartum body.

Popular discourses on postpartum bodies focus primarily on losing weight and getting back in shape, or issues of postpartum depression or anxiety that require medical attention. Pregnancy and delivery produce such visceral and embodied experiences. And such visceral sensations take hold in the birthing bodies as an aggregate of intersecting privileges and oppression, memories and desires, cultural norms and medical practices, as well as gendered and racialized narratives surrounding pregnancy and birth. The sensations—of pain, fear, calmness, shock, and the overwhelming physicality of the act of birthing—reveal so much about my intersecting positionality. I was able to choose pain partially because of the lack of other worries and concerns, but also because of the (old-fashioned and problematic) cultural narrative in Japan that a woman becomes a mother by overcoming the pain of childbirth. I yearned to connect with my mother in my home country through the sensation of pain, as a way of reaching across time and space. At the same time, I tried to reclaim my racialized and gendered body through the act of mindful birthing. How I experience and make sense of pain gives me greater insights into cultural and social conditions in which I find myself as a social and cultural subject. The sensations of birthing, then, is not purely natural, medical, or biological, but a coming-together of various forces and conditions that collide and manifest in the feeling, breathing, birthing body. Thus far, we elaborated on the sensory narratives of how various bodily sensations both reveal and materialize our lived conditions of intersectionality. In the following, we conclude our chapter by addressing the implications of our theorizing for the project of de-whitening intersectionality.

CONCLUSION

In this chapter, we provided three distinct sensory narratives that describe particular moments in which physical sensations signal the sensuous materiality of inhabiting the racialized, gendered, and sexualized bodies. Each narrative points to the fact that felt bodily sensations are not merely transient and ephemeral feelings, but a material medium through which historically ingrained relations of power, cultural memories, social norms and ideologies are invoked, remembered, and reproduced. What we feel on and through our bodies are not simply personal experiences confined within our biological bodies; rather, we feel things as recurring and habituated sensations of the particular social body that we come to occupy.

This chapter contributes to the broader attempt in this book to "de-whiten" intersectionality by paying somatic attention to the felt sensations of gendered, sexualized, classed, and racialized experiences. To "de-whiten" intersectionality, to us, means not only to re-center the role of race in the intersectional analysis, but also to de-center whiteness as particular ways of being in the world and particular ways of *being human* rooted in white normativity, cis-heterosexism, capitalism, and cognitivism. Bile (2014) pointedly argues that intersectionality should be viewed as "an epistemic *potentiality* to disrupt Eurocentric knowledge-production politics" (p. 176, original emphasis). By focusing on somatic and sensory experiences, we challenge the Eurocentric paradigm of thought in which the body remains secondary or subordinate to the mind. The mind-body dualism is still deeply enmeshed in the language, knowledge, and critique of identity politics, in that the body is largely viewed a site of inscription or the object of signification, rather than a lived, embodied subject of experience. The racialization of bodies of color often parallels the Orientalist binary between the Western mind/logic and the Eastern body/emotion. The visceral metaphor of "collision" by Crenshaw urges us to examine the materiality of lived experiences of marginalized people and identity categories they inhabit. If whiteness is built upon the paradigm of Eurocentric thought that privileges the mind over the body, reason over emotion, and logic over sensation, this chapter challenges the hegemonic epistemology of whiteness by having our felt sensations provide insight into the structures of power that shape everyday encounters. That is, the simultaneous operation of race, gender, and class in the social matrix of power is not only institutionalized, but also habituated and encoded into our lived embodiment.

In Justin's narrative, queer affect—and its racialized division—is experienced through thermal registers, through the fluctuations in temperatures or the ebb and flow of warmth that accompanies the force of "sameness" or "different-ness" that propels queer people toward or away from one another. Queer affect as heat registers, regulates, and reifies proximity and distance, attraction and aversion, inclusion and exclusion, and the very orientation of racialized queer bodies in space. That is, the geography of queer affect and desire, as registered and experienced as heat, manifests in Justin's personal experience because it has been repeated and habituated by those who navigate the racialized boundaries of queer identities. In Chris's narrative, his intersubjective connection with black performers on stage is mediated by the sensation of trauma and pain. Trauma, in this case, is not a rhetorical trope of racialized subjectivity, but the literal medium of what binds black people beyond historical and geographical distance. Black subjectivity emerges not because his body is marked as such, but because his body feels and aches with the larger collective social organ called blackness. There is no feeling into black trauma without feeling with and through other black bodies that historically and collectively remember such pain. Finally, Sachi's narrative of birthing illuminates how particular sensations of birthing came together as an aggregate of multiple forces and conditions, including socioeconomic privilege, cultural memories, diasporic yearning, and a reclamation of the racialized and gendered body that is marked as the Other. In these sensory narratives, what the bodies feel is not an idiosyncratic incident, but an unfolding of historical relations of power, cultural knowledge, acts of resistance, and ways of belonging. These felt bodily sensations in return feed into the labels and categories we use to identify and acknowledge the social location we inhabit. It is as if the collision is what forms our "identities"—the impact that cannot be undone, the impression that has been left on our skin and engraved into our tactile and epidermal memory. The category (white, black, Asian, for example) always has its sensuous content; or more precisely, the category sustains itself as an aggregate of its sensuous content.

What we feel on and through our bodies are political, however elusive, fluid, and unrecognized those feelings may be. The proposition seems simple, yet quite often disregarded in the quest for politicizing the structures of power that shape our intercultural encounters. Those felt sensations and bodily feelings—such as heat, trauma, and pain—are not neatly categorized into the grid of identity politics or the structures of oppression. After all, one's identity cannot be essentialized or reduced to any particular felt bodily sensations. Rather, the physical, emotional, affective, and visceral feelings guide, regulate, and give meaning to our social encounters. We feel the impact of collision literally and viscerally and learn how to navigate the social space in anticipation of the next collision. The grid doesn't feel—it is us, our embodied selves, who experience the series of collisions as social subjects. Our feeling bodies are molded by emergent and recurring series of impressions made on our bodies as we make contact with others, which in turn shapes the way we reach out to others.

By considering sensations, movements, and affective conditions that envelop various moments of collision, we can theorize "identity" not as a category (or a set of categories), but as emergent or recurring sequences of felt experiences that aggregate, however elusively, into a "self." To "thicken" intersectionality and move beyond the grid of identity categories, perhaps it is useful to think about identity as a series of recurring and emergent events. That means to examine *how identity happens, rather than what identity is*. As an event, identity entails all components of the environment in which it happens, including the social self, thoughts, feelings, temporal flow, texture, rhythm, smell, taste, orientation, material objects, spatial configuration, regulatory or disciplinary forces, as well as symbolic and discursive framing. An event may take place in a space that is already configured and organized, yet the temperature, movement, and nature of contact in the space vary in each encounter. What if we begin to think about intercultural encounters as an event, each having its unique configurations of sensuous qualities, rather than prescriptive and formulaic encounters of identity categories? How would it change the way we communicate across differences? Put differently, how can we examine intercultural encounters as a form of collision and carefully consider its felt dimensions, so that we gain greater insight and understanding of how others enter into, and come out of, such encounters? Thickening intersectionality, in this case, means to unravel the sensations, movements, and sequences of collision so that we learn, somatically and sensuously, from the bodies that collide.

NOTES

1. A presentation by Jeffrey McCune at the panel discussion titled "Whitening Intersectionality at Play: A Call for Re-Race(ing) Intercultural Communication" at National Communication Association (Salt Lake City, 2018) was instructive for us to return to the visceral experiences of intersectionality.

2. My use of queer throughout the manuscript draws on the insistence of Yep, Lovaas, and Elia (2003) that sexual identities are "multiple, unstable, and fluid social constructions intersecting with race, class, and gender, among others, as opposed to singular, stable, and essentialized positionings" that typically accompany the use of terms like "gay" or "lesbian" (p. 4). In this sense, queer invokes an intersectional understanding of sexuality as it manifests in/on/around bodies colliding with others.

3. Dr. Tim Berry is an associate professor and the director of the Center for Educator Partnerships and Student Support at Minnesota State University, Mankato.

REFERENCES

Alexander-Floyd, N. G. (2012). Disappearing acts: Reclaiming intersectionality in the social sciences in a post-Black feminist era. *Feminist Formations, 24*(1), 1–25.

Ahmed, S. (2004). Collective feelings: Or, the impressions left by others. *Theory, Culture & Society, 21*(2), 25–42. https://doi.org/10.1177/0263276404042133.

Ahmed, S. (2006). *Queer phenomenology: Orientations, objects, others.* Durham, NC: Duke University Press.

Bardacke, N. (2012). *Mindful birthing: Training the mind, body, and heart for childbirth and beyond.* New York: HarperCollins.

Bilge, S. (2014). Whitening intersectionality: Evanescence of race in intersectionality scholarship. In W. D. Hund, & A. Lentin (Eds.), *Racism and sociology: Racism analysis yearbook 5* (pp. 175–205). Berlin: Lit Verlag/Routledge.

Brown, C. (2016). "Black like me, Black like I already am": The language and memories of race in higher education. K. Sorrells & S. Sekimoto (Eds.), *Globalizing intercultural communication: A reader* (pp. 115–21). Thousand Oaks, CA: Sage.

Calafell, B. M. (2009). "She ain't no diva!": Reflections on in/hospitable guests/hosts, reciprocity, and desire." *Liminalities: A Journal of Performance Studies, 5*(5), 1–18.

Crenshaw, K. (1989). Demarginalizing the intersection of race and sex: A Black feminist critique of antidiscrimination doctrine, feminist theory and antiracist politics. *University of Chicago Legal Forum, 1*, 139–67.

Crenshaw, K. (1991). Mapping the margins: Intersectionality, identity. In K. Crenshaw, N. Gotanda, G. Peller, & K. Thomas (Eds.), *Critical race theory: The key writings that formed the movement* (pp. 357–83). New York: The New Press.

Crenshaw, K. (1991). Mapping the margins: Intersectionality, identity politics, and violence against women of color. *Stanford Law Review, 43*, 1241–99.

Crenshaw, K. (2003). "Traffic at the crossroads: Multiple oppressions". In Robin Morgan (Ed.), *Sisterhood is forever: The women's anthology for a new millennium* (pp. 43–57). New York: Washington Square Press.

Eguchi, S. & Baig, N. (2018). Examining embodied struggles in cultural reentry through intersectional reflexivity. *Howard Journal of Communications, 29*(1), 33–48.

Howe, D. (2012). Re-visualizing anthropology through the lens of the ethnographer's eye. In I. Heywood & B. Sandywell (Eds.), *The handbook of visual culture* (pp. 450–54). Oxford, MA: Berg.

Hunter, L. & Emerald, E. (2016). Sensory narratives: Capturing embodiment in narratives of movement, sport, leisure, and health. *Education and Society, 21*, 28–46. doi: https://doi.org/10.1080/13573322.2015.1065244.

Jones, R. G. (2015). Queering the body politic: Intersectional reflexivity in the body narratives of queer men. *Qualitative Inquiry, 21*(9), 766–75. https://doi.org/10.1177/1077800415569782.

Jones, R. G. & Calafell, B. M. (2012). Contesting neoliberalism through critical pedagogy, intersectional reflexivity, and personal narrative: Queer Tales. *Journal of Homosexuality, 59*(7), 957–81.

Jung, C. G. (1933). *Modern man in search of a soul*. New York: Houghton Mifflin Harcourt.

Massumi, D. (2002). *Parables for the virtual: Movement, affect, sensation*. Durham: Duke University Press.

Pink, S. (2013). Engaging the senses in ethnographic practice. *The Senses and Society, 8*, 261–67.

Pollock, D. (1998). Performative writing. In P. Phelan & J. Lane (Eds.), *The ends of performance* (pp. 73–103). New York: New York University Press.

Puar, J. K. (2007). *Terrorist assemblages: Homonationalism in queer times*. Durham: Duke University Press.

Puar, J. K. (2012). "I would rather be a cyborg than a goddess": Becoming-intersectional in assemblage theory. *philoSOPHIA, 2*(1), 49–66.

Rudnick, J. (2018). Bodies in dialogue: Arriving at thresholds of dialogic connections. *Cultural Studies ↔ Critical Methodologies, 19*(4), 288–96.

Saldanha, A. (2007). *Psychedelic white: Goa trance and the viscosity of race*. Minneapolis: University of Minnesota Press.

Sedgwick, E. K. (2003). *Touching feeling: Affect, pedagogy, performativity*. Durham: Duke University Press.

Sekimoto, S. (2012). A multimodal approach to identity: Theorizing the self through embodiment, spatiality, and temporality. *Journal of International and Intercultural Communication, 5*(3), 226–43.

Sekimoto, S. & Brown, C. (2016). A phenomenology of the racialized tongue: Embodiment, language, and the bodies that speak. *Departures in Critical Qualitative Research, 5*(2), 101–22.

Sekimoto, S. (2018). Race and the senses: Toward articulating the sensory apparatus of race. *Critical Philosophy of Race, 6*(1), 82–100.

Sekimoto, S. & Brown, C. (2020). *Race and the senses: The felt politics of racial embodiment.* London: Bloomsbury Academic.

Shotwell, A. (2011). *Knowing otherwise: Race, gender, and implicit understanding.* University Park: Pennsylvania State University.

Stewart, K. (2007). *Ordinary affects.* Durham, NC: Duke University Press.

Sullivan, S. (2014). The hearts and guts of white people: Ethics, ignorance, and the physiology of white racism. *Journal of Religious Ethics, 42*(4), 591–611.

Yep, G. A. (2016). Toward thick(er) intersectionalities: Theorizing, researching, and activating the complexities of communication and identities. In K. Sorrells & S. Sekimoto (Eds.), *Globalizing intercultural communication: A reader* (pp. 86–94). Thousand Oaks: Sage.

Yep, G. A. & Lescure, R. (2018). A thick intersectional approach to microaggressions. *Southern Communication Journal.* DOI: 10.1080/1041794X.2018.1511749.

Yep, G. A., Lovaas, K. E., & Elia, J. P. (2003). Introduction: Queering communication: Starting the conversation. *Journal of Homosexuality, 45*(2–4), 1–10. doi:10.1300/J082v45n02_01.

Chapter 10

Microaggressions in Flux

Whiteness, Disability, and Masculinity in Academia

Haneen Ghabra and Shahd Al Shammari

As I (Haneen) began to write this piece, I felt my heart start racing. I was terrified of writing an autoethnography that would reveal a piece of myself that I try to sometimes hide as an international scholar in fear of hurting my U.S. American academic family. I was terrified that whoever had fed into the logics of whiteness would read this piece and would not understand the international component. Being an international scholar has certainly scarred me, made me feel odd when I go back to the National Communication Association (NCA) Conference each year. I am expected to know everything in the United States, but no one is expected to know anything about me. The logic of whiteness does not expect U.S. academics or academics based in the United States to know anything about me. But, what if I asked another scholar to write with me? What if there was another Kuwaiti scholar who shared my Palestinian blood but had different social and cultural oppressions? What if I asked Shahd? Would she want to write this piece with me? What if our intersections would create a wider spectrum of privilege and oppression? I call her and ask her if she would want to submit to a call on de-whitening intersectionality and she replies excitedly, "I would love to." Her answer lays my uneasiness to rest, her answer allows us a space to speak transnationally, locally, and globally through the intersections of our identities.

We come to this narrative through our differences. Theorizing through our bodies and identities as Kuwaitis may mark us as similar but are in fact sites of disparities. We both occupy academic spaces of privilege as assistant professors who are also reminded that we are female and too young to offer anything. The stigmatization of our femaleness stems from a deep-rooted patriarchal system where we are always believed to be "less competent."

I (Haneen) am an assistant professor of communication in a predominately Kuwaiti department while I (Shahd) am an assistant professor of English literature in a predominantly white department (European) in Kuwait. As Kuwaiti PhD holders, we strive to be constantly aware that being Kuwaiti is both a citizenship and class privilege that automatically places us in a system that oppresses Others. For instance, being Kuwaiti in Kuwait is synonymous with whiteness in the United States. On a national level, this means access to free health care, education, jobs, and economic welfare. It also means performances of what Tracy Owens Patton (2004) terms "hegemonic civility," a process which suppresses and silences others in favor of maintaining hierarchies. For instance, as white civility teaches bodies to perform civility, we are reminded that white civility is a global system. When translated onto our bodies, we perform similar acts of white civility. This is directly conflated with class and citizenship. Even though we are reminded that being women means we cannot pass on citizenship to our children, as this is a right only granted to Kuwaiti men ("Kuwait: Give women equal citizenship" n.d.), we are also reminded that there are Other communities that are stateless or non-Kuwaiti that have no benefits whatsoever.

As we navigate privilege and oppression through our hybridity, our voices are one but are part of the collective. Our voices are not one but multiple. We follow Collins's discussion here where black women have a shared history of oppression but experience it differently (2000). This is mainly due to the intersections of other identities such as sexual orientation, class, age, and so forth. These women are binded by oppression but are in fact experiencing oppression differently (Collins, 2000). Like Calafell (2013), we theorize through experience, history, and relations that are written through our bodies. Our histories are both personal and collective as we theorize through the intersections of masculinity, disability, hybridity, and Otherness. Our bodies carry the burden of displacement, pain, and Otherization. Our bodies carry the wounds of hegemony and imperialism. We came to this space through academia. We came to this space through privilege, pain, and contestation through deprivation. As we write onto this chapter, we are seeking spaces of allyship through experience and through microaggressions. We offer our narratives as a means to expand race and intercultural communication. We believe that the gap between intercultural communication lies in the overlap of disparate identities laced through the transnational. Like Ghabra and Calafell (2018), we ask, "What would be the most feasible way to measure the voices of agony and heartache? Can pain be quantified" (p. 1)? What measurement have power structures provided us when erasure remains the largest quantifier for all marginalized identities? If the common denominator is the sum of our microaggressions then how can we find moments of resistance and decolonization?

In this chapter, we connect the international to the local in order to demonstrate that Middle Eastern transnational feminisms are constantly in flux. We are aware that our usage of the term "Middle Eastern" might reinforce Orientalist terms; however, by using the term "Arab World," we risk alienating countries like Turkey, Iran, and Afghanistan. Therefore, we use the term "Middle Eastern" throughout the chapter. We also use the word "Muslim" because the narrative of the Muslim women has been a global archetype that has taken center stage in the global limelight (Abu-Lughod, 2013). Through academia we connect microaggressions to larger power structures. We offer autoethnography and performative writing as a means to theorize our bodies as local, international, political, and cultural. We write together as Kuwaiti's who face different privileges and oppressions simultaneously. Our collaboration allows us to reveal the multifaceted intersections of privilege and oppression. We begin with a discussion of intersectionality and whiteness, then demonstrating its connection to the performative. We offer three key moments of experiences as Kuwaiti women; how our bodies are disciplined through academia, how our bodies are disciplined through Kuwaitiness and masculinity, and how we can navigate privilege and oppression through Otherness. We conclude with departure points and future trajectories for practicing a transnational and collective Otherness through intersectionality.

INTERSECTIONALITY AND PERFORMATIVE WRITING

As we navigate privilege and oppression, we realize that intersectionality lies at the heart of these theorizations. Our experiences are products of interlocking patterns of racism, classism, and sexism (Crenshaw, 1991). One way in which to understand this is through the matrix of domination, a roadmap that assists us in understanding the power dynamics of intersectionality (Collins, 2000). This matrix allows us to understand the intersecting nature of privileges such as upper class, white, male, heterosexual, cisgender, and ability (Collins, 2000). First, these privileged positionalities work to keep those in marginalized identities in their place of marginalization (Collins, 2000). Second, these power dynamics circulate through a number of power domains (Collins, 2000). For instance, the hegemonic domain is where ideologies circulate to keep power moving at a higher but immaterial level (Collins, 2000). Additionally, the structural domain applies the laws and regulations that will keep marginalized identities in their place, while the disciplinary reinforces them through academia and so forth (Collins, 2000). Additionally, the interpersonal domain is where we see power at a micro level (Collins, 2000). We often ignore power at a micro level when it is cloaked in more power and oppression than imaginable. Many have voiced the agony that the micro can bring forward (Abdi, 2014; AlShammari, 2017; Calafell, 2007; Ghabra, 2015; Lemaster, 2014; Eguchi, 2014). Microaggressions are moments of contention, agony, and sites of erasure by hegemonic structures. These sites of erasure work to silence the micro when the macro becomes more visible. Often we can pinpoint moments of oppression and erasure by larger structures, for instance, the firing of faculty based on their political views. However, the micro often gets overlooked. It is in the everyday that we find the most painful moments of oppression.

For this reason, understanding how power works allows one to understand how the move against identity has also been a move against intersectionality. Intersectionality encourages alliance building (Ghabra & Calafell, 2017). Critics have voiced that intersectionality is inadequate (Hutchinson, 2001; Kwan, 2002; Puar, 2007), however, we argue that the attack against intersectionality is an attack on women of color. It is no coincidence that critics identify theories of intersectionality as inadequate they have been developed by women of color (May, 2015). Ideas that are from voices of privilege will seldom be critiqued. Thus, common sense will align with hegemonic norms (May, 2015). For this reason, theories developed by those in marginalized identities will be dismissed. Therefore, it is important to name both who is critiquing intersectionality and why they are critiquing it. Most often these critiques are largely the result of systems of power and whiteness. These critiques are also products of "violent ecologies" and "neoliberal institutions like the university" (King, 2015).

For this reason, we approach whiteness as a hegemonic force that we attempt to decolonize. We define whiteness as a "Historically embedded or contextual sociological category" and as the "History of group formation" (Alcoff, 2015, p. 22). Whiteness is not fixed and has varied meanings. As it seeps into other categorical identities, it is strategic (Wander, Martin, & Nakayama, 2002). By defining whiteness as strategic, we locate whiteness as an imperialist ideology that is able to adapt dependent on what will benefit its goals. For instance, the narrative of Muslim women as oppressed is beneficial for the project of whiteness to capitalize, economically, strategically, politically, and militarily in the Middle Eastern region. Whiteness is also relational (Frankenberg, 2001). In this context, we say "Muslim" because the reinforcement of global stereotypes of Middle Eastern women in the popular culture and the media is usually reinforced by labeling them as "Muslim." We argue, this relational dialectic will only put whiteness and other categories (gender, class, sexuality, ability, education) in a zero sum relationship. Extending this further, whiteness has become a parallel dimension to other privileged categories such as class privilege (Ghabra, 2018).

Applying this to our own privileges has allowed us to understand the narratives we are working against (Muslim women as oppressed) and what new narratives we can produce without reifying the Orientalist discourses that have confined Muslim women into one category. We recognize that there is oppression in our region, as well as globally, but our privileges never make it to the global narrative. If our privileges do make it to global narratives we have to perform whiteness and speak out in the name of Muslim women that are oppressed (Ghabra, 2018). In other words, we aim to highlight the axis of privilege and oppression of Middle Eastern Feminism both locally and transnationally as always in flux. We decenter the narrative of "Muslim women as oppressed" by performing our intersectional experiences as both collective and individual. There remains a lack of literature on Middle Eastern feminisms used as culturally specific rather than ethnocentric, without whiteness clouding the narrative. If intersectionality is hierarchical then it has failed. One category cannot be ranked higher than the other. Consequently, we urge for the international to not be erased. For instance, Ghabra and Calafell (2017) have argued that when a conversation in a U.S. classroom is about Third World women's oppression, the conversation suddenly shifts back to U.S. women's oppression. For this very reason, we insist on naming and marking our bodies as in flux, constantly adapting to privilege and oppression. Whiteness often privileges Muslim women's racialized bodies and narratives as static and as one. This Western patriarchal nature of whiteness reduces Muslim women to the position of oppressed and living in violence due to the hijab (Abu-Lughod, 2013; Ghabra, 2018). As Muslim women are stuck in discourses between both Eastern and Western patriarchies, there becomes a need to define the difference between white and Middle Eastern masculinity. First, masculinity in general, is an "excess" and is not static (Lemaster, 2014). Masculinity is enacted on Other bodies through the intersections of sex, class, religion, race, sexuality, higher education, and nationalism (Lemaster, 2014). In this chapter, we locate Middle Eastern masculinity as different but similar to white masculinity. It is similar in the way that masculinity is a global and imaginative positionality that is also hegemonic (Beasley, 2008). However, masculinities are multiple and are not equal as well (Beasley, 2008). For instance, the way I deal with white masculinity and Middle Eastern masculinity differs across the intersections of race and gender (Ghabra, 2015b). Middle Eastern masculinity is not cloaked behind "hegemonic civility" (Patton, 2004). This is due to the fact that hegemonic civility has overlays of whiteness. The act of performing "civility" is a way in which white masculinity works. On the other hand, Middle Eastern masculinity is more blatant. In Kuwait, this can range from silencing or interrupting women, disciplining them when they speak out, to marrying more than wife (even though this is uncommon). Taking this to the structural level, women cannot pass on the Kuwaiti nationality to their children or husbands ("Kuwait: Give women equal citizenship rights to men," n.d.). At the micro level, as professors, part of our jobs entails dealing with the microaggressions that women face from their brothers, fathers and husbands. Due to the fact that Kuwait is a collective society, masculinity remains controlling whether at the macro or micro level. For this reason, we define Middle Eastern masculinity as a deep-rooted collective and overted system of domination. It is more hidden in modernized and upper-class families as opposed to middle class and more tribal areas because in this context it becomes cloaked with whiteness. As women have become tools by both Western and Eastern patriarchies, we contend that whiteness and masculinity cannot be separated. Whiteness has also become a parallel dimension to the act of being *Hathari* (Modernized) and *Aseel* (Pure Kuwaiti). To act *Aseel* and *Hathari* is to perform white civility and it is for these very reasons that whiteness is both strategic and relational. This performance of whiteness means also performing ability. If one were to perform ability that includes performing accepted gender roles in a civil manner. Those of that have disabilities are not seen as modern or Kuwaiti enough and are further stigmatized through both whiteness and masculinity. For instance, a Kuwaiti women with a disability must still conform to both beauty and traditional femininity in order to not be stigmatized.

In these moments of *Aseelness*, Kuwaitiness and masculinity we use performative writing and more specifically autoethnography to guide our method. We define performative writing as a method that encompasses both autoethnography and poetry and one that reveals the intersectional nature of power in relation to dominant ideologies. Within performative writing, we allow the performative writing to take its course while undertaking the rhetorical process of deconstructing and analyzing hegemonic texts (Ghabra, 2018). As we enter into the performative, we define the performative as the performance of the emotive and pain in relation to power.

We argue that autoethnography is "messy, sometimes contradictory, sometimes complicated" (Boylorn, 2008). We also negotiate our bodies as marked in differing locations of social engagement (Eguchi, 2014). Through performative writing, we showcase our intersecting experiences individually to reveal how power structures and hegemony are at play. Additionally, we argue that performative writing needs to have a reflexive dimension.

Performative writing serves as a means to both rhetorically critique these power structures thus de-whitening the pervasive nature of whiteness. For instance through continuing critical cultural dialogues, one may reflect on the ways in which they embody ideologies as well as privileges and oppressions (Lemaster, 2018). For these very reasons, reflexivity needs to be both transnational and intersectional (Calafell and Ghabra, 2018). For example, through reflecting on moments of failures, we may be able to recognize moments of alliance building (Calafell and Ghabra, 2018).

Through writing, listening, and witnessing our pain and our students' voices, we establish the performative. As Steele (2000) argues "To witness means to decide to participate—not only with the head but with the heart—in the experience of another, an experience so painful that it must be shared in order to be confronted. Those in positions of power in our society have a tremendous ability to bring Others from pain to possibility. And the beginning lies in poetry, for poetry provides access to pain." Steele (2000) finds pedagogical value in reading the poetry of women writers who have written from the body and about the body. Poetry allows us room to tap into our memories, trauma, and attempt to explore the violence that is a part of our lives, not just as women, but men, children, and the larger society as a whole.

For this reason, we aim to locate how whiteness shifts geographically and advocate for the performance of whiteness and intersectionality as theoretical and methodological sites in which to locate tensions within Middle Eastern Transnational Feminism. As we weave in our voices together as one and as two, we aim to relate our experiences to transcultural pains. Like Ghabra (2015a), as we perform, we are performing onto this chapter, revealing the wounds, the pain and, the privileges that we have been carrying on our shoulders for years.

FROM INTERNATIONAL TO LOCAL AND LOCAL TO INTERNATIONAL: DISCIPLINING OUR BODIES THROUGH ACADEMIA

From NCA to the Classroom

As I (Haneen) hide behind my laptop, frantically typing away. I am typing away the pain and contestation that I have carried through my body both geographically and transnationally. My intersectional identities as a Kuwaiti female professor are constantly in flux as I navigate between Kuwait and the United States my entire life. Spatial and temporal boundaries remind me that location is another added tension to my ever-shifting identities. However, these boundaries have allowed me to nourish and embrace the ever-changing geographical adjustments of microaggressions that haunt my body on a daily basis. Like Anzaldúa (1981), I live in a "state of psychic unrest, in a Borderland" that constantly reminds me that this borderland is movable but temperamental and volatile. Anzaldúa (1981) defines the borderlands as "a vague and undetermined place created by the emotional residue of an unnatural boundary. It is in a constant state of transition" (p. 3). It never feels that the borderland is one specific place, instead it is in a liminal space. Anzaldúa allow us to envision our own borderlands, once that at times can provide peace and comfort in knowing that it is ok to be in an in-between space.

> To live in the Borderlands means to put chile in the borscht,
> eat whole wheat tortillas,
> speak Tex-Mex with a Brooklyn accent;
> be stopped by la migra at the border checkpoints. (Anzaldúa, 194)

To live in my borderland is to speak Kuwaiti-Palestinian with an American accent making my Arabic accent sound lighter. Can I live in-flux? Will I be chastised for being a child of the borderlands? I hide behind my laptop again and start typing. For this is where I can lay the anxieties of my borderlands to rest.

As I navigate privilege and oppression, I am reminded that being a women of color shifts geographically. The microaggressions differ and are not static. In the United States, I am the international woman with the accent, to some I am seen as less intelligent because my accent is not American enough. At times, it feels as if I am respected enough when in fact I have to do triple the work to be heard. Everytime someone introduces me as Dr. Ghabra, I want to say it's Dr. Haneen, we use first names in Kuwait but the problem with privilege and oppression lies in the inability for those that have privileges to even ask a transnational scholar what they use locally or how they pronounce their name. I stay silent in fear of alienating myself from my colleagues in the United States. I don't want to upset them because of our cultural nuances and intersectional differences. I am also tired of correcting everyone. I want to feel similar but at times I feel so different. My devotion to attending the conference and reconnecting with Others at NCA puts me in a constant state of disconnect. I feel a disconnect across continents. I am across borders. It feels so far even when I remain in touch and active within NCA. My geographic location somehow makes me feel unavailable and out of touch with my academic family. My location also makes me less intelligible, easier to disregard, and easier to silence. If you aren't from a country that is European or American, you are automatically deemed less intelligible. Kuwait, a Muslim country, would certainly not make it to the top of that list. These are the violent maskings of hegemony and whiteness. I have to succumb to whiteness. I have to adapt, and I have to learn everything the white American way.

Being a respondent at NCA feels like a battle. I remember the countless poster sessions I had to give feedback to as my role as a respondent at NCA. How dare I recommend to a white male or female student to cite anyone other than the white canon? How dare I recommend work by women of color or queer scholars? The violence in these moments was almost invisible to Others standing round, presenters turning away from me while I was speaking and welcoming a white professor who was also assigned as a respondent. I find myself going to the posters that doesn't have a bunch of American or white professors standing around, in fear of being sidelined and disciplined for being an international woman of color critiquing a white man. As soon as they see my name and my affiliation (Kuwait University) on my badge, the discomfort becomes highly visible. I am already marked by my brown body, marked again by my badge, and then again with my accent.

At one point a white young man decided it was okay to cut me off and disagree with me, so I cut him off and said, "Listen I am the respondent and you are the presenter why don't you listen to my feedback without cutting me off?" The invisibility and masking of these micro moments of whiteness are what make them so violent. My accent, brown body, international affiliation, and his white American masculinity perpetuates the intersections of domination.

Am I not worth your time?
Does my accent and brown skin offend you everytime?
Have I threatened your maleness with my femaleness?
Are you disappointed I am Kuwaiti and not catering to your U.S. Americanness?
Disciplining me with your body language, like unwanted baggage
Disciplining me with your whiteness and masculinity, controlling my femininity
I can see you. . . . Can you see me?
I can see through your true colors, sidelining me with the Others
You see nothing, I see something
You see nothing, I see oppression, pain and heartache . . .
While you hide behind your mask of nonaggression, I see repression...
I see a mistake. That I did not speak back to you. . .
But . . .
I do speak back . . . Now you see me. . .
You see the angry woman of color. . . . You see the irrational scholar
And I still see you. . .
but you still see nothing because you will never see past your privilege.

As I aim to name the oppressive conditions that discipline my body on a daily basis, I am reminded of the complexities of speaking back.

"Naming oppressive realities, in and of itself, has not brought about the kinds of changes for oppressed groups that it can for more privileged groups, who command a different quality of attention" (hooks, 1984, p. 75).

Localizing Disability from the United Kingdom to Kuwait

As an assistant professor of English literature, I (Shahd) am the youngest woman in my predominantly white (English) department. On the outside, I look like a fully able-bodied woman, one who has managed to overcome any oppressions. One who is privileged enough to be able to teach at an undergraduate private university. But that is only part of the story. I received my PhD at the age of twenty-eight. Ten years before that, at the age of eighteen, I was diagnosed with a disabling neurological disorder: Multiple Sclerosis (MS). At that fragile and young age, my male neurologist informed me that I would have fewer years to live, and that I would not make it past the age of thirty. A fatal blow. Youth was not an available option for me, and neither was academia. I remember my undergraduate years as years of pleasure and pain, distress and disharmony, and a desire to graduate only so that I could say I attended university. A few years later, I was on my way to the United Kingdom for graduate school. I went to England primarily because a degree at a U.S. school would have cost me many more years—time, which I did not have. I had a clock ticking behind me, reminding me of my mortality, my functionality, and that my quality of life would be deeply embedded in my body's deterioration. Upon starting my PhD, my supervisor, Stella Bolaki, introduced me to Disability Studies. Disability Studies was a field I had never heard of. I asked her how Disability Studies could exist in a world that was ableist. I didn't even know the term "ableist" at that time. I had brought my baggage of a shamed body with me. A burdened and heavy body. Disability Studies was unheard of in Kuwait and the Middle East. "Disability" was not a term to be thrown around—there was nothing popular about disability. Disability is still seen as tragic, a curse, and in a collectivist society, it does not represent the individual but rather the family and/or tribe. By the time I was halfway done, I was training myself in Disability Studies rhetoric. Doors opened for me, and I was welcomed into the world of academic scholarship. Still, I am constantly navigating new ways of performing my identity as a disabled scholar, while dealing with microaggressions in the workplace and society at large.

Teaching for me resembles a war zone. Bodies everywhere. I look around me and I think to myself, how can I navigate the classroom today? The crowded halls? Can I walk to class without tripping? Without losing my balance? I am always on alert, always waiting to see when the next attack will come, and who and where the next shot will come from. As Brune and Wilson (2013) note, "nearly all disabled people confront, often routinely, the choice of hiding their disability or drawing attention to it and the question of what to do when others overlook it. Going to the root of a disability identity, their decisions weigh issues of stigma, pride, prejudice, discrimination, and privilege but rarely put the matter to rest" (p. 1).

Because of my doctorate degree, I was perceived as someone to respect. I moved between male-dominated spaces and women-only spaces. I found a sense of strength in that ability to move fluidly between the segregated spaces. This remained the case until one day my leg was dysfunctional and my movement was affected, again. I had to use a cane at university and walk around the hallways with my cane gripped tightly. At that moment, the dean at the time saw me hobbling along and made a comment about how women should not be spoiled. To him, women acting as "princesses" and too weak meant being spoiled. The following narratives highlights the distinction between being "tough" and being a "princess."

"It does not suit you Diktoorah! You know better than to be spoiled! Toughen up!"

The words fired at me and burnt deep into my skin. I felt a surge of tears threatening to humiliate me. No more humiliation. Don't cry, don't cry. Everyone is looking. The students heard him, the administrative assistant heard him. I have to keep it together. Get to your office, hide inside your office.

I was disciplined because I had failed to perform ideal femininity. Women did not hobble. At that moment, I realized that while I was privileged to be a Kuwaiti PhD holder, I was still a woman living with a disability that would not always be concealed and that there would be someone constantly waiting to put me back in place, to remind me of my position of inferiority. I was striving to reach an inaccessible state of being. A place of acceptance and belonging that I could not find. However, being that I had intersecting privileges of being both Kuwaiti and a PhD holder, I knew that I had to create a safe space for Other students that needed the support. Calafell (2007) states, "I'm walking through all of these people .talking about Otherness in the experiences of faculty of color, but I think it is time for me to ground some of this in my experience and my body. Where do I begin? Teaching? Research? Service?" (p. 428). Feeling the heaviness of my failing body, I recognized the potential to liberate myself and Others through teaching and research. I had to give back where I could.

Masculinity and Kuwaitiness: "Inti Mu Aseela"

I (Haneen) am reminded that the way I encounter Middle Eastern masculinity and Kuwaitiness in educational settings and it certainly differs from white masculinity. Kuwaiti masculinity is certainly not hidden. I remember my students who suddenly don't show up to community service because their husbands or father's won't allow them. I remember the controlling nature of masculinity when I had to speak to my student's father to allow her to attend to a community service session or the student that dropped out of university the last week of the semester because her father didn't want her to attend university anymore. I am upset at defending my culture against white imperialism, while I see my own flesh and blood being wounded by masculinity.

I want to take everything I said back. I remember how three of my female students want to remove their hijab but can't because their parents would not allow it. However, I also am reminded of my students who wear the hijab in order to deflect the male gaze. White masculinity appears to be more progressive on the surface level, more accepting of minorities and marginalized groups, especially when appearing in pop culture and other communication mediums. However, I don't remember being treated any better when encountering white masculinity. Instead, I remember feeling threatened because of my gender, my race, and certainly my religion (Ghabra, 2015b). However, Kuwaiti masculinity hurts so much more because it's closer to home, it's my blood. I spend all year writing and speaking out against stereotypes of Middle Eastern masculinity only to regret it when they oppress me. I regret it when I have to find a way to support my female students who can't come to class one day because her father was having a bad day and didn't want to drive her to university.

I have been trained and educated in the United States, my body is a product of colonization but it is also a privilege of mobility. My Kuwaiti nationality allows me to travel worldwide making it easier; however, my nationality (being from a Muslim country) also hinders me subjecting me to hours and hours of investigations at local airports in the United States. My English is also a product of colonization. However, I teach in a government university with Kuwaiti professors with exception to one Jordanian. I have to translate everything into Arabic for my students. I have to teach myself the terminology that I learned in the United States while decolonizing the canonical literature. I navigate between speaking Palestinian, Kuwaiti, and English but am chastised if I mix any of the three together. I am reminded that this chastising lies at the intersections of masculinity and Kuwaitiness. Like Shahd, I also live in a war zone. My body is torn between being visibly seen as Iranian, Palestinian, or a foreigner. I certainly don't look Kuwaiti, I am too light skinned. The combination of my Kuwaiti and Palestinian accent does not sound right to people. This is where the war begins. Tearing me apart, creating an unsettling feeling that can never settle because society needs to put me in a purity box. I make sure I speak Kuwaiti really loudly when in public. Usually people stop for a second confused and baffled thinking who is this foreigner speaking Kuwaiti? If they really focus on my dialect they can hear the Palestinian overlays clouding my Kuwaitiness. That's when the questions start. Are you Iranian? Oh no you must be from Bahrain because you have this accent clouding your Kuwaiti words. I reply, "I am Kuwaiti" but you aren't speaking pure Kuwaiti. I reply again, "Can you explain to me what pure means?"

Similarly, if I speak Palestinian to Palestinians I am stigmatized for throwing in Kuwaiti or English words. I am too Kuwaiti to be worthy of being

Palestinian. How dare I say I am Kuwaiti and ignore my roots? How dare I say I am Kuwaiti without saying I am originally Palestinian? I am disciplined on a daily basis through my body, my skin color, and my accent. The war zone continues. The battle inside me tears me apart, exhausts me. My language, my dialect, and my body is chastised in multiple ways, but it doesn't end there.

I teach approximately 200 students a semester and desperately want to translate all the material that I had learned while studying in the United States into booklets written in Arabic. I never knew that navigating between three dialects/language would prove to be both exhausting and one of the most painful and violent spaces of un/belonging, even among my students at time. However, in my media and society class I bring in a week about language and how it can be a method of control. This both explains to the student that language can be a way of oppressing someone and somehow lays some of my anxieties to ease. One day during office hours, two of my favorite students came into my office with the booklet that I had made them. The booklet that I have spent endless nights trying to translate, the booklet that gave me nightly migraines because Arabic was much harder to write for me then English. One of the students said, "Dr. Haneen I wrote a list of all of your *Badliyat* for you." For a second, I thought that he meant all the times I got tongue-tied while lecturing and laughed about it or had a slip of a tongue so I laughed and said, "Okay, show me." So he started reading a long list of words. Two out of these long lists were funny, the rest were all Palestinian words. I was stunned. I went silent. My own student was disciplining me through both masculinity, Kuwaitiness, and language. I looked at him and said, "Do you know that this is a Palestinian word?" He responded, "No it's not." I looked at him and said, "Do you remember what we talked about in class, about language and privilege?" He refused to acknowledge and kept insisting that my words were all wrong even though he didn't speak Palestinian. His masculinity allowed him a free pass to keep refuting my answers. His masculinity and Kuwaitiness allowed him the privilege of telling me all my Palestinianness was wrong; how dare I say those words in class, let alone in Kuwait? I gave him a lecture about privilege. However, this talk haunted me throughout the rest of the semester as he sat every day in the first seat, I could see his eyes glisten everytime I said a Palestinian word. I could see it in his eyes, he didn't have to say anything. Being *mu aseela* means we aren't pure Kuwaiti. Kuwaitiness is equated with whiteness, the act of being pure is a worldwide phenomenon; it just manifests differently from country to country. However, it is in these moments of disciplining that we find spaces of resistance.

My pain is like an open wound,
never able to heal

Privilege peels away the layers until they get deeper, concealing the wound . . . no one can see it.

no one can see my oppression . . . bleeding deeper and deeper..

I become a dreamer . . . Dreaming of those days when we would all be aware of our privileges.

Trying to heal those wounds, but everytime I heal them I am reminded that open wounds can

never heal unless we have Collective allyship. Collective reflexivity and

collective souls

Deviancy and Teaching

Living in a body that is marked as deviant and unfeminine, unpredictable, and at times, dangerous, is an act of transgression. Able-bodiedness functions as a place of whiteness, a place of purity, and a place for healthy individuals to exist. As a Kuwaiti Bedouin woman, I am a hybrid (my mother is Palestinian and my father is Kuwaiti Bedouin). I come from a tribal background and I have always lived in in-between spaces. Not far from Gloria Anzaldúa's (1981) space for the *mestiza*, this space is a place of crossing borders and boundaries. It started off for me as a linguistic and cultural crossing of boundaries, of blending a new language, one that navigates between Kuwaiti and Palestinian, but adds English as a crossing bridge in-between. Culturally, my two backgrounds have always been at odds: one liberating, the other conservative, and at times, oppressing. The tribe relies heavily on disciplining bodies—both women and men's bodies represent the tribe, the family lineage, and to deviate from the norm puts you at risk of shaming the tribe. Bodies that are deviant are shamed, hidden, concealed—not spoken about, unheard of, and remain out of sight. Disability then taints the family's (and by extension, the tribe's) image of purity, health, and *Aseelness*. Disease is a symptom of unhealthy blood, quite literally, blood that is tainted, impure, mixed, the result of an unknown cause. The ideal female body is challenged while the disabled female body calls attention to itself, demands to be heard and seen. As such, I have always felt deviant, simply living in this body, simply holding a cane in public and this has extended to the classroom and my presence in academia.

Teaching is an act of transgression in my case because this is not what white (Kuwaiti) ableist academia looks like, and even more so, is occupying different spaces of identity all at once. I am reminded of bell hooks' *Teaching to Transgress: Education as the Practice of Freedom.* hooks (1994) contends that education is a place of possibility and we have "the opportunity to labor for freedom, to demand of ourselves and our comrades, an openness of mind and heart that allows us to face reality even as we collectively imagine ways to move beyond boundaries, to transgress" (p. 206). Having felt so stigmatized against and ostracized throughout my life and my journey with my life partner (MS is my life partner, always there, part of my experience of the world), I have felt unwelcomed in most spaces. Academia was no exception. Academic ableism is very real, it seeps through the everyday microaggressions that are unseen by the naked eye. Stairs that are narrow, elevators that are too far from my classes, doors that are heavy and need to be pushed with full-body force, papers to squint at and mark—these are just a few of my favorite things of academic ableism.

"You look sick, Shahd. You don't look well. You are way too young to look this burnt out! Be happy. . . . Or maybe some more makeup?"

"I'm fine, really! Thanks for asking!" I respond, for the fifth time this month. And there are still thirteen more weeks to go in the semester.

"I am worried about you. All of us are. You are the youngest one here!"

I know they all care. I know they have made my declining health their concern. But I am reminded that I am failing to look healthy, fresh, young. Is it the dark circles under my eyes I can't seem to hide? My eye muscles are failing so my eyelids are drooping—there is no way around it, my neurologist tells me.

I have tried wearing the eyeglasses, the sunglasses, the face that smiles. . . . Nothing works. Nothing stops the invasive comments. Young female academics are to look good. Sick is not an option.

Academic ableism is regarded as a nonissue in most universities. You will not be discriminated against, you will still get the job. But you will be reminded every day of how this is a privilege for someone like you. So, I hide my body and my presence, I run to my office, pick up my books, hoping that I won't lose my grip on them. The classroom is my only hope, the only place I can transgress these boundaries of health and disability.

In the classroom, I am not afraid of being kicked out of academia. I do not fear failing. I have studied, I know the material. I am the expert on this subject. My teaching philosophy begins with my desire to incorporate pedagogical practices of love and vulnerability. I will not pretend to be wholly privileged or a complete being. I consider the multiple ways in which academia and teaching has helped me navigate society. I am reminded of Calafell and Chuang's (2018) work on moving into the classroom through a love politics, expanding the self to move to the "we" Calafell states that "As instructors of color, both domestic and international, we make ourselves vulnerable by simply setting foot into predominantly White universities" (p. 111). I would build on this vulnerability by emphasizing that as women of color who are hybrids, of mixed race, and living with a disability, vulnerability is heightened. There is almost no way out. The only way out is through the class in which a process of transformative love takes place. I reveal to my students my disability and my Otherness in the department as well as a society that demands healthy able-bodied women. Calafell (2018) calls this process "modeling" and highlights that by modeling we create "moments of symmetry, connection, and possibility" (p. 111). Because of my openness and vulnerability, I am able to reach out to students who feel Othered by their peers and the larger social circle. I am aware that the students I teach are more privileged than students at public institutions and some of them see me as the non-pure Kuwaiti disabled academic, and at times, I can see smirks on these faces, while on Others I see a flicker of hope. A silver lining. I hold on to that silver lining for a living.

SAFE SPACES: NAVIGATING PRIVILEGE AND OPPRESSION

Speaking "With" and Within the Classroom

As I hold onto Shahd's silver lining, that our students provide us. I am reminded of the privileged space I have as a professor. A space that I have to use to both protect myself and my students. Sometimes, I replay incidents in my head. If this student disciplined me with my masculinity, at least I might be able to silence him back with my academic privilege. My classroom, my rules, my office, my rules. If he wants to discipline me, I can also discipline him back but I remind myself not to respond with my privileges because this would be reenacting the cycle of violence. However, there are tensions that occupy spaces of privilege and oppression. For to use my privilege sometimes can create a safe space for Othered students. In Kuwait, certain marginalized identities get swept under the rug. Not only can we not speak about some of these identities, but it becomes a whole different ball game about how to create a safe space for unspoken identities while staying within the boundaries of the law. What is this Otherness? What can we speak about? What are you the reader understanding and what am I the writer trying to do here? I am obligated to give them a voice, my privilege owes them silence, secrecy, and security. We need to advocate for them behind closed doors. How can we work from within the closet and instead create spaces of allyship? More importantly, we need to protect ourselves while protecting our Other students. It's a whole different spectrum of privilege and oppression.

Most classes at Kuwait University are segregated. On the last day of class, my male students had their final presentations. I was constantly worried in this class because I had a number of Otherized students and was extremely protective of them in this hypermasculine classroom of about forty-five men. One of these students came to me before class, he was worried that someone would laugh at him while he was presenting because he didn't fit the role of hypermasculinity. I told him not to worry because it was the right thing to say. However, I was anxious. How would I protect him, what if something horrible happened? What if I defended him and someone filed a complaint against me? This is yet another complication of the intersections of privilege and oppression. I strategized as if I was preparing for a final exam. I absolutely could not let down my student who felt and voiced to me that I was his safe space in a culture where these issues go unspoken. It was their time to present and the students walked to the front of the room. I immediately felt the shift in the chairs, I felt the tension in the air. It made me angry and furious, all the privilege and oppression lessons and I could feel the discrimination in the room. It was like a bad energy flowing around the classroom. I got up and went to the front side of the classroom and stood there the whole twenty minutes while the group presented. I made sure that I stared at the young man who refused to watch the presentation because he wasn't watching because this student didn't fit his perception of masculinity. He understood and started paying attention. I made sure I stared at every single student the whole entire twenty minutes. I watched like a hawk, waiting for someone to flinch, move, smirk, or laugh. But they couldn't. My privilege wouldn't allow them.

These are not the only incidents where I have had to create safe spaces. I have found myself desperately trying to navigate the rigid boundaries of a university that barely provides the right facilities for my disabled students. When the university refused to change my theater-style classroom because my disabled student who was in a wheelchair could only sit near the door, I shifted the classroom to the top of the classroom. When this very same student was giving D's by other professors, my privilege allowed me the flexibility of registering her with professors that were "okay" and not fearful of her disability. I had to navigate the system in a way that felt like bending the rules. However, these are the side effects of neoliberalism, marginalized identities are already excluded from the system. For this reason we need to find ways to include them in the system through our own privileges. I often ask myself, how do I navigate these spaces with my students? How do I assure my *munaqabat (wearing a face veil)* students are safe in my classroom and that I won't discriminate against them with my unhijab modern-looking privileged body? For instance, when my *Bidoon* students inform me that they are stateless, it is my ethical responsibility and privilege not to share with Other students or professors their status. There is a sense of mutual trust that needs to be developed. Often I am in situations where I can help them navigate the system; however, I need to remind myself that I have the privilege of mobility while some of them cannot leave the country. These are the violent tensions of race, politics, and intersectionality. It creates new layers of intercultural communication that causes more difficult spaces to navigate. Speaking "with" and not "for" (Alcoff, 1991). Protecting but not speaking "for" but instead "with."

It is in these moments that we can use our privileges to create safe spaces for Others. For silence is oppression, Silence is an invisible killer. To not use your privilege is to be an enemy, not an ally. A warzone means fighting battles that aren't even ours. It means fighting battles with marginalized groups even when we don't share the same oppression. It means creating safe spaces for all of our students. This is the beauty of teaching. This is the beauty of allyship.

Bridging the Gap and Witnessing Pain

The classroom for me functions as a space filled with tensions, the undoing of microaggressions, and holds within that very space the potential for healing and transformation. We (the students and myself) come to the classroom with preconceived notions of the Other. We start the semester by tiptoeing around each other, unsure of this definition that I have proposed: safe space. A place where microaggressions are not to take place. A place of affirmation of voices and selves that are struggling to make sense of both privilege and oppression. My first thought is what does my position as an academic, a mentor, a teacher leading the class entail? I recognize my privileges within this space and the power that comes along with my position. All those who are in a position of power also hold the power to witness. My work has been invested in witnessing my students' journeys from the margins of their own lives to the center of their own lives. Silence is so pervasive, so common, so encoded within our genes. Speech in itself is an act of rebellion, a daring act, a form of intercultural communication that involves the intersections of race privilege and oppression. My teaching is, I have always felt, is embodied activism. I speak from my body as a Kuwaiti academic, one who lives with a disability, day in and day out, and performs ableism to navigate a patriarchal and able-bodied world. There is little room for me anywhere. I squirm and squiggle in to narratives, and by extension, bring my students along for the ride. I witness their transformations from silence and trauma to survival and a reclaiming of a voice. That voice is also mine. That voice is also theirs. It becomes a voice that is shaped by a politics of love, a politics of mentorship, guidance, and a desire to bear witness to their lives. That is allyship for me. I believe that "to be present, to exist, is to heal" (Alshammari, 2017, p. 64). This politics of love is reminiscent of Calafell's (2007) vision of mentorship as love. For example, when we look at Sylvia Plath's poetry, a white author who seems so distant from my Arab students, I need to contextualize and make the text familiar. I need to find bridges between Plath's struggles and their own. While Plath suffered from mental illness and a suffocating environment, her experiences are altogether different from nonwhite students and women of color. But the universal aspect of trauma and pain inflicted by patriarchal values and white masculinity remains a dominant theme.

Aggressive responses in class such as, "But she's a white woman! She's different!" don't startle me anymore. I remain calm in the face of anger, for to be a mentor, a guide, is to help walk through the darkness of the damaging effects of whiteness and masculinity. Similarities are diminished when we think of us versus them. To break through these boundaries and dismantle white hegemony is a long process that requires the desire to feel the pain of Othered bodies, to think critically about responses and where they come from, and to help find a new language to express pain. We must walk in this journey together. I urge my students to think about voice and agency. Who gets to speak and are they listened to when they do speak? What makes Plath's experiences different from their own Kuwaiti experiences? I localize these experiences and ask them to think about a bridge, a bridge of common experiences. Rather than highlight the differences (which they see so clearly), I want to foster a sense of connection to humanity and even more specifically to women's experience worldwide. It in this process of connecting through intercultural communication that we bear witness to each other's pain and testimonies of silent traumas. And the relationship is one of witnessing. I bear witness to their journeys, and silently, unknowingly, they do the same for me. I exist with every utterance, every speech act, every poem that is read in class. The words, the language, the inspired eyes that look back at me affirms my presence in the world and takes me away from bodily pain. My disability begins to fade into my peripheral vision.

Future Trajectories: An Intersectional Transnationalism

As we come together as academics that occupy spaces of privilege, our PhD's may grant us the power to create safe spaces and sometimes forget about our oppressions. However, our marginalized students have the power to teach us far beyond what a degree could offer anyone. Away from the structure of administrative chaos and oppression and away from the messiness of human relationships and microaggressions, our students are our teachers. We inhabit a collective borderland, one in which we can use our privileges to create safe spaces for our Otherized students.

Our students gifted us the experience of shared pain, shared agony, shared heartache. The pain rips away at our souls, tearing us apart, ripping us away from power structures. We navigate with our oppressed identities but the pain intensifies when we try to create safe spaces. We our prisoners of our own spaces, prisoners of a hegemonic system that forces us to navigate oppression while protecting our own marginalized students. The emotional labor tears at us both physically and emotionally but that labor is the only way we can resist microaggressions. We have the privilege of deciding when to put our bodies on the line. What risks do we take? But when we remind ourselves how oppression feels, the act of putting our bodies on the line becomes an act of resistance stemmed out of pain. Privilege is powerful, dark, and domineering. Privilege is also oppressive. The pain of protecting our students and ourselves remains an everyday battle. These acts of resistance when putting our bodies on the line are a form of intersectionality. For without advocating for the body as a means of communication, we fail to theorize from the flesh. Intercultural communication when looked at transnationally has many layers and tensions to unravel. For this reason, we advocate for an *intersectional transnationalism*. An *intersectional transnationalism* is one that locates privilege and oppression across borders. Constantly in flux an *intersectional transnationalism* adapts both locally and globally. One's privileges and oppressions are tensions that constantly fluctuate. For this reason, intercultural communication needs to allow space for reflexivity and awareness of geographical shiftings in privilege and oppression. Privilege and oppression is never static, it shifts from hour to hour, day to day, country to country, and region to region. By locating race, whiteness, intersectionality as constantly evolving, oppressing and being oppressed one may be able to theorize a more nuanced form of de-whitening intersectionality.

As we aim to introduce Other formations of intersectional identities, our Kuwaitiness marks our bodies in certain ways. Being women, academics, Kuwaiti and Palestinian, we seem similar but our identities overlap and are fraught with tensions of the body, language, and oppression. For instance, being at different institutions in the same country marks our privileges and oppressions as disparate and allows us room to reflect on new forms of a power praxis. For this reason, we advocate for both individual and collective experiences.

We are one but we are many. We are individuals but we are collective. Our oppressions are collective but our embodied experiences are disjointed. Our pain manifests in different ways both locally and globally, dispersed through various intersections. It is through the recollection of these parts that we become whole. It is through intersectionality that we combat erasure. It is through intersectionality that we measure the unsurmountable effects of microaggressions. The invisibility of our identities is crystallized through moments of allyship to decolonize whiteness. Thus, *we* extend this chapter to rupture the clouds of hegemonic forces and hope that our *we* extends into a transnational *we*.

REFERENCES

Abdi, S. (2014). Staying I(ra)n: Narrating queer identity from within the Persian closet. *Liminalities: A Journal of Performance Studies*, *10*(1), 1–20.

Abu-Lughod, L. (2013). *Do Muslim women need saving*. Boston: Harvard University Press.

Alcoff, L. (1991). The problem of speaking for others. *Cultural Critique*, *20*, 5–32.

Alcoff, L. (2015). *The future of whiteness*. Malden: Polity.

AlShammari, S. (2017a). A hybridized academic identity: Negotiating a disability within academia's discourse of ableism. In S. Kerschbaum, L. Eisenman, & J. Jones (Eds.), *Negotiating disability: Disclosure and higher education* (pp. 25–38). Ann Arbor, MI: University of Michigan Press.

AlShammari, S. (2017b). Alshammari, Shahd. Troubling Academe. *Journal of Middle East Women's Studies, 13*(3), 458–60.

AlShammari, S. (2018). Writing an illness narrative and negotiating identity: A Kuwaiti academic/author's journey. *Life Writing*, *16*(3), 431–38.

Anzaldúa, G. (1981). *Borderlands: The New Mestiza = La Frontera*. San Francisco: Spinsters/Aunt Lute.

Beasley, C. (2008). Rethinking hegemonic masculinity in a globalizing world. *Men and Masculinities*, *11*(1), 86–103.

Boylorn, R. (2008). As seen on TV: An autoethnographic reflection on race and reality television. *Critical Studies in Media Communication*, *25*(4), 413–33.

Brune, J., & Wilson, D. (1-12). Introduction. In J. Brune & D. Wilson (Eds.), *Disability and passing: Blurring the lines of identity*. Philadelphia: Temple University Press.

Calafell, B. (2005). Pro(re-)claiming loss: A performance pilgrimage in search of Malintzin Tenépal. *Text and Performance Quarterly*, *25*(1), 43–56.

Calafell, B. (2007). Mentoring and love: An open letter. *Cultural Studies ↔ Critical Methodologies, 7*(4), 425–41.

Calafell, B. & Kai-Chun Chuang, A. (2018). From me to we: Embracing the coperformative witnessing and critical love in the classroom. *Communication Education*, *67*(1), 109–14.

Chesebro, J. & Fuse, K. (2001). The development of a perceived masculinity scale. *Communication Quarterly*, *49*(3), 203–78.

Collins, P. H. (2000). *Black feminist thought: Knowledge, consciousness, and the politics of empowerment*. New York: Routledge.

Crenshaw, K. (1991). Mapping the margins: Intersectionality, identity politics, and violence against women of color. *Stanford Law Review*, *43*(6), 1241–99.

Eguchi, S. (2009). Negotiating hegemonic masculinity: The rhetorical strategy of '"straight-acting"' among gay men. *Journal of Intercultural Communication Research*, *38*(3), 193–209.

Eguchi, S. (2014). Disidentifications from the west(ern): An autoethnography of becoming an other. *Cultural Studies ↔ Critical Methodologies*, *14*(3), 279–85.

Frankenberg, R. (2001). The mirage of an unmarked whiteness. In B. Rasmussen, I. Nexica, & E. Klinenberg (Eds.), *The making and unmaking of whiteness* (pp. 72–96). Durham: Duke University Press.

Ghabra, H. (2018). *Muslim women and white femininity: Reenactment and resistance*. New York: Peter Lang.

Ghabra, H. & Calafell, B. (2017). From failure and allyship to feminist solidarities: Negotiating our privileges and oppressions across borders. *Text and Performance Quaterly*, *38*(1/2), 38–54.

Ghabra, H. S. (2015a). Disrupting privileged and oppressed spaces: Reflecting ethically on my arabness through feminist autoethnography. *Kaleidoscope: A Graduate Journal of Qualitative Communication Research*, *14*, 1–16.

Ghabra, H. S. (2015b). Through my own gaze: An arab feminist gaze, struggling with patriarchal arabness through western hegemony. *Liminalities: A Journal of Performance Studies*, *11*(5), 1–16.

hooks, B. (1984). *Feminist theory: From margin to center*. Boston: South End Press.

hooks, B. (1994). *Teaching to transgress: Education as the practice of freedom*. New York: Routledge Press.

Hutchinson, D. (1999). Rights for gay whites: Race, sexual identity, and equal protection discourse. *Cornell Law Review*, *85*(5), 1358–91.

King, T. (2015). Post-indentitarian and post-intersectional anxiety in the neoliberal corporate university. *Feminist Formations*, *277*(3), 114–38.

Kuwait: Give women equal citizenship rights to men. (n.d.). Retrieved from Equality Now website: https://www.equalitynow.org/kuwait_give_women_equal_citizenship_rights_to_men.

Kwan, P. (2002). The metaphysics of metaphors: Symbiosis and the quest for meaning. *UMKC Law Review, 71*(2), 325–30.

Lemaster, B. (2014). Telling multiracial tales: An autoethnography of coming out home. *Qualitative Inquiry*, *20*(1), 51–60.

Lemaster, B. (2018). Embracing failure: Improvisational performance as critical intercultural praxis. *Liminalities: A Journal of Performance Studies*, *14*(4), 1–21.

Patton, T. O. (2004). In the guide of civility: The complicitous maintenance of inferential forms of sexism and racism in higher education. *Women's Studies in Communication, 27*(1), 60–87.

Puar, J. (2007). *Terrorist assemblages*. Durham: Duke University Press.

Strasser, D. (2016). "You might want to call your father": An autoethnographic account of masculinity, relationships, and my father. *Journal of Family Communication*, *16*(1), 64–75.

Wander, P., Martin, J., & Nakayama, T. (2002). The roots of racial classification. In P. Rothenberg (Ed.), *White privilege: Essential readings on the other side of racism* (p. 34). New York: Worth, Print.

Yep, G. (2003). The violence of heteronormativity in communication studies: Notes on injury, healing and queer world-making. *Journal of Homosexuality*, *45*, 11–59.

Section III

TRANSNATIONAL CIRCUMFERENCES

Chapter 11

Remembering Julia de Burgos

Faithful Witnessing as Decolonial Feminist Performance

Sara Baugh-Harris

INTRODUCTION

As the lights come up, two women appear on stage. The backdrop is comprised of alternate panels, some panels painted black with white scribbled lines and cursive text, difficult to decipher from the audience. The effect is frantic, manic. Between these panels, there is another, painted in vibrant blues, oranges, and reds, which blends into the scene painted on the stage floor: the colors appear to move, creating a depiction of flowing water. On stage right, there is a window box, draped with a painted representation of the Puerto Rican flag. At the top of stage left, there is a wooden desk, with old, weathered books piled precariously high. There is paper and a pen on the center of the desk, turned just slightly to the right as if one were to begin writing. Next to the desk, one of the women sits, slightly bent over, clutching her white shawl to her body almost as if in pain. Wearing a tan, simple dress, her dark hair is parted in the center, pulled tightly back into a bun. It is Julia de Burgos. She looks to stage right, her body and face tense, as if in frightened anticipation of the other woman. The second woman is standing in the background, speaking even before the lights are up. In contrast to Julia, the woman's dark hair is free, flowing down her shoulders. She is garbed all in white, in a casual dress which drapes almost to her feet. Where Julia is hunched, hiding, this woman stands erect. Her voice is clear, and as the scene progresses, she moves toward Julia as if to emphasize each line. This character is the WOMAN (Davidranauth, 2014a, 00:06).[1]

The above scene opens Act II in Carmen Rivera's play *Julia de Burgos: Child of Water.* Rivera (1998) describes the WOMAN as "Julia's Soul" in the character list (p. 4). Within this production, the WOMAN is portrayed as an alter ego of poet Julia de Burgos, one whom Gloria Waldman (1998) describes as the "Soul, who embodies the artist, the fighter, the champion of personal and political freedom" (p. xi). This is evident as the scene progresses; the audience witnesses the WOMAN performing the poem "A Julia de Burgos," or what Waldman (1998) describes as Burgos's "Latin American feminist anthem" (p. xii). As WOMAN performs the poem, she speaks angrily at/to Julia's character. This scene, which encompasses Julia's angry reaction, illuminates the embodied materiality of Burgos's struggle to overcome oppression by theorizing a decolonial imaginary through her poetry. Indeed, Rivera's (1998) explicit script direction that WOMAN "must NOT appear like a Soul but as a regular person" (p. 4) is significant, for Burgos's struggle must be fought from and through the body.

This scene is also significant because it serves as a unique commemoration of Burgos's life and work through performance. Whereas public memory projects hinge upon, in Nora's (1992) terms, a "notion produced, defined, established, constructed, decreed, and maintained by the artifice and desire of a society fundamentally absorbed by its own transformation and renewal" (p. 6), Rivera's play is something entirely outside of those bounds. In an epigraph to the play, Torres Barreto (1998) describes the play as an act of "witnessing." She writes that Rivera has tapped into Burgos, as Rivera honors Burgos in a "truly genuine and sensitive way. Rivera not only gives us the space to discover Burgos, but also offers us the sacred space to discover the dualities within ourselves." Rivera, as a writer and playwright, has worked toward this goal in numerous projects. Yet, her tribute to Burgos is significant because it works against the ways in which public memory projects typically appropriate marginalized icons, often merely tying into intersectionality as a buzzword concept by melding narratives to fit nostalgic or nationalistic ideals. In reflecting on the goal of this edited collection to examine and imagine a political space beyond the white appropriation of intersectionality, often under the veil of inclusion, I argue Rivera's commemoration project of Burgos offers important insight into the ways in which colonized women of color understand and resist dominant regimes. Importantly, by bearing witness through her craft, Rivera creates characters who embody Burgos's difficulty in constructing compatible identities in a body too often silenced and erased in the space of dual colonialism (López Springfield, 1994).

Rivera's goals in the play are both deeply personal and political. In a second epigraph to the play, Ramírez describes Rivera's play as "an antidote for an apathetic nostalgic gaze for Puerto Rico's past." Touching on Burgos's inability to locate a space of belonging, Ramírez (1998) continues, "In *Child of Water*, the iconic poet Julia de Burgos is caught in an intermediary state of longing for and longing to; attempting to recreate what was, while attempting to break free and establish a new, politically engaged and self-actualized identity." This reading of Burgos is compatible with Rivera's own agenda and the ways in which Rivera herself has navigated her positionalities as a Puerto Rican woman living in New York. Narrative is integral to this navigation. In an interview, Rivera discusses how the role of writers in preserving memories of the Puerto Rican diaspora is critical because "we are adding to the narrative . . . We are also taking back our narrative . . . Society is telling you who you are. It is telling you who is significant and who is not. People internalize these messages. By exploring our experience, we are redefining our culture. We are affirming and declaring who we are" (Acevedo, 2015). It is the negotiation of defining and declaring an identity, despite a hegemonic narrative, which draws me to Rivera's play. In it, I see veins of memory creation which both are influenced by and bear witness to Julia de Burgos's violent, embodied struggle within a nexus of oppression as a poor Puertorriqueña, constantly read as excessive due to her sexuality, her race, and her rejection of colonial mores.

Performance is critical in understanding Burgos's struggle. In her investigation of the breadth of Burgos's legacy among writers, Pérez Rosario (2014) contrasts "lifeless statues" and other public projects with the liberatory possibilities of narrative, poetry, and performance (p. 107). These commemorations, tributes, and critical reflections are inherently connected to these Latina authors' own intersectional identities and "politicized awareness of their structural position" (Pérez Rosario, 2014, p. 107). As she traces various authors who have engaged Burgos, Pérez Rosario (2014) notes that this politicized awareness often allows these women to create and generate spaces of possibility in a way similar to Burgos. Just as Burgos used her poetry to revisit and bear witness to the pain of colonization in Puerto Rico while also forging a path of possibility for poor women of Afro-descent, subject to the erasures of a dual colonialism, Pérez Rosario (2014) argues Puerto Rican diaspora writers engage the "stories of their ancestors . . . to re-create the past and envision a more hopeful future" (p. 113). She continues by noting that these stories allow writers and artists to "break the historical silence that has characterized their place in society, while offering the infinite possibilities of self-invention" (Pérez Rosario, 2014, p. 113). Citing poets and performance artists like Mariposa and La Bruja, Pérez Rosario (2014) reiterates the need to disrupt and break the silence, and she argues that remembering Burgos serves as "a way to connect to the past and imagine a better future beyond annihilation and silence" (p. 120). Pérez Rosario (2014) is particularly invested in the role of performance in remembering Burgos as a "poet of presence and authenticity, rejecting the modernist impersonality through oral performance, passion, and rebelliousness" (p. 122). Moreover, Pérez Rosario (2014) argues that performance allows writers, like Rivera, to use Burgos's memory to "mediate their relationship to history in the process of inventing new identities, new languages, and new ways of thinking" (p. 122).

Thus, in this chapter, I argue that understanding how we perform memory within an intercultural context is a significant step in cutting through whitewashed notions of intersectionality. Below, I work to bridge performance studies and the decolonial concept of faithful witnessing as I analyze how Rivera's play engages Burgos as way to both interrogate Rivera's own lived experience while also bearing faithful witness to Burgos's (dis)embodiment rhetoric in her poetry. Performance is integral to Rivera's ability to bear such witness, and Rivera's own performance of negotiation is a significant example of a decolonial feminist memory project. In bearing witness to Burgos's ability to find liberation in the interstice, Rivera's uses performance to commemorate Burgos (and herself) as an artist who finds liberation through invention.

PERFORMANCE THEORY

As I work within this chapter to decenter whiteness, I am particularly invested in listening to "what has been silenced" as I work to meet Burgos and Rivera in their own localized contexts using pluriversal methods (Wanzer, 2012, p. 653). Thus, I first theorize how Rivera utilizes performance through faithful witnessing as a commemorative antidote to public memory projects which subsume and assimilate rich, complex intersectional histories into a flat dominant narrative. Informing this project, Calafell's (2007) work on performance explores avenues of analysis which engage the body and the everyday, no longer privileging the text or perpetuating the exclusion of marginalized people (p. 3). She centers on performance studies and notes how performance scholars "have long been concerned with the ways historically marginalized people resist the interpellative power of dominant discourse" (Calafell, 2007, p. 74). In her work, then, Calafell (2007) calls for an "embodied approach" in which the reader "feels" the text (p. 5). The body and performance are central to this call.

Calafell builds her approach from performance scholars like Conquergood (1998), who argues that against a "scriptocentric" academy, we can draw "some oppositional force, some resistance" from performance (pp. 25–26). Conquergood (1998) argues performance as a paradigm "insists upon immediacy, involvement, and intimacy as modes of understanding" (p. 26). As an alternative means of knowing, Conquergood (1998) claims "performance is a more conceptually astute and inclusionary way of thinking about subaltern cultural practices and intellectual-philosophical activities" (p. 26). Conquergood (1998) emphasizes Frederick Douglass's call for "*listening to and being touched by*" performance (p. 27, emphasis Conquergood's). Indeed, here we again see the significance of feeling, which is paramount in Calafell's (2007) approach. Moreover, both scholars view performance as breaking free from stagnant, normative traditions.

The body is central in performance. Advocating for theorizing from embodied experience, Anzaldúa (2012) argues, "the work of the *mestiza* consciousness is to break down the subject-object duality that keeps her a prisoner and to show in the flesh and through the images in her work how duality is transcended" (p. 80). Moraga (1983) expands on the significance of theories of the flesh, writing "theory in the flesh means one where the physical realities of our lives—our skin color, the land or concrete where we grew up on, our sexual longings—all fuse to create a politic born out of necessity" (p. 23). Theory in the flesh, then, is one which requires "bridging" contradictions (Moraga, 1983, p. 23). This is especially true for Latinas in the United States, whose identities are marked by what Valdivia (2004) describes as radical hybridity (p. 6). Valdivia argues that the "Latina body as a floating signifier represents the identity crisis of a nation forced to acknowledge its heterogeneity, hybridity, and continued racism" (p. 16). Thus, in working to bridge these embodied contradictory identities, Moraga (1983) advocates for "naming our selves and by telling our own stories" (p. 23). She concludes that Chicana and Latina feminists who theorize from the flesh use "flesh and blood experiences to concretize a vision that can begin to heal our 'wounded knee'" (Moraga, 1983, p. 23).

Bridging performance studies and Chicana feminist theory, Calafell (2007) centers her approach in theories of the flesh. She argues theories of the flesh "privilege subjectivity and embodied knowledges as sites of fruitful theory building, giving women of color back the power to speak as authorities of their own experiences" (Calafell, 2007, p. 8). This concept is critical in my choice to analyze Rivera's play as she crafts a memory of Burgos from Burgos's own words and lived experience; Rivera gives Burgos authority to recount her life beyond the myths and cautionary tales. Yet, there is much of Rivera's own lived experience in the performance as well. I selected Rivera's play because she is a Puerto Rican woman and writer, navigating her identity from a diasporic subjectivity wherein she has to reconcile what it means to be in the United States and "from" the island, belonging simultaneously to both/neither. Thus, by considering how Rivera remembers Burgos, I argue Rivera builds from a diasporic intimacy that informs an embodied knowledge of Burgos that is absent and incomprehensible in state-sponsored commemorative projects, such as the USPS Hispanic Subject stamp series which "honored" Burgos in 2010.

Intimacy is integral to embodied performance, and it is also deeply embedded in the self-liberation Burgos imagines within her poetry. Calafell (2007) outlines the importance of intimacy as she draws from the work of Muñoz, noting how the "affect or space of possibility is a mode of belonging made possible through a mode of identification or disidentification" (p. 27). Calafell (2007) continues by arguing that these modes result in an "anti-normative effect compounded by our feelings of estrangement as a result of being in a new space" (p. 27), and she concludes that the feelings enabled by these performances of estrangement reveal "a shared sense of loss," or what Boym calls "diasporic intimacy" (Calafell, 2007, p. 27). Within Boym's (1998) terms, diasporic intimacy is constituted by "uprootedness and defamiliarization" (p. 499). She writes that such intimacy is only accessible through "indirection and intimation, through stories and secrets" (Boym, 1998, p. 499). Arguing along with Boym (1998) that this intimacy supersedes the private and can be "framed by art, embellished by memory" (p. 500), I find that Rivera's play utilizes such silences and intimations. Working from within Burgos's words and context, Rivera directs an embodied performance of both, utilizing movement and physical contestation to reveal a deeper understanding of the ways in which Burgos, and by extension Rivera herself, uses the body to negotiate her positionalities.

Boym's (1998) theorization of diasporic intimacy is also significant to my project in that it is void of nostalgia. Boym (1998) argues diasporic intimacy is not a utopic space of connection (p. 499). As she points out, such intimacy is not "a comforting recovery of identity through a shared nostalgia of home" (Boym, 1998, p. 501). Rather, diasporic intimacy is situated in a dystopic hopefulness that hinges upon "chance encounters" which help exiles form "collective frameworks of memory" (Boym, 1998, p. 499). Here, even as they are "haunted by images of home and homeland," the diasporic subject is also cognizant of "the furtive pleasures of exile" (Boym, 1998, pp. 499–500). Within Boym's (1998) theory of diasporic intimacy, there is an emphasis on survival, and those who share in it understand that "the illusion of complete belonging has been shattered" (p. 502). Ultimately, diasporic intimacy does not build from or prize a utopic "nostalgic narrative"; rather, it emphasizes a shared sense of surviving the "common loss and pain of displacement" to "inhabit exile" (Boym, 1997, pp. 523–24). Yet, while Boym (1998) is careful to caution against reading such intimacy as a nostalgic reconstitution of past identity, she does note that this "common wound could become a community bond" (p. 523).

Calafell (2007) articulates community by again engaging the significance of feeling, writing that our identities are often "established through a connection with a feeling" (p. 15). These feelings derive from many methods of representation wherein marginalized subjects are read through hegemonic frames. Importantly, Calafell (2007) explores how this occurs through the body, acknowledging the many ways in which people of color are read as excessive. Citing how Bhabha, Muñoz, and Lancaster theorize performances of excess as resistance, Calafell (2007) concludes that "excess serves as a point of identification that enables community not only resistance" (p. 18). Adequately accounting for the ways in which this shared identification through excess manifests requires "a reflexive participatory knowledge" (Calafell, 2007, p. 20). This type of knowledge "privileges not only less traditionally accepted practices of theorizing but also Other ways of knowing by challenging the mind/body split," including "cultural performances, which have been overlooked because of a bias of textuality" (Calafell, 2007, p. 20). Here, Calafell (2007) advocates for a "participatory perspective" because of the value it places on everyday practices and the affect created from such practices (p. 20).

As part of this project, Calafell (2007) builds "toward the performative possibilities of memory to re-center difference" (p. 27). She centers narrative as a means of renegotiating memories (Calafell, 2007, p. 66). Citing her own pilgrimage experience, Calafell (2007) notes how present, past, and future are opened through the "performance or re-embodiment of memory" (p. 66). Just as Burgos works through embodied trauma as a means for new future possibility, so, too, does Calafell (2007) as she calls upon "trauma to become susceptible to critique through its telling, this performance, this pilgrimage enables a re-storied history that is activated in each step I take" (p. 66). Inherent in this performance is Calafell's (2007) understanding of "using personal experience, body knowledge, and reflection to bear upon my history and theorizations" (p. 66). As I argue below, Rivera also approaches her remembrance of Burgos through a similar understanding, as she depicts Burgos's life and work within a frame which also accounts for Rivera's own experience and reflections. Indeed, as Calafell (2007) notes, how Latinas remember is often dictated by the ways in which our bodies "negotiate historical trauma and systemic violence" (p. 93). Burgos was constantly negotiating the impact of colonialism as a diasporic Puerto Rican woman, whereas Rivera, though born in New York, carries the legacy of these traumas (Calafell, 2007, p. 93). Thus, rather than being "socialized, molded, or modified to fit the expectations" of society (Calafell, 2007, p. 75), wherein "discourses of whiteness and white identity by default get to occupy multiple space or possibilities" (Calafell, 2007, p. 79), Rivera's play engages memory as a means to delve into the complexity of Burgos's (and Rivera's) lived gendered, racialized, and colonized trauma. Yet, Rivera is able to avoid replicating a memory of Burgos "immunized against alterity" (Taylor, 2003, p. 19) by utilizing Lugones's (2003) concept of faithful witnessing.

FAITHFUL WITNESSING

Lugones (2003) performs scholarship as a pilgrimage toward coalition. She states that her goal is to identify liberatory levels of possibility (Lugones,

2003). These levels range from the personal, where we are "opening ourselves to each other, levels of intimacy, and large and sometimes dispersed solidarity" (Lugones, 2003, p. 1), to the political, which Lugones (2003) describes broadly as encompassing "the manyness of the past and present by both dominators and those resisting domination" (p. 4). Driving her scholarship is a "commitment against utopianism" (Lugones, 2003, p. 5), which exists when there is no means of resistance. Instead, Lugones tells her reader:

> to live differently in the present, to think and act against the grain of oppression. I write from the belief that it is only from that ground that the next possibility can be entertained socially, at the edge of realism. My perspective is in the midst of people mindful to the tensions, desires, closures, cracks, and openings that make up the social. (p. 5)

As a decolonial scholar, Lugones (2003) is attentive to what she calls "active subjectivity," which she theorizes as neither presupposing an individual subject, nor a collective intentionality, but rather outlined through "a consciousness by a moving with people," wherein intentionality is derived from "paying attention to people and to the enormously variegated ways of connection among people without privileging the word or a monological understanding of sense" (p. 6). Lugones (2003) is particularly concerned with the ways in which we, as scholars, tend to overly assert our agency as we "move with others" (p. 6). Thus, her project works to identify ways in which we can safeguard against:

> falling into a politics of the same, a politics that values
> or assumes sameness or homogeneity;
> without mythologizing place;
> attempting to stand in the cracks and intersections of multiple
> histories of domination and resistances to dominations? (Lugones, 2003, pp. 6–7)

Building from this concern, Lugones (2003) offers faithful witnessing as a means of moving away from universal or monosensical systems. In contrast to collaborators, who witness on the side of power, Lugones (2003) argues that faithful witnessing occurs "against the grain of power, on the side of resistance" (p. 7). She says that to witness faithfully, we "must be able to sense resistance, to interpret behavior as resistant even when it is dangerous, when that interpretation places one psychologically against common sense, or when one is moved to act in collision with common sense, with oppression" (Lugones, 2003, p. 7). While Lugones (2003) cautions us that faithful witnessing is difficult because it requires us to navigate through hard-to-detect "oppressive and fragmenting meanings" (p. 7), it is also a role which allows us to engage innumerable possibilities for coalition because it approaches the subject as plural, many. Lugones (2003) specifically cites bicultural people as those who have to navigate the role of victim and dominant, wading through the disparate desires, traits, thoughts, emotions, and performances which "are different in one reality than in the other" (p. 57).

Lugones (2003) also argues that liberatory possibility lies within memory and "readings of history that reveal unified historical lines as enacting dominations through both linearity and erasure" (pp. 58–59). Liberation, then, is possible only by acknowledging the many worlds which we might occupy, accepting bodily multiplicity wherein we occupy spaces as both oppressed and oppressor. Lugones (2003) argues that "the task of remembering one's many selves is a difficult liberatory task" (p. 59). She continues, "Self-deception and mystification are among the many forms of control of our memory of our other selves. All oppressive control is violent because it attempts to erase selves that are dangerous to the maintenance of domination over us" (Lugones, 2003, p. 59). Yet, echoing the work of scholars like Anzaldúa (2012), Pérez (1999), and Sandoval (2000), who argue for the possibility of liberation in an interstitial space, Lugones (2003) contends that one has the clearest critical perspective on all worlds by inhabiting the "limen, the place in between realities, a gap 'between and betwixt' universes of sense that construe social life and persons differently, an interstice" (p. 59). Lugones (2003) argues that this space, and the capacity it grants for recognition of our own multiplicity, also allows the formation of "liberatory syllogisms" from other worlds to "attempt to make actual in the worlds in which one is oppressed" (p. 59). Yet, again, Lugones (2003) cautions us that these syllogisms cannot transfer, and she states that the oppressed "know themselves in realities in which they are able to form intentions that are not among the alternatives that are possible in the world in which they are brutalized and oppressed" (p. 59). We see this in Burgos's poetry as contextualized against her life. Though Burgos was able to theorize her liberation, moving from the nostalgic containment of her world toward an inward space of reflection and embodied wholeness through her writing, Burgos's ability to theorize from a "third space" did not manifest in material alteration of her oppression.

Lugones (2003) accounts for this thusly, "Merely remembering ourselves in other worlds and coming to understand ourselves as multiplicitous is not enough for liberation: collective struggle in the reconstruction and transformation of structures is fundamental" (p. 62). Therefore, we might read Burgos as the forebear of the collective; her writing gives voice to her oppression and creates a path toward liberation from her interstitial perspective. Yet, in her moment, Burgos is alone in giving voice to the weight of her oppression. Indeed, Lugones (2003) notes the collective is "born of dialogue among multiplicitous persons who are faithful witnesses of themselves and also testify to, and uncover the multiplicity of their oppressors and the techniques of oppression afforded by ignoring that multiplicity" (p. 62). Even among her

Puerto Rican contemporaries who also rejected U.S. imperialism, Burgos was surrounded by adherents to a nostalgic nationalist identity steeped in racialized and gendered concepts borrowed from Spanish colonialism. As this nostalgia actively worked to discipline and silence Burgos, it was not an identity to which she had access. Only allowed to fully exist in the interstice, Burgos bore faithful witness to the multiplicity of her oppressors out of necessity. However, as her (male) peers had the luxury of engaging in colonial nostalgia as a means of resistance, they were incapable of joining or participating with Burgos in a collective struggle. Still, as I shift to my analysis of how Rivera melds performance with the role of faithful witness in commemorating Burgos, I assert that the efforts of Rivera and others to intimately engage Burgos's memory within an interstitial space play an integral role in continuing Burgos's project for Puertorriqueña liberation.

MEMORY AS PERFORMANCE, PERFORMANCE AS MEMORY

Carmen Rivera's play *Julia de Burgos: Child of Water* was first staged by the Puerto Rican Traveling Theatre in New York on May 12, 1999. The first production was eventually videotaped for the archives at the Lincoln Center Library for the Performing Arts (Rivera, 1998, p. 83). For the purposes of this chapter, I am relying on selections of a recorded performance of a 2014 centennial production, directed by Carmen Rivera's husband Cándido Tirado at the Bernie West Theater in Manhattan (Rivera, 2003). Of note, in its original run, *Julia de Burgos: Child of Water* was performed in English on weekday showings and in Spanish on the weekends (Bruckner, 1999). Tirado's 2014 staging is performed in English. Thus, for the purposes of this chapter, I analyze the English-language version, referencing Rivera's published script when relevant. Yet, in moving forward, I consider Taylor's (2003) words that the repertoire, the fluid performance of embodied memory, "requires presence" (p. 20). I take to heart her conceptualization of presence as a space where "people participate in the production and reproduction of knowledge by 'being there,' being a part of the transmission" (Taylor, 2003, p. 20). While I find it useful and important to analyze the available recording of the staged performance of Rivera's play, I also acknowledge the limitations of experiencing it solely in a relatively archived, static form.

Creative Context

In her acknowledgments for the play, Rivera begins by describing her fear in approaching this commemorative project. After being commissioned by the Puerto Rican Traveling Theatre, Rivera (1998) writes that she was "overwhelmed with joy, then quickly terror set in" (p. 81). Her fear was based in the fact that Burgos remains an icon in the Puerto Rican community. As Rivera (1998) notes, Burgos is a "Puerto Rican and Feminist SHero and literary genius. How would I be able to dramatize her life? At the beginning of the writing process I was paralyzed for several months" (p. 81). Rivera (1998) dedicated months of her life to understanding who Julia de Burgos was, meeting Burgos on her own terms. Rivera (1998) describes the process of locating Julia as a complex woman: "As I studied her poetry, interviewed people who knew her and scholars who researched her work, I slowly discovered a human being underneath all the layers of her mythology. Julia, the Woman emerged" (p. 81). Rivera (1998) continues, outlining the various facets of Julia the Woman: one "angry at the cruelties of the world"; who "believed that Social Justice and Freedom were basic human rights"; who "loved too deeply"; who "loved laughing and didn't stop herself from crying"; and who "saw, felt and heard all too clearly" (p. 81). Rivera (1998) argues that the many complexities of Burgos "plagued her and caused her to doubt her gift," and that "as witnessed through her work, she (Burgos) could never reconcile the Woman with the Artist" (p. 81). From this understanding, Rivera (1998) constructs her memory of Burgos. She writes: "I posit that these two sides of her psyche where frequently at odds throughout her lifetime. Once this level of consciousness opened up for me, JULIA DE BURGOS: CHILD OF WATER began to take shape" (Rivera, 1998, p. 81).

Child of Water is spread over two acts, with eighteen scenes divided equally between both acts. The play is set primarily at the end of Burgos's life in 1953, though Julia and the WOMAN move through scenes of dramatized memories in Burgos's life, beginning as early as 1929 with a final conversation between Julia and her mother. In her set directions, Rivera (1998) writes that it must be "surrealist and minimalist" as the play occurs "in a world between life and death, and the set must reflect this and NOT be grounded in a realistic way" (p. 3, emphasis Rivera's). As another production note, Rivera (1998) writes that "lights will be very important for the play in invoking the surreal nether world that Julia de Burgos finds herself in" (p. 3). This in-between space is critical in invoking themes found in Burgos's poetry, and it allows Rivera (1998) to interrogate the ways in which Burgos wrestled with and within the division between the public-facing persona and the poet crying out for liberation. Rivera (1998) is highly cognizant of this division, and she situates the play within that struggle, where Julia confronts and is confronted by her soul in the guise of the WOMAN character. Having duly described the character WOMAN as Julia's Soul, Rivera (1998) describes the interactions between Julia and her soul (through the embodied WOMAN) as a search for "integration and peace" only possible in the break between "time and space . . . in the chasm between life and death" (p. 3).

Performing Memory

As a guiding essence throughout the play, Rivera scripts a voice-over character who interjects lines from Burgos's poetry to frame the performance. The voice-over is described as "Julia's voice in the infinite," though Rivera (1998) writes that if "voice-overs cannot be recorded; they may be performed by the Soul" (p. 4). In the 2014 Tirado production, poems from the infinite are performed by WOMAN. As Act 1, Scene 1 begins, most of the stage lights are down, save one, shining on the WOMAN. She is standing behind one of the dark, scribbled panels, which in this scene is revealed to be transparent. The lighting against the panel creates the effect of shattered glass, an intimation to the audience that the performance is staged in a ruptured world, in the in-between. The WOMAN recites lines from Burgos's poem "Agua, vida y tierra" [Water, Life & Earth], setting the stage for what the audience is about to witness. Quietly, languidly, the WOMAN, as the infinite, states: "I was a strong outburst of the forest and river, and as a voice between two echoes, I climbed the hills. From one side the water's hands stretched towards me, and the mountain's roots took hold of me from the other. From there my voice of the present, bare of language, spreads over the world as it came from the earth" (Davidranauth, 2014b, 00:06). The light dims and briefly goes black. From this opening scene, Rivera and Tirado welcome the audience into the rupture, where Burgos's voice is experienced as she herself imagined its greatest potency, unbound from the constraints of her contextual vocabulary, free to engage the present.

Following our first introduction to the infinite voice of Burgos, coughing echoes through the theater as another light comes up on the stage. Behind another transparent panel, a different woman, Julia, is bent over. She is wearing a hospital gown, and she is gasping for air as she coughs. Between coughing fits, she is panicked, her movements frantic as she clutches her hands to her face. She is loudly talking to herself as she states: "They think they can keep me locked up . . . They can't do that . . . they don't know who I am! I'm not going back! Okay I gotta get to . . ." (Davidranauth, 2014b, 00:25). As her voice trails off, she stumbles from behind the panel, bent over and coughing, and she emerges onto the center of the stage. More stage lights come up, though they are initially dim and cast blue shadows on Julia. As she moves farther out on the stage, the stage lights also become brighter. A wheelchair is visible on stage, a nod to the many hospitalizations Burgos underwent immediately prior to her death from complications with pneumonia. Julia continues to cough and turns her back to the audience, screaming, "I hope they're gone! Leave me alone! I'm not going back!" (Davidranauth, 2014b, 00:41). The scene progresses as Julia is frightened, crying as she moves across the stage, searching for a river. She moves around the stage, alternately screaming and crying. The scene ends with Julia, clearly disconcerted, attempting to discover if she is alive or dead.

The circumstances of Burgos's death have played a large role in maintaining her mythic status. The fascination with her death also often serves to frame academic forays into her life; thus, there is little surprise that Rivera would begin her play at Julia's end. Given the public fascination with Burgos's untimely death, it is critical that Rivera utilize a cultural moment of recognition in remembering Burgos. Yet, where Burgos's demise often outstretches her contribution, Rivera uses this juncture, the nether space between life and death, to introduce her audience to Burgos. Returning to Calafell's (2007) reading of Muñoz, I consider how Rivera negotiates the myth of Burgos. Rivera builds from the identification her audience members might have with the story of Burgos's death, but she disrupts the common narrative. Rather than portraying Burgos's death as the end of her story, or even the springboard to an embellished mythic status, Rivera disidentifies with common readings of Burgos's life and instead uses it to welcome her audience into the intimate spaces between the lines of Burgos's life, history, and writing. Regarding disidentification, Calafell (2007) writes of the power of the "anti-normative effect, compounded by our feelings of estrangement" in creating community (27). While Calafell (2007) discusses difference and disidentification in the broader sense of Latinidad, Rivera works through this process on a more intimate, micro level as she works to make new meaning with her audience. Through this act, Rivera is creating space for the audience to engage Burgos on a new plane, absent of nostalgia or myth.

Burgos's death is not the only space where Rivera taps into vernacular perceptions of Burgos. She also incorporates the notion of Burgos as the broken-hearted woman whose talent is spoiled or diminished because of her lost love, Juan Isidro Jimenés Grullon. While Rivera builds from a common trope, that of the jilted woman of color marked for poverty and death, she reconstructs it in a way that recenters the split between Julia and her soul, embodied by WOMAN. In Act 2, Scene 1, described at the outset of this chapter, the WOMAN performs "A Julia de Burgos." Of note, where the script directions call for the WOMAN to recite the poem before Burgos comes on stage, Tirado's production has the WOMAN speaking directly to Burgos while she recites. With pages in her hand, the WOMAN moves toward Burgos, then the audience, as Burgos looks away from her, ashamed, sometimes toeing the ground with her foot, sometimes clutching the shawl tighter. As the recitation continues, the WOMAN again turns toward Burgos, and her voice becomes sharper, angry. She begins to move swiftly toward Burgos as she states, "You do *not* govern yourself; *everyone* governs you" (Davidranauth, 2014a, 01:40).[2] Once she reaches Burgos, the WOMAN bends over her, almost menacingly, raising her voice as she lists the people and things to whom

Burgos is beholden: "your husband, your parents, your relatives, the priest, the dressmaker, the theater, the casino, the car, your jewels, the banquet, champagne." As the list goes on, the WOMAN becomes louder, eventually shouting "HEAVEN AND HELL" into Burgos's face (Davidranauth, 2014a, 01:43). The WOMAN then pulls back, lowers her voice, and mocks Julia and her concern for "society's 'what will they say?' " (Davidranauth, 2014a, 01:45). She then pivots and walks away as she proclaims: "Not me, only my heart rules me, only my thoughts." The WOMAN walks to stage right, turns back to face Julia, and she again raises her voice, points to her chest, and says "The one who rules in me is I" (Davidranauth, 2014a, 01:50).

As the WOMAN moves into the next stanzas, Julia begins to react. She is no longer looking away, passive or ashamed. She starts interjecting lines like "Stop it!" and "What the hell are you doing?" (Davidranauth, 2014a, 2:34). The WOMAN continues through the poem's end, and there is canned applause (also noted in the script) which causes Julia to rise from her seat and confront the WOMAN, yelling, "STOP IT!" Julia then turns to the audience and angrily points around room "All of you! Stop it!" (Davidranauth, 2014a, 02:38). The two women then face one another and begin to argue. Julia blames the WOMAN for ruining her life, ripping pages from WOMAN's hands as Julia yells at her to leave and to never read her poems again. The WOMAN reminds Julia that she tried to separate from her before: "You tried to throw me away, and you tried to destroy us. I have a right!" Julia tells her "You have no right" and that she does not want to live her life with the WOMAN. As the WOMAN begs Julia to let her back in, Julia crumples the pages and throws them down, turning away from the WOMAN. WOMAN follows her, speaking to her back, "You had your chance to live your life. Were you happy, peaceful?" Here, the WOMAN (and Rivera) turn to Burgos's love affair with Grullon. But rather than centering the love story as the cause of Burgos's downfall, Rivera implies it was instead Burgos's choice to split from her soul which left her abandoned and destitute. In rejecting her soul to make her lover happy, Julia is reminded that her capitulation to Grullon's demands, namely that she give up her writing and perform a more submissive, "womanly" role, gained her nothing. The WOMAN tells Julia: "That was not living, you were broken" (Davidranauth, 2014a, 03:03).

Rivera's play frequently weaves Burgos's own words into familiar narratives. While the scene above is just one of the contentious interactions between Julia and the WOMAN, it is representative of the way in which Rivera bears faithful witness to Burgos's struggle as a diasporic woman, subject to the trauma of migration while continuously navigating dual repressive expectations within the United States and within the patriarchal nostalgia of her peers and lover. As Figueroa (2015) notes, faithful witnessing "challenges singular narratives or dominant perspectives," and within this process "understands that there are many worlds, that sees/reads many perspectives, particularly the perspectives of those who are dehumanized or rendered invisible" (p. 643). Rivera's narrative decision to embody both Julia and her soul, depicting their struggle in a surrealistic interstitial space, reveals a highly cognizant level of engagement with Burgos's poetry and the embodied resistance revealed throughout. Rivera dissects the split persona in much the same ways as Burgos does, and ultimately, they reach the same conclusion: liberation can only become possibility by turning inward, engaging the struggle at its most intimate level.

Yet, where Burgos served as a forebear in this struggle, Rivera's role is essential in moving beyond the first step of multiplicitous self-recognition described by Lugones. As noted above, Lugones (2003) cautioned that recognition is not enough for liberation; liberation requires a collective struggle, built through the dialogue of faithful witnesses who acknowledge their own experience and also "testify to" others who dwell in a space of multiplicity (Lugones, 2003, p. 62). Through her play, Rivera uses performance to testify to Burgos's vision for liberation, while also drawing her audience into the collective.

In the final two scenes of the play, Julia and the WOMAN negotiate Julia's farewell. In Act 2, Scene 8, nearing her end, Julia has returned to the hospital. This is depicted by her redonning the hospital gown from the first scene of the play. In the script, Rivera notes that this scene takes place in 1953. As the scene progresses, we can tell Julia and the WOMAN have reconciled. They are facing one another, embracing arm in arm, as Julia laughs to herself and recites fragments of verse from her poem "Después" [After]: "When everything awakens the lilies will announce it . . . they will say: 'It is the fatal conscience of that girl, she had many sins because she always lived in verse.'" The WOMAN smiles as she tells Julia, "I hope they will all say that." The WOMAN, too, recites a verse from "Réplica" [Rejoinder]: "You will always be a poem, Julia de Burgos, the one that has nothing of a bourgeois, the one that breaks centuries in her clothes, and frees her life through the stars!" The WOMAN pointedly tells Julia, "That was all you!" Julia smiles and tells her: "Us." "Us," the WOMAN happily echoes (Davidranauth, 2014c, 00:09). Here, Rivera joins the two, body and soul reunited, but also two voices amplifying Burgos's call for liberation.

As the scene continues, Julia again recites verse as the WOMAN takes the hospital gown off her body, revealing a nude dress. The WOMAN folds the hospital gown and she and Julia grab an end and carry the gown toward the back of the stage; the lights dim, leaving only one spotlight on both women. They lay the gown on the stage, symbolizing Julia's death. They maintain eye contact as Julia continues to cite verses from "Adiós en Welfare Island." With the final lines in the scene, the WOMAN looks unflinchingly at Julia, and she recites verse from "A plena desnudez" [In Total Nudity]: "One day I will go to dance with you to a faraway place where no law exists, nor reason rules; where the water is breeze, where the bird is flower; where everything pure and natural is fused in God's grace" (Davidranauth, 2014c, 00:47). Yet, where the script calls for an end of scene, and a slow dimming of lights as a recognition of Julia's passing, Tirado's production transitions seamlessly into the final scene of the play. As the WOMAN finishes reciting the lines, she and Julia stand, hold hands and walk, together, to the center of the stage, crossing into a new plane.

In the background, there is recorded sound of birds twittering, along with a low rush of water. The WOMAN and Julia stand hand in hand, and she tells Julia that she is home. Julia has returned to the Rio Grande de Loíza. It is in this final scene where Rivera breaks the fourth wall when Julia acknowledges the audience's presence, asking: "Who are all these people?" The WOMAN laughs as she tells Julia: "They came to the river for you." As Julia remains confused, the WOMAN tells her it is a tribute, "a tribute for your life . . . it's time to go now Julia." However, Julia remains still, staring at the audience. She admonishes the audience: "Don't remember me!" The WOMAN, too, addresses the audience, revealing her reunified spirit with Julia's body, as she urges them: "Feel me!" (Davidranauth, 2014c, 01:14).

In watching these women play to the audience, even once-removed from the participatory experience, I reflect back on Calafell's (2007) call to "feel" the text in an embodied way. Within this performance, Rivera's understanding of and approach to remembering Burgos springs from a similar sentiment. In reflecting on Boym's (1998) diasporic intimacy, it is clear that there is no sense of nostalgia in Rivera's commemoration. The narrative she seeks to tell is drawn directly from Burgos's embodied discourse, and there is an underlying kinship between the two writers which illuminates a shared understanding of the impermanence and trauma associated with diasporic subjectivity. As the WOMAN (and Rivera) call the audience to "feel," Rivera is also illustrating the power of performance in constructing memory from a decolonial space.

Rivera adheres to Figueroa's (2015) call for a decolonial attitude, wherein Rivera recognizes the dual nature of performance. Rivera is not only building memory performance for an audience of participatory observers, but she is also performing the role of witness through that memory construction. Contrary to a flat Burgos narrative, such as those often found in state-sponsored public memory projects like the USPS Hispanic Stamp Series, which neither anticipates a diasporic audience, nor generates any sense of self-recognition in the observer, Rivera's narrative adheres to the concept of faithful witnessing as articulated by Lugones (2003). Rivera (1998) herself describes the process of coming to this project, sitting with

Burgos's words as she waded through the "fragments" to create a tribute to Burgos (p. 81). In this way, Rivera faithfully witnesses by refuting the "unified historical lines" of erasure (Lugones, 2003, p. 59), doing the work to "sense resistance" within Burgos's poetry (Lugones, 2003, p. 7). While the play is only loosely biographical, it is a faithful commemoration in its adherence to Burgos's search for liberation, working diligently to locate meaning within the ruptures of Burgos's life.

CONCLUSION

Documenting the whitening of intersectionality, Bilge (2013) builds from Hall and Ferguson as she claims that absorption of difference is deemed necessary for the survival of neoliberalism. Bilge (2013) writes: "Crucially, this new form of economic power lives culturally through difference and . . . is constantly teaching itself with the pleasures of transgressive Other, while at the same time absorbing and neutralising, at least partially, disruptive difference" (p. 181). Bilge (2013) argues minority hegemonic criticism paradoxically works to expand hegemonic power, as "minority affirmation making substantial criticism of hegemonic authority now also provides through its incorporation unprecedented opportunities to power to rearticulate its hegemony" (p. 182).

Bilge (2013) is concerned with the ways in which the academic institutionalization of minority knowledges, specifically intersectionality, results in stripping said knowledges of their power and further marginalizes its "racialized knowers—women and queers of colour, have been marginalised in the very spaces of knowledge and activism they have built through their struggle" (p. 182). Bilge expands this argument to engage postcolonial studies. She writes, "Threatened by the cultural empowerment of the marginal and the local that these newly acquired, through struggle, speaking positions have generated, discourses of power fought back with a double move of diversification and absorption" (Bilge, 2013, p. 182). Citing Tuhiwai Smith and Mignolo, Bilge (2013) cautions against perpetuating academic colonialism and erasure, and she turns to decolonial post-disciplinarity as a remedy. Indeed, Bilge (2013) argues for epistemic disobedience:

> Counter-hegemonic knowledge builders must work with the incoherencies and interstices of institutionalizing processes and practices, and remember that what is at stake is not a thematic inclusion, a content diversification—the add-and-stir approach incorporating minority issues as subject matter to extant disciplines in their conventional frames, but an epistemic disobedience. (p. 183)

My goal in this chapter is not to argue that Rivera exists outside of the neoliberal market of "diversification and absorption" (Bilge, 2013, p. 1). Rather, I argue that Rivera, similar to Burgos, has found a way to commemorate Burgos's fight for liberation by giving the narrative back to Burgos, embodying her lyrics and her struggle. Instead of opting for the more common commemorative trope for marginalized figures, wherein she is appropriated as an exemplary (albeit still marginalized) heroine, Rivera pays tribute to the material and spiritual violence Burgos endured as a poor, sexual Afro-Latina, dually punished by the patriarchal systems of her colonial contemporaries and U.S. imperialism. In this way, Rivera builds from Burgos's intersectional identities to amplify both Burgos's critiques of colonial oppression and her calls for liberation from within the interstice.

Using performance and faithful witnessing, Rivera's play provides an example of what we might look for in resisting the erasure that too often attends calls for intersectionality. Importantly, as a model for a decolonial memory project, Rivera's understanding of memory is inherently tied to the ways in which narrative can both build or erase communal identity. Rivera is particularly aware of the importance of narrative in constructing identity within the Puerto Rican diaspora. Thus, in drawing from Ruth Trinidad Galván's (2016) work, I argue that Rivera's lived experience informs her role as dual witness. Galván (2016) argues "underscoring the collective memory of colonization and oppression," while also "foregrounding the knowledge the female brown body possesses," is critical in "decentering dominant epistemologies" (p. 348). Rivera privileges Burgos's embodied knowledge throughout the play. Moreover, she builds from this knowledge to construct a collective within her audience.

By including the familiar narratives and myths which are associated with Burgos, Rivera credibly generates a space of negotiation within Burgos's memory. She decenters the power of these myths by focusing attention on the ways in which Burgos manifested a split persona to navigate systems of oppression. Generations removed, Rivera's play echoes Burgos's embodied struggles, amplifying her excesses by physically embodying her spirit, while also demonstrating the difficulty of reconciling the multiplicity of systemic expectations placed on a diasporic woman of color. In this way, Rivera invites her audience to unlearn traditional narratives of Burgos, to delink from the nostalgia that Burgos herself rejected. In Muñoz's (1999) terms, Rivera works to help her audience collectively disidentify with these myths, accessing a "transformative politics" which "enables subjects and groups to imagine" (p. 161). Thus as scholars, we should build from Rivera's model as a first step in imagining a liberatory collective for decentering white, Western, heteronormative patriarchal strictures on who, what, and how we approach intercultural communication.

NOTES

1. The WOMAN character is always written in capital letters in Rivera's script.
2. Emphasis added to reflect WOMAN's pointed tone for these words.

REFERENCES

Acevedo, B. (2015, May 21). La historia as theatre: Interview with playwright, Carmen Rivera. *La Respuesta*. http://larespuestamedia.com/.

Anzaldúa, G. (2012). *Borderlands = La frontera* (4th ed.). San Francisco, CA: Aunt Lute Books.

Bilge, S. (2014). Whitening intersectionality: Evanescence of race in intersectionality scholarship. In W. D. Hund, & A. Lentin (Eds.), *Racism and sociology* (pp. 175–205). Muenster, Germany: LIT.

Boym, S. (1998). On diasporic intimacy: Ilya Kabakov's installations and immigrant homes. *Critical Inquiry, 24*(2), 498–524.

Bruckner, D. J. R. (1999, May 31). Picture of a fiery Puerto Rican. Review of *Julia de Burgos: Child of water*, by Carmen Rivera. *New York Times*, pp. E5.

Calafell, B. M. (2007). *Latina/o communication studies: Theorizing performance*. New York, NY: Peter Lang Publishing.

Conquergood, D. (1998). Beyond the text: Toward a performative cultural politics. In S. J. Dailey (Ed.), *The future of performance studies: Visions and revisions* (pp. 25–36). Annandale, VA: National Communication Association.

Davidranauth. (2014, May 11a). *Julia de Burgos: Child of water* [Video file]. Retrieved from https://www.youtube.com/watch?v=OdbgXUZ83cU.

Davidranauth. (2014, May 11b). *Julia de Burgos: Child of water* [Video file]. Retrieved from https://www.youtube.com/watch?v=28wfRXLKjKU.

Davidranauth. (2014, May 11c). *Julia de Burgos: Child of water* [Video file]. Retrieved from https://www.youtube.com/watch?v=l_YSIvHeZMY.

Figueroa, Y. C. (2015). Faithful witnessing as practice: Decolonial readings of *Shadows of your Black memory* and *The brief wondrous life of Oscar Wao*. *Hypatia, 30*(4), 641–56. https://doi.org/10.1111/hypa.12183.

Galván, R. T. (2016). Collective memory of violence of the female brown body: A decolonial feminist public pedagogy engagement with the feminicides. *Pedagogy, Culture & Society, 24*(3), 343–57. https://doi.org/10.1080/14681366.2016.1166149.

López Springfield, C. (1994). 'I am the life, the strength, the woman': Feminism in Julia de Burgos' autobiographical poetry. *Callaloo, 17*(3), 701–14. doi: 10.2307/2931846.

Lugones, M. (2003). *Peregrinajes/pilgrimages: Theorizing coalitions against multiple oppressions*. Lanham, MD: Rowman and Littlefield.

Moraga, C. (1983). Theory in the flesh. In C. Moraga & G. Anzaldúa (Eds.), This bridge called my back: Writings by radical women of color (pp. 20–23). Latham, NY: Kitchen Table: Women of Color Press.

Muñoz, J. E. (1999). *Disidentifications: Queers of color and the performance of politics*. Minneapolis, MN: University of Minnesota Press.

Nora, P. (1992). Introduction. In L. D. Kritzman (Ed.), *Rethinking the French past: Realms of memory* (pp. 1–20). New York, NY: Columbia University Press.

Pérez, E. (1999). *The decolonial imaginary: Writing Chicanas into history*. Bloomington, IN: Indiana University Press.

Pérez Rosario, V. (2014). *Becoming Julia de Burgos: The making of a Puerto Rican icon*. Urbana, IL: University of Illinois Press.

Rivera, C. (1998). *Julia de Burgos: Child of water*. New York, NY: Red Sugarcane Press.

Sandoval, C. (2000). *Methodology of the oppressed*. Minneapolis, MN: University of Minnesota Press.

Taylor, D. (2003). *The archive and the repertoire: Performing cultural memory in the Americas*. Durham, NC: Duke University Press.

Valdivia, A. N. (2004). Latinas as radical hybrid: Transnationally gendered traces in mainstream media. *Global Media Journal*, *2*(4), 1–24.

Waldman, G. (1998). Foreword. In C. Rivera (Ed.), *Julia de Burgos: Child of water* (pp. xi–xiii). New York, NY: Red Sugarcane Press.

Wanzer, D. A. (2012). Delinking rhetoric, or revisiting McGee's fragmentation thesis through decoloniality. *Rhetoric & Public Affairs*, *15*(4), 647–58.

Chapter 12

De-Whitening Intersectionality through *Transfeminismo*

Raquel Moreira

Laysa Fortuna was a twenty-five-year-old transwoman who was always in high spirits, according to her friends. During the election season that elected Jair Bolsonaro president of Brazil, Laysa was stabbed to death in the streets of the Brazilian Northeast city of Aracaju, right in front of its Vulnerable Person's Assistance Department ("Homen que matou Mulher," 2018). According to trans activists, the sequence of events that led to her death illustrates Brazil's institutional and cultural transphobia and cisnormativity: first, Laysa was wounded right outside the public institution that was supposed to aid her, but they are closed at night; second, the perpetrator was known in the neighborhood for harassing transwomen and had been shouting Bolsonaro's name to frighten them; third, the chief of police in charge of the crime misgendered Laysa as well as the trans*[1] activists pleading on her behalf; fourth, this same chief of police did not collect witnesses' statements; finally, Laysa was both treated at the hospital and buried by her family under her given name because she did not have "appropriate papers," despite not using her given name socially ("Militantes Reagem," 2018). Laysa was an advocate for her community, just like the trans* folks who showed up at the crime scene, police station, and hospital to advocate on her behalf. Laysa was an indigenous mestiça, like many folks from the Brazilian Northeast. Analyzing her gender identity alone may conceal other important dynamics that played out in this episode, such as institutional racism and classism.

Transfeminismo is an emerging perspective that would help analyze the multiple injustices perpetrated against Laysa. This story also demonstrates the growing visibility among trans* people in Brazil, who in the past were not heard when speaking for their communities. This growing visibility is not just political; it is also epistemological. The provisional result of these articulations is what I examine in this chapter. As an emerging political and scholarly field in Brazil, *transfeminismo* has the potential to challenge misinterpretations of intersectionality, while espousing a decolonial approach to knowledge and politics. This approach could ultimately benefit (intercultural) communication theory, practice, and politics as the field continues to push for the de-centering of whiteness and the West.

Intersectionality has become a (white) feminist buzzword, to the point that feminists of color suggest that it is as though *everyone* is doing intersectional work—or that the word itself stands in for actual intersectional analysis (Cooper, 2016; Puar, 2012). Recent scholarship revisits Crenshaw's (1989, 1991) original work to challenge feminist misreadings of the framework, while attempting to salvage it from being subsumed under neoliberal fantasies of post-racism and multiculturalism. It has been up to feminists of color, especially black feminists, to interrogate and challenge the ways in which intersectionality has been diluted by white feminists.

This chapter starts with an overview of the debate around (mis)interpretations of Crenshaw's (1991) intersectionality. Next, I briefly review scholars' call for intercultural communication's engagement with intersectionality to then analyze how the concept traveled to the Global South, specifically to Brazil. Finally, most of the present chapter is dedicated to analyzing how Brazilian *transfeminismo* has avoided the mistakes (white) feminists have made in their use of intersectionality to build an epistemological and political project that concurrently defies colonial understandings of identity—especially gender identity—while beginning to reimagine different systems of identification. This project, I believe, could be useful in the continuous push for the de-whitening and decolonizing of intercultural communication.

THE WHITENING OF INTERSECTIONALITY

The use of intersectionality as a feminist concept might be as popular as its multiple (mis)interpretations. Over the past few years, black feminist scholars started reviewing the most common ways feminists across different disciplines used the concept. A few tendencies developed within feminist studies' appropriation of intersectionality, according to Bilge (2013) and Cooper (2016): first, scholars tended to conflate intersectionality with a theory of subjectivity. Second, and consequently, this approach whitened intersectionality by decentering its concern around structural, political, and representational oppression, turning the framework into a synonym of "diversity." Finally, intersectionality became devoid of its black feminist origins. Emptied from its original concerns with intersecting, simultaneous oppression, the framework became a simple rhetorical nod in the neoliberal academy.

Building on the work of black feminists before her, Crenshaw (1989, 1991) conceptualized intersectionality as an antidote to approaches to gender and race discrimination bounded by, respectively, white women's and black men's experiences with structural, political, and representational oppression. Crenshaw noticed the inadequacy of feminist and antiracist initiatives that consistently framed gender and race oppression as mutually exclusive—or through single-axis analyses—thus deeming the experiences of black women unknowable to identity politics (1991, p. 1242). To remedy the invisibility of how women of color experience structural violence and invisibility within political movements that seek social justice, Crenshaw (1989) coined the concept of intersectionality. In her subsequent piece, "Mapping the Margins," the scholar expanded on the framework by highlighting three aspects of intersectionality: structural, political, and representational (Crenshaw, 1991). Crenshaw (1991) illustrates each dimension in concrete ways, focusing specifically on how identity politics were failing black women in each of those three realms.

The popularity of the framework, especially within feminist studies, has grown significantly since Crenshaw's (1989, 1991) seminal pieces. In fact, Cooper (2016) speaks of intersectionality's ubiquitous presence in the field as giving the impression "that 'everyone' does intersectional work" (p. 1), though there are many disagreements over the framework's meaning and effectiveness. Many of these disagreements stem from the ways in which feminists in multiple disciplines have misunderstood the framework (Bilge, 2013; Calafell, 2014; Cho, Crenshaw, & McCall, 2013; Cooper, 2016). Below, I review rebuttals to the most common misunderstandings of intersectionality.

The most reproduced inaccuracy around intersectionality is that the framework is supposed to be an all-encompassing account of identity and difference. Crenshaw (1991) herself warned against this interpretation, stating that intersectionality is not intended "as some new, totalizing theory of identity" (p. 1244). Yet, this understanding of intersectionality has been reproduced in feminist studies ad nauseum, generating in turn critiques that intersectionality essentializes identity. Cooper (2016) responds to these accusations by posing that "never did [Crenshaw's] work indicate that intersectionality was an effective tool of accounting for identities at any level beyond the structural" (p. 4). On that note, Cooper (2016) adds that intersectionality's project was never to fully account for black women's identities; instead, Crenshaw's work concentrates on "the problem of recognition rather than a problem of subjectivity" (p. 6). Intersectionality is thus concerned with making these experiences with structural oppression *knowable* to institutions.

Puar (2012) offers a somewhat similar critique when she contends that intersectionality became a rhetorical mode that replaces intersectional analysis itself. Specifically, as it has been "mainstreamed" in feminist studies, intersectionality seems to indicate "difference from," with white women as the essential center of gender identity: "many white feminists, although hailing intersectionality as [a] primary methodological rubric continue to take gender difference as foundational" (Puar, 2012, p. 53). This, Puar reiterates, is not an issue that stems from Crenshaw's (1991) original work; rather, it is a consequence of intersectionality's reproduction in (white) feminist studies.

At best, the tendency to obscure the contingency of intersectionality's emergence results in misunderstanding the framework. As argued by Cho, Crenshaw, and McCall (2013), "some of what circulates as critical debate about what intersectionality is or does reflects a lack of engagement with both originating and contemporary literatures on intersectionality" (p. 788), a point that is also supported by both Bilge (2013) and Cooper (2016). At worst, however, this lack of engagement with intersectionality's original texts reproduces the oppression the framework seeks to expose.

In tandem with questions regarding intersectionality's applicability to multiple identities are uses of the framework as synonym for diversity. Bilge (2013) provides a thorough account of how intersectionality in neoliberal times is subsumed under "diversity" initiatives. Likewise, Puar (2012) wonders, "What does an intersectional critique look like—or more to the point, what does it do—in an age of neoliberal pluralism, absorption and accommodation of difference, of all kinds of differences?" (p. 53). Puar further questions if current emptied accounts of difference serve to further reify white liberal feminism. Calafell (2014) makes a similar point when she poses that making feminist scholarship in communication studies intersectional requires more than "using the words *diversity* and *intersectionality* as signals or placeholders for commitment" (p. 266), which often amount to very little actual structural change in academic institutions.

In communication, the field's foundation on white Western epistemology (Halualani, Mendoza, & Drzewiecka, 2009; Nakayama & Krizek, 1995) has limited its engagement with intersectionality more broadly and race-related issues more specifically, in turn generating a series of critiques in its subfields. Scholars of color in intercultural communication, for instance, have made important efforts over the years to dislocate the discipline's "white problem," or the tendency to re-center, even if unconsciously, white Western knowledges and concerns (Moon as cited in Holling & Moon, 2015, p. 3). Eguchi and Asante (2016) firmly assert that "The U.S. American capitalistic heteronormative circulations of power recurrently patrol and protect the boundaries of intercultural communication theory" at the expense of LGBTQ+ people of color (pp. 171–72). Additionally, other scholars have interrogated intercultural communication's reliance on single-axis analyses while also calling for the subfield's critical engagement with race, queerness, and cisnormativity, among others (Chávez, 2013; Eguchi & Asante, 2016; Johnson, 2013; Yep, 2010). Johnson (2013), for instance, contends that intercultural communication's critical task to uncover power relations cannot be accomplished without the inclusion of trans* identities, especially as they intersect with race and class.

Several assessments and uses of intersectionality may coexist (Cho, Crenshaw, & McCall, 2013). Shifting away from discussing what intersectionality *is*, Cho, Crenshaw, and McCall (2013) concentrate instead on what they identify as the three general ways in which intersectionality has been utilized, resulting in what they call a field of intersectionality studies. The first heuristic category they identify is the application and expansion of intersectionality as a framework to analyze multiple context-specific situations in which a single-axis frame of analysis is insufficient. The second subfield of intersectionality studies investigates its theoretical and methodological reach and limitations, "and whether intersectionality's contextual articulations call either for further development or for disavowal and replacement" (Cho, Crenshaw, & McCall, 2013, p. 785). One notable example of this application of intersectionality is Yep's (2013) assessment of another scholar's failed intercultural analysis that focused primarily on a subject's gender and sexuality, relegating race, class, and nation to the analysis' background. In a previous piece, Yep (2010) had already warned communication scholars against treating intersectionality as a decontextualized series of boxes to be ticked; instead, he proposes the concept of "thick intersectionalities," in which scholars engage with intricate "particularities of individuals' lives and identities associated with their race, class, gender, sexuality, and national locations by understanding their history and personhood in concrete time and space, and the interplay between individual subjectivity, personal agency, systemic arrangements, and structural forces" (Yep, 2010, p. 173). Yep's concept thoughtfully rebukes the neoliberal tendency to simply absorb all kinds of difference—which is akin to checking boxes—and instead theoretically engages with contextual and structural specificity.

A final trend in intersectional studies deals with the practical application of the framework by activists engaged with varied movements (Cho, Crenshaw, & McCall, 2013). As Cho, Crenshaw, and McCall (2013) point out, these tendencies are not mutually exclusive, but very much interrelated. In this chapter, I take the previous points into consideration in order to analyze how intersectionality has impacted the development of Brazilian *transfeminismo*, and how intercultural communication may benefit from this emerging field and movement. First, however, I briefly outline concerns over scholarly exchanges between metropoles, or the Global North, and peripheries—or the Global South.

WHEN THEORIES TRAVEL: INTERSECTIONALITY IN BRAZILIAN FEMINIST STUDIES

Globalization has generated consequences that go beyond economic and political factors. Costa (2000) emphasizes how an increasingly complex "migration" of theories provides displacement and appropriation, resistance and transformation as part of the development of a transnational academic community. One of the consequences of this theoretical migration is that a "global division of labor" has also been established in academia. Based on the work of Chilean cultural critic Nelly Richard, Costa notes that the academy is too impacted by an unequal flow of theoretical work: in this unbalanced division of labor, the Global North produces original theoretical thought while the Global South "is expected to supply it with case studies" (as cited in Costa, 2000, p. 740). In feminist studies, this division has generated particular challenges, especially in a neoliberal context.

The global emergence of neoliberalism further complicates this scenario. Mohanty (2013) claims that postmodern feminist projects become especially limited—and even problematic—in neoliberal contexts. In investigating how her own work to decolonize feminist theory has traveled, Mohanty (2013) notes that a common critique of her approach, namely that systemic analyses of power operations are inevitably "reductionist" and "totalizing" (p. 967), is indeed an expression of the unfortunate combination of postmodernist projects and neoliberalism. As a result, she states that there is a "proliferation of depoliticized multiplicities that is a hallmark of neoliberal intellectual landscapes" (p. 968). A much more dangerous consequence according to Mohanty is the domestication of "power differences, transforming systemic projects of resistance into commodified, private acts of rebellion" (p. 968).

Concerns over the intersection of globalization and neoliberalism in the academy are extended to the uses of intersectionality. As the framework travels to other geographical locations, such as Europe, as "new" and "cutting-edge" following a neoliberal logic, its adoption might inadvertently render the work of postcolonial feminists invisible (Puar, 2012). Puar (2012) believes that "the U.S. is reproduced as the dominant site of feminist inquiry through the use of intersectionality as a heuristic to teach difference" (p. 55), so intersectionality's (white) feminist misreadings crosses borders as well, including the idea that intersectionality prescribes which identity categories should be salient in intersectional analysis. However, as Cho, Crenshaw, and McCall (2013) remind us,

> Intersectionality has . . . been posed more as a nodal point than as a closed system—a gathering place for open-ended investigations of the overlapping and conflicting dynamics of [inequalities]. . . This seems to us to be a more apt

> description of intersectionality's starting point than one that frames intersectionality as only categorically, spatially, or temporally rooted in specific relations or superficially preoccupied with "difference." (p. 788)

Back to postmodern feminist projects, these global movements have impacted concepts such as social and geographical location as well as experience in Latin America. Costa (2000) narrates how poststructuralist approaches' skepticism in universalist approaches to feminist theory may have adversely created the essentialized category of "the third-world woman as a repository of unadulterated difference that is oftentimes translated as authenticity" (p. 741). But instead of shying away from the concept of experience, Latin American feminists have responded to this trend by further politicizing and historicizing difference, *especially* through the concept of experience. In Costa's (2000) words, "Acknowledging the historicity, partiality, and contingent nature of our truth claims (e.g., that they are effects of social struggles) leads feminists ultimately to a recognition of the existence of other voices and worlds until now suppressed in the dominant epistemes of the West" (p. 734). More than an acknowledgement, this paradigmatic shift meant that differences were understood as the "effects of multiple oppressions" (p. 734). In Brazil, this idea laid the ground for the theoretical migration of intersectionality.

In Brazilian feminist studies, intersectionality is used in varied ways, some of which reproduce similar problems as in certain strands of feminist studies in the United States, and some of which remain truthful to Crenshaw's (1989, 1991) intent. In the following paragraphs, I first briefly examine the early tendency to apprehend intersectionality as a theory of subjectivity to then analyze how the framework has been used more recently, including its profound impact on the development of *transfeminismo*.

Early uses of intersectionality in Brazilian feminism suggest the concept is a qualifying noun (even though the Portuguese word is clearly an Anglicism—"interseccionalidade"), usually in relationship to feminist theories of subjectivity and difference. Leading feminist scholars Costa and Ávila (2005), for example, used the terms "intersectional difference" and "intersectionality" in writing about Gloria Anzaldúa's (2007) *La Conciencia de la Mestiza*. The authors do so to point to Anzaldúa's important contribution to theories of subjectivity from a feminist perspective, for which the authors rightfully credit being part of a scholarly movement led by women of color in the United States, eventually "opening up, in the 1990s, the course to intersectional gender analysis" (Costa & Ávila, 2005, p. 692). The authors, however, base part of their analysis of Anzaldúa on the value white feminists like Susan Friedman, Judith Butler, Nancy Frasier, and Teresa de Lauretis place on the queer Chicana author's work. But what is really noteworthy is the absence of any reference to Crenshaw's (1989, 1991) work, even as the term she coined—"intersectionality"—is abundantly mentioned throughout the article. Here, we see the materialization of both of Bilge's (2013) and Cooper's (2016) critiques: first, by using the terms associated with Crenshaw's scholarship without any actual reference to her work seems to reproduce Bilge's concerns over the erasure of black women's intellectual legacy and the reproduction of power differentials as theories travel to transnational contexts. Second, by using the term in the context of theorizing subjectivity, and *not* intersecting systems of oppression, Costa and Ávila replicate the confusion over the fact that "the framework never claimed to be an affirmative assertion about how subjectivity is constituted" (Cooper, 2016, p. 5).

More recently, intersectionality became central in articulating Brazilian black feminism. While Afro-Brazilian feminists were active scholars and advocates starting in the late 1970s, "feminismo negro" (black feminism) as a field of activism and scholarship identified as such is relatively recent in Brazil (Silva, 2018, p. 253). In reflecting on the different generations of black women in Brazil and their respective work, Silva (2018) challenges the tendency of younger black feminists in the country to "credit to Kimberlé Crenshaw the concept of intersectional feminism" (p. 254), even though Brazilian black feminists, such as Lélia Gonzalez, were writing about gender, race, and class oppression in the 1970s without necessarily using the term "intersectionality." She adds, "Although [Gonzalez] did not coin the term intersectional feminism, the genesis of the concept was already infused in her scholarly work and political intervention" (p. 254). Like Crenshaw herself, who firmly advocates for the black feminist genealogy of intersectionality, Silva proposes a context-specific genealogy of intersectional work by Brazilian black feminists who are made invisible in the migration and importing of theories from the Global North. Without a doubt, the concept of intersectionality as the understanding of how systems operate together to produce simultaneous, multiple oppressions is foundational for the recent articulations of black feminism. In this chapter, however, I turn to another scholarly and political project influenced by intersectionality, *transfeminismo*.

THE FOUNDATIONS OF BRAZILIAN *TRANSFEMINISMO*

Unlike white, Western feminist movements, *transfeminismo* blossomed out of intersectional questionings, such as the ones proposed by black feminists in both Brazil and the United States, especially over interrogations around who is the subject of feminism. As a product of these inquiries, *transfeminismo* has been not only able to avoid the single-axis, (white) feminist traps

Latin American feminisms fell for, but it has been able to challenge feminism's epistemological and political projects as well. This section outlines a series of essays about *transfeminismo* by Brazilian and other Latin American transfeministas, with a focus on two interconnected commonalities in their diverse approaches: the commitment to disrupt biological essentialism, and the purpose of doing so via intersectionality.

Transfeminismo's existence is simultaneously justified and propelled by the historical exclusion of transwomen from feminist spaces. Coacci's (2014) work traces *transfeminismo*'s origins to the heated debates in Latin American and Caribbean feminist conferences of the 1980s, which, among other issues, discussed how race, ethnicity, class, and sexual orientation interact with gender oppression. The core of these conversations questioned who the subject of feminism should be, who could claim to be feminist, and whose political agenda feminism should adopt. It was not until the late 1980s and early 1990s, with their continuing invisibility within the feminist movement, that lesbians, indigenous, and black women started organizing their own regional and continental conferences (Coacci, 2014). By the end of the 1990s, the question of inclusion had already shifted to a question of how to deal with these new "subjectivities and feminisms" (Coacci, 2014, p. 139). Coacci poses that there was considerable pushback against these other feminisms over the fear that accounting for differences would fragment the movement. Hence, the preference was still given to the "general cause in favor of [cisgender] 'women' " (p. 139).

While the account in the above paragraph is widely known among those who study feminisms in Latin America and the Caribbean, the absence of trans* individuals from these stories/histories is noteworthy. Were trans* people not present in Latin American feminist spaces? Adrião, Toneli, and Maluf (2011) suggest that while trans* people were indeed present in various feminist spaces, it was not until 2005 that visible tensions around their participation in the largest feminist conference of Latin America and the Caribbean emerged (p. 666). Scholars agree that at the heart of debates surrounding the place of transwomen specifically within feminism was the questioning of feminism's subject itself (Adrião, Toneli, and Maluf, 2011; Coacci, 2014). Or yet, the question was whether or not the category "woman," like the designation "feminist," could be the product of self-identification.

Historically part of feminist spaces, Brazilian *transfeministas* did not articulate the idea of feminism from a trans* perspective until the late 1990s and early 2000s. Coacci (2014) credits activist Aline Freitas with adopting the term *transfeminismo* around the same time. The term then became popular in the mid- and late 2000s in Spanish- and Portuguese-speaking countries, especially through the writings of Kim Perez and Beatriz Preciado (Coacci, 2014). A *transfeminista* critique of feminism has been growing and developing over the years, with trans* people connecting especially via social networks (Coacci, 2014; Jesus, 2014). Jesus and Alves (2012) link recent scholarly and political developments of *transfeminismo* to the growing political consciousness of trans* people as a social group and their ability to connect online and on the streets.

Transfeminismo can be defined as a feminist project that challenges the "morphological subordination of gender (as a psychosocial construct) to sex (as biology), conditioned by historical processes, criticizing it as a social practice that justifies the oppression of any persons whose bodies do not conform to binary notions of gender" (Jesus, 2014, p. 243). It is simultaneously a philosophical and epistemological endeavor as well as a political movement that seeks to interrogate feminisms from a trans* perspective (Jesus, 2014, p. 248). Vieira (2018) understands the importance of this project based on both the invisibility and hypervisibility of trans* people, which is expressed through a "lack of imagination" or an "excess of imagination in the form of stigmas" (p. 345). Either way, the result is erasure and depreciation of "the concrete existence of trans people in society" (Vieira, 2018, p. 345). Here, I first briefly delineate *transfeminismo*'s commitment to dismantling biological essentialism to then connect this approach to another related foundational aspect of it, intersectionality.

Disrupting Biological Essentialism

In examining the "usefulness" of *transfeminismo*, Jesus (2014) suggests that there are particular issues cisgender people may experience that potentially overlap with some of the challenges trans* folks face. Similarly, Vieira (2018) establishes connections with feminist activism and scholarship, stating that "the fight against machismo unites society as a whole" (p. 346). *Transfeminismo* then emerges as a way to "affirm subaltern identities and femininities forgotten by cisgender feminism" (Vieira, 2018, p. 358). Jesus (2014) compares the personal account of a ciswoman's hysterectomy and the subsequent questions about "womanhood" she received with the experiences of transwomen: "Mayer experienced an oppression that is daily imposed on transwomen: that they are . . . not women because they are missing a female *essence*," usually attributed to reproductive organs, such as a uterus (p. 244). A *transfeminista* perspective notices these connections, and pushes against a normative system of gender that "suffocate people of all genders and social identities" (Jesus, 2014, p. 244). In an interview with Coacci (2014), *transfeministas* Aline Freitas and Viviane Vergueiro agree that their feminism is concerned with the deconstruction of biological essentialism, specifically as it relates to diverse and nonconforming bodies, and the ability to "claim masculinity and/or femininity [or neither] without necessarily having to go through medical processes" (p. 153). This last point is especially critical for Brazilian *transfeministas*.

Though there is no absolute agreement around the idea of *transfeminismo* as a social movement, *transfeministas* articulate demands for what they understand to be basic rights, other than supporting diverse trans* movements. One of these demands relates precisely to their fight against the colonial legacy of biological essentialism. As Jesus and Alves (2012) explain, the fight to detach one's assigned biological sex to a person's self-identified gender impacts trans* folks' ability to obtain government-issued identification—a basic civil right. In the recent past, the process to obtain what is called a "social name" in Brazil was difficult to acquire without psychological and medical evaluation, which often prescribed affirmation surgeries. In 2018, as a result of trans* movements' struggles, a Brazilian high court issued a provision which facilitates trans* people's access to a "social name" on government-issued identifications by not requiring psychological and medical evaluations and interventions (Lopes, 2018). Yet, the absence of a concrete law about gender identity continues to make this process inaccessible for poor trans* people of color, like the transwoman mentioned in the introduction, Laysa Fortuna. The aforementioned provision still depends on a trans* person's ability to petition a legal name change (which is usually easier with the help of a paid lawyer), which then depends on a particular judge's interpretation of the situation, and of course, as Vieira (2018) points out, the judge might be cissexist and transphobic: "It is still common for judges to require psychiatric evaluations attesting to a person's 'transsexualism' and even the requirement of surgeries so that trans people can have documents updated, which constitute a severe attempt against trans people's rights" (p. 349). Self-identified black/trans activist Santana (2016) draws parallels between the name change process in Brazil and the relationship between the country's judicial system and Afro-Brazilians by stating, "The feeling of being on trial in the name change process is part of the same logic of judgment Black bodies experience for the purpose of incarceration. Both processes are punitive in that our humanity [is] judged by oppressive institutions" (para. 4). *Transfeminismo* is a "theoretical-activist" project that emerged out of necessity; its goal is to both challenge hegemonic ideas about identity and to advocate for the rights and dignity of trans* people under the current system.

Transfeminismo sheds light on gender essentialism and cisnormativity as integral aspects of Brazil's colonial legacy. Vergueiro (2015a), who identifies as an "intersectional transfeminista," points out that cisnormativity intersects with other parts of the colonial project in the Americas, which are "historically genocidal, white supremacist, and committed to myriad forms of subordination and biopolitical control" (Vergueiro, 2015b, p. 38). A decolonial perspective, thus, questions and destabilize first and foremost the colonial logic of subordination, including the articulation of hierarchized binaries and ethnocentric medical discourses, to then reclaim indigenous and other non-Western perspectives around what is now known as gender (Vergueiro, 2015b). Vergueiro (2015b) is explicitly committed to an intersectional decolonial effort that simultaneously foregrounds the colonial nature of cisnormativity while undoing the internalization of colonial forms of subjectivation.

Transfeminismo must be committed to dismantling societal hierarchies that intersect with cisnormativity, including those related to race, sexuality, ability, and so on. Jesus (2014) touches on the importance of intersectionality to critique cisnormativity when she states: "Transmen, transwomen, *travestis*, and other transgender people tend to be considered only in terms of their gender identification as trans*, being disregarded as human beings with gender, sexual orientation, race, age, geographical origin, ability, etc." (p. 254). Like many *transfeministas*, Jesus is fully aware of the need to interrogate knowledge, social movements, and representation of trans* people that conceal the intersectional character of their oppression. *Transfeminismo* is thus committed to structural, political, and representational intersectionality, as examined in the following section.

Transfeminismo and Intersectionality

Intersectionality and *transfeminismo* connect in their challenges to essentialist approaches to structural violence and political agendas. In her "archeology of *transfeminismo*," Jesus (2014) identifies several lines of feminist political and epistemological contributions as foundational to the ongoing development of *transfeminsmo*, including black feminism's critique of white feminism's essentialism, as well as its focus on "processes of political consciousness and resistance" (p. 243). Black women's critiques of feminism's blind spots opened the door for other marginalized identities to question who is the movement's subject, including indigenous women, poor women, women with disabilities, and of course, trans* women (p. 247). An example of such connection is Juno Creminini's *transfeminista* manifesto in which the activist clearly articulates the origins of *transfeminismo*: "my feminism has been influenced by black feminism and its annotations about intersectionality. . . this is important to me because it puts into perspective who we are, what we fight for, and how all of that created trans* feminism" (as cited in Jesus, 2014, p. 247).

Transfeministas use the concept of structural intersectionality to theorize about and advocate on behalf of their community in all of its multiplicity. Vergueiro (2015b) understands intersectionality's shaping of identity as a result of interlocking systems of structural oppression that intersect in ways that create normative identities. Vergueiro further argues that "the critical analysis of cisgender normativity can only be done via intersectionality" (p. 193). The author explicitly suggests that she is challenging homogenizing accounts of trans* experiences in Brazil because "to comprehend the plurality in our voices means to complexify simplifications about any social group and, consequently, articulate fights for social justice from the paradigm of diversity, and not from the supposed common agenda within groups" (p. 31). It is clear that Vergueiro's intention is to make trans* experiences *knowable* to systems and social movements while fighting to dismantle these systems.

Similarly, Jesus's (2014) account gives a sense that *transfeminista* perspectives are indeed multiple, though firmly grounded in political intersectionality's idea of coalition. She claims, however, that for a project to be considered *transfeminista* it must be committed to at least four principles: first, the dismantling of essentialist links between gender and biology, as mentioned above; second, the ratification of the intersectional character of oppressions; third, the recognition of the historical fight of *travestis* and *transexuais*[2] as well as "the personal experience of the transgender population in general as fundamental elements for the comprehension of feminism" (p. 249); finally, *transfeminismo* accepts contributions from all persons, trans* or otherwise, who do not fit within cissexist societal models. Moreover, "transfeminismo recognizes the intersection of identities" in the oppression of nonconforming bodies who fall outside of racist and sexist ideals (p. 249).

A compelling motivation for *transfeminismo* is the alarming physical and structural violence trans* people face in Latin America in general, and in Brazil specifically. Jesus (2014) cites reports from global organizations such as Transgender Europe that paint a horrific picture of the violation of basic human rights of trans* people, including that Brazil was responsible for roughly 50 percent of all murders of trans* people in Latin America between 2008 and 2011. An updated 2018 report from Transgender Europe tracking murders of individuals under the trans* umbrella in seventy-two countries suggest that this violence has not receded since Brazil continues to occupy the first position in their rank. Trans*-led Brazilian NGO Rede Trans Brasil monitors these acts of violence more thoroughly, breaking the general number down into other demographic categories, such as gender identity, race, and age. According to their 2018 report, most of those murdered were *travesti*-identified, or feminine-presenting, black/Afro-Brazilian, and younger than thirty-five years old (Rede Trans Brasil, 2019). The report draws parallels between these numbers and the ongoing extermination of cisgender black people in Brazil (Rede Trans Brasil, 2019). Ultimately, *transfeminismo* propels the message that monitoring and denouncing structural violence against trans* folks is the result of *their own* political organization and activism (Jesus, 2014).

Transfeminismo is not directly connected to social movements historically formed by *transexuais* and *travestis*, though the respect and support for them is a *transfeminista* commitment (Jesus, 2014; Vergueiro, 2015b; Vieira, 2018). One tension that mediates *transfeminismo* and these social movements is the discussion around de-pathologizing trans* identities. As a coalitional perspective that aims to represent diverse trans* and other nonconforming identities, *transfeminismo*'s advocacy in this respect has divided positions (Coacci, 2014). Some folks under the trans* umbrella, especially *transexuais*, defend pathologizing trans* identities as means for receiving free medical treatment in the Brazilian universal health-care system—they usually identify with the gender binary, which is in line with this medical approach that postulates that one must be either/or gender (Coacci, 2014). De-pathologizing could mean loss of access to health care for poor *transexuais*. Vieira (2018) and many other *transfeministas* (Coacci, 2014; Vergueiro, 2015b; Jesus, 2014) take an intersectional approach to this issue by concurrently recognizing the importance of access under the present system while also challenging "these protocols [...] that end up excluding or criminalizing trans people who do not fit rigid social expectations of gender, like *travestis*," an extremely vulnerable group of trans* people (Vieira, 2018, p. 348). In this case, trans* folks' material realities are impacted differently by specific policies especially at the intersection of class and race, and their political decisions reflect these structural constrains (Jesus, 2014, p. 254). Additionally, the fact that this is an ongoing issue between *transfeminismo* and other trans* movements does not mean that other political and epistemological projects are not emerging in tandem with current, established perspectives. Santana (2016), for instance, suggests that while some black trans* activists do not use "the language of transfeminismo," they *practice* an embodied "abolitionist *transfeminismo*" that is just as powerful (para. 7).

Other issues of structural violence that *transfeministas* shed light on through both structural and political intersectionality are related to areas in which current provisional policies do not reach, namely the familial space, the school, and the workplace. In the case of the home, Vieira (2018) wonders what role public policies could have in protecting trans* people who have been rejected by their families, and what role the government has in promoting education around the importance of accepting and welcoming trans* family members. Vieira (2018) understands that such familial violence against trans* people "will extend itself and produce effects in several social spheres" (p. 349). Similarly, schools too are oppressive environments where trans* people report being abused not only by classmates, but also by teachers and administrators. Vieira (2018) asserts that there is no right to education in a transphobic society. Though the narrative is that trans* people "evade" formal education, the reality is that they are expelled from it (Vieira, 2018,

p. 349). Most importantly, efforts to address cissexism and transphobia in the classroom are generally met with fierce opposition.

The growing visibility of transphobic, cissexist conservative discourses has schools as its preferred target. In Brazil, the 2018 election of far-right conservative Christian Jair Bolsonaro is a culmination of the transphobic and queerphobic discourses that have been circulating in the country for many years. Evangelical Christians across several countries have coined the term "ideologia de gênero" (gender ideology) to refer to any modest efforts to promote discussions around gender identity and sexuality in educational settings (Rangel, 2018; Saldaña, 2018). I would like to use two recent events to illustrate the popularity and now structural sanction of the fight against this so-called gender ideology in Brazil. In October 2017, philosopher Judith Butler was scheduled to give talks in São Paulo about her recent work around Jewishness and Zionism. News of her talk was shared in online conservative circles that credited her as the creator of "gender ideology." As a result, Butler was met with harassment and protests, to the point that demonstrators burned an effigy of the scholar amid shouts of "burn the witch" and "not in Brazil" (Aragão, 2017). Next, in January 2019, Bolsonaro's appointed Secretary of Human Rights Damares Alves, who like the president is a conservative Christian and a fervent opponent of "gender ideology," stated that Brazil was entering a "new era" in her inauguration speech, one in which "boys wear blue and girls wear pink" (Pains, 2019). The current conservative landscape in Brazil works to expose, simultaneously, the structural violence to which trans* people are subjected and the need for a *transfeminista* political agenda.

A final recent development in *transfeminismo* relates to representational intersectionality. Often a less discussed aspect of Crenshaw's (1991) work, representational intersectionality is a crucial aspect of *transfeminismo*'s political articulations. Crenshaw (1991) establishes connections between the structural oppression and political exclusion of black women to their dehumanizing representation in popular culture. This dehumanization happens concomitantly via the production of popular culture images as well as through failed intersectional criticism, which tends to ignore the ways in which sexism and racism intersect to produce damaging images of black women. Jesus, in an interview with Vieira (2018), evaluates the recent shift in trans* representation in Brazilian media as "not just any kind of representation. . . it is a conscious, informed representation" (p. 370). Jesus affirms that though not all visible trans* people in media are clearly *transfeministas*, their work consciously or unconsciously provides a *transfeminista* perspective. However, there are artists whose activism in media is visible and intends to challenge cissexism, machismo, racism, and classism, such as in the case of black *transfeministas* Linn da Quebrada, Liniker, MC Xuxú and others (pp. 370–71). What is noteworthy in this modest trend is that these artists reclaim subaltern femininities, such as *travesti* femininity, a political identity formed in the streets of Latin America and which is not associated with a specific gender—or sexuality, for that matter, given that Western scholars have erroneously linked *travestis* to "homosexuality" (Belizario, 2019).

Transfeminismo is a movement under construction in Latin America. More than simply reproducing imported scholarship on intersectionality, *transfeminismo* "is being ressignified and adapted to the voices and realities transwomen and transmen, *travestis* and other trans people in these lands *al sur del mundo*" (Jesus, 2014, p. 254). Like Vergueiro (2015a, 2015b), Jesus (2014) highlights *transfeministas'* creativity in adapting and at times rejecting established theories from the Global North to the contingency of trans* people's lives and experiences in Latin America, a move that "is in opposition to the colonial tendency of introjection of and subordination to concepts from cultural metropoles" (p. 254). Together, intersectionality and decolonial approaches to identification have aided *transfeministas* in articulating the structural violence against and political invisibility of trans* people while rethinking foundational Western assumptions about gender identification. Here, intersectionality is used as a sensibility, as intended by Crenshaw (1991). *Transfeministas* understand the dynamism of the framework and do not feel trapped or frozen by supposedly predetermined salient categories of identity. Beyond making their experiences knowable to systems of oppression, *transfeministas* are committed to dismantling and reimagining these systems.

INTERCULTURAL COMMUNICATION NEEDS *TRANSFEMINISMO*

The modest space *transfeministas* are carving out is the result of both their political organization and also of their contributions to scholarship. As a political project, *transfeminismo* embodies Bilge's (2013) call for a "radical intersectional praxis" in coalition-building, which is a difficult task in a neoliberal "diversity regime" in which social movements are "now required to compete with each other, rather than collaborate" (p. 406). Jesus (2014) urges *transfeministas* to continue to take on the challenge to think and write to a diverse and heterogenous publics, including social movements and varied institutions, such as the academy. Previous research on trans* identities was largely conducted by cisgender people, many of whom were Western scholars, and most of whom imposed their Western lenses on their subjects' experiences (Belizario, 2019; Yep, 2013). As a result, many of these studies were committed to "uncovering" how certain practices and bodies fit binary categories of gender and/or sexuality familiar to Western academia, much in the same way communication studies continues to do (Chávez, 2013; Johnson, 2013). The absence of trans* scholars in academia aids in the reproduction of social injustices against trans* people in general (Johnson, 2013; Vieira, 2018). The *transfeministas* highlighted in this chapter illustrate the necessity of having trans* people writing about their experiences with structural oppression, while deconstructing cisnormativity and reenvisioning different systems of identification. It will be crucial to see how these contributions are going to impact the future of trans* and feminist movements and their demands, as well as the landscape of queer and feminist scholarship. For now, however, the field is established enough that it could potentially benefit intercultural communication.

Accounts of power relations in intercultural contexts will not be comprehensive if scholars overlook how trans* people's existence is shaped by intersecting systems of oppression, such as race, class, nation, immigration status, and so on (Eguchi & Asante, 2016; Johnson, 2013; Yep, 2013). Concurrently, intercultural communication scholars should pay attention to trans* people's knowledge production about non-oppressive ways to reconceptualize Western systems of gender and sexuality, as well as the political strategies these groups generate under precarious structural conditions that both seek to alleviate their existence under the current system while reimagining a political project in which trans* people are fully entitled to human and civil rights. Instead of directing their attention to the Global North, *transfeministas* increasingly focus on those who have been surviving and challenging coloniality, racism, and transphobia through their lived experiences in Latin America. It seems like a similar movement from intercultural communication scholars could help address the field's "white problem." Additionally, as Eng, Halberstam, and Muñoz (2005) contend, the supremacy of U.S.-based scholarship reproduces dynamics that go beyond academia, in which meanings of queerness, and gender and sexuality categories more broadly, are subsumed by "U.S. nationalist identity and political agenda globally" (p. 15). In paying attention to *transfeminista* work in Brazil, intercultural communication scholars could potentially help shift the field's Western-centric tendencies and develop a more nuanced understanding of power relations within context-specific structures, all while learning from the theoretical, political, and coalitional contributions *transfeministas* have to offer. These possibilities fall perfectly in line with what critical scholars have demanded from intercultural communication over the recent years (Chávez, 2013; Eguchi & Asante, 2016; Johnson, 2013; Yep, 2010).

Transfeminismo's purposes of dignity and self-determination may seem modest, but in a context of white supremacist cis-heteronormative violence—from the need to "pass" to the high murder rate among trans* people—these objectives become radical. On that note, I would like to conclude through the words of *transfeminista* Viviane Vergueiro (2015b), who has strongly advocated for an intersectional decolonial approach to trans* studies and politics:

> We have an immense intersectional challenge in institutions and in sociocultural constructions disseminated to erase us, or to push us to exist under their conditions: in silence, in secret, in confession, in condescension, in the passibility that allows us an always-intersectionally threatened survival through cisnormative violences of unconsented medical interventions, documents, reports, and guns turned against our bodies and identities. (p. 223)

Transfeminismo is a good example of preserving intersectionality's original, critical contributions while envisioning innovative ways to apply the concept as a sensibility in the Brazilian context and beyond. Like critical scholars in intercultural communication, *transfeministas* too are concerned with the violence of normative identities; to that end, scholars whose intellectual and political work seek to dismantle cissexist and other interlocking systems of oppression, such as white supremacy and heteropatriarchy, should be done with the awareness of power imbalances in transnational knowledge production. Ultimately, this project must also function in tandem with more generative decolonial aspirations to reconceptualize identity.

NOTE

1. Trans* activists in Brazil use this prefix to indicate an umbrella term that is more appropriate for the Brazilian context than the term "transgender." The term *transsexual* is still widely used in the Brazilian trans* community; it is usually claimed by older activists who identify with the gender binary.
2. The term *transexual* is still widely used in the Brazilian trans* community; it is usually claimed by older activists who identify with the gender binary.

REFERENCES

Adrião, K. G., Toneli, M. J. F., & Maluf, S. W. (2011). O movimento feminista brasileiro na virada do século XX: Reflexões sobre sujeitos políticos na interface com as noções de democracia e autonomia. *Estudos Feministas*, 3, 661–81.

Anzaldúa, G. (2007). *Borderlands/la frontera: The new mestiza* (3rd ed.). San Francisco, CA: Aunt Lute.

Aragão, A. (2017, November 8). Please watch this insane footage of Judith Butler being called a witch in Brazil. *Buzzfeed News*. Retrieved from https://www.buzzfeednews.com/article/alexandrearagao/judith-butler-brazil.

Belizario, F. (2019, March 7). Gênero: Feminilidade travesti. *Medium*. Retrieved from https://medium.com/@febelizario/g%C3%AAnero-feminilidade-travesti-aaffaf7fb386.

Bilge, S. (2013). Intersectionality undone: Saving intersectionality from feminist intersectionality studies. *Du Bois Review, 10*(2), 405–24.

Calafell, B. M. (2014). The future of feminist scholarship: Beyond the politics of inclusion. *Women's Studies in Communication, 37*, 266–70.

Chávez, K. (2013). Pushing boundaries: Queer intercultural communication. *Journal of International and Intercultural Communication, 6*(2), 83–95.

Cho, S., Crenshaw, K. W., & McCall, L. (2013). Toward a field of intersectionality studies: Theory, applications, and praxis. *Signs, 38*(4), 785–810.

Crenshaw, K. (1989). Demarginalizing the intersection of race and sex: A black feminist critique of antidiscrimination doctrine, feminist theory and antiracist politics. *University of Chicago Legal Forum, 1*, 139–40.

Crenshaw, K. (1991). Mapping the margins: Intersectionality, identity politics, and violence against women of color. *Stanford Law Review, 43*(6), 1241–99.

Coacci, T. (2014). Finding Brazilian transfeminism: A preliminary mapping of a rising branch. *História Agora,* 15, 134–61.

Cooper, B. (2016). Intersectionality. In L. Disch and M. Hawkesworth (Eds.), *The Oxford handbook of feminist theory* (pp. 1–15). New York, NY: Oxford University Press.

Costa, C. L. (2000). Being here and writing there: Gender and the politics of translation in a Brazilian landscape. *Signs, 25*(3), 727–60.

Costa, C. L. & Ávila, E. (2005). Gloria Anzaldúa, a consciência mestiça e o "feminismo da diferença." *Estudos Feministas, 13*(3), 691–703.

Eguchi, S. & Asante, G. (2016). Disidentifications revisited: Queer(y)ing intercultural communication theory. *Communication Theory, 26*, 171–89.

Eng, D. L., Halberstam, J., & Muñoz, J. E. (2005). Introduction: What's queer about queer studies now? *Social Text, 23*(3–4), 1–17.

Halualani, R. T., Mendoza, S. L., & Drzewiecka J. A. (2009). "Critical" junctures in intercultural communication studies: A review. *The Review of Communication, 9*(1), 17–35.

Homem que matou mulher trans gritou o nome "Bolsonaro" (2018, October 24). *Pragmatismo Político*. Retrieved from https://www.pragmatismopolitico.com.br/2018/10/homem-que-matou-mulher-trans-gritou-o-nome-bolsonaro.html.

Jesus, J. G. (2014). Gender without essentialism: Transgender feminism as a critique of sex. *Universitas Humanística, 78*, 241–57.

Jesus, J. G. & Alves, H. (2012). Transgender feminism and movements of transsexual women. *Cronos, 11*(2), 8–19.

Johnson, J. (2013). Cisgender privilege, intersectionality, and the criminalization of CeCe McDonald: Why intercultural communication needs transgender studies. *Journal of International and Intercultural Communication, 6*(2), 135–44.

Lopes, I. (2018, September 20). Direito ao nome da população transsexual no Brasil. *Brasil de Fato*. Retrieved from https://www.brasildefato.com.br/2018/09/20/direito-ao-nome-da-populacao-transexual-no-brasil/.

Militantes reagem a morte de mulher trans no Sergipe. (2018, October 22). *O Globo*. Retrieved from https://oglobo.globo.com/sociedade/militantes-reagem-morte-de-mulher-trans-no-sergipe-23177708.

Mohanty, C. T. (2013). Transnational feminist crossings: On neoliberalism and radical critique. *Signs, 38*(4), 967–91.

Moon, D. G., & Holling, M. A. (2015). A politic of disruption: Race(ing) intercultural communication. *Journal of International and Intercultural Communication, 8*(1), 1–6.

Nakayama, T. K., & Krizek, R. L. (1995). Whiteness: A strategic rhetoric. *Quarterly Journal of Speech, 81*, 291–309.

Pains, C. (2019, January 3). "Menino veste azul e menina veste rosa", diz Damares Alves em vídeo. *O Globo*. Retrieved from https://oglobo.globo.com/sociedade/menino-veste-azul-menina-veste-rosa-diz-damares-alves-em-video-23343024.

Puar, J. (2012). "I would rather be a cyborg than a goddess": Becoming intersectional in assemblage theory. *PhiloSOPHIA, 2*(1), 49–66.

Rangel, S. (2018, December 17). Bolsonaro pede disciplina e critica "ideologia de gênero" em entrega de colégio da PM. *Folha de São Paulo*. Retrieved from https://www1.folha.uol.com.br/educacao/2018/12/bolsonaro-pede-disciplina-e-critica-ideologia-de-genero-em-entrega-de-colegio-da-pm.shtml.

Rede Trans Brasil. (2019). *Diálogos sobre viver trans – monitoramento: Assassinatos e violação de direitos humanos de pessoas trans no Brasil*. Brasil. Retrieved from: http://redetransbrasil.org.br/wp-content/uploads/2019/01/Dossi%C3%AA-Rede-Trans-Brasil-2018-Portugu%C3%AAs.pdf.

Saldaña, P. (2018, October 23). Saiba como surgiu o termo "ideologia de gênero." *Folha de São Paulo*. Retrieved from https://www1.folha.uol.com.br/cotidiano/2018/10/saiba-como-surgiu-o-termo-ideologia-de-genero.shtml.

Santana, D. (2016, June 28). "Conversa Entre Manas": Por um transfeminismo abolicionista e anti racista." *Blogueiras Negras*. Retrieved from http://blogueirasnegras.org/2016/06/28/conversas-entre-manas-por-um-transfenimismo-abolicionista-anti-racista/.

Silva, C. (2018). Feminismo negro. In H. Buarque de Hollanda (Ed.), *Explosão feminista* (pp. 252–72). Rio de Janeiro, Brazil: Companhia das Letras.

Vergueiro, V. S. (2015a, October 26). Despatologizar é descolonizar. *Global action for trans equality*. Retrieved from https://transactivists.org/viviane-vergueiro-despatologizar-es-descolonizar/.

Vergueiro, V. S. (2015b). *Por inflexões decoloniais de corpos e identidades de gênero inconformes: Uma análise autoetnográfica da cisgeneridade como normatividade*. Unpublished master's thesis, Universidade Federal da Bahia, Bahia, Brazil.

Vieira, H. (2018). Transfeminismo. In H. Buarque de Hollanda (Ed.), *Explosão feminista* (pp. 343–78). Rio de Janeiro, RJ: Companhia das Letras.

Yep, G. A. (2010). Toward the de-subjugation of racially marked knowledges in communication. *Southern Communication Journal, 75*(2), 171–75.

Yep, G. A. (2013). Queering/quaring/kauering/crippin'/transing "other bodies" in intercultural communication. *Journal of International and Intercultural Communication, 6*(2), 118–26.

Chapter 13

Dark Looks

Sensory Contours of Racism in India

Pavithra Prasad and Anjana Raghavan

Pavi: December 2007, Baga Beach, Goa, Western Coast of India

A group of my friends from Chennai are visiting Goa for the New Year's Eve. They are staying in Baga where the tourist crowds are mostly made up of middle-class and working-class Indians who have come to walk on the beach, try jet-skiing, and eat well on the oceanfront. I take a break from the white hippie enclaves in Anjuna and Vagator where I am doing fieldwork on rave tourism, and head south to meet them. It is winter, but the heat presses the thick ocean air onto my skin. The loose palazzo pants and a tank top I am wearing stick to me in spots—I pull them away from my sun-darkened body and put on a pair of shades to shield my eyes from the midday sun. It is a relief to get on my scooter and let the speed of my ride lift the sweat off my neck. The thirty-minute ride to Baga also brings with it a palpable shift away from the orientalism and racism of trance freaks toward Indians that I've been documenting for the past six months. The bodies get browner, the crowds get denser, and the style of clothing get less pseudo-tribal boho chic the closer I get to Baga.

I ride up to a beach shack to meet my friends, but they are not there yet. I settle down at a table just off the sand and order a snack while I wait for them. I am not nervous, but I do notice that I am the only woman in the less-than-busy tent. Small groups of young and middle-aged men sit at a few tables on either side of me. I don't own a smartphone so I look at the sea instead. A few minutes pass by and I turn to find a middle-aged man in a polo shirt tucked into full pants standing by me and smiling with all his teeth. I glance at him with a reluctant half-smile and turn back to the ocean view. "Excuse me, madam," I hear him say his voice dripping with a kind of obsequiousness that sets my hair on end. I tense up immediately but turn toward him anyway. "Madam, you don't mind . . ." He gestures to a camera in his hand and simpers through his leering smile, "One photo please?" I swallow a rising panic—I know what he is asking, but I try to play dumb and reach for the camera and look around him to his companions. "No problem, I can take a photo of you all." "No, no!" he says. "You," he says pointing at me. I shake my head, no, but he is already clicking away. Still simpering, he says, "Thanks-ah, thanks" and walks away hurriedly to join his table where is greeting with hand-slaps and guffaws. I feel myself glowing bright red, ashamed and self-conscious about my bare arms, my exposed clavicle, cursing myself for forgetting another layer of cover. "At least he asked," I tell myself as I shrink into the plastic chair, the cheers of the men slapping at my back like the rough waves of the ocean in front of me.

I become acutely aware of how my body is being seen. A sunburned brown woman, by herself, wearing sunglasses and a tank top, showing her arms, exhibiting brazenness reserved only for white bodies—to be alone and just sitting, to be alone and spending money, to be alone and dressed in Western clothes, to be alone and unafraid, to be alone and brown and female. An oddity, a novelty, a freak just like the white hippies, a testament to the "freedom" of expression that is possible in Goa. A sight to be seen. A souvenir.

Anjana: January 2019, Kochi Biennale, Kerala, Southern India

I am wearing a turquoise blue, crushed cotton, sleeveless dress. It is ankle length, and flowy. The relative lightness of my skin-tone, my clothes, and other, less obvious, but deeply embodied cues mark my caste and class privileges in this southern Indian city. The women's bodies are like mine, but they are dressed mostly in podavai or salwar kameez. I make eye-contact with all the not-white women I see. My transnational and caste privileges enable me to do this; my exhaustion with relentless whiteness encourages me to do this. Those presenting as women mostly return my smiles. I am trained not to make eye-contact with those presenting as men. I have not left home so long as to forget this. Evening falls, dusk gathers, and suddenly I can feel eyes everywhere. This dress was a mistake. I feel the v-neck gaping too much, I feel my arms, with no sleeves to hide them, grow grotesquely large. I see the white bodies around me sauntering around in teeny-tiny shorts, and transparent sarongs, bustiers, and tank tops. They move with a freedom I find offensive just now.

I walk into a shop. In the corner I spot a black couple; a man and a woman, both look to be in their sixties, and are dressed in Western clothes. I notice them being watched. I catch their eye and smile. There is also a young woman, no more than sixteen, a local who will most likely be identified as working-class, with the brown-black skin common in this part of the country, who is being watched. I smile at her, too. Across from us, a clutch of white tourists, both men and women, are exclaiming loudly over some trinkets. The shopkeepers are entirely preoccupied with them, but they watch all of us. They are most suspicious of the young local woman. They are suspicious of the black couple; but wait to see if they will buy things. They tolerate me because they know I can afford to buy things. They do not volunteer to speak with any of us, but look me up-and-down, their eyes glinting with part disgust—part leer. I feel myself shrink, and grow enormous, all at once.

BETWEEN SELF AND SCHOLARSHIP: THE SCOPE AND LIMITS OF THIS CHAPTER AND ITS MILIEUS

The desires to cowrite this piece are messy, thorny, and viscous. We write our opening narratives and what follows from complex and variegated privileges of *savarna* caste,[1] English language ability, economic and symbolic class, and global-northern geographic locations, and careers in academia. We write from the margins of gender-sexual-political queerness, brownness, transnational liminality, Tamilness, and radical anti-caste/anti-national/decolonial feminisms. The brief anecdotes we narrate above illuminate intersections that we were always aware of, and many that we are still learning about, as we examine our own privileges and locational blank-spots. In doing so, we seek to complicate the understanding of race, color, and caste in India through the affects generated by a violent form of looking. We began this chapter with two such affective moments, not to center ourselves in this analysis, but to reveal the extent to which women's bodies that do not conform to rules of invisibility (even ours that have caste and class privileges), move into a field where gaze and touch blur together through hierarchies of power. We also speak from a place which recognizes that our articulations are firmly located in our caste, class, and locational privileges; knowing that our capacities to "voice" are inextricably linked with the enforced silence upon Dalit, Bahujan, Adivasi, queer, and other marginalized subjectivities in the Indian context. We work from a position of resistance to these cultural norms, not to overgeneralize the scopic culture of India, but to point to the embedded colonial, antiblack, casteist, white-supremacist vestiges of colorism that inform this culture. While this might appear as an obvious space of intersectional inhabitation, this chapter explores the particular need to reconnect with and build on Dalit and black feminist articulations and practices of intersectionality, even as we resist the relentless ways in which whiteness appropriates intersectionality as part of its ever-expanding tool kit. The resistive core of black feminist thought that emerges throughout mutigenerational works from Sojourner Truth to Toni Morrison and many more informs our own resistance to centering whiteness as the point of departure when mapping injustice and oppression. Rather than bifurcating feminist and anti-racist work, we attempt to map the ways in which caste-based and antiblack racism in India coincides with the variegated oppressions of women[2] in public spaces. Furthermore, we elaborate how the privileges of speaking from the global north inflect how we understand feminist concerns in the global south.

We write as transnational academics experiencing mobilities of symbolic and spatial capital and from spaces defined by mobility. We begin with our experiences in tourist contact zones, where we necessarily come face to face, with our racialized selves. Sekimoto (2018) observes that racial awareness is activated by sensorial experiences, thereby framing the body as "an anchor of sensory knowing vis-à-vis race" (p. 84). In this vein, we strive to lay open the contours of a pervasive scopic culture that inflects public life in India, from which caste and class privilege enormously protect us, even while they do not totally immunize us. We argue that when othered subjects across a spectrum of privilege move through fields of visibility, they are touched by a "haptic visuality" (Marks, 2000) that is felt on the body in violent ways. We explore how the gaze that strikes women's bodies in India reveals a complex web of relationality between casteism and racism. We do so with an acute awareness of how our experiences as women living in the global north can never be approximated alongside the depth of trauma experienced by Dalit, Bahujan, Adivasi, and black women living in India. While we cannot and do not speak for or as these women, what we can show is that a manner of *being looked at* coats the surface of discriminatory violence across a range of our identities and bodies. We, therefore, also map a growing anecdotal archive of phobic experiences that black bodies experience while moving through India, not to conflate these experiences with ours, but to question the global north's logic of racism that is unable to grapple with the very real color/caste/class nexus of oppression in India. Since color/caste/class operate as variable nodes of intersectional identities, it is extremely difficult to make clear the relationships between each of these markers. Here, we use the phrase intersectional identities to denote the embodied-performative iterations of intersectionality, which cannot be reduced to neatly demarcated categories of experience. Color does not always correspond to caste, just as caste does not always reveal social-economic class. As Jayawardene (2016) notes, "Constitutive of colonial racist ideology and the ensuing onto-colonial sociality of the present moment, colorism in South Asia is not simply characterized by a yearning for lighter skin, but is far subtler and severe" (p. 338). The nexus between caste, color, race, class, and gender are deeply complex, and historically blurry.

While Jayawardene conditionally accepts the "Aryan" theory of colorism in India,[3] scholars like Darity and Deshpande (2003) and Pandian (2007) are much more ambivalent about this view. What is agreed upon, however, is that coloniality and European discourses of white supremacy are deeply embedded and intertwined with those of caste supremacy in contemporary Indian sociopolitical life. Additionally, one must also account for the complexities of color and race that came with the Indian Ocean Slave Trade, and Mughal rule in India, which account for Indian and Sri Lankan communities of African heritage in present-day South Asia (Jayawardene, 2016). In contemporary South Asia, there is also medical, educational, and economic migration from the African continent, as well as the movement of black peoples by way of tourism from the global north. In parallel, there is steadily growing anger, articulation, and resistance lead by Dalit, Adivasi, and Bahujan communities in response to Hindutva (Hindu Fundamentalism) articulations of an exclusionary and heteronormative "Indianness." While this is in no way an exhaustive examination of contextual complexities and nuances, it helps to remind us that doing the work of radical intersectionality, particularly in postcolonial spaces, often involves a morass of external and internalized discourses of coloniality, violence, and racialization.

Radical intersectionality, as we articulate it here, requires us to hold intersections as different, yet intimately connected to one another, without conflating, or flattening the politics of any one inhabitation. For example, the critiques of colorism in India tend to foreground the idea of a collective aspirational whiteness. However, as Prasad (2018) has shown, the complex epidermalization of the Indian aspirational class can also shift the meanings of darker skin color toward an upwardly mobile class aesthetic and a performance of neoliberal power. The intersections of class, caste, and color in India, therefore, defy generalization, and yet exert a palpable force on people's everyday performances of identity. To understand how these forces play significant roles in how sexism is felt and sensed in public spaces, we must adopt a radically fluid deployment of intersectional method, which reflects this slippery terrain and resists a neocolonial codification into a lexicon of the "other." So rather than use whiteness as a point of departure to talk about color-based sexism in India, we instead seek to center the geopolitical location and socioeconomic mobility of brown bodies between the global north and south, which reveal how certain privileges complicate the understanding of antiblack/caste/regional sexism in India. We write this piece as an interruption to a scopic regime, revealing how the privileges afforded by a relationality to the global north coproduces sexism, desire, and xenophobia. We frame this writing as a preliminary, and speculative exploration of optics: the politics of gazing, being seen, and being invisible. This introductory section has provided some reflections on positionality, as well as how and why we want to do this work of reimagining intersectionality in the specific context of haptic visuality in India. The next section will focus on locational, sociocultural, and identity-based specificities that are essential to any fruitful practice of intersectionality in a global context.

INTERSECTIONAL CONTOURS IN INDIA

This section is intended as a broad contour of contexts. We recognize that the preliminary work we are undertaking, along with fellow scholars in thinking through anti-blackness and casteism in India, is a tall order. The ways in which racialized hierarchies operate mean that postcolonial societies cast in the "middle" of the racial pyramid by extant racial logics are often characterized by complex desires for whiteness that are deeply rooted in anti-blackness. In India, these complexities are exacerbated by casteism, sexism, regionalism, colorism, as well as religious multiplicities. Jayawardene (2016) articulates the intersections of race, coloniality, caste, and class as "racialized casteism," which is the frame she uses to articulate the intimacies between anti-blackness, caste, and coloniality in India and Sri Lanka. She examines the ontological politics of communities of African heritage in both Sri Lanka and India. Noting that the Siddi community in India is listed as a Scheduled Tribe by the Indian government, she writes, "Society conceives of them as inferior alongside the Sudra and Dalits (untouchables) who are also in similar socioeconomic positions and are lower castes" (p. 335). Jayawardene's astute, nuanced, and intersectional analysis, however, does not discuss the specificities of regional and linguistic politics of identity that reflect more informal taxonomies beyond the juridical—such as the coding of South Indian and Sri Lankan Tamils as also black-skinned and socially inferior in the national consciousness. In the context of Tamil peoples of southern India and Sri Lanka, we see on the one hand that dark skin is celebrated as a marker of Dravidian cultural-political identity, while on the other, Tamil popular culture, television, and film constantly equate fairness of skin-tone with beauty.[4]

The internalization of whiteness as an ideal, Nadeem (2014) argues, is less about a hatred for the self and more about an "anxious love for the other" (p. 225), where she describes the desire for whiteness as a desire to liberate oneself from the barriers of caste, class, and region that are inscribed into skin color. This desire for liberation is a complicated one, as in contemporary India, the valorization of "fairness" involves an intricate dance of amnesia in regard to whiteness. The elision of race and whiteness from the vocabulary of fairness is not accidental. For fairness of skin to emerge as a neoliberal-cosmopolitan ideal of freedom, its connections to whiteness must necessarily be forgotten (Paul, 2016). This forgetting then allows for the discourse of fairness to be reinscribed into purely "local" systems of violent categorization, thus rendering coloniality and whiteness irrelevant to casteist-regionalist colorism.

Precolonial systems of caste used violent discourses of othering and purity/pollution, which varied between regions and kingdoms (Darity & Deshpande,

2003). Combined with Empire's use of eugenics and race-science, caste was further transformed into a logic of socioeconomic categorization and hierarchy, yielding what Jayawardene terms "racialized castesim" (p. 341) in contemporary India. Suna (2018) makes the important point that whiteness and coloniality were deeply complicit and invested in systematizing casteist hierarchies, thus aligning themselves with existing savarna hierarchies and institutions of power. Behl (2011), in her work, alludes to the deep embeddedness of casteism when she discusses the ways in which her Sikh participants adopt a "caste-blind" approach to casteism, thereby ignoring the foundational structures that already privilege those from savarna lineages, regardless of religion. With privileged-caste Hindu communities we see a wide spectrum ranging from explicit bodily caste supremacy and violence to more sophisticated forms of epistemic and symbolic caste violence, as well as a nonrecognition, and forgetting: a caste-blank approach. These mechanisms of privilege and denial are a serious impediment to challenging structural violence, as well as to coalition building. It is in this context that Dalit feminist Lata P.M.'s (2015) reminder serves us well: "Dalit-Bahujan feminist thought articulates the primacy of caste, class and gender in the Indian context [. . .] Any materialist and layered analysis of our lived reality has to engage with the voices, analyses and theories of Dalit Bahujan feminists" (para. 8). Prashad (2000), in turn, discusses antiblack racism among South Asians, noting that South Asia internalized the racist matrix in the particular modality of the "model minority." This modality of internalizing white supremacy is closely tied to the hierarchical quality of racialization, which produces a particular form of fictive seduction for those who are not at the very bottom of the hierarchy. "It is of course," as Prashad notes, "far better to be acknowledged as having some value than to be denied having any at all" (p. 160). This fictive seduction of belonging operates with great efficacy in India, particularly through narratives of violent nationalism. The composite of caste-race-class-gender in contemporary India is also deeply affected by these imaginaries of nationalist-xenophobic-belonging (Prashad, 2000; Bannerjee, 2005; Ramaswamy, 1997). The combination of internalized white supremacy, casteism, and classism, which produces the desire for fair skin, aligns perfectly with contemporary Hindutva nationalist agenda that is essentially invested in producing a hyper-patriarchal, xenophobic, exclusively savarna nation-state.

These observations draw our attention to the ways in which different identifications are always in contact and tension with one another, producing heteromasculinities and heterofemininities which, if not adhered to, have deadly consequences particularly for dark, femme, queer, trans, Muslim, and many Other bodies. While the deeply patriarchal-misogynistic narrative of fundamentalist and nationalist discourses of Hindutva are well established (Bacchetta 2002, 2004; Bedi 2006), it is also important to note that these movements and political parties actively solicit the support and participation of women as well. In her work, Bedi (2006) notes that Hindu women, who join the ranks of Hindutva parties like the *Shiv Sena*, perform a complicated set of negotiations which involve internalizing misogyny and patriarchal nationalism. This manifests as social and material attacks against Dalit women (Rege, 1998, 2000) on the one hand, and performing agency and resistance against savarna male cadres, on the other. In her incisive critique of the savarna portrayal of "marginalized women" in the film *Lipstick Under My Burkha* (2016), Rahmath E. P. (2016) notes this complexity to powerful effect. Noting the stereotypical, fetishistic, casteist, and Islamophobic ways in which the women in the film are portrayed, Rahmath simultaneously teases out the ways in which the focus on "marginalized" women's bodies by savarna lenses is also an erasure of the violences that savarna patriarchy visits upon savarna women. She asks, "Why are they hiding the damn Brahmin patriarchy? Why wasn't even a single women from this class/caste portrayed in this movie? [. . .] Why don't they bother about the sexual lives of savarna women? Why don't you show that boldness to talk about the widows in Vrindavan or women under khap panchayats?" (para. 10). This nuanced and contradictory understanding of the ways in which women are simultaneously weaponized and victimized is key to unpacking the haptic-optic complexes that are projected on to women's bodies, which forms the basis of the next section. Rahmath's critique is also why we narrate and locate our own positionalities in relation to our experiences. The ways in which we, as savarna women, are consumed by patriarchal haptic visuality must be held together with the ways in which we are constantly also protected by the structural privileges put in place by that very same patriarchy. The work of de-whitening and decolonizing intersectionality lies primarily in the *practice* of intersectionality. In this particular case, that requires understanding intersectionality as applicable *both* to privilege as well as marginality.

The messy privileges of both women who conform, and the explicit dangers that beset women who do not, demonstrate the ways in which institutionalized misogyny is an inherent part of the dynamics of anti-blackness and casteism in the Indian context. In the next section, we examine how being "looked at" functions as a method of disciplining the othered bodies of women through hypervisibility. Specifically, we theorize toward an understanding of the "haptic gaze" as a prosthetic for physical touch, wherein the hypervisible markers of color, race, caste, and class on gendered bodies become justifications for varying degrees of symbolic and literal invasion, abjection, and physical violence these bodies experience as they move through public space.

THEORIZING HAPTIC-OPTICS IN THE MATRICES OF RACE-CASTE-GENDER

The feeling of being looked at is not to be conflated with that of being seen. Intersectionality demands we see rather than merely look at the many vectors of difference that shape our lives. It demands an empathic being with those who ask to be seen in their multifaceted subjectivities. To be looked at, however, presumes an ontological separation and distance between the subject and object of a gaze. To be looked at as woman is to be constructed as an object of pleasure, especially while we are also expected to derive pleasure from it. Mulvey (1989) constructs "woman . . . as bearer of meaning, not maker of meaning" (p. 7) in the context of scopophilia, which then opens up space to consider what the implications of a "bearer" are. What is being borne and what kind of body is able to be seen as doing the bearing? Metzl (2004) in his critique of the psychological framings of scopophilia reminds us to be cautious about the distinction between normative and pathological scopophilia, as itself being a symptom of institutionalized misogyny. While Mulvey suggests that "we can begin to make a break by examining patriarchy with the tools it provides" (p. 7), we follow Lorde's (1984) important declaration that the master's tools are ontologically violent. Rather than examine scopophilia on its terms, we use the resistant methods of feminists of colors, to expose the ways in which the gaze constructs its subjects in a careful hierarchy, privileging certain bodies over others. This hierarchization of the body is underpinned by an immutable, essentialist view of the body in patriarchy. Ahmed and Stacy (2001) call for a "skintight politics" to critique feminist discourses of the body that frame bodily difference as resolute and irrevocable, rather than constantly coming into being. They write, "For in some sense, the very argument that 'the body' has been elided, negated and devalued in masculinist thought can fetishize the body, can allow it to appear as if it is an object that could be simply missing" (p. 3). We follow this call to ask how the body, skin, and color emerge interstitially, shifting between locations of subjectivity, especially when they are being looked at. For instance, our opening narratives indicate the movements between when our skin "disappears" and "reappears" in various contexts, where we are read either as dark, fair, savarna, Indian, Western, shaping what parts of our subjectivities are on display and when. This has less to do with our own sense of identity, than it does with how we are marked by others' desire, disgust, fascination, or scorn. The kind of scopophilia we recount does not simply land on our skin, but sweeps across it with a palpable affect. The skin, therefore, is not merely marked by color but also by a form of deferred touch, much in the way that Marks (2000) remarks about "haptic visuality" where "the eyes themselves function as organs of touch." She writes that haptic visuality "more inclined to move than to focus, more inclined to graze rather than gaze" (p. 162). While Mulvey and Marks are concerned with cinematic image, we extend their thinking to argue how scopophilia does in fact construct the body/skin as a screen upon which pleasure and desire are projected via a haptic gaze. This kind of looking at does not seek depth or even touch, rather a morbid and prosthetic extension of a panoramic vision that takes in not just the body but also its surrounding context. The woman's body in a public space is available as a screen because it is moving in public—the color or quantity of her skin also absorbing and projecting those who surround it. It is an image so real that you can reach out and touch it.

Scopophila[5] undergirds the deployment of the haptic gaze in India. Women's bodies are paradoxically constructed as objects to be looked at while simultaneously being expected to repel the optical touch. Chawla (2017) recounts incidents from her childhood, in which her mother chides her for smiling back at a man in the market where they are shopping, saying "who knows what people want" (p. 9). The implication that touch cannot be far behind the gaze sits heavy in the admonition. Indeed, returning a gaze itself is somehow constructed as an engagement with and acquiescence to being touched by vision, an accusation that is often heard under patriarchy in any part of the world—that a woman being looked at or stared at is implicitly asking to be touched or assaulted. Our own introductory anecdotes, and those that we have gathered via conversation or reading reflect this same knowledge, a lesson taught very early and held very deeply within the bodies of those presenting as women, though of course varying significantly in degree. The corporeal burdens of visuality are of course not the same for all bodies, in fact, we note that color and race often predicate how a body becomes visible or invisible, touchable or untouchable. Ironically, in India, where fair skin is exalted, meeting this standard of desirable color is accompanied by the expectation that women use their color to "disappear" into the "privilege" of not being stared at. Some have the class privilege to disappear from the public spaces of roads, busses, and trains, by quite literally becoming invisible inside cars with tinted windows.[6] Haptic vision seeks out unruly bodies that are dark, black, Dalit, fat, queer, poor, foreign, or diasporic and reaches out to touch them with impunity.

Our bodies come into a differential awareness of identity when we meet a haptic gaze. Marks notes, "The haptic image forces the viewer to contemplate the image itself instead of being pulled into narrative" (p. 163). Reversing this perspective to consider the living body as the haptic image, we might see how narratives of identity and experiences that construct the *subject* are elided in favor of viewing eye's terms of engagement and contemplation with the *object*. Our narratives that began this chapter demonstrate at least for a short temporal span, how a sense of how we were being looked at transports us unwillingly into a field of perception that is not our own. The haptic gaze encroaches on women's bodies; an encroachment which often breaches into actual physical violence, ranging from self-harm to sexual assault. However, we must return to an intersectional analysis of this violence to reveal how black, Dalit, Bahujan, and Adivasi women experience this violence differently from savarna women like ourselves. In the next section, we hold space for the experiences of women whose bodies are assaulted by haptic violence in different ways, and for whom such violence is deeply racialized. While we account for the differential experiences of women (including trans and nonbinary people), we recognize that under a Hindu nationalism aligned with white supremacy, misogyny, and Islamophobia, we cannot offer a simplified white/brown/black lexicon with which to understand haptic visuality in India. Instead, we decode the heterogeneous contexts under which critical intersectional analysis leads us to decolonial solidarity.

DARK LOOKS, DARK BODIES: AN INTERSECTIONAL ARTICULATION OF HAPTIC-VISUAL VIOLENCE

We began thinking about the resonances between our shared yet different experiences of the haptic gaze, after the publication of an article by the BBC. In the piece, Butterfield (2018) articulates what it was like to travel in India and endure the affective violence that touched her black female body. She writes,

> I had been travelling around Asia since August 2017. Like many tourists venturing into communities lacking diversity, I've been used to being stared at, but the attention I received in India felt different. The looks didn't seem like expressions of curiosity. They seemed sinister and unwelcoming. When people (young and old) see someone with black skin they stare, point, laugh, make jokes, clear paths, run as if you are chasing them, and fix their face to display an overall look of disgust. Too many people were rude, incredibly childish and treated me poorly. When not being ostracised, I was fetishized. (para. 30)

What Butterfield narrates is not singular in its observations. The blogosphere abounds with similar accounts of black women charting the challenges of "traveling while black" (Chideya, 2014) in India, in which their being looked at generated everything from acute discomfort to physical harm. A Duke University student doing fieldwork in India notes, "In India, the staring is quite ridiculous. Whether they are walking or driving, people slow down to catch a long glimpse. They get close and look at you straight in the face and look away when you look back" (Barry, 2018, para. 6).

A solo-traveler, Le'Ana Freeman says,

> Being a Black woman in India was a multifaceted experience. I did find myself more sexualized here because most people's only real frame of reference of black women were from music videos, media, and pornography (so I was told) [. . .] You also get quite a few stares and people asking to take photos with you; especially when you travel the rural areas. (qtd. in Taylor n.d, para. 4)

While white women have also documented this haptic gaze, their narratives account for their whiteness as the source of fetish that results in sexual harassment, preferential treatment, or even distance, rather than in the particular sensation of a proximal haptic gaze itself (Merelli, 2017). The narratives offered by black women are distinct in their naming of the affect as threatening, uncomfortable, and aggressive. Travel writer Maya (n.d.) notes,

> Usually when people ask to take a picture with you, it's pretty harmless. But in India I found it to be overwhelming. I'd say yes to one person and soon people were lining up to take a picture with me, making seeing some sites a lengthy process. While there were some families that asked for pictures, the majority were groups of young men. I said yes to some, but after a guide told me that many men Photoshop the pictures to look inappropriate, I started declining. I don't know how much truth there is to this claim, but I do know that it didn't feel right. (para. 3)

We note here, the use of black bodies as screens upon which fictions about blackness are projected (Young, 2010). The material remnant of the groping gaze, the photograph, turning the body from flesh into image. The affect the gaze produces for bodies, to whom the photograph is never available, is significant precisely because it alone remains as evidence of the encounter. This affect is also expressed uncomfortably through narrative, for narrative often fails to capture the visceral familiarity of this gaze. These singular narratives instead reflect the alienation and isolation experienced by the black women who write them, heightening their visibility even to themselves. Maya writes, "It may seem strange, but I had never been so conscious of the fact that I'm a black woman as I was in India" (Maya, n.d., para. 1).

The narratives of travel we include here are written by black women from Europe and the United States. We make this distinction because this transitory mobility renders visitors' bodies visible in very different ways than resident black diasporic communities. The gaze that falls on the black tourist body ascribes and projects a much different version of "touchability" and fetish than it does on black bodies that live and work in India. The markers of the global north tourist/backpacker are subtle, yet candidly apparent in women traveling by themselves, a rarity among resident populations. The class-consciousness of the gaze sees what we sometimes miss in our exclusive focus on race. Chideya (2014) writing for the *New York Times* recollects,

> Brown skin that's often perceived as "otherness" in parts of America is not seen that way in much of the world [. . .] I experienced it in southern India, where many people were similar shades of brown as me or darker. I was not mistaken for being a local, but I could circulate less conspicuously than fair-skinned visitors. I took advantage of my skin color (and some common-sense cultural and street smarts, like dressing modestly, showing no valuables and staying alert) to go solo and explore low-income areas of Mumbai that the guards at my luxury hotel had warned me against visiting. My reward: I was invited to lunch at the home of a family, where an older couple and their son and daughter-in-law shared a two-room house. (para. 13)

Each of these narratives also reflects a particular mode of mobility—the ability to travel as citizens of the global north. An attention to global class hierarchy reveals the experiences of black travelers, while targeted in specific ways by the haptic gaze, still reenact some other familiar projections—the global north's images of an "authentic" India located in the dissonances between luxury and poverty. The very appearance of global north travelers as socioeconomically advantaged complicates our reading of how the haptic gaze negotiates with racialized bodies. Very many of the women travelers we acknowledge here distinguish themselves as members of a mobile class—Ivy league scholars, Fulbright fellows, or upper middle-class professionals. Boutique travel companies and collectives, like Travel Noire and Nomadness Travel Tribe, specifically characterize black travel as rite of empowerment, vision, and symbolic wealth. However, class identity makes black travelers visible to locals in ways that foregrounds their race and gender alone. The haptic gaze takes in their class as well as race, where class privilege potentially subdues far more aggressive engagement, like that experienced by African diasporic subjects living in India.

African diasporic peoples living in India have been subjected to visceral violence as a manifestation of anti-blackness. Across the country, there have been attacks against black people, both professionals and students, living and working in major cities (Jaiswal, 2016; Prabhu, 2017). Stephen (2016) in her reportage of anti-blackness in India documents African diasporic peoples in India describing the ways in which they experience antiblack violence in India, how surprised they are at the levels of ignorance about Africa in Indian media and educational discourses, and that Indians appear to associate Africans with "drugs, violence, and prostitution" (Stephen, 2016, para. 10). While we do not have the space to articulate the full depth of African diasporic people's experiences in India, we want to mark this narrative as connected to, yet different from the previously discussed narratives of black women from the global north *traveling* in India. Once again, we see how the complex nexuses of white supremacy, savarna-supremacy, colorist, and gender produce a very specific discourse of anti-blackness in the Indian context.

The amputation from a Hindutva nation is even more acutely experienced by Dalits, especially women (Pasricha, 2015). While women with class, caste, and/or color privilege do feel flashes of the haptic gaze, we are able to step out of those in ways that dark skinned and black-skinned Dalit women cannot. The gaze lands on these bodies in far more visceral and violent ways. The distance between gaze and touch collapses as Dalit women are simultaneously hypervisible as "non-caste" and "impure," while also being vigorously erased from visibility. The highly visible narrative platforms that we as diasporic savarna women, black women tourists, and fair-skinned upper class/caste Indian women are afforded are denied to Dalit women. Their narratives do not circulate in the academy or global platforms, despite the violence they face for being "seen" in spaces, and despite the violability that is projected onto their bodies being well documented. The ubiquity, frequency, and normalization of violence against Dalit and Bahujan women's bodies in India cannot be emphasized enough. As Thaali (2015) notes, "punishing Dalit women is the duty of caste patriarchy" (para. 7).

Like Butterfield, Kumar (2017), a Dalit feminist scholar-activist, writes of her own recollections of festival time. We find points of connection to Butterfield's narrative, and also points of deep unarticulated distinction and specificities, which separate the two.

> I had seen men dance like this on the road during Ganesh Chaturthis. And when I watched the men, there was always a distance that I had to keep—sitting by the window of a moving car, I'd gape at them enviously, safely. On the bike, too worried—there was always the fear of being groped by one of the thousands of hands dancing in the air—fear of an anonymous hand plucking at my body—afraid of the helplessness that'd come from not knowing whom and how many to fight if a hand did grope. Perched safely in balconies, I'd also watched men dance like this at Holi. (para. 41–42)

The consequences for Dalit women, and for Kumar, as we read her account, are distinctly different from those for Butterfield, even as we can sense the connections in the sense of danger, violation, and fear. When Kumar writes of the "helplessness that'd come from not knowing whom and how many to fight," she is writing of a long, horrific, and traumatic enactment of caste violence, both as history, and as present. Rege (1998) argues that this is precisely why Dalit women need to and do talk, and act "differently." She writes that this " 'different voice' of the Dalit women is not an issue of identitarian politics; some 'authentic direct experience' but from a long lived history of lived struggles" (p. 42). The hyper-sexualization of Dalit and Bahujan women, and the marking of their bodies as sexually accessible, and "promiscuous" is, in part, "because of their participation in social labour" (Rege, 1998, p. 44), and the ways in which savarna caste hierarchy systematically dehumanizes Dalit and Bahujan women's bodies. Rege's observation connects powerfully with the ways in which black feminism critiques the race-blankness of white supremacy, and these shared understandings of resistance—of knowing that no woman is free when a black or Dalit woman is violated—are illustrative of the importance of intersectional coalitions, and activism. Soundararajan (2014) makes precisely this link when she writes: "Just as there is no way to understand sexual violence in the history of the United States without understanding racism, there is no way to understand the frequency and lack of punishment of violence against women in India right now without understanding caste" (para. 2).

In her complex, nuanced, and powerfully critical work, Rege (2000) argues for the centering of Dalit Feminist Standpoint theory, arguing, in similar lines to black feminism, that the violence of casteism, and savarna oppression of Dalit, and Bahujan communities are foundational to the possibility of coalition, justice, and liberation of any kind. She reminds us that the transformation of our own subjectivities, and the dismantling of privileges is the first step in intersectional practice. We want to conclude this section with this complex, and difficult understanding of intersectional practice; of our own complicity as savarna women, and our simultaneous commitment to doing the work of dismantling privileges, and building ethical, and accountable coalitions. We want to follow Rege (2000) in her reflection that internal/reflexive critique is neither about "freezing" nor an "uncritical celebration," nor a submission to "authenticity politics" "it means a recognition of connections of power that exist between women. It means speaking, not just 'as one' or 'for the other' but within and about the space between the 'self' and the 'other' " (p. 493).

ENACTING RADICAL, INTERSECTIONAL COALITIONS

The import of this work within intercultural communication leads us to a critical intervention—to rethink how identity is written about in relation to geopolitical location. While scholarship in intercultural communication has made great strides to identify the many forms of oppression using intersectional approaches, it must also contend with how to map intersectional privileges. Here, we strive to show how our positions speaking to and through Western academic discourses of intersectionality interrupts monolithic understandings of South Asian, black, and Dalit experiences. We argue that the deterritorialized global north (vis-à-vis traveling bodies) must be entered into the field of interrogation, particularly when dealing with the visibility or invisibility of certain violences against women. For intercultural communication to be cleaved from whiteness as its point of departure, we must more thoroughly understand how race, caste, and class arranges bodies of color in relation to *each other*.

Thus, as we examine the contours of these stories, what emerges is not just a map of widespread anti-blackness, and casteism in India, but also a map of a very familiar affect that coalesces around the very experience of being stared at. Women of all backgrounds report anecdotally on this "culture of staring" that touches us in varying ways. And yet, we struggled to find writings that theorized this experience in ways that acknowledged the anecdotal nature of how these experiences were being documented. We ourselves were frequently paralyzed as we grappled with how to describe these anecdotes that defied generalization or categorization. This is not to obscure or deny the everyday resistances, solidarities, and emergent resistances that othered bodies enact everyday, but rather to draw attention to the absence of both the articulations of haptic-optic experiences, and the resistances and solidarities that are responses to them.

The intersectional feminist framing of the gaze demands a thick, long-form narrative—narratives that account for our differential experiences. How then do we theorize the immediacy of haptic-optics that unfold and close at a rapid pace? How do we contend with the inability to document these moments that generate an affect so palpable yet fleeting arising in one instance only to be redacted by another (either by an act of kindness or indifference)? How do we remain allied to each other through failures, as we resist the imperative to "gloss over difference because cultures of domination teach us to"? (Ghabra & Calafell, 2018). To do this work of transnational, interracial, and anti-caste solidarity we defend the anecdote, as an empirical locus of coalition rather than as detritus of the Western academic archive. We approach anecdotes of experience as synapses from which to theorize. The flashes of haptic-optics that encroach onto bodies unfold with an immediacy that is best documented retroactively. The body registers these synapses before anything else happens. These are deep, yet brief, affective flashes that offer intersectional analysis another layer where we see experiences coalesce before they diverge. Anecdotes of optical affects thus permits us to explore the experiences of identity markers like caste, class, race, gender, sexuality, age, and disability in a form that does not demand, or privilege linearity of narrative, or even a verbal-written articulation. These experiences are viscerally embodied, and often, women and queer peoples traverse and navigate the optics of dangerous, desiring, and despising gazes with no time, or space to speak. We also want to clarify that in referring to a politics of optics, we are not performing a form of "ocularcentrism" (Ono, 2000, p. 136) that equates "seeing" with "knowing." Rather, we are using the politics of seeing and being seen as a way of displacing the legitimacy of the spoken/written, and to open up the interiority of the experience of the gaze, which is not always co-constructed. Tracing and understanding the extent and variegated contexts of caste, coloniality, nationalism, gender, class, and region are crucial to an intersectional analysis of anti-blackness in South Asia. Simplifying or flattening any of these identifications, or conflating one with another might mean that we use a frame of "race" as it operates in societies where whiteness visibly inhabits a space, to understand "color" in a society where whiteness and blackness are not highly visible tourists, but an invisible ontological-epistemological measure. Dismantling these structures of violence to form effective and meaningful coalitions will take enormous work because "solidarity is not 'natural' " (Prashad, 197), no matter how deeply we desire it.

NOTES

1. The term *savarna* collectively refers to various caste communities self-identifying as "higher" castes. Derived from the Sanskrit word for "color" and "caste," *varna*, savarna stands in for privileged caste groups who benefit from systemic social, economic, and cultural privilege. The literature and distinctions between *varna* and caste are complex, and we do not have room to address these here. For this chapter's purposes, we wish to highlight that those who do not conform to savarna categories, such as Dalit, Bahujan, and Adivasi (indigenous) peoples, call for the naming of savarna privilege as crucial to any discussion about injustice and inequality in India and the diaspora. For an incisive Dalit feminist reading on savarna accountability, see Soundararajan and Varatharajah (2015).

2. We acknowledge that our discussion does not directly address *hijra*, *thirunangai*, transgender, and nonbinary wymxn and peoples who are also very much harmed by the scopic regime we map. However, our positionalities and the scope of this chapter limit our ability to honor those experiences. We hope in this writing, however, to hold space and openings for their experiences.

3. The "Aryan/Dravidian" discourse in India has a complex and contentious status. Scholarship (Deshpande, Jayawardane, Klass, Ghurye, Thapar, Pandian, etc.) remains undecided on the unipolar understanding of "Aryans" as a "fair-skinned" people who dominated "darker" skinned, indigenous peoples. While the migration of "Aryan" peoples into India, and the subsequent othering of local peoples is generally agreed upon, it is not unilaterally agreed that skin color was a clear marker of differentiation.

4. See also Parameswaran & Cardoza (2009), Verghese (2017) and Guha Ray (2010) for discussions of skin-lightening across regions in India.

5. Since this chapter is not concerned directly with Mulvey's framing of cinematic scopophilia, we want to leave room for different negotiations and interpretations of the term.

6. The complexity of these intersectional positionalities can be traced in the coverage of the 2012 Nirbhaya case, where a young savarna woman was brutally raped to death on a public bus. Nirbhaya was both savarna and lacking the privilege of being able to "disappear" into the safety of more private modes of transport. Dalit feminist activists provided a critical intersectional intervention here, in pointing out that similar cases involving Dalit victims who were both violently erased by caste and class received little to no such attention locally or globally.

REFERENCES

Bacchetta, P. (2002). Hindu nationalist women imagine spatialities/imagine themselves: Reflections on gender-supplemental agency. In P. Bacchetta, & M. Power (Eds.), *Right wing women: From conservatives to extremists around the world* (pp. 43–56). London and New York: Routledge.

Bacchetta, P. (2004). *Gender in the Hindu nation: RSS women as ideologues*. New Delhi: Women Unlimited.

Banerjee, S. (2005). *Make me a man!: Masculinity, Hinduism, and nationalism in India*. Albany, NY: State University of New York Press.

Barry. D. (2018, July 31). Traveling while black: India. [Blog post]. Retrieved from https://blogs.nicholas.duke.edu/internshipblogs/traveling-while-black-india/.

Bedi, T. (2006). Feminist theory and the right-wing: Shiv Sena women mobilize Mumbai. *Journal of International Women's Studies*, *7*(4), 51–68.

Behl, N. (2011). Understanding difference blindness: Minimization of casteism in the Sikh community. *American Political Science Association Annual Meeting Paper*. Available at SSRN: https://ssrn.com/abstract=1902291.

Butterfield, A. (2018, April 30). Ostracised and fetishised: The perils of travelling as a young black woman. *BBC News*. Retrieved from https://www.bbc.com/news/stories-43877568.

Chawla, D. (2017). The migration of a smile. *Departures in Critical Qualitative Research*, *6*(2), 4–15.

Chideya, F. (2014, January 3). Traveling while black. *The New York Times*. Retrieved from https://www.nytimes.com/2014/01/05/travel/traveling-while-black.html.

Darity, W., Jr. & Deshpande, A. (Eds.) (2003). *Boundaries of clan and color: Transnational comparisons of inter-group disparity*. London, NY: Routledge.

Ghabra, H. & Calafell, B. M. (2018). From failure and allyship to feminist solidarities: Negotiating our privileges and oppressions across borders. *Text and Performance Quarterly*, *38*(1–2), 38–54.

Guha Ray, S. (2010, March 23). India's unbearable lightness of being. *BBC News*. Retrieved from http://news.bbc.co.uk/.

Jaiswal, N. (2016, February 25). Being black in India can be deadly. *Public Radio International (PRI)*. Retrieved from https://www.pri.org/stories/2016-02-25/being-black-india-can-be-deadly.

Jayawardene, S. (2016). Racialized casteism: Exposing the relationship between race, caste, and colorism through the experiences of Africana people in India and Sri Lanka. *Journal of African American Studies*, *20*(3–4), 323–45.

Kumar, V. (2017, December 25). Sure, you could say I went to a Dalit women's conference but woah it was a zingat party. *The Ladies Finger.* Retrieved from http://theladiesfinger.com/dalit-women-conference/.

Lata, P. M (2015, May 8). Silenced by manu and mainstream feminism: Dalit Bahujan women and their history. *Round Table India.* Retrieved from: https://roundtableindia.co.in/.

Lorde, A. (1984). The master's tools will never dismantle the master's house. In *Sister outsider: Essays and speeches* (pp. 110–13). Berkeley, CA: Crossing Press.

Marks, L. (2000). *The skin of the film: Intercultural cinema, embodiment, and the senses.* Durham, NC: Duke University Press.

Maya. (n.d.). Black female solo travel to India. [Blog post]. Retrieved from http://www.mayatheexplorer.com/black-female-solo-travel-india/.

Metzl, J. (2004). From scopophilia to survivor: A brief history of voyeurism. *Textual Practice, 18*(3), 415–34.

Mulvey, L. (1975). Visual pleasure and narrative cinema. *Screen, 16*(3), 6–18.

Nadeem, S. (2014). Fair and anxious: On mimicry and skin-lightening in India. *Social Identities, 20*(2–3), 224–38.

Ono, K. A. (2000). Re/membering spectators: Meditations on Japanese American cinema. In D. Y. Hamamoto, & S. Liu (Eds.), *Countervisions: Asian American film criticism.* Philadelphia, PA: Temple University Press.

Pandian, M. S. S. (2007). *Brahmin and non-brahmin: Genealogies of the Tamil political present.* New Delhi: Permanent Black.

Parameswaran, R. & Cardoza, K. (2009). Melanin on the margins: Advertising and the cultural politics of fair/light/white beauty in India. *Journalism and Mass Communication Monographs, 11*(3), 213–74.

Pasricha, J. (2015, December 10). Violence against Dalit women: How caste intersects with gender-based violence. *Feminism in India: Intersectional Feminism Desi Style.* Retrieved from https://feminisminindia.com/2015/12/10/violence-dalit-women-caste-intersects-gender-based-violence/.

Paul, A. (2016). Beyond the pale?: Skinderella stories and colourism in India. *IDEAZ Journal: Centre for Tourism & Policy Research, 14*, 133–45. Kingston, Jamaica: Arawak Publications.

Prabhu, M. (2017, May 3). African victims of racism in India share their stories. *Al Jazeera.* Retrieved from: https://www.aljazeera.com/.

Prasad, P. (2018). Sunburned: Color lines in the sand. *Departures in Critical Qualitative Research, 7*(1), 101–22.

Prashad, V. (2000). *The karma of brown folk.* Minneapolis: University of Minnesota Press.

Rahmath, E. P. (2017, August 10). Why not Janeu under my kurta? *Round Table India.* Retrieved from http://roundtableindia.co.in/.

Ramaswamy, S. (1997). *Passions of the tongue: Language devotion in Tamil India 1891-1970.* Berkeley and Los Angeles, CA: University of California Press.

Rege, S. (1998). Dalit women talk differently: A critique of 'difference' and towards a Dalit feminist standpoint position. *Economic and Political Weekly, 33*(44), 39–46.

Rege, S. (2000). Real feminism and Dalit women: Scripts of denial and accusation. *Economic and Political Weekly, 35*(6), 492–95.

Sekimoto, S. (2018). Race and the senses: Toward articulating the sensory apparatus of race. *Critical Philosophy of Race*, *6*(1), 82–100.

Soundararajan, T. (2014, June 9). India's caste culture is a rape culture. *The Daily Beast.* Retrieved from https://web.archive.org/web/20140612001327/http://www.thedailybeast.com/witw/articles/2014/06/09/india-s-caste-culture-is-a-rape-culture.html.

Soundararajan, T. & Varatharajah, S. (2015, February 10). Caste privilege 101: A primer for the privileged. *The Aerogram.* Retrieved from http://theaerogram.com/caste-privilege-101-primer-privileged/.

Stephen, C. (2016, June 15). Indians don't realise how their racism towards Africans damages the country's international image. *The Wire.* Retrieved from https://thewire.in/external-affairs/inherent-racism-is-harming-international-image-of-indians.

Suna, J. (2018, April 30). The politics of civilizing the savage: British colonialism and anthropology. *Round Table India.* Retrieved from http://roundtableindia.co.in/.

Taylor, D. (n.d.). The black expat: 'Stereotypes about India are unfair' [Blog post]. Retrieved from https://legacy.travelnoire.com/the-black-expat-stereotypes-about-india-are-unfair/.

Thaali, P. (2015, April 9). Academic untouchability: The Dalit woman experience. *Round Table India.* Retrieved from http://roundtableindia.co.in/.

Varghese, J. (2017). Fair & lovely: Ideas of beauty among young migrant women in Chennai, India. *Women's Studies Journal, 31*(1), 59–69.

Young, H. (2010). *Embodying black experience: Stillness, critical memory, and the black body.* Ann Arbor, MI: University of Michigan Press.

Chapter 14

"We Had to Sink or Swim"

Privileging and Intersectionalizing Racialized Ethnic Identifications among Asians and Asian Americans

Yea-Wen Chen

According to Pew Research Center (2013), Asians/Pacific Islanders and Asian Americans are the fastest growing racial group in the United States and make up the largest share of recent immigrants, including undocumented migrants. Yet, it is quite puzzling to tease out what *Asian (American)* means and who is included and/or excluded across historical, ethno-cultural, linguistic, religious, socioeconomic, and geographical borders. For instance, Ocampo (2016) wonders why "Filipinos are rarely the first people that come to mind" when hearing the word "Asian" (p. 3), which leads to his categorization of Filipino Americans as "the Latinos of Asia." Filipino Americans are sometimes treated as Asian and/or mistaken as Latinx, and they are not other times. Historically, pan-Asian groups emerged in the 1960s during the Civil Rights era to mobilize a collective voice and a political movement to advance pan-Asian interests (Kibria, 2000). Nevertheless, the "pan-Asian" or "Asian pan-ethnic" subject position is fraught with dilemmas, tensions, and paradoxes (Otis, 2001). Furthermore, discourses about Asians and Asian Americans conjure up ambivalent, contradictory, and paradoxical images and perceptions such as "the model minority," "the yellow peril," "forever foreigners," and/or "honorary whites" (Kawai, 2005; S. J. Lee, 1996; Tuan, 1998). To challenge monolithic, hegemonic, and whiteness-reproducing—or whitening—discourses, I examine in this chapter (counter)stories of how Asian/immigrant/American community leaders and members experience and narrate their identities in partnership with a nonprofit organization in Cincinnati, Ohio.

Racism is one of the unifying themes that cut across Asian immigrant and Asian American experiences in the United States (S. S.-H. Lee, 2014). Even though racism represents a shared struggle among Asians/immigrants/Americans in the United States, Asian ethnic groups, however, experience racism *differentially* across time, space, phenotype, skin color, ethnicity, immigration status, sex and gender, sexuality, education, location, and more. Throughout history, Asian/immigrant/American groups and communities have become *differentially racialized* as "Asian" in the United States—often in service of reproducing white U.S. nationalism (e.g., the Chinese Exclusion Act of 1882, the internment of Japanese Americans during World War II, and the shifting racial classifications of Indian Americans over time). Racialization can be understood as the processes of (re)creating races and (re)producing racial meanings that are historical, political, sociocultural, and materially consequential (Bonilla-Silva, 2004, 2006). To deploy "pan-Asian-ness" as strategic essentialism for political mobilization against racism and interlocking oppressions, it demands conversations about hierarchies and (in)equities within and across Asian/immigrants/Americans that are intentional and deliberate rather than secondary and tangential. In the context of a pan-Asian service agency in the U.S. Southwest, Chen (2014) evidences that, when competing discourses across intersecting identity positions are not addressed, intra-Asian hierarchies become masked and reproduced in service of the nonprofit-industrial complex only to reify an essentialized subject position of (educated/affluent/assimilated) Asians and Asian Americans as the model minority. Thus, it is necessary to situate and examine discourses of Asianness in the context of racism, whiteness, and intersectionality.

Rooted in black feminist thought, intersectionality has been developed out of a need to confront and address racism/heterosexism/classism within and across feminist movements (Collins, 2000; Crenshaw, 1991). As a legal scholar, Crenshaw (1991) first conceived intersectionality to understand the interlocking injustices and oppressions that structure the raced and gendered bodies. It stresses a standpoint epistemology to understand and legitimize the experiences of the marginalized from particular and specific localities that traverse and/or bridge multiple axes, epistemologies, and power lines. Responding to the critique that intersectionality has been depoliticized, neutralized, and weakened for social and racial justice (e.g., Bilge, 2013), I, in this chapter, return to and embrace the intellectual root of intersectionality by focusing on how (antiblack) racism/classism/colonialism becomes embedded in *racialized ethnic* identifications among Asians/immigrants/Americans (Tuan, 1998, p. 23). Following Tuan (1998), I use the term "racialized ethnic" identifications to acknowledge "the problematic nature of ethnicity for individuals who reside in the racial margins" who always already struggle with and are positioned between self-defined and racialized identities (p. 23).

Toward the book's goal of de-whitening intersectionality, I privilege and centralize how Asians/immigrants/Americans avow and experience their identities as an effort to de-center whiteness, while reclaiming intersectionality that has often been erased in discourses about Asians/immigrants/Americans. In particular, my analysis focuses on de-whitening the dominant discourses about Asian America such as the model minority myth at the particular intersection of race, gender, and immigration status. While acknowledging that sexuality is a particularly challenging and necessary topic within Asian and Asian American communities, I did not wish to tokenize the singular voice of the only self-identified LGBTQ participant in this study.

Theoretically, this chapter is guided by several underlying commitments that seek to de-whiten and intersectionalize the model minority discourse, which has continued to deflect, mystify, and deny the situated-ness of the Asian/immigrant/American experiences since the mid-1960s. To de-whiten the model minority myth means, on the one hand, to demystify how Asians/immigrants/Americans experience racial discrimination in the service of white supremacy, and, on the other hand, to confront how Asians/immigrants/Americans participate in perpetuating antiblack racism. Further, to de-whiten the model minority discourse *intersectionally* is to draw inspirations from black feminists to challenge white supremacist impulses within Asian/immigrant/American communities. Ultimately, de-whitening and intersectionalizing the model minority discourse is to pledge loyalty to and alliance with browner and more disenfranchised Asians/immigrants/Americans and other groups of racial minorities (e.g., blacks, Latinx, Native Americans, etc.).

RESEARCH CONTEXT

This is part of a larger project in collaboration with a pan-Asian nonprofit organization, Asian Community Alliance (ACA), in Cincinnati, Ohio. In 2000, the concept of ACA was birthed "around the kitchen table" when four founding women "got together and started talking about the idea of Asian empowerment." Since then, ACA has grown into a registered 501(c)(3) nonprofit organization. At its core, ACA's mission is to "educate, empower, inspire, and create healthy Asian families and communities" through working with community leaders and local agencies to develop and offer needed programs and services. In 2017, Asian American communities accounted for 2.8 percent of Ohio's total population (Ohio Department Services Agency). Though relatively small in size, Ohio's Asian population has been steadily fast-growing.

ACA's work was and continues to be shaped by and grounded in the local context of Cincinnati. Relevant to ACA, one of the founders and a number of Asian community leaders and members were employed by Procter & Gamble (P&G), one of the largest employers in Cincinnati. For instance, one of P&G diversity and inclusion practices is promoting affinity groups such as "Asian Pacific American Leadership Team." Also, during the time of this research, University of Cincinnati's president was an Asian/Japanese/Canadian man, Dr. Santa Ono, who served as its twenty-eighth president from August 2012 to July 2016. One ACA staff mentioned that Dr. Ono's wife supported and was involved with ACA at the time of this research. In 2015, one local event relevant to ACA's work was the death of a Cincinnati police officer, Sonny Kim, who was "shot and killed in the line of duty" on June 19, 2015, leaving behind his wife and three children (Knight, 2018). Officer Kim was a respected figure both inside and outside Asian communities in Cincinnati.

Funded by an internal grant, this research focused on community engagement as a concept that bridged and connected ACA's initiatives from youth leadership, senior assistance, to domestic violence. My involvement with ACA began in January 2013 when I volunteered and became involved with one of ACA's initiatives: Project HOPE (Helping Our People through Empowerment) that aimed to raise awareness of domestic violence within Asian communities and connect victims/survivors with needed resources. This research grew out of my volunteering experiences. In partnership with ACA staff members who recruited all the interviewees, I interviewed a total of thirty individuals across Asian communities in the greater Cincinnati area in the summers of 2014 and 2015.

Researcher Self-Reflexivity

My collaboration with ACA was informed by my intersecting identity positions as a first-generation immigrant, a racialized Asian, a working mother, a politically Taiwanese and culturally Chinese cisgender woman, and a critical intercultural communication scholar. Since embarking on my journey in the United States in 2004, I have experienced multiple changes in my immigration status from a F-1 student, a H-1B worker, and to a permanent resident (a.k.a. green card holder). While my intersecting positionality assisted my collaboration with ACA in terms of rapport, access, and commitment, I strove to as self-reflexive in this work as possible so that I could listen/feel/understand experiences shared with me as intended—rather than as what I wanted to hear/feel/know. Following Brookfield's (1995) approach that interrogates power relations, assumptions, and practices, I exercised as much self-reflexivity as possible in asking myself how this collaboration could benefit not just me but the people and communities that ACA aimed to serve and empower.

Procedures

This research was supported by an internal grant at Ohio University, which provided lodging in Cincinnati, gift cards as research incentives, and transcription support. An Institutional Review Board (IRB) approval was obtained prior to conducting one-time, semi-structured interviews with community leaders and members recruited by ACA staff members. In the summers of 2014 and 2015, all interviews were conducted in locations of interviewees' choosing such as their individual home, at a conference room, or at a public coffee shop. Interviews followed IRB protocol, were recorded with consent for accuracy, and lasted between thirty and ninety minutes each. Participants were asked general questions about their lived experiences, their intersecting identities, and their views of an organization like ACA. This process resulted in 718 pages of single-spaced transcriptions. This chapter focused on portions of the transcripts where the participants discussed their preferred racial and/or ethnic identifications and their experiences as Asians and/or Asian Americans in Cincinnati.

Participants

A total of thirty self-identified leaders and members of the Asian communities in the greater Cincinnati area participated in this research. Six of the thirty participants were interviewed with a family member or community partner, which resulted in a total of twenty-seven interviews. Participants in this study were fifteen heterosexual men and fifteen heterosexual women, and came from various Asian communities: Chinese, including those from Taiwan or whose parents were from Taiwan (n=5), Vietnamese (n=4), Japanese (n=4), Korean (n=3), Filipino (n=3), mixed-race and transracial (n=3), Bhutanese (n=2), Indian (n=2), Laotian (n=1), Pakistani (n=1), Indonesian (n=1), Taiwanese (n=1) (see table 14.1). Following one of the participant's categorization of "1.5 generation" referring to individuals who immigrated as a child, the participants varied in immigration status: fourteen first-generation immigrants, eight immigrated as a child (a.k.a. 1.5 generation), and eight second-generation immigrants who were born in the United States.

Analysis

Consistent with critical race scholarship, my analysis was guided by the lens of (re-)racialization as the repeated processes of (re)signifying and (re) ascribing racial groups and meanings that are historical, political, sociocultural, and materially consequential and intersect with sex and gender and immigration status (Bonilla-Silva, 2004, 2006). In particular, I went through

Table 14.1 ***Participants' Demographic Background***

	Sex	*Self-identification*	*Immigration Status*
Participant 1	Man	Bhutanese (American)	1st generation /Permanent resident Immigrated as a refugee
Participant 2	Woman	Korean American	1.5 generation Immigrated at the age of 2
Participant 3	Woman	Chinese	1st generation /U.S. citizen
Participant 4	Man	Asian/Chinese/Taiwanese	2nd generation/U.S. citizen
Participant 5	Man	Indian	1st generation/U.S. citizen
Participant 6	Man	Chinese	1st generation/U.S. citizen
Participant 7	Woman	Chinese (from Taiwan)	1st generation/U.S. citizen
Participant 8	Man	Korean American	1.5 generation Immigrated at the age of 11
Participant 9	Man	Vietnamese American	1.5 generation/U.S. citizen Immigrated as a child and refugee
Participant 10	Man	Korean	1st generation/Permanent resident
Participant 11	Woman	Japanese	1st generation
Participant 12	Woman	Mixed-raced Indian/Asian	1st generation/U.S. citizen
Participant 13	Woman	Indian	1st generation/U.S. citizen
Participant 14	Woman	Asian/Laotian and American	1.5 generation/U.S. citizen
Participant 15	Man	Bhutanese	1st generation Immigrated as a refugee
Participant 16	Woman	Vietnamese American	2nd generation/U.S. citizen
*Participant 17	Man	Japanese (American)	1st generation/U.S. citizen
*Participant 18	Woman	(American)	1st generation/U.S. citizen
Participant 19	Woman	Filipino American	1st generation/U.S. citizen
*Participant 20	Man	Vietnamese American	2nd generation/U.S. citizen
*Participant 21	Man	Vietnamese American	2nd generation/U.S. citizen
Participant 22	Man	Japanese American	1.5 generation/U.S. citizen Immigrated at the age of 9
*Participant 23	Woman	Filipino American	1st generation/U.S. citizen
*Participant 24	Man	Filipino American	2nd generation/U.S. citizen
Participant 25	Woman	Taiwanese American	2nd generation/U.S. citizen
Participant 26	Man	Pakistani American	1.5 generation/U.S. citizen Immigrated at the age of 1
Participant 27	Man	Hapa	2nd generation/U.S. citizen
Participant 28	Woman	Chinese American	2nd generation/U.S. citizen
Participant 29	Woman	Indonesian American	1.5 generation Immigrated at the age of 11
Participant 30	Woman	Transracial adoptee	1.5 generation/U.S. citizen Immigrated/Adopted at 5 months

*Indicates participants who were interviewed with a family member or community partner a critically informed two-step process of open coding and closed coding that attended to both participants' worldviews and dominant discourses about race relations (Lawless & Chen, 2019). In the opening coding process, I coded discourses that were significant and meaningful to the participants as how they understood their racialized ethnic identifications. Then, I interrogated dominant discourses that were embedded in the participants' interviews about Asians and Asian Americans' positions in the U.S. society. In other words, I unpacked how the participants' identifications reified and/or resisted the status quo and/or the subject positions of Asians/immigrants/Americans in the United States with particular attention to intra-ethnic hierarchies, historical relations, and contradictions that functioned to uphold white supremacy, sexism, and xenophobia.

(COUNTER)STORIES OF RACIALIZED ETHNIC IDENTIFICATIONS

Predominantly, the interview discourses in this study reveal the (re-)racialization of Asians/immigrants/Americans as processes of homogenizing and masking intersectionality within racialized ethnic identities to blur, negate, and render meaningless and gradually unconscious any meaningful difference within racialized Asian ethnic groups (e.g., sex and gender, class, and immigration status). Specifically, my analysis highlights that racializing discourses also function to "feminize" Asian women and men similar to Eguchi's (2011) argument that "the 'feminized' perception of gay Asian men works to construct racialized stigmatizations toward them" (p. 38). Participant 11's comment below evidences a normative process of "racializing Asians" vis-à-vis negating differences within and across ethnic groups while neglecting other identities:

> I'm Japanese. I'm dark. I have big eye. I don't have brown hair so I don't look Japanese. So, a lot of people qualified me as Thai, Vietnamese, Malaysian, Korean, everything but Japanese. So, I kind of actually enjoy looking like everybody else.

As the process of racializing Asians/immigrants/Americans became normalized, participant 11, a self-identified first-generation Japanese woman, exemplified learning to accept race as the primary category of identification without considering other identities. Participant 19's remarks below echo the process of becoming a racialized Asian who was encouraged to see "no breakdown":

> When I arrived here in '89 it was very tough here in Cincinnati. The Midwest is not so familiar with Asians. We're a bunch of foreigners, it's a phrase I've

> always remembered. "You're a bunch of foreigners." So anyway, we were like—you know—it didn't matter if you came from the Philippines or if you came from Korea. We were all Chinese, because Chinese is Asian. That's how I saw how Americans saw Asians as Chinese. There's no breakdown, you know?

The stereotype of Asians and Asian Americans as "forever foreigners" was evoked here also. Specifically, language use plays an important role in (re) constructing and (re)racializing individuals and groups into monolithic "Asian" Others that erase complex gender and other differences within. Participant 30, a self-identified transracial adoptee born in South Korea and raised in a white family, was called "Asian" in high school. She commented, "My nickname literally in high school . . . not in a bad way, and I thought it was fine, but it was just 'Asian.' It was just like 'Hey, Asian, ha-ha!'" Overall, my analysis identified three overlapping themes: (a) racializing and feminizing discourses of the "good" Asian (ethnic); (b) fragmentations and hierarchies within racialized ethnics; and (c) pan-Asian organizing as "togetherness-in-difference."

Racializing and Feminizing Discourses of the "Good" Asian (Ethnic)

Historically, the "success" story of the Chinese, Japanese, and Asian Americans becoming the (feminized) model minority emerged in the mid-1960s, which has continued to (re)shape perceptions of Asians and Asian Americans as self-reliant, highly disciplined, and family-oriented model citizens (Kawai, 2005; E. D. Wu, 2014; F. H. Wu, 2002). Race making of the Asian (American) identity is "profoundly shaped by understandings of blackness and whiteness" (E. D. Wu, 2014, p. 7). Speaking as an Indonesian American/1.5 generation immigrant/Muslim/woman, participant 29 evoked the discourse of the "good" Asian: "You're a good kind of Asian. You're a good mix of Asian and American." Collectively, the participants in this study were not just conscious of the model minority stereotype, but were critical of the various ways in which it had constrained and/or hurt individuals and communities, including themselves. The particular emphasis on "goodness" highlights that gendered/feminized nature of racial discourses toward Asians/immigrants/Americans. That is, the racializing discourse of the "good" Asians function to simultaneously feminize both Asian women and man. In this study, more women than men were aware of and associated the discourse of "goodness" with Asian-ness.

Many of the participants in this study discussed narrow career expectations—either implicit or explicit—for Asian (American) youth and young adults as measures of "success" in life, especially stricter expectations for women. Participant 16, a self-described Vietnamese American woman, discussed the common pressure to become a medical doctor, "For example, going into college, they [parents] expected me to have a medical degree, which is huge common stereotype for Asians, or the expectation at least." Similarly, participant 22 evoked the expectation of becoming successful in business when describing his mother, "My mom, she's always been a sort of delinquent of the family where everyone was typical Japanese, 'you must be a successful business person.' She was kind of the outcast of the family. She was into the alternative culture." While participant 16 as a woman talked about strict career expectations that her parents had of her, participant 22 as a man discussed his mother being the outcast who defied family expectations. Both examples imply that Asian women might experience stricter expectations following gender norms. Also, both discourses illustrate how the perceived close family ties associated with the model minority stereotype functioned to restrict career paths just as there were limited ways of being the "good" Asian.

The racializing/feminizing model minority discourse in this study discouraged and denied healthy expressions of negative feelings and emotions that did not uphold "goodness." The participants shared how the (feminized) good model minority stereotype had negatively influenced themselves and communities that they knew, particularly around mental health and suicides among Asian (American) youth. At a community level, participant 16 discussed how asking for help was frowned upon, "Typically, they [Vietnamese community] don't like to ask for help because it's then showing that they need help, and other people might see that they're, I guess, vulnerable." Regarding mental health and emotional well-being, participant 13 explained the harmful effect of being racialized and feminized as the model minority on Asian American youth,

> We are first seen as the model minority . . . You are gonna excel in all these different ways and there are no problems for this particular minority. And we kind of go to fulfill that expectation and act in that way. So, you have to just deny any emotional issue and just focusing on the academic career achievements. . . . I know so many Asian kids who are falling apart.

Participant 25 echoed how she struggled with the expectation of not being/feeling emotional, especially given her childhood experiences of not just being held back for not speaking English but also being bullied for looking different. Paradoxically, the racialized and feminized Asian ethnics were not allowed to be emotional. She remarked:

> I feel like we're taught just to agree and internalize our feelings. Not be emotional, you know, always respect your parents and not disagree and back talk to

> them. So you couldn't express your feelings and that's where I feel like a lot of times I have trouble still to this day.

Speaking as the president of a Filipino American Association, participant 24 shared struggling with mental health as a teenager who "was born here of two Filipino parents,"

> I didn't want to have anything to do with Filipinos, so it was a very difficult time growing up. . . . So much to the fact that I didn't even eat Asian food. So, my parents had to go out and buy me Burger King or McDonald's, because I grew up on burgers as an Ohio meat and potatoes guy. . . . Trying to develop that Asian American identity was very difficult. I was one of those teenagers who felt like I wanted to commit suicide at the time because of how hard it was.

Wu (2002) argues that "the model minority myth ought to be rejected" partly because it "is based both to deny that Asian Americans experience racial discrimination and to turn Asian Americans into a racial threat" (p. 49). This study adds that the model minority myth is simultaneously a racializing and feminizing discourse. Interview discourses in this study highlight the emotional costs, if not traumas, associated with being racialized and feminized as the "good" model minority who are allowed to express positive emotions. Additionally, the model minority discourse did not just promote certain images of/about Asians/immigrants/Americans but also rendered undesirable and/or invisible other ideas. For instance, what was often less considered were areas where Asians/immigrants/Americans might be lagging behind. Participant 17 framed this issue as "bamboo ceiling" in that "when it comes to managerial areas, Asian Americans face ceiling." Collectively, the participants problematized the negative impacts of racializing and feminizing Asians/immigrants/Americans as the "good" model minority.

"We Had to Sink or Swim"

Discourses in this study indicate that the (feminized) model minority myth only exacerbated and rendered more precarious, if not dangerous, the conditions for those who were further *othered* such as Japanese Americans during and after World War II, refugees from lower socioeconomic status, and "browner" Asians. Participant 22 discussed how his adopted grandmother, a second-generation Japanese American, taught him to be "more American than the typical American."

> When I first came to the States and my mom made lunch for me, my father's mother was very surprised, "If you take that to school you'll get bullied." That's the extent to which they had to keep a low profile because after World War II

> and the internment camps and all that, they had to be more American than the typical American.

This exemplified how the "good" model minority discourse encouraged unquestioned assimilation at the expense of Asians/immigrants/Americans. Similarly, participant 9 explained that the model minority myth further framed those who were also economically disadvantaged refugees with polarized options of either overcoming inconceivable hardships to achieve the American dream or falling into the crack without anyone's knowledge. Speaking as a Vietnamese American/refugee whose family was sponsored by a church to immigrant to the United States, he remarked on the hardships he and his family had to overcome:

> A long story short, *we had to sink or swim*. And learn how to survive and thrive, as is—as are most Asian families. School is important. It isn't like Asian families can, parents especially my mom, she never helped us in schoolwork. We had to figure it out for ourselves.

Speaking not just as a refugee but also as a daughter raised by a divorced man, participant 14 recalled that "I got picked on a lot in my own community." The excerpts here suggest that the "good" model minority stereotype functioned to divide and further marginalize Asians/immigrants/Americans who already resided in the margins (e.g., refugees, single-parent households, and religious minorities). As Kawai (2005) argues, the model minority myth has perpetuated color-blindness in the service of strengthening white supremacy.

Fragmentations and Hierarchies within Racialized Ethnics

Within and across racialized Asian ethnic groups, the model minority myth functions to fragment and further divide an already heterogeneous group in the service of white supremacy (F. H. Wu, 2002). Specifically, the participants in this study underscore particular fragmentations and hierarchies within, in-between, and across the racialized Asian ethnic groups while erasing identities that could serve as points of unification for resistance (e.g., gender and socioeconomic status). In this study, participants not only avowed their racialized ethnic identities in various ways, but also questioned the normative process of who should, or should not, be considered Asian (American). To illustrate, participant 14 stated: "I hate the Asian American terminology. . . . Does that mean if I was just Asian, I don't mean anything? My ethnic background is Asian. I'm not Asian American." Similarly, participant 6, who grew up in China and was a naturalized U.S. citizen, identified "as Chinese. Just Chinese." To him, the label "Chinese American" referred to those born in the United States like his son, but not him. In contrast, participant 3 avowed as half Chinese and half American: "I'm a Chinese who came over here and later on I became a naturalized citizen. And so I still love China. I am still Chinese. . . . I'm half American too because my kids are born here." Born to students who were born in China and were raised in Taiwan, participant 4 viewed himself this way: "I call myself Asian American. I'm not one, not the other; I'm both." In juxtaposition, participant 24 stated, "I sometimes call myself an American Asian." Challenging homogeneity, the diverse identifications reflect what might hold particular meanings to individuals as well as how belonging, lived experiences, and intersecting social forces such as immigration could shape understandings of the self.

Some participants highlighted a tendency for fragmentations whether within or across communities. Ultimately, the status quo of white supremacy benefits from fragmentations that prevent groups from building coalitions that can challenge the status quo. Participant 8 pondered why certain racialized ethnic communities did not interact with others, and said: "I think Korean Americans, for various reasons, has been exclusive. They don't want to mingle without other Asian groups." Participant 14 remarked on religious differences within a racialized ethnic community, "The Vietnamese community is split between the church and Buddhism." Similarly, participant 23 evoked hidden tensions within when describing herself, "I am a Filipino, but I am also 25% Chinese. So, what's interesting is that in the Philippines, Filipinos with Chinese blood tend to be discriminated." Here, fragmentations and divisions among racialized ethnic Others could function to render invisible and/or unconscious the particular ways in which racialized Asians shared racial discriminations.

Together, the participants in this study highlighted particular hierarchies within Asian and Asian American communities. First, many participants commented on tensions occurring around intersecting forces such as English hegemony and geopolitical relations. Participant 8 touched on the intersection between geopolitical relations and English hegemony. Identifying as a Korean American man belonging to the church, he stated,

> For me, I think there was a different classification between Indian American and truly East Asian, North Asian. Indians are taught very well. They're very articulate. They come across as very intelligent. They have very strong opinions. English in a certain sense is their first language.

Speaking as a heterosexual man, participant 8 seemed to view difference in English proficiency competitively. Participant 10, a self-described Korean man, echoed the linguistic advantage for Indian Americans, stating: "English is their native language. So, they have some issues but they can deal with it themselves." As an Indian American, participant 5 affirmed this sentiment and said, many Americans viewed "Indians, original, [as] very intelligent people. Not only that, we can communicate better than Mainland Chinese people. . . . We can communicate better so we can get better jobs." On the one hand, the linguistic advantage for native English immigrants like Indian Americans ought to be acknowledged given the power of English hegemony in the U.S. society. On the other hand, this emphasis ignores racial discrimination that Indian Americans might face as "browner Asians" in relation to phenotypical East Asians.

Second, several participants discussed differences around complex geopolitical relations either historical or contemporary, which supports Wu's (2014) observation that "National conversation about the model minority demonstrate that Asian Americans' social standing remains inextricably bound to global forces" (p. 253). Nakayama (2016) suggests that "we cannot understand the experiences and histories of Asian Americans outside the context of *both* domestic and international contexts" (p. 30). Participant 17 brought up colonial history between Japan and Korea: "That's the difference between Japan and Korea. Japanese government, colonizing Korea was not good." Speaking as a Bhutanese American, participant 1 discussed a nuanced struggle between Bhutanese and Nepalese peoples given their recent history. He stated: "I like Columbus too but there's too many Nepalese people. Too many, like 2,000 Nepalese people are there. So, if we sit together, then my boys they will learn good things." Participant 1 and his family lived as refugees in Nepal for eighteen years where his children were born. Given the tensions, participant 1 had requested the following with his children's schools: "Please don't tell our children they're Nepali. Tell them Bhutanese, so that they can remember, 'I am Bhutanese.'" Participant 15 echoed and explained a stigma of being labeled "refugees" resulting from tensions between Bhutanese and Nepalese, "During our stay in Nepal for about 15-20 years, there were classes between the refugees and the people of Nepal. The people of Nepal and our people had some clashes, more classes, and then our people would be called 'refugees.'"

Third, many participants talked about how the differences in immigration status and generation mattered. Participant 28 talked about identifying more as Asian American than Chinese American given her experience growing up in Ohio and connecting more with second-generation Asian Americans. She explained:

> Since I was born and raised in the U.S., I haven't really identified as being Chinese or Chinese American. When I decide who to socialize with, really, I connect with most other Asian Americans, regardless of whether they're from Pakistan, or China, or Japan. And really children of immigrants in general, I feel that I connect to that experience as well—of being second generation.

Speaking as a "proper Indian," participant 13 described how immigration status could matter for identification. She explained,

> There's a difference between Indians who come here for their undergraduate and pre-undergraduate and Indians who migrated to this country for a job or for their post-graduate Degrees because I think when you come here for undergraduate Degree I think you assimilate into the culture that are here more or less deeply because I think part of it is that you live in a dorm for four years obviously, you know what I mean and you still don't regard what happens to us. You've been surrounded by the mainstream culture so I knew people also coming here at eighteen or nineteen which is a much more impressionable age than in the mid-twenties or thirties. So, I think that's the difference.

In general, not much attention has been paid to how Asians/immigrants/ Americans experience themselves intergenerationally.

> Two issues were less discussed among the participants in this study. Among the thirty participants, participant 26 was only person who talked about 9-11 as a Muslim/Pakistani Indian/American. Simultaneously, he talked about not being "allowed to be American to some extent" and being "tough for him as a Pakistani Indian to identify as Asian" given how he looked. He explained, "I feel like the word Asian really carries this East Asian context to it. . . . And there's quite a difference between East Asians as well as the Indian subcontinent." Sexuality is another understudied issue. Participant 2 shared her challenge of finding a supportive community, "I identify as lesbian and queer and, for me, finding a Korean-American community that was open to, sort of, accepting someone who was Korean-American and lesbian, was challenging."

Mixed-Race Asians

The experiences of mixed-race Asians stood out—highlighting tensions between racialized ethnic groups and also racial groups. The voices of mixed-race Asians underscore a long neglected need for racialized Asian ethnics to engage in intergroup coalition building, particularly with other historically marginalized groups. Identifying as a transracial adoptee born in (South) Korea and growing up with white parents, participant 29 explained the liminal, in-between space that she experienced herself, "Of course, I identify as Asian because I'm Asian—but at the same time, I don't totally identify as Asian. My body identifies as Asian, but my culture is, I don't know, white, I guess." Speaking as Hapa who was born to a German father and Korean mother who met in the United States, participant 27 described how his identifications had evolved over time:

> I first started out growing up in all suburban white neighborhood, so I really just didn't see myself as different from anyone else. I just thought I was white,

> I saw my dad, I was like 'ok, I must be white.' . . . Eventually another group of East Asians came and they came from Asian, so all of a sudden I realized I was Asian. And they started inviting me—our families became really close—and I started understanding Asian culture outside of what my mom would just talk about but then other people's Asian culture, so I started identifying as Asian. Soon after that, though I got really involved in everything Asian, certain groups started discriminating against me, because I wasn't full Asian and they could tell. So that's kind of when it came full circle and I realized, well, I'm not just white American, I'm not just Asian American, but I'm both, and I have to forge my own identity there as Hapa.

Born to parents and grandparents from UK and growing up in India, participant 12's identification as Asian was often challenged,

> I may not look Asian. . . . With ACA when I went into the community, they would always question me about where I am from. . . . They know my accent is Asian. There's an Asian accent when I speak, but they would never say I'm from India or they always would think I'm not Asian.

Given the increasing number of intermarriages between Asians and non-Asians, mixed-race Asians hold a special position in reinforcing and/or challenging the model minority discourse.

Pan-Asian Organizing as "Togetherness-in-Difference"

The core of pan-Asian organizing rests on Ang's (2001) notion of living "togetherness-in-difference" that "is not only about fusion and synthesis, but also friction and tension, about ambivalence and incommensurability, about the contestations and interrogations that go hand in hand with the heterogeneity, diversity, and multiplicity" (p. 200). Existence of nonprofit organizations like ACA is simultaneously enabled and constrained by persisting and shifting stereotypes of Asians and Asian Americans as the (feminized) model minority, forever foreigners, and more. As participant 12 (and a board member of ACA at the time) explained, "What we [at ACA] have realized is that there are a lot of disparities that exist, social economic backgrounds across the Asian communities. There are a lot of people who need help and there are a lot of people who are doing really well." While no participant would dispute the merit of pan-Asian organizing, few participants offered concrete ideas for how to organize meaningfully across the fragmentations and hierarchies discussed earlier. Participants 21 and 22, two brothers and successful restaurant owners, were the only ones offer specifics. Speaking as a second-generation Vietnamese American, participant 21 stated, "My thought was to do as many Asian restaurants as possible. I always identified myself as—not as a restauranteur—just someone who's trying to do Asian-American advocacy. Doing business is a part of that." Participant 22, who is participant 21's sibling, further explained what motivated them,

> Something that I've noticed like way different from the kids out in the West Coast, L.A., Orange County area, they don't feel ashamed of their culture. They embrace their Vietnamese-ness, Korean-ness, whatever. When we moved here, we noticed a lot of the Asian kids were either trying to be White or Black.

The racialized (and gendered) ethnic identifications reflected the particular context and localized race relations in Cincinnati, Ohio, where Asians/immigrants/Americans struggled with invisibility, representation, and belonging. In this context, pan-Asian organizing toward "togetherness-in-difference" would need to simultaneously bridge fragmentations and address hierarchies in building an equitable community while resisting the feminized model minority stereotype in service of white supremacy.

DISCUSSION

As an effort to de-center whiteness while reclaiming intersectionality, this study examines interview discourses of racialized/feminized ethnic identifications among Asians and Asian Americans in partnership with a pan-Asian nonprofit organization. Analysis of interviews with thirty self-identified Asians/immigrants/Americans reveal three overlapping themes regarding the normative yet differential processes of racializing and feminizing Asians as the "good" model minority. First, all participants in this study are critical of the discourse of the "good" Asian in terms of how it restricts career paths for Asian youths and negative impacts the mental, emotional, and cultural well-being of individuals as well as communities. Given that Asian (American) identity is "profoundly shaped by understandings of blackness and whiteness" (E. D. Wu, 2014, p. 7), the participants seem to be more aware and critical of the reality that Asians are racialized and feminized as inferior to white men. However, there seems to be less awareness of how the racializing and feminizing model minority discourse also privileges Asians/immigrants/Americans above other minorities. As Wu (2002) puts it, the model minority discourse "conceals within it an invidious statement about African Americans along the lines of inflammatory taunt: 'They made it; why can't you?'" (p. 49). Without such awareness, Asians/immigrants/Americans can perpetuate antiblack racism without realizing it.

Second, findings in this study underscore diverse, if not divisive, racialized ethnic identifications. On the one hand, the diverse identifications signal a tendency toward fragmentations within Asian and Asian American communities, which makes community building challenging. On the other hand, the diverse identifications also reveal hidden hierarchies based on native English speaker status, colonial histories/geopolitical relations, and immigration status. The hidden hierarchies represent power lines of differences that matter across racialized ethnic groups (e.g., lighter vs. browner Asians; descendants of colonizers vs. the colonized; refugees vs. voluntary immigrants, etc.). Both the fragmentations and hierarchies have been neutralized in the service of white supremacy. Critically reclaiming them through an intersectional lens can offer new possibilities of reimagining what being Asian/immigrant/American can mean in the twenty-first century.

Third, returning to the work of pan-Asian organizing as this research would not have been possible without the support and partnership of ACA, the first two themes suggest a fruitful direction of framing pan-Asian organizing as building "togetherness-in-difference" (Ang, 2001). Consistent with a dialectical view of intercultural communication (Martin & Nakayama, 1999), this approach to pan-Asian organizing advocates a broad and encompassing framework of holding simultaneously contradictory ideas, tensions, and pushes and pulls. Further, finding from this study echo Chen's (2014) concerns that pan-Asian organizing might function to privilege and reproduce white supremacy when it fails to consider culturally specific and ethically relevant experiences of Asians, Asian Americans, or American Asians within their local and global contexts.

De-whitening Racialized Ethnic Identifications across Intersecting Oppressions

Consistent with the theoretical commitments that guide this chapter, the findings offer several directions for thinking about de-whitening racialized and feminized Asian ethnic identifications across intersecting injustices and oppressions. First, I recommend that discussions of racialized/gendered ethnic identifications include conversations about how to confront antiblackness within and across Asian/immigrant/American families and communities. Guided by intersectionality for social justice (Bilge, 2013), such discussions should address sexism, English hegemony, and xenophobia as well. Second, I urge more conversations unpacking how the racialized "good" Asian ethics are simultaneously gendered (feminine). That is, the racialized ethnic identifications are also gendered and classed phenomena (e.g., the stereotypical trope of "[educated] tiger moms"). Third, findings in this study suggest a need to rethink pan-Asian organizing as "intersectional organizing" that begins with race and extends to bridge across sex and gender, sexuality, socioeconomic status, generations of immigrants, and more.

Limitations and Future Research

The findings of this study should be interpreted with in mind the particular ways in which it was conducted. Recruited by the nonprofit partner, I have only interviewed one self-identified LGBTQ participant even though sexuality remains a particularly challenging topic within Asian and Asian American communities. Future research should examine the intersection of race/ethnicity, sexuality, and immigration status within and across Asian and Asian American communities, particularly browner Asians and LGBTQ/refugee/Muslim Others who cross more borders and margins than the racialized phenotypical (East) Asians.

REFERENCES

Ang, I. (2001). *On not speaking Chinese: Living between Asia and the west*. New York, NY: Routledge.

Bilge, S. (2013). Intersectionality undone: Saving intersectionality from feminist intersectionality studies. *Du Bois Review: Social Science Research on Race, 10*(2), 405–24. doi:10.1017/S1742058X13000283.

Bonilla-Silva, E. (2004). From bi-racial to tri-racial: Towards a new system of racial stratification in the USA. *Ethnic and Racial Studies, 27*(6), 931–50.

Bonilla-Silva, E. (2006). *Racism without racists: Color-blind racism and the persistence of racial inequality in the United States* (2nd ed.). Lanham, MD: Rowman & Littlefield.

Brookfield, S. D. (1995). *Becoming a critically reflective teacher*. San Francisco, CA: Jossey-Bass.

Chen, Y.-W. (2014). Pan-Asian organizing for empowerment? Unpacking nonprofit discourses across organizational status position. *The Howard Journal of Communications, 25*, 350–71. doi: 10.1080/10646175.2014.924451.

Collins, P. H. (2000). *Black feminist thought: Knowledge, consciousness, and the politics of empowerment*. New York, NY: Routledge.

Crenshaw, K. W. (1991). Mapping the margins: Intersectionality, identity politics, and violence against women of color. *Stanford Law Review, 43*(6), 1241–99.

Eguchi, S. (2011). Negotiating sissyphobia: A critical/interpretive analysis of one "femme" gay Asian body in the heteronormative world. *The Journal of Men's Studies, 19*(1), 37–56. doi: https://doi.org/10.3149/jms.1901.37.

Kawai, Y. (2005). Stereotyping Asian Americans: The dialectic of the model minority and the yellow peril. *The Howard Journal of Communication, 16*, 109–30.

Kibria, N. (2000). The contested meanings of 'Asian American': Racial dilemmas in the contemporary US. *Ethnic and Racial Studies, 21*(5), 939–58.

Knight, C. (2018). Officer Sonny Kim was killed three years ago today. *Cincinnati Enquirer*. Retrieved from https://www.cincinnati.com/story/news/2018/06/19/officer-sonny-kim-killed-three-years-ago-today/714967002/.

Lawless, B. & Chen, Y.-W. (2019). Developing a method of critical thematic analysis for qualitative communication inquiry. *The Howard Journal of Communications, 30*, 92–106. doi:10.1080/10646175.2018.1439423.

Lee, S. J. (1996). *Unraveling the "model minority" stereotype: Listening to Asian American youth.* New York, NY: Teachers College, Columbia University.

Lee, S. S.-H. (2014). *A new history of Asian America.* New York, NY: Routledge.

Martin, J. N. & Nakayama, T. K. (1999). Thinking dialectically about culture and communication. *Communication Theory, 9*(1), 1–25.

Nakayama, T. K. (2016). Dis/orienting identities: Asian Americans, history, and intercultural communication. In A. González, & Y.-W. Chen (Eds.), *Our voices: Essays in culture, ethnicity, and communication* (6th ed., pp. 29–34). New York, NY: Oxford University Press.

Ocampo, A. C. (2016). *The Latinos of Asia: How Filipino Americans break the rules of race.* Stanford, CA: Stanford University Press.

Ohio Department Services Agency. *Ohio Asian Americans.* Retrieved from https://development.ohio.gov/files/research/P7004.pdf.

Otis, E. M. (2001). The reach and limits of Asian panethnic identity: The dynamics of gender, race, and class in a community-based organization. *Qualitative Sociology, 24*, 349–79.

Pew Research Center. (2013). *The rise of Asian Americans.* Retrieved from http://www.pewsocialtrends.org/2012/06/19/the-rise-of-asian-americans/.

Tuan, M. (1998). *Forever foreigners or honorary whites? The Asian ethnic experience today.* New Brunswick, NJ: Rutgers University Press.

Wu, E. D. (2014). *The color of success: Asian Americans and the origins of the model minority.* Princeton, NJ: Princeton University Press.

Wu, F. H. (2002). *Yellow: Race in America beyond Black and White.* New York, NY: Basic Books.

Chapter 15

Crazy Sexy Asian Men!

Masculinities in Crazy Rich Asians

Zhao Ding and Kamela Rasmussen

The mainstream U.S. media increasingly produce programs featuring racial minority casts. For example, one of the major TV networks, the American Broadcasting Company (ABC), has introduced two sitcoms that depict Asian American families and Asian migrants' experiences in 2015, *Dr. Ken* and *Fresh Off the Boat*. In August 2018, the Warner Bros. Pictures released the romantic comedy-drama film *Crazy Rich Asians*. It was adapted based on the same titled novel written by Kevin Kwan. Kwan is a Singaporean American novelist who is widely known for his novels *Crazy Rich Asians*, *China Rich Girlfriend*, and *Rich People Problems*. The film *Crazy Rich Asians* follows a Chinese American Economics professor named Rachel Chu (played by Constance Wu), who accompanies her boyfriend Nick Young (played by Henry Golding) to his home country Singapore for his friend's wedding and to meet his family. During their trip, Rachel is surprised to find that her boyfriend's family is one of the wealthiest in Singapore. Swamped in the isolated world built upon old money, Rachel has to deal with all the barriers that come with dating her crazy rich boyfriend. Along with its national and international release, *Crazy Rich Asians* swept the global box office, generating a gross of $230 million worldwide (Rodriguez, 2018). It became a huge success as a romantic comedy. The film has been seen as the first major Hollywood film to feature a majority Asian and Asian American cast to appear in twenty-five years since *The Joy Luck Club* was released in 1993. *The Joy Luck Club* had been indicated as a milestone as it centered on relationships between Chinese American women and their Chinese immigrant mothers (Change, 2018).

Crazy Rich Asians has been widely applauded for its breakthrough of redefining Asian/American masculinities (Tso, 2018; Chow, 2018). Media representations of Asian/American masculinities have emasculated and marginalized Asian/American men in TV and films. Images of Asian/American men are often limited to strangely nerdy, incompetent, and asexual (Eng, 2001; Ono & Pham, 2009), such as the Korean immigrant Han Lee from the CBS sitcom *2 Broke Girls* (2011) being portrayed as a small, emasculated, broken-English, workaholic who runs a dive diner. Simultaneously, Asian masculinities have also been portrayed as hypermasculine, such as the martial arts fighters Bruce Lee and Jackie Chan (Chan, 2000). Furthermore, Asian masculinity has been portrayed as more effeminate and weaker than white masculinity and the former is hardly ever shown as a romantic interest in TV and movies (Lopez, 2014). Nakayama (1994) also contends, "white heterosexual masculinity organizes and drives the narrative, constructing and constraining the range of potential meanings" (p. 167). He deems that the construction of Asian/American masculinity serves to re-center the white hetero-patriarchy and masculinity in U.S. popular culture.

However, *Crazy Rich Asians* portrays Asian/American men as romantic lead roles, which have often been exclusively roles for white actors. Kevin Kwan, the executive producer and the author of the novel expects this film to be a "watershed moment" to break down those stereotypes of Asian men (Chow, 2018). Since the release of the film, media have been cheering for the success of portraying Asian masculinities as sexually attractive and confident in *Crazy Rich Asians*. Some reviewers suggest that the film redefines Hollywood's Asian men as everyone's desires (Abad-Santos, 2018; Chow, 2018). Some argue that *Crazy Rich Asians* does not only challenge stereotypes surrounding Asian men, but also redefines North American beauty standards by putting more Asian men and women on the center stage, portraying them in a different perspective (Singh, 2018; Tso, 2018).

As critical intercultural communication scholars, we acknowledge the effort of this film to reframe performance of Asian/American men as sexy, masculine, and natural as their white male counterparts who often represent the beauty standards. These standards are often judged by white/Western beauty standards. They are transnationally circulated along with Americanized globalization and white imperialism and coloniality. Therefore, ideals and performance of beauty are profoundly racialized. As discussed above, media portrayals of Asian/American men are often either emasculated or hypermasculated. Accordingly, we are concerned with the film, which celebrates desirable and attractive Asian men and masculinities as a neutralizing strategy to mask and maintain the existing racial order. As Eguchi and Ding (2017) argue in their critical reading of ABC's *Dr. Ken*, "uncultural" narratives of Asian/Americans reinforce the stereotypical construction of Asian/Americans and mask the historical and contemporary realities of racism to maintain the existing hierarchies and dominant powers. The neutralizing strategy adopted by *Crazy Rich Asians* continues to Otherize Asia and Asian masculinities. This strategy also serves to reproduce the hierarchy of masculinities in the United States where white hetero-patriarchy and masculinities are re-centered and normalized. To demonstrate our argument, we analyze the representations of Asian masculinity in *Crazy Rich Asians* for this critical engagement. We are interested in examining how the film redefines Asian men and masculinities through interactions and relations among Asian male and female characters. By doing so, our larger goal is to challenge the hierarchy of masculinities presented in *Crazy Rich Asians* as it strategically draws our attention away from its reproduction of white hetero-patriarchal and masculine norms at the expense of Asian and Asian Americans.

In what follows, we first situate intersectionality as our conceptual lens to analyze the representations of Asian masculinities in *Crazy Rich Asians*. Then, our analysis follows two major themes: neutralization of Asian masculinities and Orientalization of Asian masculinities, organize our analysis. With such demonstration, we conclude this chapter by redirecting our attention to the larger implication of intersectionality that the film offers.

INTERSECTIONALITY

Intersectionality focuses on the reciprocity of major social categories, such as race, gender, sexuality, class, nation, religion, age, and ability, impacts the construction and production of people's experiences in the society. The concept of intersectionality came from Crenshaw (1989), to critically examine legal, cultural, and political systems that maintain power to discriminate black women. She emphasizes black females' complex experiences that have been informed by race, gender, and class in institutional contexts. Collins (2000) further complicates the concept in her theorization of black feminist thought. She asserts the various levels of privilege within the oppressed group and that the early and continuing feminist movements are primarily concerned with only the oppression faced by the most privileged (white women) in this oppressed group.

The notion of intersectionality is also important to and has influenced communication research in intercultural contexts (e.g., Calafell, 2013; Abdi & Van Gilder, 2016; Eguchi, Calafell, & Files-Thompson, 2014). As Yep (2013) addresses, intersectionality helps intercultural communication scholars "to unpack the cultural perspectives and constructions of normativity of their projects" (p. 123). Abdi and Van Gilder (2016) adopt intersectional approach to make sense of stories and experiences of queer Iranian-American women in cultural, familial, and relational discourses, as well as their ways of coping with challenges brought by their intersectional identities. Through the conceptual lens of intersectionality, authors are enabled to understand the rather complex and fluid experiences of queer women of color. Furthermore,

Washington's (2016) research on the representation and commodification of the success of PSY's *Gangnam Style* explores the conditional visibility of Asian/American and Asian/American masculinities through the lens of intersectionality. Washington argues that the seemingly positive yet conditional embrace to Korean popular culture and PSY is an alternative frame of "yellow peril" discourse in the white heteronormative U.S. society.

Meanwhile, we also need to be cautious when we use intersectionality in our research to not fall into the trap of using it as a check box. Yep (2013) indicates, "Intersectionality should not be treated in a superficial and roster-like fashion in which the individual's race, class, gender, sexuality, nationality [and other vectors of difference] are simply listed as categories of identity" (p. 123). Puar (2007) further argues that the misunderstanding and misuse of intersectionality dissolves the examination of race and whiteness, and fails to meet the appeals of postcolonial and transnational feminist thoughts. Similarly, Blige (2014) asserts that to de-whiten intersectionality, we need to disrupt Eurocentric knowledge-production politics and uncover the invisibility of race. As Eguchi, Calafell, and Files-Thompson (2014) argue in their research on African American male same-sex relationships in film *Noah's Arc: Jumping the Broom*, it is important to identify dominant ideologies and power structures surrounding intersectionality, such as whiteness, heteronormativity, and class privileges, especially in the seemingly progressive media product featuring racial, gender, and sexual minorities. Thus, as a part of the collective effort to de-whiten intersectionality in intercultural communication research, we situate intersectionality as our conceptual lens in a careful and nuanced way, to address the complexity of the construct of Asia and Asian masculinity by considering the historical and contemporary reality of power relations (Yep, 2010). Our goal in this chapter is to call out what affect and constitute representations of Asian masculinities and to expose the hidden power relations in the film *Crazy Rich Asians.*

READING *CRAZY RICH ASIANS*

Recognizing *Crazy Rich Asians* as a cultural and ideological product allows us to pay attention to the hidden assumptions about Asian masculinities produced and presented in the show. *Crazy Rich Asians* depicts a romantic story when Nick Young, the son of one of the wealthiest family in Singapore and a NYU professor, invites his girlfriend Rachel Chu, an Economics professor at NYU, traveling back to Singapore to attend the wedding of his best friend Colin. In Singapore, while Rachel is visiting her college friend Peik Lin, Rachel is surprised to find from Peik Lin and her dad Wye Mun Goh that Nick's family is extremely rich and his family and his friends do not seem to approve of their relationship because of their socioeconomic status differences. During the stay, Rachel learns about the sacrifice of marrying into a crazy rich family and she finds out the truth about her missing dad. With this background in mind, now we enter into reading the intersection of race, gender, sexuality, nation, and class around the representations of Asian men and masculinities in *Crazy Rich Asians*.

Neutralization of Asian Masculinities

Based on our review and analysis of the film, *Crazy Rich Asians* has produced different depictions of Asian masculinity performances for Western audiences. *Crazy Rich Asians* neutralizes Nick Young's masculine performances and his physical appearances as a strategy to whiten/Westernize Asian masculinities that appear not threatening to their audiences. Simultaneously, the film Otherizes Nick's family and friends in Asia and Asian masculinities by depicting them as effeminate, hypersexual, awkward, and hetero-patriarchal, in order to maintaining the existing racial hierarchy that informs the construct of masculinities. As Projansky and Ono (1999) argue, reproducing whiteness depends on the Othering representation of nonwhite as deviant from and thus subordinate to the dominant group. By applying and accenting the stereotypes of nonwhites, the mainstream media and cultural industry mark and preserve the invisible domain of whiteness (Griffin, 2015). This film utilizes Nick Young's character as a façade, to promote the illusory propaganda of diversity and inclusiveness in Hollywood and the United States, while driving the audience's attention away from its reproduction and normalization of white hetero-patriarchy and masculinities.

Contrary to the historically emasculated and effeminate media representations of Asian American men, Nick Young's character is cheered on by the audience. In the film, Nick is depicted as desirable, crazy rich, sexy, and masculine. The character is a romantic, gentle, and caring lover to his girlfriend Rachel Chu. He understands that Rachel may get overwhelmed by his family, so he reserves a hotel room for him and Rachel to stay instead of living with his family during their visit. At Nick's family party, Nick introduces Rachel to his family and friends, and carefully protects her from their unpleasant background interrogations. After learning Rachel gets pranked by his ex-girlfriend at the bachelor party of Colin's fiancée, Nick apologizes to Rachel for not informing her about his family before, and confesses how important she is to him. These caring and affectionate acts performed by Nick break the stereotypical media images of Asian American men as either awkward and shy or hypermasculine.

Here, Nick's performance is neutralized for showing his character being nonthreatening to the (white) dominant structure. Nick is depicted as a professor at New York. Although his vocation cannot provide as much wealth as his family business can, being a university professor with a highly educated background still does not free Nick's character out of the model minority construct. Career options of (East) Asian Americans are often limited to medicine, law, engineering, higher educational institutions, or additional degrees that indicate Asian Americans "successful" present (Hyun, 2005). Furthermore, Nick's performance is shown that he has adopted and embraced the ideals of individualism that value personal merit and choices and heteronormative structure of kinship (Eng, 2010). Unlike his cousins and friends who live closely with their family in Asia, Nick lives in New York and wants to have a family with his girlfriend Rachel, instead of going back to Singapore and running his family business. When Rachel is sitting in the first-class private suite on an airplane to go to Singapore and holding a glass of champagne, she first realizes that her boyfriend Nick may come from a really rich family. She is struck by this new finding and surprised by Nick's frugal lifestyle that does not show his identity of being the heir to one of the largest fortunes in Singapore. So, she confronts Nick, "I mean, you have a Jamba Juice card. You use my Netflix password. You play basketball at that Y that kind of smells." Nick replies, "Yes, my family has money, but I've always thought of it as theirs, not mine." These portrayals of Nick's intersectional positioning mirror norms of white hetero-patriarchal capitalist ideals and remind U.S./Western audience of a familiar image of an ordinary thirty-ish white middle-class abled man.

In addition, Nick is set up as less foreign than the other Asian men in the film through his physical appearance. Nick, played by Henry Golding, fits into the Western idealized masculine body image of large, defined muscles, above average height, and "strong" facial features including a wide jaw and thick eyebrows (Law & Labre, 2002). In comparison to other characters, Nick is taller, more muscular, and more Western compared to other men in the film, positioning him as the ideal romantic partner. The physicality of other male characters, who the audience only sees in an Asian setting, serves to further neutralize Nick. Nick's closest comparison in terms of romantic desirability, Colin, performs as a slightly less masculine version of Nick, allowing Nick—as the more masculine appearing—to escape from stereotypical depictions of Asian men as feminine. Colin, played by Chris Yang, stands at 5′11″ while Nick stands at 6′1″. Colin has a narrower jaw and lighter skin while Nick has a wider jaw and tanner skin. Colin is thinner than Nick while Nick possesses more muscle mass. Colin serves to maintain the racial hierarchy where the feminine Colin is less masculine than Nick. Eng (2001) explains that the feminized physical appearance of Asian males assists the mainstream framings of inferior Asian bodies to whites. Here, Colin's relatively more feminized physical appearance serves to neutralize and whiten Nick's manhood and masculinity, so that the latter will be more desired. Through showcasing the comparison between Nick and Colin, the film reproduces and secures the dominance of white masculinity.

Moreover, the neutralizing strategy reproduces the construct of Asian/Americans as almost white. We identify almost white as this ambiguous territory for Asian/Americans in which they are positioned near to the power center preserved by whiteness through their material success (Eguchi & Ding, 2017). The almost white structure reinforces the existing power hierarchy where whiteness maintains the center. Of the characters with major speaking parts, Cousin Oliver has the darkest skin. This has much to do with the casting of Filipino Actor Nico Santos in the role of Cousin Oliver. Cousin Oliver reveals to Rachel in the first few moments of meeting her that his branch of the family has mostly lost their fortune and that he makes a living doing odd jobs for the family. He is given the job of servant; therefore, marking him as less than the rest of the family. Other roles featuring darker skin actors are the security guards who initially refuse access to Nick's grandmother's home and the vendors at the open market. The security guards, unlike the other men, are bearded and carry weapons. Their masculinity is threatening to Rachel and Peik Lin Goh and they are shown to be one of very few characters that do not seem to understand English. Even in Singapore, there is an expectation that all the characters understand and speak English, so when the security guards do not immediately seem to understand what Rachel and Peik Lin are saying, they are marked as Other and foreign. This, in combination with their weapons and aggressive stance, conflate foreign-ness and darkness with threatening. In comparison, the other Asian characters understand English and are safe. At the open market, men and women with dark skin tones are shown as cooks and service workers. Rachel, Nick, Colin, and Araminta stand out in the crowd as both wealthy and lighter skinned. While they are shown to have familiarity with the workers in this open market, this visit is marked by tourism. This juxtaposition allows the audience to see the *Crazy Rich Asians* as almost white and visitors in this foreign place.

The construction, comparison, and contrast of masculinities among Nick, Colin, and their cousins are to further reproduce, maintain, and circulate the (white) dominant values and ideals. Although Nick and Colin are portrayed as sexy, attractive, and desirable, the difference between them marks the invisibility of whitened masculinities. The neutralized performance reassures that the film is nonthreatening to the dominant social, political, cultural, and economical structures, and it further imposes U.S./Western values and beliefs on non-Western cultures within and outside of Western countries (Chavez, 2013; Eguchi, 2014; Eguchi & Ding, 2017). Thus, we argue that the neutralized performance and physical appearance in *Crazy Rich Asians* is presented to remain the historical continuum of Otherized Asian American media representation.

Orientalization of Asian Masculinities

Representations of Asia and Asian identities remain to be regulated and Otherized by Western ideologies embedded by white hetero-patriarchal and masculine norms. Asia, Asian people, and Asian Americans are continuously to be fantasized by the West. Media representations of Asian masculinities are constructed as Oriental. Asian American images have been conflated with Asians due to the historically anti-Asian sentiments (Ono, 2005). The fear of Asia being a threat to the white dominance on culture, economy, politics, and military leads Asian Americans being used as both scapegoats and spectacle for social issues by mainstream media (Osajima, 1988). Therefore, there is inevitably historical and continuous connection between Asia and Asian America, as well as their media images. Although *Crazy Rich Asians* presents all Asian male characters that seemingly complicate and de-whiten the dominant depiction of Asian manhood and masculinities, their images are still informed by the stereotypical media construction of Asian/American males. The film still makes Asian male characters and masculinities Othered.

The film *Crazy Rich Asians* represents Asian masculinities as awkward. It reinforces the historical feminization and subordination of Asian men through the dominant Hollywood gaze. For example, the Goh family provides a weird, awkward, and feminized performance of Asian masculinity. Wye Mun Goh, the father of Rachel's college roommate, is immediately extremely invasive and sexual toward Rachel upon their first meeting. Rachel is visibly uncomfortable as Wye Mun calls Rachel a "hottie," dateable, and the "gold standard." He constructs Rachel's presence as a potential sexual or romantic encounter for his awkward son. Despite being sexually aggressive toward Rachel, he is outwardly flamboyant. He speaks with a higher pitch and comes off much more feminine than the other men in the film. Like Colin, he has a smaller jaw and body type than Nick but unlike Colin and Nick, he dresses in typically feminine clothing and attempts to be the center of attention. He maintains a heterosexual image in the film, being one of the few characters to engage in any sort of sexual contact with a significant other; however, his significant other is the least attractive and their sexual interaction is awkward and the characters who witness it are repulsed.

Also portrayed as awkward is P.T. Goh, Wye Mun's son. P.T. shares the same physical characteristics as his father and is regarded by Rachel as unattractive, but harmless. This harmlessness is in contrast with Nick's apparent safety as Nick is safe in that he *will* not harm Rachel while P.T. is harmless in that he *can*not harm Rachel, or any other woman for that matter. Wye Mun broadcasts P.T.'s lack of a love or sexual life to Rachel before P.T. has said anything to her. P.T. then engages in creepy behavior such as telling Rachel he loves her (and little else) while eating with his family, taking pictures of Rachel while she is unaware, and making a heart shape with his hands when Rachel leaves. This behavior is laughed off or ignored by the other characters, indicating that while creepy, P.T. poses no danger and could not interact with a woman in a normal way. These performances are crafted from the Asian nerd stereotype. This stereotype relies on a combination of overwhelming sexual desire, typically for Asian or white women, and an overwhelming lack of sexuality to render the Asian nerd unable to be sexual.

The film *Crazy Rich Asians* reproduces Asian masculinities as flamboyant. Bernard Tai and Cousin Allistair Wang represent a totally opposite depiction of Asian masculinity than that of the Goh family. Bernard Tai is first characterized as a "douche-nozzle" by Nick while Cousin Allistair is shown to be an incompetent director only interested in having sex with his actress girlfriend when Nick describes his family to Rachel. In contrast to the harmless Goh family, who could not bed anyone of a "gold standard," Bernard and Cousin Allistair are hypersexualized. Both men were present at the bachelor party and the wedding. Bernard is portrayed as having seized control of the bachelor party despite Colin's wishes. While Colin tells Nick that he wanted a small, tame party, Bernard plans a large party a boat with tons of women and alcohol. Also presents are pageant winners in swimwear from the United Kingdom, the Netherlands, and other countries. He spends most of the bachelor party with his arms around these women and it is unclear if these women were invited guests or hired. He is loud and makes sexual jokes that are shown to make Colin and Nick uncomfortable.

Like the Goh family, these men serve the purpose of setting Nick up as the ideal partner and de-accenting Nick. The portrayals of Bernard and Allistair reproduce the historical and ideological narrative that Asian men are "yellow peril" who threaten the white dominant lifestyle on culture, economy, politics, and military (Kawai, 2005). Their performance indicates the white/U.S. American/Western gaze of Asia as the "underdevelopment," which further Otherizes Asia and Asian masculinities away from the white hetero-patriarchal norms (Eng, 2001). Bernard and Allistair are revealed to be unsuitable mates during their introductions and are not redeemed as the movie goes on. Bernard is said to have been a bully who was beaten up by Nick as a child. The audience never hears Bernard's recollection of this event and is given no choice but to understand Bernard as weaker than Nick. Bernard is also portrayed as incapable of forming a loving, romantic relationship. Much of his screen time is focused on shallow and sexual conquests. In comparison, Nick is shown as being able to have many women desiring him romantically and be capable of having a loving and functional relationship. Cousin Allistair is in direct competition for inheritance with Nick. However, he is characterized as unfit to lead the family in business compared to favorite grandson Nick. His girlfriend is then swayed to pursue Nick as Nick will inherit much more than Cousin Allistair, showing that Cousin Allistair is only capable of having a romantic relationship when (a) Nick is not interested and (b) the woman believes she will gain some sort of monetary or social value by dating him. In contrast, Rachel had no idea of Nick's wealth until well into their relationship and this wealth was more of a detriment than an asset.

In addition, the representations of gender and (homo/hetero)sexuality further construct the Otherized Asian masculinities. In the film, Cousin Oliver introduces himself to Rachel as the "rainbow sheep" of the family. This phrase, derived from the rebellious black sheep of the family, alludes to Cousin's Oliver's sexuality. Although never stated explicitly, Cousin Oliver seems to be understood as gay. The casting of Nico Santos in this role perhaps compounds this. Santos, who may be best known to U.S. American audiences for his role of the openly gay Mateo on NBC's *Superstore*, is an openly gay actor who typically plays gay roles. Like Wye Mun Goh, he speaks in a higher-pitched voice and wears more feminine clothes than other men. In the book series, he is never depicted as having a serious romantic or sexual relationship. His sexuality could be considered "accepted" in that it is never problematized by the family.

Cousin Oliver represents another nonthreatening Asian masculinity. He serves primarily to passively guide Rachel through this new world she has found herself in. He first serves as her narrator, engaging in gossip to fill in the gaps in Rachel's knowledge of the family. He later serves as her stylist and confidante when she is unsure of herself before the wedding. He also serves the family in the same manner, supplying them with the rare things they need. When Nick's mother asks Cousin Oliver to supply her with information that will break up Rachel and Nick, Cousin Oliver passively agrees. Cousin Oliver is given no significant plot lines of his own and exists mainly to serve the heterosexual characters.

The ambiguity of Oliver's sexuality is constructed through the dominant Western closet paradigm in which "coming out" is emphasized and imperative (Yep & Lescure, 2014). It imposes Western/U.S. American ideology of sexual visibility that values individualism, economic independence, and personal visibility (Yep & Lescure, 2014). As Eng (2001) and Yep (2013) argue, the construct of individuals' sexual identity always associates with their race, class, gender, and national locations. In the film, Oliver has never "come out." However, his verbal and nonverbal performance, such as stylish appearance, vocalism, and girls' best friend, corresponds to stereotypes associated with asexual and effeminate Asian gay men. Furthermore, the (in)visible negotiation and acceptance of Oliver's queerness reproduces the hetero-patriarchal assumptions often associated to Asian cultures. Thus, Oliver's portrait maintains hegemonic constructions of U.S./Western imperialist (hetero/homo-) masculinity which regards U.S./Western as the progressive and civilized better culture and race than "othered" Asia. In contrast to the ambiguous depiction of Oliver's sexuality, the film emphasizes the depiction and representations of hetero-patriarchal romantic relationships and masculinities.

In *Crazy Rich Asians*, most romantic relationships are presented as heterosexual. None of the characters, aside from Cousin Oliver, are hinted at being anything other than straight. The participants of these relationships are required to engage in normative gender patterns with Peik Lin Goh being chastised by her father for her masculinized appearance and mannerisms. Interestingly, the way the characters engage in heterosexual relationships is very polarized. Relationships are either entirely sexual or not sexual at all. Cousin Allistair and his girlfriend, Kitty, are shown to be an extremely sexual couple but they are never shown to have genuine affection between them. Their decrees of love after fighting at the wedding are interrupted by passionate kissing and their relationship is framed more through sex than any other connection. Bernard is also shown to be incapable of any relationship that is not sexual.

The three romantic couples in the movie (Nick and Rachel, Colin and Araminta, and Michael and Astrid) engage each other in very little physical contact. While the movie points to a fairly conservative culture several times, with Nick introducing Rachel as his friend and little talk about romance outside of marriage, Rachel is American and therefore unencumbered by this conservatism outside of the Asian setting and the other couples are shown to not be sexual inside of marriage. For example, the first scene between Michael and Astrid features Michael nude in the shower. He is shown to have a similar, if not more muscular, physique to Nick and the sweeping angle of the camera allows audience members to see him as sexy. Astrid arrives home during this shower and goes about having her staff hide her purchases from him and reading to their child. Astrid is sitting on the bed when Michael walks into the bedroom wearing only a towel. Instead of engaging in romantic conversation or sexual contact as Astrid seems to desire, Michael begins an argument with her. Here, Michael is shown to be uninterested in having a sexual relationship with his wife. While Astrid later believes that Michael is having a sexual relationship with another woman, this is shown to be false in the book series and it is in fact Astrid who has an extramarital affair (while still believing Michael has cheated on her).

This representation of Asian masculinity as either completely sexual or not sexual at all furthers an existing stereotype in the American consciousness of Asian men being unfit partners. It shows Asian men as being only capable of doing one or the other, a trope that is common in U.S. American television as well. The television series *Selfie*, which had a white female lead and an Asian American male lead, portrayed its Asian American male lead as unwilling to talk about or have a sexual relationship with his white female counterpart despite his clear interest and romantic desire for her. Before she decides he is even a possible romantic partner, he spends much of the series trying to stifle her sexuality. The series was then cancelled in the middle of its first season before the characters decided to engage in a relationship. Other U.S. American medical dramas depict the relationships between black men and Asian women as either sexual or romantic, leaving relationships with white men as the only relationships capable of being both sexual and romantic (Washington, 2012). While Season 15 of *Grey's Anatomy* has introduced an Asian American character, who is in a relationship that is both sexual and loving, this relationship is also with a white man. The only relationship that is shown to be both romantic and sexual is that of Wye Mun Goh and his wife. However, this relationship serves primarily as comic relief and is shown to be repulsive to the other characters. Taken together, this leaves the audience with the sense of Asian masculinity as not being able to perform normal romantic heterosexual relationships compared to their white counterparts.

Crazy Rich Asians depicts Asian masculinities as hetero-patriarchal to promote Nick Young's character being open-minded, caring, and supportive of gender equality. Patriarchy is a socially constructed system in which males are considered dominating and superior than anyone deemed weak, such as females. The patriarchal-structured society demands females to serve and to be submissive to males, and it suppresses their capability of thinking and providing for family and the society (hooks, 2004). The masculinities of Asian and Asian American men have been taught and confined by racial, gendered, and sexual orders (Shimizu, 2012). White hetero-patriarchal ideologies have been imposing onto representations of Asian and Asian American masculinity portrayed in the U.S. popular culture, and constructing Asian and Asian American masculinity as effeminate and emasculate yet vicious, sultry, and oppressive to their women (Eng, 2001; Shimizu, 2012).

In *Crazy Rich Asians*, we notice that to secure Nick Young as nonthreatening and being almost white, the framing of Asian masculinity reconstitutes the hetero-patriarchal tradition. For example, Michael Teo, Astrid's husband who used to be a military captain, has been struggling with his patriarchal manhood throughout the movie. He married into Astrid's family, and feels inferior because his wife is richer and more famous than him. His manhood remains to be hurt as Astrid offers to help his failing business, as well as she keeps hiding her luxurious expenses, which he cannot afford to buy for his wife. Their marriage is eventually ended when Astrid finds Michael's affair with another woman and confronts it with him. However, the last straw that breaks Michael is Astrid's reaction to his affair. Although Astrid is saddened by his husband's affair, she tells him that they should stop talking about it to not make a scene in front of her family at Colin's wedding. Michael insists that Astrid deems her and her family more important than him and their marriage. At the end of the film, Astrid moves out of their apartment because she owns fourteen department buildings and she does not need the apartment bought by her husband. Before she left, Astrid confronted Michael's manhood, "It's not my job to make you feel like a man. I can't make you something you are not."

Without further investigating and complicating the tensions and conflicts between Astrid and Michael, the film implies Michael as the sole blame for his failed marriage, due to his insecurity on his manhood shaped by "Asian" hetero-patriarchal ideals. Scenes described above show that Michael cannot tolerate his manhood and masculinity being continuously challenged by his wife's wealth and confidence. In order to reaffirm his patriarchal power as a husband and male, Michael refuses Astrid's financial assistant and cheating on her with another woman that eventually ends his marriage. Therefore, although this film intends to de-whiten the stereotypical images of Asian men by portraying Michael Teo as a physically sexy man, it still did not shake the yellow-peril informed construction of Asian men who threaten the white dominant structure.

In a similar vein, Eddie Cheng, Nick's cousin, is depicted as an aggressively hetero-patriarchal playboy who shows no affection to women. At Colin's bachelor party, Eddie quite disdains with Nick's concern over Rachel. With a woman who is not his wife in his arm, Eddie mocks Nick, "Oh my God, Nick! What are you worried about? You don't have to keep Rachel happy. She's just lucky to be here." Colin tries to stop him, but Eddie continues to denigrate Rachel for not coming from a rich family. He says, "Oh what? So we're gonna pretend like that's not the truth? Are we in some kind of fairy tale story that I don't know about? Did you find a shoe at midnight and jump in a pumpkin? Yo, I got so much shit about marrying Fiona, and her parents own the biggest shipping company in Hong Kong. Hey, Araminta's adorable, but you think your dad would be spending millions on this wedding if her parents didn't own a billion dollar resort chain? What's Rachel bringing to the table?" "Small tits!" Allistair quips. This scenario, once again, (re) produces the vicious and sultry hetero-patriarchal construction of Asian masculinity, in which men are considered weak if they show affection to women (hooks, 2004). The hypermasculine portrait of Eddie and the contract showed between him and Nick, re-whiten and re-center the neutralized performance of Nick's manhood and masculinity that is caring, affectionate, sexy, and desired.

The invisible fathers in the film further visualize the Orientalization of Asian masculinities. Although the film does not show father, their roles and functions that indicate and construct the hetero-patriarchal kinship, society, and cultures are detectable from the interactions and relationships among other characters. The depiction of the fathers' absence covers the reproduction of Western/U.S. American superiority on race, gender, sexuality, class, and nation over Asia.

Crazy Rich Asians depicts three families in which "the father" is absent: Rachel's father, Nick's father, and Peik Lin's father. Although Rachel's and Nick's fathers never show up in the film, their existences are well explained by the female characters. Rachel's father, as we learn from the film, had not died, as Rachel doesn't know in the beginning. She finds out the truth about her "father" at Colin's wedding when she is confronted by Nick's mom and grandma. Eleanor and grandma are informed by the private investigator they hired that Rachel's dad is still alive. Eleanor tells Rachel, "Your mother's husband is very much alive. During her marriage she cheated on him, and became pregnant with another man's child. And before he found out, she ran away to America." Rachel's mother later confirms it and tells Rachel more behind the story, "My husband wasn't a good man. He hurt me. But an old schoolmate of mine helped me through things, and we fell in love, and I got pregnant with his baby. That's you. I was so afraid my husband would find out and kill us both, so I just took you and I ran to America." In this complex and troubled past, although Rachel and her mother seem to be the victims of this abusive hetero-patriarchal structure, they become the blame for their failed and scandalous relationships.

According to the film, Nick's father is not there because he was called to business in Shanghai. We learn from the film that Nick's father is a very successful and diligent businessman. Later in the film, at the scene of Nick's family making dumplings, the conversation between Rachel and Nick's mother inform us more about Nick's father and the family. In the scenario, Rachel leaves the table and goes to look for the bathroom when Nick's mom Eleanor catches her from behind. Using her own story, Eleanor tries to talk Rachel out of her relationship with Nick. Eleanor says, "You asked about my ring. The truth is Nick's father had it made when he wanted to propose to me because Ah Ma wouldn't give him the family ring. I wasn't her first choice. Honestly, I wasn't her second." Rachel is surprised by Eleanor's confession and shows her sympathy. Eleanor continues, "I didn't come from the right family, have the right connections. And Ah Ma thought I would not make an adequate wife to her son." "But she came around, obviously," says Rachel. "It took many years, and she had good reason to be concerned. Because I had no idea the work and the sacrifice it would take. There were many days when I wondered if I would ever measure up. But having been through it all, I know this much. You will never be enough," Eleanor ends the conversation assertively, and leaves Rachel standing there ashamed and perplexed. This scenario and the intensive conversation between the mother and soon-to-be daughter-in-law offers us a peak into this traditionally hetero-patriarchal-ruled kinship depicted through the lens of the West.

In the hetero-patriarchal kinship structure, father and son are the backbone, the hope and the only heir of the whole family, while their mother, wife, and daughter-in-law are always the outsiders who need to depend on their husband and son to secure their position in the family (Wolf, 1972). This film utilizes the negotiation between Rachel and Nick's mom to reconstruct the Orientalized Asian family and Asian fantasies. The conflicts between Rachel and Nick's mom, between Western ideologies and Asian ideologies, and between Western masculinity and Asian masculinity, are ended with the victory of Rachel and the engagement party of Rachel and Nick. In doing so, the film again validates the superiority of the West over the East, which is the forever Orient.

Different from the absence of Rachel's and Nick's fathers that we have discussed above, the father of Rachel's college friend Peik Lin, Wye Mun Goh, does appears in the film. We argue that the "father" is also missing in Peik Lin's family, because Goh's appearance and performance somehow is more like a comedian, not the traditional image of Asian father depicted passively and seriously as Rachel's and Nick's ones. Wye Mun Goh may be the most positive and advanced portrayal of an Asian father in the U.S. mainstream media. Contrary to Nick's father who inherits his fortune from the "old money," Goh represents the "new money." He was born poor but achieved success later. He also used to study at Cal State Fullerton in the United States. Unlike many Asian men depicted in the film who married young pretty model-like trophy wives, Goh is happily married with a chubby, older woman who uses her chopsticks to feed the dog at the dining table. Goh and his family are kind as they generously help Rachel deal with Nick's family. In contrast to many of Nick's family and friends who only care if Rachel comes from a rich family, Goh values Rachel's educational and professional success. Goh is very impressed when Rachel tells him that she is an Economics professor, and gently scolds his daughter who needs to be more like Rachel. He also tells his son that Rachel is the "Goh standard" that his son needs to find a girlfriend who is as smart as Rachel. We argue that Goh's liberal yet ridiculous father's portrayal is utilized to further validate the "real" image of Asian fathers and the Orientalized construct of Asian families and Asia.

Hetero-patriarchal structure indicates that father's role symbolizes the prosperity of the family and the nation (Chan, 2001). Looking back in the modern history of China, "father's" role had always been absent because of their sickness or death due to the wars, crimes, or addiction to opium. The absence of "father" led to numerous intrusions from Western countries. As the antithesis of the West who thinks of itself as "masculine-big guns, big industry, big money," China and even the whole Asia had been fantasized as the Oriental East which is effeminate, emasculate, weak, poor, and obsolete (Eng, 2001, p. 1). Thus, these invisible father images represent the obsolete, hetero-patriarchal, Oriental values that need to be liberated by Western modernity and globalization (Eng, 2010). The movie uses the logic of the absence of father reconstitutes the Oriental images of Asian masculinity and Asia.

CONCLUSION

In this chapter, we have attempted to interrogate the ways in which Asian men and masculinities are redefined in the film *Crazy Rich Asians*. Through the conceptual lens of intersectionality, we identify and critique the neutralizing strategy applied to generate desirable and attractive images of Asian men and masculinities. That is, the film neutralizes the leading character Nick Young's masculine performance and physical appearances as a strategy to (re-)whiten/Westernize Asian masculinities that appear not threatening to their audiences. Simultaneously, the film Otherizes Nick's family and friends in Asia and Asian masculinities by portraying them being effeminate, hypersexual, awkward, and hetero-patriarchal. We argue that the neutralizing strategy masks and maintains the existing racial order and continues to Orientalize Asia and Asian masculinities. Even further, this strategy serves to draw attention away from its reproduction of the hierarchy of masculinities at the expense of Asian and Asian Americans in which white hetero-patriarchy and masculinities are re-centered and normalized.

Since 2015, we have observed an increase in Asian/American characters in the mainstream media products, with the consecutive release of ABC's *Fresh Off the Boat*, *Dr. Ken*, and Warner Brother's *Crazy Rich Asians*, as well as many other TV and film products in which Asian/Americans are featured in leading roles. In many of these TV programs and films, Asian/Americans' identities, femininities, and masculinities are discussed. It is vital for us to cautiously welcome and critically celebrate such "progress." It is vital to interpret such "progress" through the lens of intersectionality, in order to examine how are "othered" subjects constructed. The universally cheered "progressive" Asian masculine image constructed by the film *Crazy Rich Asians* is harmful because it intends to erase the existing racial hierarchy and unequal power relations among race, nation, gender, and class. Masculinity is intersectional and it needs to be considered among historical and political relations, economics, race, gender, and nation at local and transnational contexts (Yep, 2013).

This chapter contributes to the ongoing conversation of de-whitening intersectionality in the discipline of intercultural communication. It follows the call to re-center the origin of intersectionality as a conceptual tool that deconstructs and contests power structure in and across the international and intercultural contexts by engaging seemingly "inclusive" and "progressive" popular cultural products. Through the intersectional lens, this chapter decenters white/Western hetero-patriarchal and masculine productions of U.S. mainstream film industry at the expense of Asian and Asian Americans. More specifically, we come to an understanding that the neutralizing strategy adopted in the film is a site where racialized masculinity is covered and reproduced through Asian characters. Accordingly, Asian males (such as Nick) become the production of a white man, which makes the rest of Asian male characters (such as Nick's family and friends), who are portrayed as effeminate, hypersexual, awkward, and hetero-patriarchal, a representation of otherized and deviant masculinity in comparison to whiteness. Intersectionality utilized in this chapter also illuminates and contests the existence of masculinity hierarchy that is crucial for preserving white hetero-patriarchal masculinity as the center and the norm, which makes it even more vital to deconstruct the constructed Asian masculinity in the context of Hollywood liberalization. As critical intercultural communication scholars, it is vital for us to interrupt white hegemony and globalization that marginalizes and erases nuances of knowledge of non-Western people of color who have often been marked as cultural Others.

REFERENCES

Abad-Santos, A. (2018, August 17). *Crazy Rich Asians* has a daring premise: An Asian man that everyone desires. *Vox*. Retrieved from https://www.vox.com/culture/2018/8/17/17682032/crazy-rich-asians-representation-asian-men.

Abdi, S. & Van Gilder, B. (2016). Cultural (in)visibility and identity dissonance: Queer Iranian-American women and their negotiation of existence. *Journal of International and Intercultural Communication, 9*(1), 69–86.

Balaji, M. (2011). Beyond Jackie Chan. In R. L. Jackson, & M. Balaji (Eds.), *Global masculinities and manhood* (pp. 186–201). University of Illinois Press.

Bilge, S. (2014). Whitening intersectionality: Evanescence of race in intersectionality scholarship. Racism and sociology. *Racism Analysis Yearbook, 5,* 175–205.

Calafell, B. M. (2013). (I)dentities: Considering accountability, reflexivity, and intersectionality in the I and the we. *Liminalities: A Journal of Performances Studies, 9*(2), 6–13.

Chan, J. (2001). *Chinese American masculinities: From Fu Manchu to Bruce Lee.* New York: Routledge.

Chan, J. W. (2000). Bruce Lee's fictional models of masculinity. *Men and Masculinities*, 2, 371–87.

Chang, J. (2018, September 5). At 25, "The Joy Luck Club" is still a captivating Hollywood movie about Asian American identity and, finally, it's no longer the only one. *Los Angeles Times*. Retrieved from https://www.latimes.com/entertainment/movies/la-et-mn-the-joy-luck-club-at-25-20180905-story.html.

Chávez, K. R. (2013). Pushing boundaries: Queer intercultural communication. *Journal of International and Intercultural Communication, 6*(2), 83–95.

Chen, A. S. (1999). Lives at the center of the periphery, lives at the periphery of the center: Chinese American masculinities and bargaining with hegemony. *Gender & Society, 13*(5), 584–607.

Chow, C. (2018, August 14). Going virile: How 'Crazy Rich Asians' redefines Hollywood Asian men. *The Undefeated*. Retrieved from https://theundefeated.com/features/going-virile-how-crazy-rich-asians-redefines-hollywoods-asian-man/.

Crenshaw, K. (1989). Demarginalizing the intersection of race and sex: A Black feminist critique of antidiscrimination doctrine, feminist theory and antiracist politics. *University of Chicago Legal Forum, 1989,* 139.

Eguchi, S. (2014). Ongoing cross-national identity transformation: Living on the queer japan-U.S. transnational borderland. *Sexuality & Culture, 18*(4), 977–93.

Eguchi, S. (2017). Japanese male-queer femininity: An autoethnographic reflection on Matsuko Deluxe as an onē-kei talent. In S. Toyosaki & S. Eguchi (Eds.), *Intercultural communication in Japan: Theorizing homogenizing discourse* (pp. 73–85). London: Routledge.

Eguchi, S., Calafell, B. M., & Files-Thompson, N. (2014). Intersectionality and quare theory: Fantasizing African American male same-sex relationships in *Noah's Arc: Jumping the Broom. Communication, Culture & Critique, 7*(3), 371–89.

Eguchi, S. & Ding, Z. (2017). "Uncultural" Asian Americans in ABC's Dr. Ken. *Popular Communication, 15*(4), 296–310.

Eng, D. L. (2001). *Racial castration: Managing masculinity in Asian America*. Durham, NC: Duke University Press.

Eng, D. L. (2010). *The feeling of kinship: Queer liberalism and the racialization of intimacy*. Durham, NC: Duke University Press.

Espiritu, Y. L. (2004). Ideological racism and cultural resistance: Constructing our own images. In M. L. Andersen, & P. H. Collins (Eds.), *Race, class, and gender: An anthology* (5th ed., pp. 175–184). Belmont, CA: Wadsworth.

Griffin, R. A. (2015). Problematic representations of strategic Whiteness and 'post-racial' pedagogy: A critical intercultural reading of *The Help. Journal of International and Intercultural Communication, 8*(2), 147–66.

Guo, L. & Lee, L. (2013). The critique of YouTube-based vernacular discourse: A case study of YouTube's Asian community. *Critical Studies in Media Communication, 30*(5), 391.

Harris III, F. H., Wood, J. L., & Newman, C. (2015). An exploratory investigation of the effect of racial and masculine identity on focus: An examination of White, Black, Mexican, Latino, and Asian men in community colleges. *Culture, Society and Masculinities, 7*(1), 61.

Hill Collins, P. (2000). *Black feminist thought: Knowledge, consciousness, and the politics of empowerment*. New York: Routledge.

hooks, b. (1952 [2004]). *The will to change: M/en, masculinity, and love*. New York: Atria Books.

Hyun, J. (2005). *Breaking the bamboo ceiling: Career strategies for Asians.* New York, NY: HarperCollins.

Kawai, Y. (2005). Stereotyping Asian Americans: The dialectic of the model minority and the yellow peril. *The Howard Journal of Communication, 16*, 109–30.

Lee, R. (1999). *Orientals: Asian Americans in popular culture.* Philadelphia, PA: Temple University Press.

Law, C. & Labra, M. P. (2002). Cultural standards of attractiveness: A thirty-year look at changes in males images in magazines. *Journalism and Mass Communication Quarterly,* (3), 697.

Lee, R. (2014). *Exquisite corpse of Asian America.* NY: New York University Press.

Lopez, L. K. (2014). Blogging while angry: The sustainability of emotional labor in the Asian American blogosphere. *Media, Culture & Society, 36*(4), 421–36.

Nakayama, T. K. (1994). Show/down time: "Race," gender, sexuality, and popular culture. *Critical Studies in Mass Communication, 11*(2), 162–79.

Ono, K. A. (2005). From nationalism to migrancy: The politics of Asian American transnationalism. *Communication Law Review, 5*(1), 1–17.

Ono, K. A., & Pham, V. N. (2009). *Asian Americans and the media.* Malden, MA: Polity Press.

Osajima, K. (1988). Asian Americans and the model minority: An analysis of the popular press image in the 1960s and 1980s. In G. Y. Okihiro, S. Hune, A. A. Hansen, & J. M. Liu (Eds.), *Reflections on shattered windows: Promises and prospects for Asian American Studies* (pp. 165–74). Pullman, WA: Washington State University Press.

Projansky, S., & Ono, K. A. (1999). Strategic whiteness as cinematic racial politics. In T. K. Nakayama, & J. N. Martin (Eds.), *Whiteness: The communication of social identity* (pp. 149–74). Thousand Oaks, CA: Sage.

Puar, J. K., 1967. (2007). *Terrorist assemblages: Homonationalism in queer times.* Durham: Duke University Press.

Rodriguez, A. (2018, October 1). 'Crazy Rich Asians' is the top-grossing romantic comedy in 10 years. *MSN Entertainment.* Retrieved from https://www.msn.com/en-sg/entertainment/movies/news/%E2%80%9Ccrazy-rich-asians%E2%80%9D-is-the-top-grossing-romantic-comedy-in-10-years/ar-BBNNtKe.

Shimizu, C. P. (2012). *Straight sexualities: Unbinding Asian American manhoods in the movies.* Stanford, CA: Stanford University Press.

Singh, K. (2018, August 17). PSA: The men of *Crazy Rich Asians* are hunky AF. *Flare.* Retrieved from https://www.flare.com/tv-movies/live-action-barbie-movie-margot-robbie/.

Tso, P. (August 8, 2018). 'Crazy Rich Asians' is proving that Hollywood is ready for buff Asian men. *Men's Health.* Retrieved from https://www.menshealth.com/entertainment/a22674130/crazy-rich-asians-cast-representation/.

Wang, G. (2010). A shot at half-exposure: Asian Americans in reality TV shows. *Television and New Media, 11*(5), 404–27.

Wang, X. & Cooper-Chen, A. (2010). Gendered stereotypes of Asians portrayed on the websites of U.S. higher education institutions. *Visual Communication Quarterly, 17*(2), 77–90.

Washington, M. (2012). Interracial intimacy: Hegemonic construction of Asian American and Black relationships on TV medical dramas. *Howard Journal of Communications*, *23*(3), 253–71.

Washington, M. (2016). *Gangnam Style* and the Asian invasion: YouTube's politics of virality, virility, and visibility. In S. Noble, & B. Tynes (Eds.), *The intersectional Internet: Race, sex, class and culture online*. New York: Peter Lang.

Wolf, M. (1972). *Women and the family in rural Taiwan*. Stanford, CA: Stanford University Press.

Yep, G. A. (2013). Queering/quaring/kauering/crippin'/transing "other bodies" in intercultural communication. *Journal of International and Intercultural Communication, 6*(2), 118–26.

Yep, G. A. (2016). Toward thick(er) intersectionalities: Theorizing, researching, and activating the complexities of communication and identities. In K. Sorrells, & S. Sekimoto (Eds.), *Globalizing intercultural communication: A reader* (pp. 86–94). Thousands Oaks, CA: Sage.

Yep, G. A. & Lescure, R. (2014). Kuaering "home" in Ang Lee's *The Wedding Banquet*. In E. Patton, & M. Choi (Eds.), *Home sweat home: Perspectives on housework and modern relationships* (pp. 167–82). Lanham, MD: Rowman & Littlefield.

Zhang, Q. (2010). Asian Americans beyond the model minority stereotype: The nerdy and the left out. *Journal of International and Intercultural Communication*, *3*(1), 20–37.

Index

Albuquerque, 25–27, 30, 32, 35, 37–40
almost white, 269, 274
ambiguity, xxiii, 119, 120, 131–33, 272
ambiguous, xx, xxi, xxiii, 119, 120, 123, 132, 134, 135, 269, 273
anti–blackness, xxiii, 75, 127, 228, 230, 235, 236, 238, 239
appropriation, xxiv, 60, 65, 70, 74–76, 79, 83–85, 87, 139, 184, 204, 208
Arab, 161, 176
Asian, xx, xxiv, 49, 85, 102, 109–12, 114, 127, 151, 154, 229, 237, 243–60, 263–79
Asianness, xxiii, 101, 103, 106–7
assemblage, 59, 61, 63, 65–79, 140, 142
autoethnography, 53, 55, 119–21, 123, 134, 159, 161, 164

biological essentialism, 211–13
black, x–xiii, xiv, xvii–xviii, xx, xxiii, 18, 45–55, 59–62, 64–65, 68–79, 83–94, 108, 110–11, 120–22, 124–29, 131–33, 139, 141, 144, 147–48, 153–54, 160, 183, 204–5, 211, 213, 215–17, 224–30, 232–39, 244–45, 250, 258–59, 265, 272, 274
black feminism, xii, 47–48, 210, 214, 237
black feminist thought, ix, xxii, 46, 54, 84
black masculinity, 147–48
body, xvii, xx, xxi, xxiii, 9, 15, 36, 51, 53, 54, 64–66, 69, 74, 76–77, 103, 107, 113, 120, 125, 127–28, 132, 134–35, 140, 143–54, 165, 167–73, 175–76, 178, 183–84, 186–89, 197–98, 200, 223–24, 226, 231–34, 236, 238, 256, 268, 270
Brazil, xxiii, 203–4, 207–11, 213, 215, 217, 219–20
Brazilian feminist studies, 208–9, 220

Chicana, xxii, 3–11, 13–21, 25–35, 37–43, 99, 120, 131, 187, 209
cisnormativity, 203, 207, 213, 214, 219
colonization, x, xxi, 5–6, 12–13, 17, 32, 76, 170, 185, 200
colorism, 225–28, 230
coming out, 104
consciousness, xi, 10, 13, 14, 62, 70, 88, 133, 146, 193, 228, 235
Crazy Rich Asians, 263–79
culture, x, xvii, xix, xx, 5, 7–9, 11, 14, 17, 26, 28–30, 34, 40–42, 49–51, 53–55, 63, 68, 72–73, 75, 77, 79, 106, 109, 112, 113, 139, 151, 162, 169, 170, 175, 185, 217, 225–26, 228, 238, 251, 256–58, 264, 266, 269–71, 273–74, 276

Dalit feminism, 225, 237
decolonial, xxiii, 17, 29, 35, 41, 183–84, 186, 190, 198–200, 204, 213, 218, 220, 225, 233
decoloniality, 35
desire, x, 7, 12, 15, 16, 65, 73–75, 111, 114, 146, 148, 151–53, 168, 173, 176–77, 184, 190–91, 225, 227–29, 231–32, 239, 264, 269, 271, 273–75
difference, xi, xvii, xix, xx, xxi, xxii, xxiii, 4, 8, 12, 41, 48, 50, 53, 62, 63, 67–69, 72–79, 99–100, 102–5, 111, 120–23, 128–30, 134–35, 140, 142, 144, 148, 154, 159, 163, 166, 177, 189, 195, 199, 206–9, 211, 231, 238, 249–50, 254–59, 266, 269
disability, xxiii, 67, 159–60, 167–69, 172–73, 175–77, 238
disciplinary whitening, 45
disidentification, 111–13, 188, 195
diversity disclaimer, xiii

ethnic identification, xxiii, 11, 243–44, 247, 249, 258
ethnicity, xvii, 13, 18, 49, 211, 244

faithful witnessing, xxiii, 183, 186, 189–90, 196, 200
felt sensations, 140–43, 153–55
feminine principle, 4, 15
feminism, x, xi, xii, xiv, xviii, xxii, xxiii, 3–7, 9–13, 15–17, 28, 46–49, 53–54, 63–64, 76, 78, 83–84, 86, 93, 106, 161, 163, 165, 203–4, 206, 209–20, 225, 237
feminist stewardship, 48
Flint, ix

gender, xi, xii, xiv, xv, xvii, xviii, xx, xxi, xxiii, 3–6, 9–10, 12–14, 17–18, 29, 46–48, 50–52, 60, 62–65, 67, 84–93, 99, 101–2, 104–7, 110, 112–13, 120–23, 127–28, 130, 133–35, 140–41, 145, 147, 151–54, 161–64, 170, 189, 192, 203–7, 209–20, 225–26, 229–31, 235–36, 238–39, 244–47, 249–51, 253, 258–59, 265–67, 272–74, 276, 278
global north/global south, 226–27, 237

haptic gaze, 230, 232–36
haptic visuality, 226–27, 230–31, 233
hetero-patriarchy, 70, 78, 220, 264–65, 267, 274, 278
Hillary Clinton, ix, x, xi, xii
Hocicona, 25, 27–28, 30, 32

ICE, xiv
identity, x, xi, xii, xiii, xiv, xviii, xix, 4, 7, 9–11, 13, 16–18, 25–27, 30, 35, 42, 46, 49–55, 60, 62, 64–67, 69, 71, 74, 77–79, 86–88, 101–3, 105, 107, 113–14, 119–22, 126, 128, 131–33, 140–43, 146, 153–54, 162, 168, 172, 185, 187–89, 192, 200, 203–6, 208, 213–20, 227–28, 231–32, 235, 237–38, 244, 246, 250, 252, 257–58, 266, 268, 272
immigration, 86, 219, 244–45, 247–48, 254–56, 259–60
intersectionality, ix, x, xi, xii, xiii, xiv, xvii, xviii, xix, xxi, xxii, xxiii, xxiv, xxvii, 4–5, 8–11, 13–14, 16–17, 25, 27, 29, 30, 40, 45–55, 66–68, 72, 77–79, 83–94, 99–100, 104–5, 119–23, 134, 139–44, 152–55, 159, 161–63, 165, 175, 178, 184, 186, 199–200, 203–20, 225–27, 230–31, 237, 244–45, 249, 258–59, 265–66, 278–79

Jennifer C. Nash, xii

Kimberlé Crenshaw, x, xii, xvii, 86, 99, 210
Kuwaiti, 159–61, 164–67, 169–72, 174, 176–78

Latina/o, x, xx, 18
lived embodiment, xii, 72–73, 121, 134, 142–43, 153, 186, 189

masculinity, 52, 70, 76, 91–93, 147–48, 159–61, 163–64, 167, 169–71, 174–77, 212, 264–67, 269–75, 277–79
media representation, 53, 217, 263, 266–67, 270
memory, xxiii, 9, 20, 29, 31, 33, 38, 108, 140–41, 143, 154, 184–89, 191–94, 198, 200
Michigan, ix
Middle East, xxiii, 161–70
mindful birthing, 149, 151–52
model minority, 110, 229, 243–45, 250–53, 255, 257–58, 268
multiple axes of domination, x, xii, xiii, xiv
multiple sclerosis, 168
Muslim, 161–63, 170, 229, 250, 256, 260

narrative, xxii, 9, 10, 25–27, 29–34, 37, 41–42, 53–54, 61, 64, 70–71, 77–78, 107, 113–44, 122–23, 127, 132–35, 141–44, 152–54, 159–63, 169, 176, 184–86, 188–89, 195–98, 200, 216, 225, 229, 231–32, 234–36, 238
neoliberal governance, xi
neoliberal identity politics, xii, 67, 204, 227–28
neutralization, 265, 267
New Mexico, 25–27, 32, 34–35, 37, 39–40, 42
nonblack feminists of color, xxii, 83, 87, 92–93
nonprofit–industrial complex, 244
nonprofit organization, 243, 245, 258

Orientalization, 265, 270, 275
Otherization, 160

pan–Asian organizing, xxiii, 250, 257–60
power–conscious framework, 84–85, 87–92
Puerto Rico, 184–85

queer, x, xii, xiv, xvii, xviii, xix, xxi, xxii, xxiii, 9–10, 46, 49–50, 52, 61, 70, 85, 91, 99, 102–7, 109–15, 119, 121–22, 124–25, 128, 131, 133–34, 141, 144–46, 153, 166, 199, 207, 209, 217, 219, 225, 229, 232, 238, 256, 265, 272
queerness, xxiii, 10, 101, 103–4, 106–7, 109, 112, 121, 144, 207, 219, 225, 272

racialization, xiiii, 51, 55, 151, 153, 227, 229, 247
racialized casteism, 226, 228–29
racial trauma, 141, 147, 153–54, 189, 226, 252
repressive intersectionalities, 11, 17–18
restorative intersectionalities, 13, 17–18

same-sex marriage, 102, 106, 111–33
scopophilia, 231–32, 239
sexuality, xvii, xviii, 7, 9–13, 15–17, 28, 30, 32–33, 37, 42, 52, 60, 63, 65–67, 79, 85, 92, 101–7, 112–13, 121–22, 128, 133–34, 141, 148, 162–63, 185, 207, 214, 217–19, 238, 244–45, 259–60, 265–67, 271–74, 276
social justice, xviii, 10, 13, 28, 30, 36, 42, 46, 52–53, 60, 71, 76–77, 91, 134, 139, 193, 203, 205, 215, 219, 237, 244, 259

Taiwan, 101–6, 108–13, 247–48, 254
Taiwanese, 102, 105–6, 109, 112, 125, 246–48
teaching, 31, 110, 127–28, 168–69, 172–73, 176, 199
thick intersectionalities, 105, 122, 141, 207
Tommy J. Curry, xiii
Tongzhi, xxii, 101–3, 105–7, 109, 111, 113
tourism, 223, 227, 269
transfeminismo, xxiii, 203–4, 209–20

transnational, xxii, xxiii, 35, 40, 52, 85, 101, 106, 113–15, 121, 151, 159–61, 165–66, 177–78, 208, 210, 220, 224, 226, 264, 266, 278
travel narratives, 127, 234, 235
travesti, 214–16, 218

whitening, xiv, xvii, xviii, xix, xx, xxi, xxii, 4, 16, 45, 48–51, 53–55, 60, 84, 93, 99, 120, 134, 147, 152, 159, 164, 178, 199, 203–4, 230, 243, 245, 259, 278
white supremacy, x, xviii, xix, xx, xxi, 65, 69, 71, 72, 78, 147, 149, 219–20, 226, 229, 233, 236–37, 245, 249, 253–54, 258–59
white western feminisms, xii, xiv

Xicana, 4–5, 7, 11–18
Xicanisma, xxii, 3–4, 11, 13–15, 17–18

About the Editors

Shinsuke Eguchi (PhD, Howard University) is an associate professor in the Department of Communication and Journalism at the University of New Mexico. Their research interests focus on global and transcultural studies, queer of color critique, intersectionality and racialized gender politics, Asian/Pacific/American studies, and performance studies. They are a recipient of 2019 Randy Majors Award—annually recognizing an individual who has made outstanding contributions to lesbian, gay, bisexual, and/or transgender scholarship in communication studies—bestowed by the National Communication Association's Caucus on Gay, Lesbian, Bisexual, and Transgender Concerns. Their mostly recent work will appear or has appeared for publication in *Women Studies in Communication*, *China Media Research*, *Journal of Homosexuality*, *Cultural Studies↔Critical Methodologies*, *Critical Studies in Media Communication*, and *Departures in Critical Qualitative Research*. With Bernadette Marie Calafell, they are also the coeditor of *Queer Intercultural Communication: The Intersectional Politics of Belonging in and across Differences* released from Rowman & Littlefield (2020; Lanham, MD).

Bernadette Marie Calafell (PhD, University of North Carolina, Chapel Hill) is the inaugural department chair and professor of Critical Race and Ethnic Studies at Gonzaga University. Her research is focused on queer of color theories, women of color feminisms, critical rhetoric, performance studies, horror, and monstrosity. She is author of *Monstrosity, Performance, Race in Contemporary Culture* and *Latina/o Communication Studies: Theorizing Performance*, as well as coeditor with Michelle Holling of *Latino Discourse in Vernacular Spaces: Somos de una Voz* and *Queer Intercultural Communication: The Intersectional Politics of Belonging in and across Differences* with Shinsuke Eguchi. She is the coeditor along with Thomas K. Nakayama of Peter Lang's Critical Intercultural Communication Studies book series and coeditor along with Marina Levina and Kendall Phillips of the Horror and Monstrosity series through the University of Mississippi Press.

Shadee Abdi (PhD, University of Denver) is an assistant professor of communication at San Francisco State University. She is a critical cultural communication scholar whose research interests include intercultural, transnational, and diasporic communication, sexuality studies, family communication, performance studies, and performances of Iranian diaspora. Broadly, her work explores how conflicting discourses complicate and enhance our intersectional understandings of identity and power relative to race, culture, sexuality, gender, nationality, religion, ability, class, and family. She is specifically interested in narratives of resistance within familial and mediated contexts. Her work has appeared in *Critical Studies in Media Communication*, *The Journal of International and Intercultural Communication*, *The Journal of Intercultural Communication Research*, and *Liminalities: A Journal of Performance Studies*. She recently coedited alongside Dr. Haneen Al-Ghabra, Dr. Fatima Zahrae Chrifi Alaoui, and Dr. Bernadette Calafell, *Negotiating Identity and Transnationalism: Middle Eastern and North African Communication and Critical Cultural Studies* (Peter Lang, In Press), the first book of its kind in Communication Studies.

About the Contributors

Sara Baugh-Harris (PhD, University of Denver) is an instructor in the Theater Department at Agnes Scott College in Decatur, Georgia. With a background in culture and communication as well as rhetorical studies, her current research intersects at the nexus of decolonial scholarship, Latinx and Chicanx feminist studies, and memory studies.

Christopher Brown (PhD, University of New Mexico) is an associate professor and chair of the Department of Communication Studies at Minnesota State University, Mankato. His scholarly research explores discourses of white supremacy and white-male elites' constructions of race and leadership. He is a coauthor with Sachi Sekimoto of a forthcoming book, *Race and the Senses: The Felt Politics of Racial Embodiment.*

Santhosh Chandrashekar (PhD, University of New Mexico) is an assistant professor in the Department of Communication Studies at University of Denver. His research examines South Asian racialization in North America as entangled with, and complicit in, settler-colonial and antiblack logics. He is currently working on his monograph along with coediting an anthology that examines settler colonialism as a core analytic in communication studies, specifically critical intercultural communication.

Yea-Wen Chen (PhD, University of New Mexico) is an associate professor in the School of Communication and a Provost's Professor of Equity in Education at San Diego State University. Her research examines how communication—including silence—about cultural identities impacts diversity, inclusion, and social justice across contexts such as identity-based nonprofit organizations. She is the winner of numerous top paper awards at regional, national, and international communication conferences. Dr. Chen has published over forty works, including peer-reviewed articles in *Communication Monographs*, *Journal of International and Intercultural Communication*, *Departures in Critical Qualitative Research*. Also, she has coedited *Our Voices: Essays in Culture, Ethnicity, and Communication* (6th edition, Oxford University Press, 2015).

Andy Kai-chun Chuang (PhD, University of Denver) is an associate professor of Communication Studies at the LaGuardia Community College, City University of New York. His research focuses on professional identity, organizational resistance, critical qualitative research, and queer intercultural communication. He has published on *Departures in Critical Qualitative Research*, *Communication Education*, and *Journal of Management Inquiry*.

Jaelyn deMaría (PhD, University of New Mexico) is an assistant professor in the Communication & Journalism Department at the University of New Mexico. She is a multimedia storyteller originally from Albuquerque, New Mexico. Her research interests are centered in the intersections of intercultural communication, justice studies, Xican@ studies, ritual behavior, border studies, and anticolonial studies through a lens of visual communication and media justice.

Zhao Ding (PhD, University of New Mexico) is an assistant professor in the Department of Communication Studies at Dixie State University. Her research interest is in critical intercultural communication; race, gender, and sexuality; Asian and Asian American identities; and media representations.

Aisha Durham (PhD, University of Illinois, Urbana-Champaign) is an associate professor of Media and Culture in the Department of Communication at the University of South Florida. She is a cultural critic who uses autoethnography, performance writing, and intersectional approaches refined in black feminist thought to analyze representations of racialized gender and class in popular culture. This scholarship contributes to an interdisciplinary field called hip-hop feminism. Recent research about black womanhood is featured in *The Crunk Feminist Collection*, *Media Activism in the Digital Age*, and in her award-winning book, *Home with Hip Hop Feminism: Performances in Communication and Culture*.

Michelle A. Holling (PhD, Arizona State University) is a professor of Communication in the Department of Communication at California State University San Marcos. Her scholarly interests span matters of race; vernacular voices with specific emphasis on Chican@-Latin@ rhetoric; academe as a site of inquiry to explore issues of intersectionality, identity, and agency; and gendered violence. She is coeditor, with Dreama Moon, of *Race(ing) Intercultural Communication: Racial Logics in a Colorblind Era* and coeditor, with Bernadette Calafell, of *Latina/o Discourse in Vernacular Spaces: Somos de Una Voz?* She is also published in an array of peer-reviewed journals.

Haneen Ghabra (PhD, University of Denver) is an assistant professor at Kuwait University's Department of Mass Communication and author of the book, *Muslim Women and White Femininity: Reenactment and Resistance (2018)*. She recently was the recipient for the Outstanding Article of the Year Award, at the National Communication Association's (NCA) Feminist Division (November 2018) and the recipient of the 2018 Outstanding Book of the Year for the International and Intercultural Communication Division (IICD) of the National Communication Association.

Amber Johnson (PhD, The Pennsylvania State University) is an associate professor in the Department of Communication at Saint Louis University. As a scholar/artist/activist, Dr. Johnson explores the language, exigency, sound, and aesthetics of social justice. Their art, research, and activism focus on performances of identity, protest, and social justice in digital and lived spaces. As a polymath, their mixed-media artistry involves working with metals, recycled and reclaimed goods, photography, poetry, percussion, and paint to interrogate systems of oppression. Dr. Johnson is the creator of the Justice Fleet ™, a mobile justice museum that fosters healing through art, dialogue, and play and an award-winning assistant professor of Communication and Social Justice at Saint Louis University. Notable awards include the Golden Anniversary Monograph Award for their research on black masculinity and the performative possibilities of social media, the Lilla A. Heston award for Outstanding Scholarship in Interpretation and Performance Studies for their work on embodied pedagogies and social justice, and the Faculty Excellence Award for Diversity and Social Justice. Dr. Johnson has published articles in several journals including *Qualitative Inquiry*, *Critical Studies in Media and Communication*, *Text & Performance Quarterly*, *Liminalities: A Journal of Performance Studies*, and *Communication Quarterly*.

Benny LeMaster (PhD, Southern Illinois University Carbondale) is an assistant professor of Critical/Cultural Communication Studies in the High Downs School of Human Communication at Arizona State University. They draw on rhetorical and performance traditions to explore the material, discursive, and performative constitution of intersectional difference. They are especially interested in queer and trans of color cultural performance, production, and survival. Their research has been published, for instance, in *Women's Studies* *in Communication*, *Communication and Critical/Cultural Studies*, and *The Popular Culture Studies Journal*. Their pronouns are they/them/their.

Dawn Marie D. McIntosh (PhD, University of Denver) is an independent scholar located in Colorado. Her research is focused in whiteness studies, feminist of color theories, qualitative research methods, performance studies, and critical rhetoric. She is the coeditor to *Interrogating the Communicative Power of Whiteness*.

Raquel Moreira (PhD, University of Denver) is an associate professor of Communication in the Humanities Division at Graceland University. Her research focuses on the role of transgressive performances of femininity by cisgender women and queer people of color in the struggle against structural violence in Brazil. Specifically, she uses critical cultural and rhetorical methods as well as queer feminist of color theories to study the cultural production of marginalized feminine-presenting people in Rio de Janeiro's favela funk. The essay she published in *Women's Studies in Communication*, " 'Now that I'm a whore nobody is holding me back!': women in favela funk and embodied politics," in which she explores these performances as strategically employing embodied politics in order to confront gender, race, and class oppression, received the 2017 Feminist Scholar of the Year from the Organization for Research on Women and Communication.

Miranda Olzman (MA, San Francisco State University) is a doctoral candidate in the Department of Communication Studies at University of Denver.

Pavithra Prasad (PhD, Northwestern University) is an assistant professor of Performance Studies and Intercultural Communication at California State University, Northridge. Her work critically examines performative expressions of alienation, alterity, and futurity in South Asia and the diaspora. Her published works on orientalism and subculture, queer diasporic politics, and race in the global imaginary appear in *Text and Performance Quarterly*, *QED: A Journal in GLBTQ Worldmaking*, and *Departures in Critical Qualitative Research* among others.

Anjana Raghavan (PhD, Indian Institute of Technology, Madras) is a senior lecturer in Sociology in the Department of Psychology, Sociology and Politics, Faculty of Social Sciences and Humanities at Sheffield Hallam University, United Kingdom. Her work is located at the interstices of decolonial and queer feminisms, political philosophies, and critical theory-practice-performance. She has published work on decolonial spiritual practice, corporeality, cosmopolitanism, and women-of-colors feminisms. She is the author of *Towards Corporeal Cosmopolitanism: Performing Decolonial Solidarities.*

Kamela Rasmussen (MA, San Jose State University) is a PhD student in the Department of Communication and Journalism at the University of New Mexico. Her research interest is in performances of race, gender, class, and sexuality; politics of beauty; and critical intercultural communication.

Justin Rudnick (PhD, Ohio University) is an assistant professor in the Department of Communication Studies at Minnesota State University, Mankato. Their work explores the sensory and affective dimensions of queer identity and performances in/of everyday life. Their work can be found in outlets such as *QED: A Journal in GLBTQ Worldmaking*, *Departures in Critical Qualitative Research*, and *Cultural Studies ↔ Critical Methodologies.*

Sachi Sekimoto (PhD, University of New Mexico) is an associate professor in the Department of Communication Studies at Minnesota State University, Mankato. Her scholarship explores the cultural politics of the senses and the critical phenomenology of cultural and sensorial embodiment. She is a coauthor with Christopher Brown of a forthcoming book, *Race and the Senses: The Felt Politics of Racial Embodiment*, which explores how race is felt and sensed by racialized subjects.

Shahd Alshammari is an assistant professor of Literature and is the chair of the Global Studies Center at Gulf University for Science and Technology. She has published articles on disability studies, illness narratives, and women's representation in television and literature. Her latest work is *Notes on the Flesh* (2017).

Printed in Great Britain
by Amazon

79516071R00183